Contemporary Voices of Wh   ......ica

This book presents ten alarmingly candid interviews by some of the most prominent members of what editors Carol M. Swain and Russ Nieli warn is a growing white nationalist movement in America. The ten people featured in this volume make statements that are sure to shock, amuse, challenge, and provoke the typical reader. Their remarks are of particular value, Swain and Nieli believe, for understanding how the many race-conscious whites who lie outside the integrationist consensus on racial issues in America view developments that have taken place in the United States since the great victories of the civil rights movement in the 1950s and 1960s. If current trends continue, the editors predict, white nationalist ideas will become ever more popular, especially as whites become a diminishing portion of the U.S. population. What is most needed now, Swain and Nieli conclude, is for the claims of white nationalists to be aired in more open public forums, where they can be vigorously challenged and subjected to honest evaluation and refutation.

Carol M. Swain is Professor of Political Science and Professor of Law at Vanderbilt University. She is the author of *Black Faces, Black Interests: The Representation of African Americans in Congress* (1993, 1995), which was selected by *Library Choice Journal* as one of the seven outstanding academic books of 1994. *Black Faces* was also the winner of the 1994 Woodrow Wilson prize of the American Political Science Association for "the best book published in the United States during the prior year on government, politics or international affairs," the co-winner of the V. O. Key Award of the Southern Political Science Association for the best book published on Southern politics, and the winner of the 1995 D. B. Hardeman Prize of the Lyndon Baines Johnson Foundation for the best scholarly work on the U.S. Congress during a biennial period. Her latest book, *The New White Nationalism in America: Its Challenge to Integration*, was published by Cambridge University Press in 2002.

Russ Nieli received his M.A. and Ph.D. degrees from Princeton University's Politics Department, where he is presently a lecturer. Dr. Nieli authored a study of philosopher Ludwig Wittgenstein and is currently working on a book on the decline of inner-city African-American communities in the decades following the 1960s. He has also edited an important anthology on affirmative action.

Contemporary Voices of
White Nationalism in America

Edited by

CAROL M. SWAIN
Vanderbilt University

RUSS NIELI
Princeton University

CAMBRIDGE
UNIVERSITY PRESS

PUBLISHED BY THE PRESS SYNDICATE OF THE UNIVERSITY OF CAMBRIDGE
The Pitt Building, Trumpington Street, Cambridge, United Kingdom

CAMBRIDGE UNIVERSITY PRESS
The Edinburgh Building, Cambridge CB2 2RU, UK
40 West 20th Street, New York, NY 10011-4211, USA
477 Williamstown Road, Port Melbourne, VIC 3207, Australia
Ruiz de Alarcón 13, 28014 Madrid, Spain
Dock House, The Waterfront, Cape Town 8001, South Africa

http://www.cambridge.org

© Carol M. Swain and Russ Nieli 2003

First published 2003

Printed in the United States of America

Typeface Sabon 10/12 pt.   *System* QuarkXPress [BTS]

A catalog record for this book is available from the British Library.

Library of Congress Cataloging in Publication Data

Contemporary voices of white nationalism in America / edited by Carol M. Swain,
Russ Nieli.
  p. cm.
Includes bibliographical references and index.
ISBN 0-521-81673-4 – ISBN 0-521-01693-2 (pb.)
  1. White supremacy movements – United States.   2. Whites – United States –
Interviews.   3. United States – Race relations.   4. United States – Ethnic relations.
5. Racism – United States.   6. Hate groups – United States.   7. United States – Social
conditions – 1980-.   I. Swain, Carol M. (Carol Miller), 1954-.   II. Nieli, Russell, 1948-.

E184.A1 C598 2002
305.8′034073–dc21

                                                                            2002067711

ISBN   0 521 81673 4   hardback
ISBN   0 521 01693 2   paperback

Contents

Preface

Beginning in the early 1990s a new voice began to be heard in America – the voice of white nationalism. Energetic, articulate, and skilled in the use of the Internet, the carriers of this new voice now pose the most serious ideological challenge to the ideal of an integrated and racially pluralist America since the passing of the Jim Crow order in response to the great civil rights revolution of the 1950s and 1960s. Although the white nationalist movement is in an early growth stage, and its existence is not even known by some, there is reason to believe that in the decades ahead its influence will expand well beyond its current scope. If the experience of other multiracial, multiethnic societies around the world has taught us anything, it is that nationalist passions, whether ethnic, linguistic, or territorial, are a volatile and often irrational affair whose capacity for disrupting settled habits and long-term political compromises can hardly be overstated. With the passing of the Cold War and the bilateral global power alignment, issues of group consciousness and ethnic identity politics seem to have taken on a new salience and vitality in many places with consequences that may be only dimly foreseen. We believe that the time has come for mainstream political and religious leaders in America to take the threat posed by white nationalism more seriously and to address some of the underlying issues and conditions that are contributing to its growth.

The ten interviews included in the present volume grew out of a much larger project on the possibility of racial polarization in America undertaken by one of us, Carol M. Swain. Russ Nieli served as the chief interviewer. It became clear to both editors early in the interviewing process that something new was astir in America in terms of attitudes toward American nationalism and race. A new ideological landscape seemed to be opening up before us that, like a volcanic island newly emergent from the sea, was largely unexplored and to many still unknown. Situated somewhere between the mainstream right of American Conservatism, and the older racist right of organizations like the Ku Klux Klan and the American Nazi Party, this new emergent territory called out for exploration. In a separate volume, Swain examines the current white nationalist movement at great length and analyzes the salient forces that appear to be giving it life.

These interviews are here presented to the general public as both a stimulus and a warning. As a stimulus, they offer the benefit of often well-articulated views that frequently contain important insights or perspectives rarely encountered in mainstream discourse. Indeed, there is something refreshing about the candor and openness of many of those who speak in these pages, and few will come away from them without being morally and intellectually challenged in some way. This stimulus, however, comes with a warning, for ethnic nationalism, when not counterbalanced by a more inclusive moral vision, has proven itself to be a thoroughly pernicious force in modern politics, and there is no reason to believe that a triumphant white nationalism would be any exception. To lay out some of our own views on these critical issues, and to explain why we believe America has been an exception to the general rule that multiracial, multiethnic societies are doomed to eventual dissolution, the editors of this volume have included an in-depth introductory essay that addresses the challenges posed to the American commonweal by white nationalism and the new white racial assertiveness.

The ten interviewees presented here have been selected on the basis of their national prominence, their general articulateness, and the overall range of their views. The universe of white nationalist groups is a large and expanding one, and like any anthology, this volume contains only a tiny selection of all those individuals and groups who might have been included. Anyone who spends a few hours surfing the various white nationalist and white racialist websites on the Internet will discover just how vast the network of these organizations has become over the past few years. In some cases, people whom we eagerly sought to contact would not consent to be interviewed, though in general most of those that we did contact were eager to speak to us and to have their views appear in print and presented to the general public.

We have divided the interviews into three major categories. In the first group, consisting of Jared Taylor of *American Renaissance* magazine, Reno Wolfe of the National Association for the Advancement of White People, Inc. (NAAWP), and CUNY philosophy professor Michael Levin, the interviewees see themselves as defenders of the legitimate civil rights of white people against what they allege are a host of racial double standards that work to the detriment of whites. Each of the three interviewees in this section deplores current affirmative action policy and what they contend is a general practice on the part of the mainstream news media of gross underreporting of black-on-white crime. Taylor and Levin also believe, like most of the other interviewees in this volume, that there are significant genetic differences between blacks and whites, and that these differences are largely responsible for the higher black crime rate and the poorer performance of blacks in academic settings. The policy prescriptions of the people in this grouping tend toward moderation, however. None of the three people interviewed in this first section, for instance, openly support the creation of a racially separate state or believe that the basic structure of the American political regime should be radically altered because of current racial divisions.

The next section introduces the views of three prominent racial separationists, who conclude that America has become a country of at least two or three distinct nationalities (black, white, Hispanic), and that the interests of each of these groups would be better served if each had a separate nation-state of its own. Don Black of the *Stormfront* website, David Duke of the European-American Unity and Rights Organization (EURO), and the Princeton-trained astrophysicist Michael H. Hart all believe that multiracial societies are inherently faction ridden and that justice no less than expediency is on the side of their partitioning into separate territorial entities. While they agree with many members of the first group on the need for vigorous white rights advocacy, they believe such advocacy should include a more radical demand for an all-white (or at least white-dominant) nation, where European Americans can develop their common culture and common sense of peoplehood without hindrance from members of other racial groups.

The third major grouping includes three white supremacists who agree with most of what those in the separationist group say but have grafted onto their call for political separation a Social Darwinian and white supremacist ideology that draws much of its inspiration from the German Nazi movement of the 1930s. Matthew Hale and Lisa Turner of the World Church of the Creator, and William Pierce of the National Alliance, are included here among the white supremacists. Each of those interviewed in this section believes that white people are not only intellectually superior to the darker skinned peoples of the earth, but that they have some kind of right of nature to translate this superiority into an extensive white *Lebensraum*. Another feature of those in this group is a hatred of Jews that seems to exceed in intensity their generalized dislike of the world's colored peoples.

Members of the Christian Identity and Anglo-Israelite movement, who believe that the Anglo-Saxon race is a direct descendant of the lost ten tribes of ancient Israel, are an important segment of the contemporary racialist right in America, but they do not easily fit into any of the three major classifications developed in this anthology. Their manner of argument is rooted primarily in Biblical exegesis, and they are more of a social and religious force than a politically engaged one. For these reasons, the one representative of this point of view highlighted here, the articulate Dan Gayman of the Missouri-based Church of Israel, has been placed in a separate section, which we have titled White Christianity. Gayman's views on public policy issues would probably place him in the first section, since he neither calls for a white separatist state nor believes that whites have a natural right to

dominate other races. Although Gayman does not defend legal separa-
tionism, he does believe that white, black, Hispanic, and Asian people
should marry within their own group, socialize within their own group, and
attend separate religious services. Gayman also believes that whites have
shown superiority to other races in terms of morality and scientific achievement, though he attributes this superiority to their Christian religious faith
rather than to superior genes.

A word should be said here about the mechanics and goals of the interviews. All of the interviews were conducted by telephone from Princeton
University's Woodrow Wilson School of Public and International Affairs
between November 1999 and May 2000. The telephone interview format
was chosen largely because of its cost effectiveness and the relative ease it
presented in gaining access to often busy and controversial figures, who no
doubt would have been more difficult to line up for face-to-face interviewing. Every effort was made in these telephone inquiries to elicit the most
honest and forthright responses to the many controversial issues that were
raised. While probing questions – and in some cases unsettling or embar-
rassing questions – were often posed to respondents, the purpose of the
interviews, as was made clear to each of the participants from the outset,
was not to debate or condemn those interviewed but to give them the opportunity to state their particular views on controversial racial topics honestly,
openly, and in their own words. The respondents were also given the opportunity to read over the telephone transcript and to make additions or
corrections where such changes were deemed to elucidate or better explain
important ideas they were trying to convey. (Michael Levin, Michael H.
Hart, and Dan Gayman made extensive use of this editing privilege.)

The interview format, we believe, is a particularly good one for understanding how other people view the world, and in one way or another, all
the following interviews, even those that are most distasteful from our own
moral and policy standpoints, offer valuable insights into what various
people are saying today about race relations in America. To lay out some
of our own views on these critical issues and to explain why we believe
America has been an exception to the general rule that multiracial, multiethnic societies are doomed to eventual dissolution, we have included as an
introduction an in-depth interpretive essay that addresses the challenges
posed to the American commonweal by white nationalism and the new
white racial assertiveness. Anyone who takes the time to read this volume
carefully will gain important insights into the contemporary world of white
nationalism and white protest, which seems to be expanding its influence
in America at an alarming rate.

In the wake of the events of September 11, 2001, a number of people have
asked us what we think the impact will be of America's declared war on terrorism on the future of the white nationalist movement. We see two major
effects, each pulling in opposite directions. On the one hand, the direct

attack on the United States, like the bombing of Pearl Harbor sixty years earlier, has drawn the country together against a common foe. In our common vulnerability, the attacks have, for the present, heightened the sense that "we're all in this together." The sight of American flags flying alongside of – or even in place of – the Confederate battle flag on Southern pickup trucks is just one indication of how patriotic attachments to a wider concept of nationhood can displace narrower regional or racial feelings.

The events of September 11, however, were in some sense made to order for white nationalist propagandists to exploit. "This is what happens when you let nonwhites into the country," white racial advocates like David Duke have been proclaiming on their websites, and the events of September 11 have no doubt lent additional weight to white nationalist calls for ending Third World immigration into the United States. The fact, too, that America's long-term pro-Israel foreign policy is held partially responsible for the hatred so many Mideasterners feel toward the United States has not gone unnoticed by white nationalist activists, who predictably attribute this state of affairs to the pernicious influence allegedly exerted by Jews on the contours of American foreign policy.

The terrorist attacks on America have also caused a renewed interest in Harvard professor Samuel P. Huntington's "clash of civilizations" model of post–Cold War international conflict, which white nationalists find quite congenial. Even though Huntington himself can hardly be described as a racial or ethnic nationalist, his view that global conflicts in the future will take place along "civilizational fault lines" determined by ethnicity and religion, and that the European–Christian cultural heritage of the United States largely determines America's place in the scheme of rival civilizations, is one dear to the hearts of America's white nationalists. "White Christians like us in the United States have to stick together against our Islamic, Asian, and African rivals" is a message that can be easily drawn from Huntington's thesis, and white nationalists have not failed to draw it.

So on balance the events of September 11, 2001, will probably have a decidedly mixed impact on the future of white nationalism in the United States. For those committed to an integration-seeking vision of a pluralist America – an America that welcomes people of all racial and religious groups if they are willing to take part in a common civic enterprise based on a common language and a rights-based democratic political regime – the terrorist attacks on American institutions will only strengthen their resolve to stand up for what they have always believed. For those, however, who believe that the stability and coherence of the American polity is dependent largely on maintaining its white, European–Christian ethnic and religious identity, the attacks on America by nonwhite Islamists will only strengthen them in their conviction that America must remain a "white man's country," and that it must forcefully reassert the priority of its European racial and cultural heritage (if need be by creating a separatist white state).

Acknowledgments

We would like to express our gratitude to Michael Barkun of Syracuse University, Dean Kent Syverud of Vanderbilt University, Kelley Walker of Vanderbilt University, Reggie Cohen and Rob Rodgers of Princeton University, Lewis Bateman of Cambridge University Press, and our transcriber Helene Randerson of Princeton. Each provided invaluable service on this project. The funding for this research as well as its companion volume, *The New White Nationalism in America: Its Challenge to Integration*, came from a number of different sources, including the National Science Foundation, the Carnegie Mellon Foundation, and the Smith Richardson Foundation. It is acknowledged that the final product is quite different from the research proposals that some of the grant makers funded.

The principle on which this country was founded and by which it has always been governed, is that Americanism is a matter of the mind and heart. Americanism is not, and never was, a matter of race and ancestry. A good American is one who is loyal to this country and to our creed of liberty and democracy.

> President Franklin D. Roosevelt (a letter to Henry Stimson, February 1, 1943)

Deeply rooted in our religious heritage is the conviction that every man is an heir of dignity and worth. Our Judeo-Christian tradition refers to this inherent dignity of man in the Biblical term "the image of God." The image of God is universally shared in equal portions by all men. . . . Every human being has etched in his personality the indelible stamp of the Creator. Every man must be respected because God loves him. The worth of an individual does not lie in the measure of his intellect, his racial origin or his social position. Human worth lies in relatedness to God. An individual has value because he has value to God. Whenever this is recognized, "whiteness" and "blackness" pass away as determinants in a relationship and "son" and "brother" are substituted.

> Rev. Martin Luther King, Jr. (*Where Do We Go From Here: Chaos or Community*, 1967)

In my view, Government can never have a "compelling interest" in discriminating on the basis of race in order to "make up" for past racial discrimination in the opposite direction. Individuals who have been wronged by unlawful racial discrimination should be made whole; but under our Constitution there can be no such thing as either a creditor or a debtor race. That concept is alien to the Constitution's focus upon the individual, and its rejection of dispositions based on race or blood. To pursue the concept of racial entitlement – even for the most admirable and benign of purposes – is to reinforce and pre-serve for future mischief the way of thinking that produced race slavery, race privilege and race hatred. In the eyes of government, we are just one race here. It is American.

> Justice Antonin Scalia (*Adarand v. Pena*, 1995)

INTRODUCTORY ESSAY

Forging a Common Identity

*The Challenge of White Nationalism and
the New White Racial Assertiveness*

I. A Dangerous Turn

Even after two centuries of a blood-soaked history of chaos and disruption, "nationalism," declared the historian Arthur Schlesinger, Jr., shortly before the breakup of the Soviet Union, "remains the most vital political emotion in the world – far more vital than social ideologies such as communism or fascism or even democracy." Nationalism, he went on,

> continues to thrive because it taps potent emotions of history and locality to give individual lives meaning in an increasingly baffling universe. Today the nationalist fever encircles the globe. In the West the contagion convulses Ireland and Israel, divides Belgium, Cyprus, and Canada, arouses Brittany, Corsica, and the Basque country. Nationalism broke up the Soviet empire and now threatens to break up the Soviet Union itself. In the third world, nationalism, having overthrown Western colonialism, launches a horde of new states, large and micro, often at each other's throats in reenacting ancient quarrels of history. Within nation-states, nationalism takes the form of ethnicity or tribalism. In country after country across the third world – India, Burma, Sri Lanka, Indonesia, Iraq, Ethiopia, Nigeria, Angola, Trinidad, Guyana – ethnic groups struggle for power and, in desperate cases, for survival. The ethnic upsurge in America, far from being unique, partakes of the global fever.[1]

The end result of this ethnic and nationalist upsurge, Schlesinger warned, can only be – as the title of his 1991 book proclaimed – *The Disuniting of America*: "The cult of ethnicity," he wrote, "exaggerates differences, intensifies resentments and antagonisms, [and] drives ever deeper the awful wedges between races and nationalities.... The recent apotheosis of ethnicity, black, brown, red, yellow, white, has revived the dismal prospect that in happy melting-pot days Americans thought the republic

---

[1] Arthur Schlesinger, Jr., *The Disuniting of America* (Whittle Direct Books, Knoxville, Tenn., 1991), p. 21.

3

was moving safely beyond – that is, a society fragmented into ethnic groups."[2]

Writing a few years after Schlesinger, the Canadian journalist and historian Michael Ignatieff offered an equally grim picture of the chaos that rising ethnic nationalism was unleashing around the world. Reflecting on the course of violent ethnic movements in the former Yugoslavia and elsewhere, Ignatieff captured with great poignancy the sorrow and disillusionment with which he and so many other liberal democrats who had come of age during the Cold War came to realize that the passing of totalitarian communism would not necessarily portend the triumph of liberal pluralism:

When the Berlin Wall came down, when Vaclav Havel stood on the balcony in Prague's Wenceslas Square and crowds cheered the collapse of the Communist regimes across Europe, I thought, like many people, that we were about to witness a new era of liberal democracy. My generation had almost reconciled itself to growing old in the fearful paralysis of the Cold War. Suddenly a new order of free nations began to take shape – from the Baltic republics to the Black Sea, from Tallin to Berlin, from Prague to Budapest, Belgrade, and Bucharest. In August 1991, when Muscovites defended the Russian Parliament against the tanks, we believed that the civic courage which had brought down the last twentieth-century empire might even be strong enough to sustain Russia's transition to democracy. We even thought, for a while, that the democratic current in the East might sweep through our own exhausted oligarchies in the West. We soon found out how wrong we were. For what has succeeded the last age of empire is a new age of violence. The key narrative of the new world order is the disintegration of nation-states into ethnic civil war; the key architects of that order are warlords; and the key language of our age is ethnic nationalism. . . . Though we have passed into a post-imperial age, we have not moved to a post-nationalist age, and I cannot see how we will ever do so.[3]

Reflecting further on the course of ethnic disruption in Northern Ireland, Belgium, India, Czechoslovakia, and his own native Canada, Ignatieff came to equally pessimistic conclusions: "Most multinational, multi-ethnic nation-states are discovering that their populations are often more loyal to the ethnic units that compose them than to the federation and the laws that hold the state together."[4]

Can it happen here? Can the ethnic separatist forces that have so traumatized and divided other multiethnic states around the world become a significant factor in the future course of the United States? Until the editors of the present anthology began their study of the people and organizations profiled in this volume, they probably would have answered such questions with

---

[2] Ibid., p. 58.
[3] Michael Ignatieff, *Blood and Belonging: Journeys into the New Nationalism* (Farrar, Straus, Giroux, New York, 1993), pp. 4–5, 13, 243.
[4] Ibid., p. 243.

a resounding No! At the very least, they would have said that serious ethnic strife is not likely to occur in the United States in the immediate future. More elaborately, we probably would have acknowledged that racial polarization and ethnic separatism are always a possibility in a multiethnic state, but that in the case of the United States at least, such developments would go against the dominant trend set by the powerful civil rights and integrationist movements of the past fifty years, and that, for the present, they do not seem to constitute a serious threat to America's peace and repose. The growing friendships across racial lines, the ubiquitousness of integrated workforces, the steady rise in interracial marriages, and the strong national consensus against racial prejudice and racial hostility all seemed to suggest to us that Americans would be spared the kinds of racial and ethnic tensions that have so often plagued – and frequently destroyed – so many other multiethnic societies. The editors would still like to think about these issues the way they once did, but reflection on the growing racial consciousness movement among white people in America in recent years has convinced us that some of our earlier assumptions, if not wrong, were at least too facile.

Something clearly has changed. Over the past ten years, with ever increasing strength, a new white pride, white protest, and white consciousness movement has developed in America, whose potential for growth and heightened influence throughout America's European population we think is considerable. In a companion volume, *The New White Nationalism in America: Its Challenge to Integration*, Carol Swain has made an extensive effort to outline the contours of this movement, to assess the possibilities for its future growth, and to analyze the countervailing forces at work that are most likely to neutralize its harmful effects.[5] Here we will just observe that the convergence of three major factors in the latter half of the 1990s seems to have been responsible for this new white racial assertiveness. These are (1) the huge influx of nonwhite immigrants, both legal and illegal, into the United States in the 1980s and 1990s, and the resulting prospect that white European Americans may soon become – or have already become – a minority population in many parts of the country; (2) the continuing white resentment and hostility over what is perceived to be the gross unfairness of race-based affirmative action policies that grant preferences in jobs, promotions, set-asides, and university admissions to members of nonwhite minority groups; and (3) the exponential growth in the number of households that are connected to the Internet and the emergence of Web communication as a means by which like-minded people who might otherwise be marginalized or disregarded by the mainstream media can consolidate their strength, share ideas, and mobilize their resources for influencing public opinion.

[5] Carol M. Swain, *The New White Nationalism in America: Its Challenge to Integration* (Cambridge University Press, New York, 2002).

It is important to understand how this new white consciousness movement – which we, following the lead of other scholars and following the
self-designation of many of the members of the movement itself, often
subsume under the umbrella term "white nationalism" – differs from, and
yet in some ways is related to, older white nativist and white racist organizations like the 1950s- and 1960s-era Ku Klux Klan. In terms of similarities, white nationalism, like the Klan, is interested in fostering white
pride and a sense of European-American group consciousness. To accomplish this, it is also interested in celebrating the achievements of white
people around the world. Similarity can also be seen in personnel. Some
of the leaders of the new organizations that we profile here, like Don
Black (*Stormfront* website) and David Duke (European-American Unity and
Rights Organization), got their start in racial advocacy many years ago as
leaders in the Klan movement.

But we believe that the image of the night-riding Klansman – or of his
more contemporary reflection in the figure of the tattooed skinhead spewing
forth vile epithets against Mexicans, Jews, and blacks on the TV talk show
circuit – is one of very limited usefulness in trying to grasp the nature and
appeal of contemporary white nationalism in America. For white nationalism is seeking to go mainstream. And in going mainstream, it has found it
necessary to eschew most of the images and tactics of the older racist right,
as well as some of its more bizarre rituals and beliefs. While some of the
leaders of the newer racial advocacy organizations were once active in Klan
organizations, many of the key personalities involved in the leadership of
the movement bear little resemblance to the kinds of people we normally
associate with the traditional racist right in America. Most are better educated, more moderate in their language, and generally more appealing as
human beings than most of the racist figures with whom we have become
familiar through our history books or through contemporary television.
Surely figures like Jared Taylor and most of the members of his *American
Renaissance* group, or the newer Christian Identity leaders like Pete Peters
and Dan Gayman, bear little resemblance to skinheads or thuggish
Klansmen.

An important observation on this matter is made by sociologists Jeffrey
Kaplan and Leonard Weinberg. In their important book *The Emergence of
the Euro-American Radical Right,* Kaplan and Weinberg suggest that our
image of what is going on among the contemporary radical right may be
distorted by the very groups that seek to keep us informed of what they are
doing. Such watchdog agencies as Klanwatch, SOS Racisme, the Simon
Wiesenthal Center, and the Anti-Defamation League, Kaplan and Weinberg
explain, are uniformly hostile to the people and groups they monitor and
have a tendency to portray them in the worst possible light. The goal of
these watchdog agencies, they say, "is to have members of the public regard
the racist and anti-Semitic right with the same affection they would the

AIDS epidemic or the outbreak of the ebola fever." While expressing some sympathy for this tactic, Kaplan and Weinberg conclude that ultimately it is harmful. "There is a price to be paid for reducing the groups and individuals involved to screen villains straight out of Central Casting," they write. "The price is that these efforts distort the reality. The groups and individuals who make up the radical right movement may have embarked on a destructive path, but they are often more complicated, considerably more personable, and far more nuanced than is suggested by the caricatures."[6]

Syracuse University scholar Michael Barkun offers a related comment regarding members of the racist religious right. The newer leaders of Christian Identity and other white separatist organizations, Barkun says, are "not simply younger than their predecessors but better educated, more polished, and more adroit in shaping their message to a skeptical audience, having learned from David Duke's example how effectiveness, appearance, and manner can deflect hostility."[7] The upshot of what Barkun and Kaplan/Weinberg are saying here is what we have said previously: contemporary white nationalism and white racism are seeking a mainstream audience.

If the Klan and skinhead models distort the reality of the contemporary white nationalist leaders and their organizations, they are even more misleading when it comes to understanding the manner in which the newer groups seek to recruit a following. In both America and Europe, the older racist and anti-Semitic right appealed for support usually through a few well-chosen slogans endlessly repeated to evoke powerful gut reactions among a suitably susceptible audience. "Jews Get Out!," "Niggers In Their Place," "White Men Built This Country," and "Segregation Now, Segregation Tomorrow, Segregation Forever" are the sorts of slogans that formed the heart of their appeal. Fiery speeches with a great deal of emotion but little intellectual content drew many followers into the fold. In addition, secret initiations and rituals with flamboyant costumes and mass parades formed important trappings of the movement that appealed to subliminal forces in the human soul often among people with little understanding of – or little control over – the deeper currents that moved them. Throughout, there was comparatively little appeal to reasoned or sustained arguments. By contrast, the new white nationalist movement that has emerged in America over the past ten years is a movement whose major mode of operation is discourse and ideas. At least for the present, it pays little regard to rituals or mass rallies and seeks to expand its influence largely through

---

[6] Jeffrey Kaplan and Leonard Weinberg, *The Emergence of a Euro-American Radical Right* (Rutgers University Press, New Brunswick, N.J., 1998), p. 2.

[7] Michael Barkun, *Religion and the Racist Right* (University of North Carolina Press, Chapel Hill, N.C., 1994), p. 253.

argument and persuasion directed at its target audience of white Americans aggrieved over race-based affirmative action policy and impending demographic change. In this regard, it is more analogous to the parties of the Left around the world – or to the Libertarians in the United States – than to the older style of Klan and Nazi groups.

What makes some of the newer organizations so dangerous, we believe, is that they address many important issues of race and nationality that are often ignored in polite company, and they do so with a degree of candor and openness not found in more mainstream discourse. On sensitive issues of race, mainstream discourse, we believe, has become so cluttered with the baggage of political correctness and taboos that it is not an arena where many people – and certainly not white people – feel comfortable expressing openly their deepest convictions and concerns. As a result, silence and self-censorship become the order of the day. We have even seen this process at work among many college undergraduates whom we have known – young people at congenial settings like Princeton, who, one would assume, would be among the most open and least inhibited of Americans.

The great danger here is that with few legitimate mainstream arenas in which to discuss many of their deepest anxieties and forebodings, people turn to white nationalist and white supremacist groups, which may offer the only forum for candid discussions of race. This may explain the incredible popularity of such institutions as the *Stormfront* website, which since its inception in 1995 has reportedly received several million visitors. And within these groups, one-sided pictures and half-truths, which usually have the great advantage of containing at least an important kernel of the truth on the tabooed subject, come to exert considerable appeal. The danger that we are talking about was well described by an academic colleague – a social scientist specializing in black/white race relations – who read a preliminary version of some of the material presented in this volume. In a personal communication, the colleague wrote:

I read through the interviews with a mixture of fascination, disgust, amusement, and sadness. At the end, I felt unclean. Like I needed to take a shower. There is enough logic to what they argue to make it compelling. Most importantly, they address topics and give voice to views that the mainstream media never allows in the public arena. Since those arguments are never allowed in the mainstream, these leaders are able to make them on the margins without clear and systematic refutation. THAT is a real danger. In the mainstream media, when such views are given voice, they are only dismissed and not refuted. Simply saying that the views are wrong and sending Atlanta Braves pitcher John Rocker for psychological rehabilitation is counter-productive.

These are essentially our own views on the matter. We present the following ten interviews to the general public with the hope that they might help stimulate more open discussion on issues of race and nationality among people who share our own basic commitment to the civil rights era vision of integration, common humanity, and the inclusion of all in the American Dream. We think it of utmost importance that many of the topics that are now discussed openly only within the province of the racialist right be taken up and seriously addressed by more moderate voices who have not lost faith in the older ideal of an integrated America.

We might mention in this context, that we are not alone in calling for a more candid discussion about race in America. In his June 1997 commencement address at the University of California at San Diego, President Clinton announced that he was launching a new initiative on race to be headed by a distinguished multiracial panel. "Over the coming year," Clinton explained, "I want to lead the American people in a great and unprecedented conversation about race." After announcing the names of the seven panel members, he went on: "I want this panel to help educate Americans about the facts surrounding issues of race, to promote a dialogue in every community of the land to confront and work through these issues. . . . Honest dialogue will not be easy at first. We'll all have to get past defensiveness and fear and political correctness and other barriers to honesty. Emotions may be rubbed raw, but we must begin." After reflecting on the difficulties involved in the undertaking, Clinton then concluded: "But if ten years from now people can look back and see that this year of honest dialogue and concerted action helped to lift the heavy burden of race from our children's future, we will have given a precious gift to America."[8]

Unfortunately, by almost all accounts, what was to be a "great and unprecedented conversation about race" proved a monumental flop, and, if anything, the panel's activities over the following months served to reinforce the stranglehold that political correctness continues to exert in America upon open discussion of controversial racial topics. Prospect for fruitful dialogue was not helped by the fact that all the Race Initiative Panel members were supporters of affirmative action. And the panel's leader, the eminent black historian John Hope Franklin, set the tone for the panel's activities early on when he announced that he was only interested in hearing from people who supported the value of "diversity." With the boundaries of acceptable discussion set so narrowly in our national dialogue, it is not difficult to understand why so many disaffected European Americans turn to white-centered websites.

The dangers of racial division and racial extremism emerging out of this kind of situation has been illuminated recently by an important article on the mechanisms of group polarization by University of Chicago law professor Cass R. Sunstein. Drawing extensively from recent social psychology

---

[8] William Clinton, Commencement Speech, University of California at San Diego, June 14, 1997. Available on the Internet at
http://www.whitehouse.gov/Initiatives/OneAmerica/announcement.html.

research, Professor Sunstein has explained how the process of deliberation and group discussion can produce dramatically different results depending on whether the group involved is ideologically homogeneous or whether it contains a variety of contrasting or conflicting viewpoints. In the latter case, where multiple perspectives and competing views are voiced, people often come to realize after discussion that their own view is one-sided, or overly simplified, or in need of important qualification. The tendency of such discussion is often to lead people in a direction that moderates their predeliberation viewpoint, or at least opens people to the possibility that other views once dismissed out of hand may contain worthwhile insights. However, when group discussion takes place among like-minded people without the benefit of contrasting perspectives, the tendency, Sunstein explains, is for the members of the group to become more radicalized and to adopt positions more extreme than most would have adopted on their own. Under such circumstances, the members of the group tend to adopt the views of those at the fringe. Sunstein sees this process of group polarization at work in many venues including the arena of racial and ethnic conflict. On this he writes:

In a striking empirical regularity, deliberation tends to move groups, and the individuals who compose them, toward a more extreme point in the direction indicated by their own predeliberation judgments. For example, people who are opposed to the minimum wage are likely, after talking to each other, to be still more opposed; people who tend to support gun control are likely, after discussion, to support gun control with considerable enthusiasm; people who believe that global warming is a serious problem are likely, after discussion, to insist on severe measures to prevent global warming. This general phenomenon – group polarization – has many implications for economic, political, and legal institutions. It helps to explain extremism, "radicalization," cultural shifts, and the behavior of political parties and religious organizations; it is closely connected to current concerns about the consequences of the Internet; it also helps account for feuds, ethnic antagonism, and tribalism.[9]

We think that the process Sunstein describes here is clearly at work among many of the white nationalist groups that we have surveyed. We also believe that a major reason why their members and potential members have such little exposure to alternative viewpoints is because of the overall feebleness and self-censorship that continues to dominate discussion about controversial racial issues in America. We suppose that this volume will provoke all the fascination, disgust, amusement, and sadness that it did for our academic colleague. Some may even feel that they have to take a shower after reading it. But more importantly, we hope that in forcing the reader

[9] Cass R. Sunstein, "The Law of Group Polarization," *John M. Olin Law and Economics Working Paper No. 91* (published by the Law School, The University of Chicago, 1999), p. 1. The paper is available on the Internet from the Social Science Research Network Electronic Paper Collection: http://papers.ssrn.com/paper.taf?abstract_id=199668.

to confront the many tabooed claims and convictions openly expressed here, this volume will contribute to the kind of real dialogue about race in America that President Clinton called for in 1997 but so conspicuously failed to bring about.

II. American Exceptionalism: the Loyalty to an Idea

Movements and peoples often come to define themselves and what they stand for most effectively when engaged in confrontation with rival forces that they know in some critical way they do not want to emulate. The Church Fathers of the third and fourth centuries of the Christian era came to state most clearly what they stood for in their confrontation with the ancient Gnostics; the antiaristocratic republicans of the American Revolutionary era came to define themselves most clearly in their struggle with the British Crown; the German and Japanese democracies that emerged after World War II defined themselves largely against the backdrop of, and in opposition to, the fascist and militarist regimes that had previously dominated their respective societies in the prewar era. With the fever of ethnic nationalism and ethnic separatism so pronounced around the world, and with a small but growing chorus of voices even within the United States arguing that multiracial and multiethnic societies are a bad idea and must eventually come to ruin, it is perhaps an appropriate time to state clearly and concisely what it is about America that has enabled it to survive and to integrate diverse peoples as well as it has.

"No other nation," Margaret Thatcher has observed, "has so successfully combined people of different races and nations within a single culture" as the United States.[10] Many other European observers have offered similar observations,[11] and in view of the history of most other multiethnic states in the twentieth century, beginning with the collapse of the Austro-Hungarian, Czarist-Russian, and Ottoman Empires at the end of the First World War, it is not out of place to speak here of an American exceptionalism. America has done better than almost any other country of the world in integrating into one vibrant and cohesive society many racial, ethnic, and religious groups that elsewhere in the world – and in the United States, too, at times – have been at each other's throats. The British and the Irish, the Germans and the French, the Russians and the Poles, Jews and Gentiles,

---

[10] Quoted in Schlesinger, *The Disuniting of America*, p. 78.

[11] Hans Kohn, the great German–Jewish historian of nationalism who emigrated to the United States in the 1930s, remarks that "no other nation has had to face the problem of immigration and assimilation of the most diverse strains on a scale even approaching that with which the United States had to deal and which it has solved on the whole with astonishing success and tolerance" (*American Nationalism: An Interpretive Essay*, Macmillan Company, New York, 1957, p. 147).

Puritans and Catholics, Japanese and Koreans, Chinese and Thais – to name just a few of the diverse peoples that have populated America — have not always been known to get along well with each other when occupying the same or neighboring territories. To be sure, progress has often been painfully slow, old antagonisms have sometimes lingered for generations, new antagonisms have sometimes emerged in the New World that didn't exist in the Old, and it wasn't until the post–World War II era that the dominant powers in America made any real effort to remove the thicket of hindrances and prohibitions, both legal and cultural, that had long prevented the full integration of African Americans into the mainstream of American life. But the fact is still undeniable: compared to most other multiethnic societies around the world, America has done extraordinarily well in integrating diverse peoples into a generally decent and stable society.

What is responsible for America's "exceptionalism" here? While the issue is obviously a complex one, we see at least five salient features of the American experience that have had an important effect in enabling the United States to avoid the curse of so many other multiethnic societies. These include (1) a self-definition of nationhood centering around the ideals of liberty and equality; (2) the hope, optimism, and future orientation implicit in the American Dream; (3) the socially unifying force of the English language; (4) the color-blind theory of justice ringingly proclaimed by Justice Harlan in his famous dissent in the *Plessy* case; and, (5) the Biblical view that God is the creator of all mankind and that mankind is all one race. We believe it appropriate here to examine each of these at some length, because, taken together, they provide the strongest response that we know to those more pessimistic voices in recent years that seem to have lost faith in the ideal of an integrated America – or even more radically, that argue with considerable force (like Michael H. Hart in the present volume) that multiethnic societies like the United States are intrinsically unstable, and that mercy itself calls out for their dismantling into more ethnically homogeneous units.

The first of these features contributing to America's exceptionalism proceeds from the peculiar role that the ideology of liberty and equality has played throughout American history, or at least since the Revolutionary era and the signing of the Declaration of Independence (the colonial era may constitute an exception to America's exceptionalism here). After a visit to the United States, British philosopher Bertrand Russell once remarked on how differently most Americans thought of their nation than the British did of theirs. Russell was particularly struck by the many chance acquaintances he met in America who, upon learning of his British origin, would ask him questions like, "Well, what do you think of America?" or "How do you like the United States?" To a British subject, such questions, Russell thought, were quite odd, not so much because of what was meant by the questions, which was plain enough, but because of the seeming inappropriateness of posing them to a complete stranger who was a foreign national. A British citizen would no more think it right or proper, Russell explained, to ask a foreigner, "What do you think of Britain?" than he would of asking him, "What do you think of my mother?"

Russell saw the difference in the two peoples to lie in the unique role played in America by certain ideas and ideals – and by the function served in America's national identity by its official national commitment to those ideas and ideals. Whereas Britain for a Britisher was something akin to one's family, which one is related to by birthright and which one does not normally talk about freely with outsiders, America, Russell noted, was different. Alluding to the Gettysburg Address, Russell suggested that unlike most other nations, where national identity is akin to family identity, America was dedicated to a *proposition*. That proposition, of course, dealt with the ideals of liberty, equality, and the pursuit of happiness as framed in the opening paragraphs of the Declaration of Independence. While people may become Americans by birth, a central feature of the American identity, Russell discovered, is adherence to a set of principles and ideals that immigrants may readily adopt and that by their very nature peoples of all races and national-origin backgrounds can understand and appreciate. Thus Americans can ask foreigners without any sense of betraying an intimacy, "What do you think of America?" whereas a Britisher would never ask a foreigner the same question about Britain.

Innumerable other commentators have made observations similar to those of Russell. Harvard political scientist Samuel P. Huntington, for instance, notes that for most of the nations of the world, "national identity is the product of a long process of historical evolution involving common ancestors, common experiences, common ethnic background, common language, common culture, and usually common religion."[12] America, however, is very different, he points out, insofar as its civic identity has been based less on any of these factors than on a common adherence to a set of shared political ideals focusing on democracy and individual rights. It is the adherence to these political ideals, Huntington claims, which provides the basis for a kind of unity and inclusion of diverse peoples in America not found in most other countries, where common peoplehood is usually tied closely to common ethnicity and common descent. These shared political ideals provide the cement holding together otherwise disparate peoples.

"In what was truly a novel event in world history," Huntington writes,

Americans did not assert their independence because their ethnicity, language, culture, or religion differentiated them from their British brethren. The United States came into existence at a particular moment in time – July 4, 1776 – and it was the

---

[12] Samuel P. Huntington, *American Politics: The Promise of Disharmony* (Harvard University Press, Cambridge, Mass., 1981), pp. 23–4.

product of a conscious political act based on explicit political principles. "We hold these truths to be self-evident.," says the Declaration. Who holds these truths? Americans hold these truths. Who are Americans? People who adhere to these truths. National identity and political principle were inseparable. From the beginning, as [Herbert] Croly noted, the American past was "informed by an idea." And hence there was from the beginning the tendency, as a distinguished English historian put it, "to describe the national identity as allegiance to political principles; to equality, freedom, inalienable rights, and authority derived from the consent of the governed. . . . The Revolution, the Declaration of Independence, the constitutions of the states and the Constitution of 1787 explain their national existence.". . . The United States thus had its origins in a conscious political act, in the assertion of certain basic political principles, and in adherence to constitutional agreements based on those principles.[13]

As a result of this fact, Huntington goes on,

it is possible to speak of a body of political ideas that constitutes "Americanism" in a sense in which one can never speak of "Britishism," "Frenchism," "Germanism," or "Japanesism." Americanism in this sense is comparable to other ideologies or religions. "Americanism is to the American," Leon Samson has said, "not a tradition or a territory, not what France is to a Frenchman or England to an Englishman, but a doctrine – what socialism is to a socialist." To reject the central ideas of that doctrine is to be un-American. . . . In the United States, as in no other society, ideology and nationality are fused and the disappearance of the former would mean the end of the latter.[14]

Swedish social scientist Gunnar Myrdal, in his classic *An American Dilemma*, had earlier expressed views nearly identical to those of Huntington. Myrdal, as a foreign observer, was perhaps in an even better position than Huntington to assess the importance of what he called the American Creed in welding together so restless and so heterogeneous a population as that which he encountered in his extensive travels in the United States. In the very opening lines of his mammoth study, he captures well the foreigner's initial shock at America's seemingly discordant energies and bewildering diversity. "It is a commonplace," he writes,

to point out the heterogeneity of the American nation and the swift succession of all sorts of changes in all its component parts, and, as it often seems, in every conceivable direction. America is truly a shock to the stranger. The bewildering impression it gives of dissimilarity throughout and of chaotic unrest is indicated by the fact that few outside observers – and, indeed, few native Americans – have been able to avoid the intellectual escape of speaking about America as "paradoxical".[15]

[13] Ibid., pp. 24–5.
[14] Ibid., pp. 25, 27.
[15] Gunnar Myrdal, *An American Dilemma: The Negro Problem and Modern Democracy* (Harper and Brothers Publishers, New York, 1944), p. 3.

   This seemingly discordant medley, nevertheless, was not without its
harmony and unifying rhythms, Myrdal believed, which were supplied, he
said, by the nation's basic commitment to the underlying political principles enshrined in the Declaration of Independence and the Bill of Rights. It
was the shared belief in a peculiarly American view of liberty, equality, and
individual rights, Myrdal contended, that provided the unifying framework
in which America's diverse peoples could all get along:

> Still, there is evidently a strong unity in this nation and a basic homogeneity and
> stability in its valuations. Americans of all national origins, classes, regions, creeds,
> and colors, have something in common: a social *ethos*, a political creed. It is diffi-
> cult to avoid the judgment that this "American Creed" is the cement in the struc-
> ture of this great and disparate nation. When the American Creed is once detected,
> the cacophony becomes a melody. The further observation then becomes apparent:
> that America, compared to every other country in Western civilization, large or
> small, has the *most explicitly expressed* system of general ideals in reference to
> human interrelations. This body of ideals is more widely understood and appreci-
> ated than similar ideals are anywhere. . . . These ideals of the essential dignity of the
> individual human being, of the fundamental equality of all men, and of certain
> inalienable rights to freedom, justice, and a fair opportunity represent to the
> American people the essential meaning of the nation's early struggle for indepen-
> dence. In the clarity and intellectual boldness of the Enlightenment period these
> tenets were written into the Declaration of Independence, the Preamble to the
> Constitution, the Bill of Rights and into the constitutions of the several states. The
> ideals of the American Creed have thus become the highest law of the land.[16]

   Myrdal was perhaps most surprised to find that America's African population, though denied many of the benefits of the nation's high ideals, had
not turned against them in a cynical rejection of the hypocrisy of the majority. Not only did African Americans appeal to the American Creed when
pleading their case for the redress of the many wrongs done to them, they
genuinely seemed to believe in the Creed and affirm it as the basis of their
own civic identity:

> Sometimes one even gets the impression that there is a relation between the intense
> apprehension of high and uncompromising ideals and the spotty reality. One feels
> that it is, perhaps, the difficulty of giving reality to the *ethos* in this young and still
> somewhat unorganized nation – that it is the prevalence of "wrongs" in America,
> "wrongs" judged by the high standards of the national Creed – which helps make
> the ideals stand out so clearly. America is continuously struggling for its soul. . . .
> The Negro people in America are no exception to the national pattern. . . . The
> American Negroes know that they are a subordinated group experiencing, more
> than anybody else in the nation, the consequences of the fact that the Creed is not

---

[16] Ibid.

lived up to in America. Yet their faith in the Creed is not simply a means of pleading their unfulfilled rights. They, like the whites, are under the spell of the great
national suggestion.[17]

   Writing more than a decade after Myrdal, another foreign observer, the
German émigré scholar Hans Kohn, similarly attributed America's exceptionalism in successfully integrating people of diverse ethnic and religious
backgrounds to the near-universal acceptance of the Jeffersonian ideals of
liberty and equality. Immigrants to America came from diverse ethnic backgrounds, Kohn points out, and many chose to maintain their particular
ethnic character for an extended period of time. What elicited the *unum*
out of the *pluribus*, Kohn believed, was not the unity of an ethnic or genetic
type – which didn't exist in America – but the common affirmation of the
political and humanitarian ideals represented by Jeffersonian liberalism.
Immigrants of varying backgrounds readily assimilated and adopted these
ideals as their very own:

Thomas Jefferson, who as a young man had opposed immigration, wished in 1817
to keep the doors of America open, "to consecrate a sanctuary for those whom the
misrule of Europe may compel to seek happiness in other climes." . . . This procla-
mation of an open port for immigrants was in keeping with Jefferson's faith in
America's national mission as mankind's vanguard in the fight for individual liberty,
the embodiment of the rational and humanitarian ideals of eighteenth century
Western man. The American nation was to be a universal nation – not only in the
sense that the idea which it pursued was believed to be universal and valid for the
whole of mankind, but also in the sense that it was a nation composed of many
ethnic strains. Such a nation, held together by liberty and diversity, had to be firmly
integrated around allegiance to the American idea, an idea to which everyone could
be assimilated for the very reason that it was a universal idea.[18]

The immigrants [to America] often in the first genertion, certainly in the second, have
learned to share the happiness and pride of the native American in their liberty and
equality, in the institutions and opportunities of the new homeland. In view of the
multitudes who poured into America and their so different backgrounds, one can say
that the melting pot worked well. It was not a racial melting pot: the immigrants were
not assimilated to the original Anglo-American stock; for that they were much too
numerous; though cases of intermarriage have been frequent, ethnic and religious
groups have tended to preserve, at least for some time, their separate personalities.
But these immigrants were assimilated in a much deeper sense, in the sense of a spiritual transformation. They became Americans in the full sense of the word, a sense
which does not include race or ethnic origin but is based upon loyalty to an idea.[19]

---

[17] Ibid., pp. 3–4. Sociologist Robert Bellah has spoken of some of the principles that
    Huntington and Myrdal enunciate as constituting nothing less than an American "civil
    religion," but one that he sees under threat. On this, see Bellah's *The Broken Covenant*
    (Seabury, New York, 1975).
[18] Kohn, *American Nationalism*, p. 138.
[19] Ibid., p. 150.

To be sure, the pluralist/universalist model of American nationality, championed by Myrdal, Kohn, Huntington, and others, has not been without its critics. On both normative and empirical grounds it has been vigorously attacked by those who would stress the central importance of Anglo-Saxon ethnic and cultural hegemony as factors contributing to the success of the United States as a stable and progressive society. Indeed, from earliest times to the present, there have really been two traditions on this issue, with the pluralist/universalist ideal alternating in prominence with the nativist/Anglo-Saxonist one for political and social dominance. Even though the pluralist tradition is more in tune with the ideals of America's founding documents (at least if one ignores the Constitution's compromise on the slave issue and the separate status of Native Americans), it has at various times in America's past, especially during times of great national anxiety over rapid immigration and rapid ethnic change, been overwhelmed by tides of Anglo-Saxonist nativism.

The most striking instance of this was the spectacular rise of the Native American Party (or "Know-Nothings," as their opponents called them) largely in response to the huge influx of impoverished Irish Catholic immigrants in the late 1840s and 1850s. By 1855 these "Know-Nothings" had succeeded in dominating the state legislature in Massachusetts and in capturing no less than six state governorships. They declined, however, in the years immediately preceding the outbreak of the Civil War even more rapidly than they had arisen. A similarly rapid rise – and decline – in membership and influence was experienced by the anti-immigration American Protective Association in the 1890s. It grew largely in response to the growing number of eastern and southern European Catholic and Jewish immigrants flocking to America beginning in the 1880s. The early 1920s repeated the pattern with the growth of a revitalized Ku Klux Klan that at its height contained perhaps 3 million members. Its Invisible Empire stretched from its home base in the South to huge areas in the North and Midwest and, at its peak, exerted a powerful influence in several state legislatures. The Klan's target at this time was similar to the older Protective Association – Catholic and Jewish immigrants, as well as Southern Negroes, who for the first time were migrating in great numbers to other parts of the country. One of the more paradoxical effects of the Klan in this era was in the powerful reaction it provoked among many African Americans. Its racist and chauvinistic brand of Protestant white nationalism contributed significantly to the growth of a similar (though nonviolent) style of black nationalism in the form of the Garveyite movement that, like the Klan itself, enjoyed a spectacular rise in membership in the early 1920s, only to decline precipitously by the end of the decade.[20]

---

[20] The history of nativist opposition to non-Protestant immigrants is presented in John Higham's *Strangers in the Land: Patterns of American Nativism 1860–1925* (Rutgers University Press, New Brunswick, N.J., 1955).

It is important here, however, not to let our image of the Klan or the Know-Nothings obscure our understanding of some of the issues that were involved in these movements. Large-scale immigration and rapid racial and ethnic change are almost never accomplished without huge disruptions and substantial inconveniences to populations that are already settled and established. The representatives of those populations who oppose the change often have very good reasons for doing so, and the concerns they express are not to be dismissed out of hand as alarmist imaginings of xenophobes or bigots. Ben Franklin, for instance – that most genial and practical of men – was hardly a bigot when he questioned the wisdom of allowing ever larger numbers of German speakers into English-speaking Pennsylvania:

This will in a few years become a German colony: Instead of their learning our language, we must learn theirs, or live as in a foreign country. Already the English begin to quit particular neighborhoods surrounded by Dutch [the German-speaking Pennsylvania Dutch], being made uneasy by the disagreeableness of dissonant manners; and in time, numbers will probably quit the province for the same reason. Besides, the Dutch under-live, and are thereby enabled to under-work and under-sell the English; who are thereby extremely incommoded and consequently disgusted, so that there can be no cordial affection or unity between the two nations.[21]

The concerns Franklin raised about immigrants bringing with them foreign speech, foreign manners, and a willingness to work for less ("under-work and under-sell") than natives were not fanciful and would remain a constant among immigration critics to the present day. The concerns of workers over economic competition has been particularly pronounced in immigration debates since at least the 1840s with the large influx of poor Irish and Germans. An article in the November 29, 1844, issue of the *Native American*, for instance, raised issues about immigration that have always been paramount among wage earners. This Philadelphia-based nativist newspaper, which supported various measures to limit the influence of recent immigrants to the United States, protested at this time: "Our laboring men, native and naturalized, are met at every turn and at every avenue of employment, with recently imported workmen from the low wages countries of the Old World. They fill our large cities, reduce the wages of labor, and they increase the hardship of the old settler."[22] Similar complaints could be found in the areas settled by the Chinese in the 1870s, by the Japanese in the 1890s, by the Italians at the turn of the century, and by many Hispanic groups today.[23]

---

[21] Kohn, *American Nationalism*, pp. 137–8.   [22] Ibid., p. 144.

[23] For a similar assessment of the effects of the large-scale recent immigration on the nation's lowest-paid workers, see George J. Borjas, *Heaven's Door: Immigration Policy and the American Economy* (Princeton University Press, Princeton, N.J., 1999). Borjas, who is himself an immigrant from Cuba, supports cutting back foreign immigration to the levels of the 1970s.

Other critics of foreign immigration have focused less on the economic competition and more on the political and cultural differences of foreign immigrants and on the threat posed to natives when immigrants become the dominant social force in a region. Foreign-speaking immigrants in the past have often been seen as unassimilable and possessed of discordant attitudes and manners that were not consistent with the kind of orderly, Anglo-Saxon–derived democracy that was practiced in the United States. The novelist James Fenimore Cooper, for instance, wrote in 1838:

The great immigration of foreigners into the country, and the practice of remaining, or of assembling, in the large towns, renders universal suffrage doubly oppressive to the citizens of the latter. The natives of other countries bring with them the prejudices of another and an antagonist state of society; or what is still worse, their reaction; and it is a painful and humiliating fact, that several of the principal places of this country are, virtually, under the control of this class, who have few convictions of liberty, beyond those which arise from a love of licentiousness, who are totally ignorant of its governing principles, and who, in their hearts and language, are hostile to the very people whose hospitality they enjoy. Many of these men cannot even speak the language of the land, and perhaps a majority of them cannot read the great social compact, by which society is held together.[24]

Nevertheless, however understandable the concerns of immigration critics have been at various times, and however real the problems to which they sought to draw attention, the fact still remains that their fears proved hugely exaggerated. America, as Margaret Thatcher remarked, has shown itself quite adept at assimilating foreigners from diverse lands, and while inconveniences and disruptions of the native population have certainly occurred, the natives do not seem to have fared so badly in the long run. Indeed, America seems to have been enriched in countless ways by the diversity of its many immigrant peoples and their descendants. One cannot resist the conclusion in this great controversy over what it takes to be a good American, that defenders of the pluralist/universalist tradition have wound up espousing not only a more elevated and inspiring ideal than their opponents, but one that has proven practically effective as well.

This is a critical point to keep in mind. Despite its great ethnic and religious diversity, America in many ways, with its dedication to a set of core unifying political principles, has proven itself to be a more stable, less fractured society than many of the more demographically homogeneous societies of the Old World. It has certainly proven itself to be a more orderly, less tumultuous, less faction-ridden society in the twentieth century than ethnically homogeneous Germany, Italy, or Greece. "Some European observers," Hans Kohn writes,

[24] Ibid., pp. 156–7.

have emphasized and exaggerated the antipathy felt by "native" Americans toward immigrants, or at least toward some categories of immigrants, and have attributed it to the desire or need for basing the American nation on a unity of race or faith such as is supposed to exist in the formation of European nations; thereby, they apparently believe, the American nation would be endowed with a greater cohesion and strength. Yet the American idea of liberty – with its recognition of diversity in origins and religious background – has proved a stronger national cement and a more secure basis for ordered liberty and economic prosperity than bonds of common blood or religion or the uniformity of a closed society. In spite of the lesser homogeneity of the population, there is greater national cohesion in the United States – and less danger of disruptive factionalism – than in France, Germany or Italy. In America diverse people are held together by their common faith in individual liberty and equality; these carry in America a different meaning from that observable on the European continent.[25]

---

[25] Kohn, *American Nationalism*, pp. 148–9. To the defenders of Anglo-Saxon nativism, past and present, we might offer the following words of Lincoln: "Our progress in degeneracy appears to me to be pretty rapid. As a nation, we began by declaring that '*all men are created equal*.' We now practically read it 'all men are created equal, *except negroes*.' When the Know-Nothings get control, it will read 'all men are created equal, except negroes, *and foreigners, and Catholics*.' When it comes to this I should prefer emigrating to some country where they make no pretense of loving liberty – to Russia, for instance, where despotism can be taken pure, and without the base alloy of hypocrisy." (From a letter to Joshua F. Speed, 1855; cited in Werner Sollors, *Beyond Ethnicity*, Oxford University Press, New York, 1986, p. 92.) Or even more telling, we might offer those of Herman Melville, arguably America's greatest novelist: "There is something in the contemplation of the mode in which America has been settled, that, in a noble breast, should forever extinguish the prejudices of national dislikes. Settled by the people of all nations, all nations may claim her for their own. You cannot spill a drop of American blood without spilling the blood of the whole world. Be he Englishman, Frenchman, German, Dane, or Scot, the European who scoffs at an American calls his own brother *Raca*, and stands in danger of the judgment. We are not a narrow tribe of men with a bigoted Hebrew nationality – whose blood has been debased in the attempt to ennoble it, by maintaining an exclusive succession among ourselves. No, our blood is as the flood of the Amazon, made up of a thousand noble currents all pouring into one. We are not a nation, so much as a world; for unless we may claim all the world for our sire, like Melchisedec, we are without father or mother. For who were our father and our mother? . . . Our ancestry is lost in the universal paternity. . . . We are the heirs of all time, and with all nations we divide our inheritance. On this Western Hemisphere all tribes and people are forming into one federal whole, and there is a future which shall see the estranged children of Adam restored as to the old hearthstone in Eden." (From Melville's *Redburn: His First Voyage*, 1848; cited in Kohn, *American Nationalism*, p. 148.) Or finally, we might offer those of Franklin Roosevelt, who, in the middle of the Second World War, at the height of the anti-Japanese feelings in the United States to which his own administration was highly susceptible, wrote to Secretary of War Henry Stimson in support of the formation of a Japanese-American combat unit: "The principle on which this country was founded and by which it has always been governed, is that Americanism is a matter of the mind and heart. Americanism is not, and never was, a matter of race and ancestry. A good American is one who is loyal to this country and to our creed of liberty and democracy." (Letter dated February 1, 1943; cited in Schlesinger, *The Disuniting of America*, p. 14.)

III. The Universal Futurism of the American Dream

The United States, it is often said, is a country that has been settled by people who have come from many diverse lands but who all share a common desire to seek a better life for themselves and their children. This remark highlights the second feature of the American experience that we think is responsible for its exceptionalism in avoiding the kind of ethnic and religious strife that has destroyed so many other similarly diverse societies: the immigrants' break with the past, the orientation toward the future, and the common desire of most who have come to America not just to live in a land dedicated to political equality and democratic governance but also to be citizens of one that will provide the opportunity for average sorts of people who are willing to work hard and save to experience an improvement in their material condition. Much has been said about the American Dream, but it is perhaps not sufficiently appreciated just how important the widely shared goals and aspirations represented by the dream have been in providing social and political stability in a nation with such vast racial, ethnic, and religious diversity as the United States.

"The love of wealth," Tocqueville observed, "is . . . to be traced, as either a principal or an accessory motive, at the bottom of all that the Americans do."[26] "The love of well-being has now become the predominant taste of the nation."[27] "In America everyone finds facilities unknown elsewhere for making or increasing his fortune."[28] "Not only are manufacturing and commercial classes to be found in the United States, as they are in all other countries, but, what never occurred elsewhere, the whole community is simultaneously engaged in productive industry and commerce."[29] As an Old World aristocrat, Tocqueville was perhaps more attuned than we are today to understanding just how radical a break this kind of universal pursuit of an improved living standard was with Europe's past and the past of most other civilizations. Throughout most of human history, the possibilities of socioeconomic betterment have usually been available only on a limited scale, and by both custom and law, ascribed social and occupational status – one usually fixed at birth – has been a more common human arrangement than the kind of wide open possibilities for economic and occupational advancement found in the United States. The fixed-status order of European feudal society, which put a premium on family background and distinguished lineage, was superseded in America by a radically new kind of order, where the masses of common people, who could not look

---

[26] Alexis de Tocqueville, *Democracy in America*, Volume II (Phillips Bradley translation, Vintage Books, New York, 1945), p. 240.

[27] Ibid., p. 138.

[28] Ibid., p. 37.

[29] Ibid.

backward with pride to a distinguished ancestry, could look forward with eagerness and hope to the many future possibilities offered for occupational and material improvement, if not for themselves, at least for their children and grandchildren.

We can perhaps see this radical shift most easily in the peculiarly American valorization of the "self-made man," and the higher prestige that came to be associated in America with the New Money that was earned by one's own effort rather than the Old Money of family inheritance that was the source of prestige elsewhere. Historian Gordon Wood has stressed the effect of the American Revolution and the later triumph of the Jeffersonian and Jacksonian brands of democracy in bringing about this radical change. The Revolution and the changes brought about in early nineteenth-century America, says Wood, shattered hierarchical privilege in both the social and economic order. The shattering of monopolistic privileges in the economic order during the Jacksonian period was particularly important for the future development of America, Wood contends. It created, he says, "a dizzying spiral of rising aspirations and expanding opportunities, the like of which no society in history had ever experienced in such a short period of time." More than ever before, Wood says, what counted in the equation of getting ahead was enterprise and hard work, rather than family connections, political privilege, or the manners and education of a gentleman. "It was out of these developments," he explains,

that emerged the ideal of the "self-made man," a symbol that Americans in time became so familiar with that we have forgotten what a novel, indeed radical, notion it originally was. Of course there had always been social mobility in Western society, some times and some places more than others; but it had generally been a mobility of a peculiar sort in which the upward-thrusting individual sought to acquire the attributes of the social status he aspired to and at the same time tried to forget and disguise the lowly sources from whence he came. Such mobility had not been something to be proud of, as indicated by the pejorative terms – "upstarts," "nouveau riches," "parvenus" – used to disparage its participants. Now, however, in early 19th century America, independent mobile men began boasting of their humble origins and their ability to have made it on their own, without influence and patronage, even without education. . . . Because the future was filled with such promises for so many ordinary people, few Americans as yet looked back with any sense of discrepancy and nostalgia to the world they had lost. . . . They had created a society in which common ordinary people in their separate and strenuous pursuits of wealth dictated and shaped the contours and values of life.[30]

It is easy to criticize the vulgarity, materialism, and fevered pursuit of gain that men of refinement, from Tocqueville to the present, have often

---

[30] Gordon S. Wood, *Social Radicalism and the Idea of Equality in the American Revolution* (University of St. Thomas, Houston, Tex., 1976), pp. 13–14.

condemned in America. Such criticisms are at least partially warranted, but it is important to keep in mind here that there are many worse things in this world that human beings can occupy their time with than making an honest dollar. Making war and making trouble seem to be the two most common alternatives, at least for males.[31] Whatever else one may say about it, the restless quest of Americans to improve their economic condition, which has been a distinguishing feature of American life since late colonial times, has contributed substantially to the relative peaceableness of the American polity. As Tocqueville well understood, hard-working people looking out for their own material advancement have too much at stake in maintaining domestic peace and tranquility to be interested in revolutionary agitation or radical utopian projects of the kind that have wreaked such havoc elsewhere in the world. And the future-orientation toward life implicit in the American Dream has contributed greatly to an overall optimism that has enabled many of those emigrating to America to leave their often bitter historical memories behind and focus on the many new opportunities available to them in the New World.

Emigrating to America, writes Arthur Schlesinger, "was seen as a severing of roots, a liberation from the stifling past, an entry into a new life, an interweaving of separate ethnic strands into a new national design. ... The unstated national motto was 'Never look back.'"[32] Schlesinger illustrates this with the advice given by Secretary of State John Quincy Adams to a German nobleman who inquired about the wisdom of emigrating to America. Those contemplating such a relocation, Adams advised, "must cast off the European skin, never to resume it. They must look forward to their posterity rather than backward to their ancestors."[33] The salutary effect of this attitude can hardly be understated when it comes to understanding how America was able to incorporate within the same nation, ethnic, religious, and national-origin groups that in the Old World often seethed with the deepest hatreds of one another and considered themselves mutual enemies. An ancient Chinese proverb observes that "men do not live even one hundred years, yet they harbor the grief of a thousand." For many of those who were willing to uproot themselves and emigrate to America, the grief of a thousand years was put behind them as a new horizon opened with new possibilities for economic cooperation that would lead to the advancement of all. With the future filled with promise, they were less inclined to dwell on the hatreds and humiliations of the past.

---

[31] On money-making as an alternative to war-making and trouble-making, see Albert Hirschman's classic *The Passions and the Interests: Political Arguments for Capitalism Before Its Triumph* (Princeton University Press, Princeton, N.J., 1977).

[32] Schlesinger, *The Disuniting of America*, p. 6.

[33] Quoted in Schlesinger, ibid., p. 7.

This emphasis on the future in America as a factor mitigating ancient ethnic and religious strife has been explained best by Kohn, our most acute student of European nationalism. America's emphasis on the future, together with its focus on the individual, Kohn explains,

helps to create this new nation out of many nations, to strengthen the Unum in the Pluribus. European and Asian nationalists have been accustomed to look to the past and to try to revive its real or imagined splendors. Ancestral heroic deeds and cultural achievements have thrown their spell over the living generation which felt itself justified and heightened by the glories of the achievements of individuals and generations long dead. Territories settled or conquered in the past, frontiers drawn long ago and changed since, have in the age of nationalism in many cases appealed from reenactment into a new living reality and have by this confusion of the past and the present caused unbelievable suffering and disaster. Real or more often imagined humiliations and wrongs suffered in the past have haunted and disfigured the emotional life of many peoples. Americans on the other hand are not accustomed to look back upon the past. They are a new nation established on virgin soil. . . . Thomas Jefferson spoke for the American people when he wrote on August 1, 1816: "I like the dreams of the future better than the history of the past." . . . This futurist outlook in the United States was not founded only in the optimism of the Enlightenment. As a nation of many peoples and many faiths, the United States could not allow its various component parts to look too much to the past, which divided them and often set one against the other. It could unite them in liberty and tolerance only if the immigrants looked not back toward the innumerable defeats and victories, scars and triumphs of their ancestral history, but forward to a common future based upon individual activity within the framework of the common constitution and the common American ideas. . . . This community of the future, a future already realized in the present and yet ever expanding beyond all realization, was the strongest bond uniting the Americans of all generations and of all strains.[34]

The process Kohn describes has been so successful that it is difficult for most Americans today even to understand the kinds of psychic forces that drive many ethnic conflicts around the world. The spectacle of the Protestant Orangemen, still marching defiantly in their dotage through Catholic areas of strife-torn Northern Ireland, trying to relive the glories of the victory of King William and his Protestant armies over the hated Catholic James II in the Battle of the Boyne of 1690 – the spectacle strikes most Americans as pitiable if not deranged. To sacrifice the well-being of one's self and one's children, and the long-term peace and repose of the land in which one lives and seeks to make a home, for the sake of ancient quarrels that one only learns about in history books is to most Americans the height of folly. "Come, let us work and make money together and create a better life for our children" has been the dominant American way of thinking on

[34] Kohn, *American Nationalism*, pp. 150-2.

these matters, and on the whole it has proved remarkably successful in reducing the kind of internecine ethnic and religious strife that has bitterly divided so many other countries.

This aspect of the American experience was most appreciated by the British writer Israel Zangwill. In his enormously influential play, *The Melting Pot*, Zangwill, whose own parents were Russian Jews, describes the travail of a young Russian Jewish immigrant composer in New York City, who has fallen in love with a Russian Gentile woman. The composer, David Quixano, learns that his beloved, Vera Revendal, is the daughter of a now deceased anti-Semitic Russian father, who in the Old Country supported a murderous pogrom in which David's own parents and brother were killed. Despite their discordant family heritages, and despite the fierce opposition to their marriage from family members and friends, David and Vera persist in their devotion to one another. The two young Russian Americans are determined to marry and to leave the mutual animosities of their Old World heritage behind. In the final climactic scene of the play, which takes place in lower Manhattan from the roof of a settlement house with the Statue of Liberty in the background, David describes his inspiring vision for America:

DAVID: There she lies, the great Melting-Pot – listen! Can't you hear the roaring and the bubbling? There gapes her mouth [*pointing east towards the New York harbor*] – the harbor where a thousand mammoth feeders come from the ends of the world to pour in their human freight. Ah, what a stirring and a seething! Celt and Latin, Slav and Teuton, Greek and Syrian, – black and yellow –

VERA: Jew and Gentile –

DAVID: Yes, East and West, and North and South, the palm and pine, the pole and the equator, the crescent and the cross – how the great Alchemist purges them with his purging flame! Here shall they all unite to build the Republic of Man and the Kingdom of God. Ah, Vera, what is the glory of Rome and Jerusalem where all nations and races come to worship and look back, compared with the glory of America, where all races and nations come to labor and look forward!

[*David raises his hand in benediction over the shining city*]

Peace, peace, to all ye unborn millions, fated to fill this giant continent – the God of our *children* give you Peace.[35]

The play ends with the torch of the Statue of Liberty twinkling in the background, and as the final curtain begins its slow descent, choral voices with music accompaniment join in the singing of "America." *The Melting Pot* was first performed in Washington, D.C., in the fall of 1908, and became immensely popular in the United States – though not, significantly, in Old World Britain where its author had grown up. It was enthusiastically embraced as reflecting some of the best in American ideals by such

[35] Israel Zangwill, *The Melting Pot* (Macmillan, New York, 1910), pp. 198–9.

luminaries of the day as Theodore Roosevelt and Jane Addams. "More than any social or political theory," writes the literary historian Werner Sollors, "the rhetoric of Zangwill's play shaped American discourse on immigration and ethnicity, including most notably the language of self-declared opponents of the melting-pot concept."[36]

Among the most important of these self-declared opponents in Zangwill's time was the Harvard philosopher Horace Kallen. In a series of essays later brought together in a book, *Culture and Democracy in the United States* (1924), Kallen argued against the melting-pot metaphor on both normative and empirical grounds. Empirically, Kallen contended, America was hardly a melting pot, as most of its citizens married within their ethnic and religious groups, and even when they didn't, it was not accurate to speak of the formation of a genuinely new race of mankind as melting-pot adherents often did. Even if one could speak of such a genuinely new American race, it existed, Kallen said, side by side with the older ethnic and religious subdivisions, which showed no signs of disappearing. "The older types persist," he wrote, "and . . . new types come as additions to the old."[37] Most of the metals in the pot did not appear to melt very much.

Kallen opposed the melting-pot image as an ideal even more fervently than he protested its inadequacy as an actual description of fact. Most

---

[36] Sollors, *Beyond Ethnicity*, p. 66. While popularized by Zangwill's play, the melting-pot image itself, or similar metaphors, had a long tradition in America going back to J. Hector St. John Crèvecoeur and his influential *Letters from an American Farmer* (1782). America, the French observer rhapsodized, was melting the diverse strands of Europe into a new man: "What then is the American, this new man? He is either an European, or the descendant of an European, hence that strange mixture of blood, which you will find in no other country. I could point out to you a family whose grandfather was an Englishman, whose wife was Dutch, whose son married a French woman, and whose present four sons have now four wives of different nations. *He* is an American, who, leaving behind him all his ancient prejudices and manners, receives new ones from the new mode of life he has embraced, the new government he obeys, and the new rank he holds. He becomes an American by being received in the broad lap of our great *Alma Mater*. Here individuals of all nations are melted into a new race of men, whose labours and posterity will one day cause great changes in the world." (Quoted in Sollors, *Beyond Ethnicity*, pp. 76–7.) Writing two generations later, Emerson was even more effusive in his use of the melting-pot metaphor, and geographically more inclusive. In a notebook entry of 1845, he wrote: "I hate the narrowness of the Native American Party. . . . Man is the most composite of all creatures. . . . As in the old burning of the temple at Corinth, by the melting and intermixture of silver and gold and other metals, a new compound more precious than any, called the Corinthian Brass, was formed so in this continent – asylum of all nations, the energy of Irish, Germans, Swedes, Poles and the Cossacks, and all the European tribes – of the Africans, and of the Polynesians, will construct a new race, a new religion, a new state, a new literature, which will be as vigorous as the new Europe which came out of the smelting pot of the Dark Ages, or that which earlier emerged from the Pelasgic and Etruscan barbarians." (Quoted in Sollors, *Beyond Ethnicity*, p. 95.)

[37] Horace Kallen, *Culture and Democracy in the United States: Studies in Group Psychology of the American People* (Boni and Liveright Publishers, New York, 1924), p. 177.

human beings, he argued, have a very special relationship to their ethnic or ethnico-religious communities, which is established more by inheritance than by active choice or design. Even though people don't choose their grandparents, their relationship to their forbears and their ethnic heritage is usually one of very special significance to them. Indeed, it is within their ethnic communities that most people feel most at home, and there should be nothing suspect about such feelings. Ethnic groups, Kallen said, "establish the lines of association, the preferences of the herd type in which the individual feels freest and most at ease, in which he can feel relaxed and be at play." In America, he noted, "Italians and Jews and Yankees and Irishmen may have become people of a single culture, tradition, aspiration and public behavior, yet they will regularly associate with people of their own racial and familial tone, and their marriages will not so very largely overflow the boundaries set by these factors and by their churches." This kind of ethnocentric behavior is natural to man, Kallen believed, and immigrants should not be required to abandon their ethnic attachments to become fully American. In any case, they had not done so in the past, and would not be likely to do so in the future. The Americanization of the immigrants, he said, "consisted of their compenetration into the country's economic and political pattern, and of that alone. The residue of their being, where they were freest and most at home, remained continuous with their own old-worldly inheritance."[38]

Kallen's real opponents were the more extreme variety of Americanization proponents, who sought to efface all traces of the immigrants' past by prohibiting such things as the teaching of foreign languages in the schools. The demands of a politically and economically unified country, he believed, may require all to learn English and to participate in the common democratic process, but they did not require ethnic homogenization through mass intermarriage as suggested by the melting-pot metaphor, nor did they require wholesale abandonment of cherished ethnic loyalties and traditions. A freedom-loving democratic society, he contended, must leave room for what he called Cultural Pluralism, and must reject the efforts to fit everyone into the same mold. Kallen, who was a Jew, believed that human individuality, both of persons and of ethnic groups, was being suppressed in his time by a stultifying Anglo-Saxon cultural imperialism that was represented in its most menacing contours by the powerful Ku Klux Klan of his day. A 1924 article titled "Culture and the Klan," concluded with the ominous challenge, "The alternative before Americans is Kultur Klux Klan or Cultural Pluralism."[39]

Kallen's essays provided a needed corrective to the more high-handed style of Anglo-Saxonist assimilationism that gained ground during and

[38] Ibid., pp. 128, 184–5.
[39] Ibid., p. 43.

immediately following the First World War, and while Kallen clearly got some things wrong – he severely underestimated, for instance, the degree of intermarriage among third- and fourth-generation immigrants and he incorrectly portrayed the ethnic involvement of individuals as a fixed condition rather than a choice – Kallen successfully showed that one didn't have to become a WASP to become a good American. The Know-Nothingism of the Kultur Klux Klan, he correctly pointed out, would destroy the rich *pluribus* in America in its narrowly conceived view of the *unum*. Even though becoming an American did require numerous changes and adaptations – and Kallen would no doubt have placed the abandonment of Old World feuds and civil strifes and the adoption of a tolerant peaceableness toward outsider groups as preeminent among these – it did not require of immigrant groups a total forgetfulness of their past or an abandonment of their cherished group identities. Unlike the more extreme assimilationists of his time, Kallen was quite comfortable with "hyphenated Americanism," and he correctly perceived that a cohesive society no more required that Chinese Americans, Polish Americans, or Jewish Americans become culturally Anglo-Saxon than it did that they become Episcopalians.

A similar point has been made in more recent times by the sociologist and theorist of assimilation Milton Gordon. Just as Kallen spoke of the ethnic group as one in which Americans could find "the residue of their being" beyond their American national identity, Gordon speaks of ethnic attachments as constituting an "inner layer" of the personality that can coexist quite comfortably for most people with their feelings of attachment to America. This inner layer is different for people of different ethnic and religious groups – and, indeed, distinguishes them as such – though they are all equally American. In a modern complex society, Gordon writes, "ethnic identification . . . may contain several 'layers.'" The point, he says, "is not that Negroes, Jews, and Catholics in the United States do not think of themselves as Americans. They do. It is that they also have an 'inner layer' sense of peoplehood which is Negro, or Catholic, as the case may be, not 'white Protestant' or 'white, Anglo-Saxon Protestant.'"[40]

Samuel P. Huntington offers an observation similar to Gordon's. "For the immigrants," he writes,

becoming an American could mean accepting and identifying with American social, economic, and political values and institutions – whose appeal had, of course, been a principal reason for their immigration in the first place. In effect, a bargain was struck: ethnic groups retained so long as they wished their ethnic identity, but they converted to American political values, ideals, and symbols. Adherence to the latter was the test of how "American" one was, and it was perfectly compatible with the

---

[40] Milton Gordon, *Human Nature, Class, and Ethnicity* (Oxford University Press, New York, 1978), p. 175n.

maintenance of ethnic culture and traditions. The primordial or organic ties remained in large part ethnic; the political or ideological ties were American. . . . At times, descendants of earlier immigrants could and did speak contemptuously of "hyphenated Americans," but first- and second-generation Americans were better Americans for being hyphenated. . . . American political values and ideals . . . had their roots primarily in British sources, but American national identity was defined in terms of the former [i.e., specific values and ideals] rather than the latter [i.e., British ethnicity].[41]

If Zangwill's play overstated the effects of intermarriage in forming a new American racial type – and understated the degree of persistence of Old World ethnic and religious identities – it clearly got it right on the issue of the American Dream. People did come to America – and continue to come – "to labor and look forward," and to bestow the blessings of God and the bounties of America on their children and their children's children. The dream has become the defining characteristic of much of American life, and at least since the Roosevelt Revolution of the 1930s, governments at all levels have tried to bring the promise of the dream to ever larger segments of the population. Besides assuming greater responsibility for economic growth through sound monetary and fiscal policies, aggressive infrastructure creation, equitable laws of contract and exchange, and so on, government in America since the New Deal has directed its energies ever more aggressively to helping ordinary sorts of people to achieve the American Dream. Unemployment and workmen's compensation insurance; special legal protections for labor unions; laws prohibiting racial, religious, and gender discrimination in employment, housing, and public accommodations; vastly expanded educational expenditures at the primary and secondary school level; the G.I. Bill and Pell grants; Head Start and other preschool programs; the Small Business Administration loan program; the low-tuition community college system; tax incentives for home ownership – all these programs and innumerable others at the national, state, and local levels can be seen as attempts to bring the promise of the American Dream to an ever wider audience.

One issue that older theorists of integration and assimilation did not address sufficiently, however, was that of differential performance in the economic and occupational arena across different racial, ethnic, and religious groups. Many early social reformers appear to have believed (or at least to have hoped) that, with increasing opportunities for upward socioeconomic mobility opening to all, groups at the lower end would be able to raise themselves up, and that over time there would be a rough parity across all the groups in terms of their economic and occupational status. The free public school system and the increasing opportunities for a college education were seen as particularly important in providing a means of ascent by

[41] Huntington, *American Politics*, p. 27.

which the less-advanced groups could catch up with the more advanced. The G.I. Bill after the Second World War, which increased exponentially the number of people who could attend college, and the subsequent expansion of that uniquely American institution of the community college system, were seen as important components in this opportunity-enhancing strategy.

Alas, things didn't work out the way the reformers hoped. Even though many have been able to take advantage of the enhanced opportunity structure over the past fifty years, it has become apparent to all knowledgeable students of the subject that, in a free market economy, ethnic groups almost never achieve at the same rate, and that disparities often last for generations, if not indefinitely. Ironically, a major source of the difference has turned out to be the persistently different outcomes in the public schools, and in the educational arena more generally. Some groups seem to do much better than others at using the educational system as a ladder of upward mobility, and the pattern set early upon the group's arrival in the United States has often persisted for three or more generations.

These issues need to be discussed at greater length as they are critical for understanding what has kept American society together for so long. We can perhaps get a better understanding of the matter by looking at the differential performance of two of the New Immigrant groups (as they were called in their time) – southern Italians and Ashkenazic Jews. Italians and Jews came to the United States in large numbers during roughly the same time period (1880–1924), they moved to many of the same urban areas of the country, they were both poor and ignorant of the English language when they arrived in America, and they encountered roughly the same level of discrimination and hostility from the Protestant Old Stock. But Jews quickly surpassed Italians in virtually all areas of American life where book learning and educational attainment play an important role. The disparities have continued to persist into the present. Even though most school age Italians and Jews today are well into the fourth and fifth generations, and many are the products of considerable ethnic intermixing, the huge disparities in academic achievement, particularly at the upper levels, continue to be enormous. A glance at the student directory of almost any elite college or university in the country tells the same story: While there are approximately twice as many Italian Americans in the United States as Jews, at the top educational institutions Jewish-surnamed students typically outnumber Italian-surnamed ones by a factor of two-to-one or more. At Harvard and Yale, the ratio may be closer to three- or four-to-one.[42] Students with names

---

[42] Among the nation's most elite institutions, the ratio may be lowest at Princeton. For reasons that have not been entirely explained, but that probably have to do with the much higher ratio of recruited athletes to the overall student population than at other top institutions (and to the fact that Jews are probably much underrepresented among this group), Princeton in recent years has had a Jewish undergraduate presence substantially less than

like Abruzzo, Romano, Marino, and Carlucci, while as able as their peers, are simply overwhelmed in numbers by all the Bernsteins, Levys, Cohens, and Greenbergs. Similar disparities are found among the faculties and top administrators of many of these same institutions, as well as among the faculties of the leading law schools, medical schools, dental schools, journalism schools, film schools, and business schools. In addition, lists of the wealthiest Americans, of the Americans who have won the Nobel Prize for science and economics, of the top American journalists and broadcasters, of the leading publishers and filmmakers, of the most prominent doctors and lawyers, and of all the people who have made it into *Who's Who* all reveal a similar pattern: despite arriving in this country at the same time, settling in the same areas, and encountering many of the same obstacles to advancement, Jewish Americans as a group have out-achieved Italian Americans as a group in many of the most prominent areas of American life, and they have done so to an extraordinary degree. If one considers these outcomes in terms of a group contest, one can say of the Jews in their relation to the Italians what has sometimes been said in the past about the athletes Michael Jordan and Tiger Woods: They are simply in a different league than their competitors.[43]

Yet Italians and Jews are not at each other's throats. Indeed, they often get along with each other quite well, even when living in the same neighborhood and sending their children to the same public school. Italians, it would seem, have generally accepted the vastly superior Jewish economic and occupational position without great bitterness or a sense of grievance, largely, one supposes, because the Jews' superior position is seen as substantially related to genuinely superior Jewish performance, especially in the arena of education. (By contrast, Italians are often bitterly resentful of the affirmative action preferences given to African Americans and Hispanics, primarily because such preferences are seen as unmerited and the result of a fundamental breach in the rules of an equitable achievement game. Such feelings are particularly heightened among working-class and

that at Yale or Harvard. According to a 1996 student survey, 9.1 percent of Princeton freshmen identified themselves as Jews – a figure representing four times the proportion of Jews in the U.S. population but less than half of the estimated proportion of Jews among the undergraduate bodies of Harvard and Yale (and half of the estimated proportion of Jewish students at Princeton in 1973). According to a rough estimate by Nieli based on freshmen/sophomore yearbook entries, approximately 5 percent of Princeton undergraduates in 1997 had Italian surnames. (See the article in the May 14, 1999, issue of *The Chronicle of Higher Education*, "Princeton Tries to Explain a Drop in Jewish Enrollment.")

[43] On Italians and Jews, see the relevant sections of Thomas Sowell's *Ethnic America* (Basic Books, New York, 1981); Nathan Glazer and Daniel Patrick Moynihan, *Beyond the Melting Pot*, Second Edition (MIT Press, Cambridge, Mass., 1970); and the articles under "Italians" and "Jews" in *The Harvard Encyclopedia of American Ethnic Groups*, edited by Stephan Thernstrom, Ann Orlov, and Oscar Handlin (Harvard University Press, Cambridge, Mass., 1980).

lower-middle-income Italians who have the fewest opportunities and advantages in life.[44])

America as a cohesive, multiracial, multiethnic society can only endure if group differences of this kind, like individual differences, are perceived as a natural and inevitable result of diversity and freedom. While perhaps the basis for some disappointment on the part of the less-successful groups, such differences cannot be allowed to become the basis of politicized grievances or a deep sense of social injustice. If differential achievement of this kind is allowed to become the basis for intergroup bitterness, hostility, and resentment, or if it gives rise to widespread paranoia and conspiracy thinking among the less-successful groups, then a pluralistic, multiracial, multiethnic society cannot endure. Under such circumstances, the pessimistic conclusions offered by ethnic separatists become inescapable, and the partition of the country into racially or ethnically separate subdivisions would cease to be such a crackpot idea (or such a remote possibility).

What is true of the Italian/Jewish comparison in the past is probably also true if we pair up some of the lower and higher achieving nationalities among the more recent immigrant groups. The Mexicans and the Asian Indians, the Nicaraguans and the Koreans, the Puerto Ricans and the Chinese – each seem to be showing a pattern of differential achievement not unlike the Italian/Jewish one. And if history is any guide, there is no more reason to believe that the lower achieving groups will do any better in catching up to the higher achieving ones – even while all groups show substantial progress – than has been the case in the past with the Italians vis-à-vis the Jews. Past history and present trends all seem to suggest that the pattern of advancement will not be even across ethnic groups, and at the highest levels of achievement in the more education-intensive arenas, it will not even be close to even. Even though most poor immigrants in time will live to see their children and grandchildren do substantially better than themselves, huge differences in the pattern of group attainment in various areas is virtually inevitable in any free society that allows for upward socioeconomic mobility. Whether these differences in group performance are primarily due to cultural and psychological factors that have their roots in differential historical experience (as the editors of the present volume tend to believe), whether they are due primarily to genetic differences that have their origin in evolutionary biology (as most of the people interviewed in this volume are convinced), or whether they are caused by one or more of any number of alternative factors makes little difference, in one sense at least. For whatever their cause or causes, the differences in ethnic group performance that have always existed in the past are likely to determine the pattern of ethnic group performance among the newer arriving groups in

---

[44] See the outstanding ethnographic study by Jonathan Reider, *Canarsie: The Jews and Italians of Brooklyn Against Liberalism* (Harvard University Press, Cambridge, Mass., 1985).

the future. And little can be done to change this situation that is consistent with the ideals of the American regime. We believe that any multiethnic society that wants to remain stable over time must condemn in the strongest possible way that poisonous envy over superior individual and group performance that we believe is ultimately responsible for much of the anti-Semitism and anti-Asianism to be found in contemporary America (including that expressed by a number of the people interviewed in this volume).

Nathan Glazer has perhaps captured best the direction that a racially, ethnically, and religiously diverse society must take on this matter in an article written in 1969. Differences in group outcomes, particularly in occupations requiring high levels of formal education, are found around the world, Glazer notes, and seem to follow definite patterns. These differences seem to be as true for non-Western countries like Malaya, Nigeria, and Indonesia, he says, as they are for the United States. In the United States, Glazer points out, Italians and certain other ethnic groups did very poorly for many years in the public school system, while Japanese, Chinese, and Jews did outstandingly well, and the difference is not easily explained in terms of factors such as poverty or discrimination. Glazer predicted at this time – correctly as it turned out – that based on available evidence such "different levels of ethnic achievement . . . will continue into the future, even if reduced." His normative conclusion on this situation is worth repeating here. "History and social research convince me," Glazer writes, that

> there are deep and enduring differences between various ethnic groups in their educational achievement and in the broader cultural characteristics in which these differences are, I believe, rooted; that these differences cannot be simply associated with the immediate conditions under which these groups live, whether we define these conditions as being those of levels of poverty and exploitation, or prejudice and discrimination; and that if we are to have a decent society, men must learn to live with some measure of group difference in educational achievement, to tolerate them, and to accept in some degree the disproportion in the distribution of rewards that may flow from differences in educational achievement. . . . We need to press not only our research on these differences, their origins, their extent, their causes, the measures that reduce them, but also develop and strengthen a political and social philosophy that permits a society to accept them, to live with them, and be stronger because of them.[45]

We strongly endorse Glazer's comments here, and believe that learning to live with such inevitable differences in performance among racial and ethnic groups is as important to the well-being of a society as demographically diverse as the United States as the tolerance of different religious beliefs.

---

[45] Nathan Glazer, "Ethnic Groups and Education: Towards the Tolerance of Difference," *The Journal of Negro Education*, Summer 1969, pp. 187, 195.

IV. English for the Children

If the American Creed and the American Dream explain important aspects
of America's relative success in integrating people of diverse ethnic and religious backgrounds into a single cohesive society, a third and equally important factor has been the integrating role played by the English language. It
is indeed one of the sweet ironies of modern history that the United States,
the most racially, ethnically, and religiously diverse country in the world, is
also one of the most linguistically homogeneous ones. This linguistic homogeneity, moreover, has come about, if not spontaneously, at least with a
minimal level of government direction or intervention. Already by the latter
half of the eighteenth century, long before most state and local governments
had begun to establish public school systems in which foreign-language-
speaking children could be instructed in English, English had acquired the
status of a de facto national language. Not only was English the language
of the Declaration of Independence and of the Constitution, but outside of
certain isolated farming communities, it would become the language that
the children and grandchildren of immigrants, if not the immigrants themselves, would usually be most eager to learn and to speak. Americans need
only turn to Canada, their language-troubled neighbor to the north, to see
how different – and how fortunate in many ways – their own language
development has been compared to that in many other multiethnic states.

The "triumph and general adoption of the English language," declared
New York City's mayor De Witt Clinton in 1814, "have been the principal
means of melting us down into one people, and of extinguishing those stubborn prejudices and violent animosities which formed a wall of partition
between the inhabitants of the same land."[46] Clinton, who would go on to
gain fame as chief promoter of the Erie Canal that contributed so much to
linking the eastern and western portions of New York State into a unified
arena of economic activity, understood well the unifying force of a common
language. New York City and New York State over the previous century and
a half had seen the influx of immigrants speaking a cacophony of Dutch,
French, English, German, Swedish, Finish, Italian, Yiddish, and several other
European languages – not to mention the dozens of different languages
spoken by the indigenous tribal peoples whom the Europeans called
"Indians." As a facilitator of trade and commerce, as an avenue of widespread civic participation in democratic politics, and as a medium for the
dissemination of news and information to the widest possible audience,
the English language in America has played a critical role in unifying and
binding together what would otherwise be a disparate tower of Babel. This
was as true in the time of De Witt Clinton at the beginning of the nineteenth
century as it is today in the beginning of the twenty-first – indeed, it is prob-

[46] Cited in Sollors, *Beyond Ethnicity*, p. 83.

ably more important today than ever given the larger number of foreign languages spoken by recent immigrants, many of whom come from areas of
Asia, Africa, and the Middle East not represented in the earlier migrations.

From relatively early times in our nation's history, it has been the expectation – one that we think is most reasonable and worthy of strong endorsement – that immigrants, if they desire to stay in America and become full
citizens, must learn English and see to it that their children learn English
as well. In general, this expectation has been met. The general pattern
throughout most of the nineteenth and all of the twentieth century has been
for the first-generation immigrants to learn a kind of broken English that
was used in their contact with native English speakers outside the home,
while reserving for more intimate contacts between kinsmen and relatives
their native non-English tongue in which they felt much more at ease.
Native-language newspapers and periodicals often flourished among this
group, though they were frequently short lived. The second generation then
often became bilingual, speaking their parents' native tongue while at home,
while conversing in standard American English outside the home. Not infre-
quently, the greater ease with which the children learned English and the
ways of America society led to a kind of role reversal in which the second-
generation children would translate what was going on in America to their
more linguistically isolated parents. In the third generation, finally, the
grandchildren of the immigrants became exclusive English speakers ignorant for the most part of their grandparents' native tongue.

This was the general pattern with almost all the New Immigrant groups
that came to America in the period from 1880 to 1924, and despite nativist
fears of a contrary development, it appears to be the pattern of today's
immigrants as well, including most Latinos, who seem to generate the
bulk of white nativist and white nationalist concern.[47] Some groups have
been successful in maintaining their native language over more extended
periods of time, though these groups have been the rare exceptions. In any
event, they have usually cultivated English language skills alongside their
native tongue, and the process of native-language maintenance has usually
required a great deal of independent effort on the part of the groups
involved. Those successful in such bilingual endeavors have usually been
ethnico-religious groups like Hutterites, Amish, and Hassidic Jews, who
have been able to combine a strong religious commitment to their communal language with both low levels of geographic mobility and low levels
of marriage outside the group. Needless to say, these conditions are most
difficult to maintain in contemporary America.[48]

---

[47] See Linda Chavez, *Out of the Barrio: Towards a New Politics of Hispanic Assimilation*
(Basic Books, New York, 1991).
[48] See on these issues the article by Joshua A. Fishman, "Language Maintenance," in *The
Harvard Encyclopedia of American Ethnic Groups.*

The simple fact of the matter is that immigrants have the most power-ful economic and other practical incentives to learn to speak English well and to encourage their children to get the best English language education that they possibly can. Insofar as immigrants seek to realize the American Dream of upward socioeconomic mobility – and the vast majority certainly do – learning English becomes indispensable. This has been the case at least since the last third of the nineteenth century as America rapidly shifted from an agriculturally based society of rural farmers to an urban-industrial one. While many first-generation immigrants sought to preserve their native lan-guage and cultures, it usually didn't take long for even the first generation to realize that English language skills commanded a premium in America. And even if the immigrants themselves didn't at first realize this, they had the many Old Stock assimilationists who ran the settlement houses, together with the English-speaking members of their own ethnic group, to help explain it to them. A 1912 *Guide to the United States for the Jewish Immigrant* tells the universal story:

English [in America] is absolutely indispensable to the workman. He needs it in order to find work. He needs it to take direction and have his work explained. He needs it unless he is willing to work for the smallest wages with no hope of increase. He needs it when he is in difficulties to avoid interested helpers. He needs it to protect himself without requiring the help of the law. He needs it to understand words of warning and keep out of danger, for every year hundreds of immigrants are hurt or killed in America, because they do not understand the shouts of warning, or do not know how to read danger signals, when a few English words might have saved their lives.[49]

With the shift from an industrial society of urban laborers and factory workers to a postindustrial society of office workers and symbolic analysts, the incentive for learning to read, write, and speak good standard English has become even greater.

Despite the natural tendency for the children of immigrants, if not the immigrants themselves, to learn the dominant language, at various times in America's past doubts have arisen about the effectiveness of this process. During the nativist hysteria following the First World War, for instance, several states, believing that the children of immigrants might take on alien ways and fail to learn English, passed laws prohibiting the teaching of foreign languages in both public and private schools. Nebraska, for instance, passed a law in 1919 that declared: "No person, individually or as a teacher, shall, in any private, denominational, parochial or public school, teach any subject to any person in any language other than the English language. . . . Languages, other than the English language, may be

---

[49] Quoted in *Language in the USA*, edited by Charles A. Ferguson and Shirley Brice Heath (Cambridge University Press, New York, 1981), p. 16.

taught as languages only after a pupil shall have attained and successfully passed the eighth grade as evidenced by a certificate of graduation issued by the county superintendent of the county in which the child resides." In a similar attempt to force English assimilation and American acculturation, a number of states during this period also passed laws requiring all students to attend the government-run public school system.

In two decisions widely hailed by civil libertarians, however, the U.S. Supreme Court struck down both anti–foreign language laws, insofar as they were applied to private schools, and compulsory public school attendance laws. "The power of the state to compel attendance at some school and to make reasonable regulations for all schools, including a requirement that they shall give instructions in English, is not questioned," a majority of the Court declared in *Meyer v. Nebraska* (262 U.S. 390 [1923]). "The desire of the legislature to foster a homogeneous people with American ideals, prepared readily to understand current discussions of civic matters is easy to appreciate," it said. Nevertheless, anti–foreign language laws of the Nebraska type, the Court concluded, far exceeded any legitimate state interest in these matters and conflicted with both the right of parents to educate their children the way they wished and the right of foreign language teachers to pursue their profession. Both of these rights the Court located in the liberty provision of the Fourteenth Amendment's Due Process Clause under the reigning ideal of due process rights that were substantive as well as procedural. The Nebraska law, the Court concluded, trampled upon these rights and was not reasonably related to the legitimate state purpose of having all citizens learn English. Foreign languages, the Court concluded, can be learned alongside of English with no harmful consequences to the children involved. "It is well known," the Court said, "that proficiency in a foreign language seldom comes to one not instructed at an early age, and experience shows that this is not injurious to the health, morals, or understanding of the ordinary child."

Compulsory public school attendance laws were invalidated by the High Court two years later. The case involved a challenge by representatives of private and parochial schools to a 1922 Oregon law requiring all school children in the state to attend its public schools. "Under the doctrine of *Meyer v. Nebraska*," a unanimous Court declared, "we think it entirely plain that the [Oregon] Act of 1922 unreasonably interferes with the liberty of parents and guardians to direct the upbringing and education of children under their control. . . . The fundamental theory of liberty upon which all governments in this Union repose excludes any general power of the State to standardize its children by forcing them to accept instruction from public teachers only. The child is not the mere creature of the State; those who nurture him and direct his destiny have the right, coupled with the high duty, to recognize and prepare him for additional obligations" (*Pierce v. Society of Sisters* 268 U.S. 510 [1925]).

If *Meyer* and *Pierce* established the rights of parents to have their children learn non-English languages alongside of English in private schools, it accorded no such right to have native-language instruction in the public schools or at taxpayer expense. In the late 1960s, however, a number of Latino activists, together with their allies among white liberals, sought to rectify this situation by successfully imploring Congress and many state legislatures to pass bilingual education laws that provided funding for students from non-English-speaking homes to receive instruction in their parents' language within their local public school systems. The justifications for these programs, like the programs themselves, varied widely. Some believed that by adopting the child's home language as the initial instructional language in the public schools, children from non-English-speaking homes would not only come to learn nonlanguage subjects like math more rapidly but also would come to like school better and be more highly motivated to learn. They would, it was said, develop higher self-esteem as the school showed respect for their home language and, as a result, would eventually both learn English more readily and display higher achievement in their nonlanguage subjects as well. For many ethnic activists, these pedagogical considerations were secondary to the goal of maintaining the generational continuity of their language and culture against what they perceived to be the threat of American assimilation. These activists, however, probably saw no contradiction or trade-off between the two sets of goals – those initially receiving non-English instruction in the public schools would eventually, they believed, learn English as well or better than comparable students in monolingual programs, and they would probably surpass them in other subjects, too.

Unfortunately, the actual experience with bilingual programs proved much different than the hope. An early evaluation in 1978 by the independent American Institutes for Research (AIR) commissioned by the U.S. Office of Education showed that few if any of the promises of bilingual education were actually borne out. Surveying over 11,000 Hispanic students who had been enrolled in federally supported bilingual programs for at least four years, the AIR study found that bilingual students, while they increased their Spanish-language skills, were losing ground in their English-language competency to those in English-only instruction. Moreover, they did not seem to be developing higher self-esteem or any greater eagerness to learn, and their performance in math was only slightly better than the very low level of achievement of other Hispanics in monolingual instructional programs.[50] Surveying some of this early research in the late 1970s, political scientist Gary Orfield struck a note of alarm:

[50] Abigail Thernstrom, "Language: Issues and Legislation," in *The Harvard Encyclopedia of American Ethnic Groups*; Chavez, *Out of the Barrio*, Chapter 1.

There is nothing in the research to suggest that children can effectively learn English without continual interaction with other children who are native English speakers, yet the Federal money has supported programs with only about one-tenth Anglos in the average class. In a society where Spanish surname children are now more segregated than blacks . . . a program that tends to increase separation, raises very serious questions.

Orfield warned that many of the existing bilingual programs "pursue not successful integration into American society but deeper cultural and linguistic identity and separation."[51]

Orfield's uneasiness was increasingly shared by many Americans, and by the early 1980s a movement was under way to replace bilingual programs with English-immersion instruction. A related movement, whose early leader was the California Senator S. I. Hayakawa – an American of Japanese descent – sought to have English declared as the official language of the United States. Both of these movements in time would prove at least moderately successful, particularly at the state level. By 1990, sixteen state legislatures had passed laws declaring English their official language, while in four other states (California, Arizona, Colorado, and Florida), each with large Spanish-speaking populations that had enough clout in the state legislatures to thwart such legislation, voters approved "official English" declarations by statewide referenda.

The California case was particularly instructive as it set a trend that other states would soon follow. The English Language Amendment to the state's constitution, voted on in November 1986, stated as its purpose to "preserve, protect and strengthen the English language, the common language of the people of the United States." It instructed the state's legislature to assure the status of English as the state's official language and to pass no law diminishing this role. While vague, the symbolic significance of the proposed amendment was lost on no one. After a vigorous campaign in which most of the state's political establishment, including its Republican governor, and an impressive array of interest groups including the Chamber of Commerce, the AFL-CIO, the state's Roman Catholic bishops, the League of Women Voters, and the ACLU all opposed the measure, the amendment was passed overwhelmingly by the statewide electorate. Almost three out of every four voters approved the amendment, including a majority in every California county. In exit polls, 58% of Asians said they supported it, 67% of blacks, and 72% of whites. And although the amendment had been vigorously portrayed by its opponents as anti-Latino and anti-immigrant in intent, and despite opposition by almost all prominent Hispanic leaders, support for the measure among Hispanic voters reached almost four in ten. As political scientist Jack Citrin and his colleagues have remarked, summing

---

[51] Quoted in Thernstrom, ibid., p. 625.

up the experience with "official English" referenda in California and elsewhere:

The political Right is the core of the English-only movement, but it attracts support from all along the ideological spectrum. Despite the condemnation of party leaders, civil rights organizations and other powerful interest groups, a majority of Democratic and black voters have approved English Language Amendments. . . . To the mass public, English remains an important symbol of national identity. Regardless of ethnicity, most Americans take for granted that English is the national language.[52]

Two years after the California vote, a statewide poll revealed the depth of the public consensus on the importance of English as America's common language. Asked whether speaking English is "very important," "somewhat important," "not too important," or "not important at all" in "making someone a true American," an amazing 94% of respondents said it was either "very important" or "somewhat important," with the vast bulk of these offering the "very important" response. In all, 76% of those asked said speaking English was very important to being a true American, including 66% of Hispanics, 71% of Asians, 77% of whites, and 83% of blacks. By contrast, only 52% of respondents said that speaking up for the country when it is criticized is very important to making someone a true American.[53]

California also proved to be a battleground state in the drive to dismantle bilingual education programs. Proposition 227, a 1998 ballot initiative dubbed "English for the Children" by its supporters, called for the replacement of bilingual instruction in the public schools with programs that would immerse most children from non-English-speaking homes immediately in an English-speaking environment. Despite being outspent by its opponents by a factor of as much as 25 to 1, Proposition 227 was approved by over 60 percent of California voters. Ron Unz, the Silicon Valley software entrepreneur who led the drive to pass the initiative, explained the successful strategy he and backers of Proposition 227 used to gain voter support. "The story we emphasized," Unz writes,

was one that pitted the common sense of ordinary people – white and Latino, Democrat and Republican – against the timid political elites of all these groups, unwilling to challenge the special interests that benefited from a failed system. Our message to the media was populism without xenophobia, and it resonated widely. Every poll

[52] Jack Citrin, Beth Reinhold, Evelyn Walters, and Donald Green, "The 'Official English' Movement and the Symbolic Politics of Language in the United States," *The Western Political Quarterly*, Volume 43, September 1990, pp. 548, 557.
[53] The poll is discussed and analyzed at great length in Jack Citrin, Beth Reingold, and Donald P. Green, "American Identity and the Politics of Ethnic Change," *The Journal of Politics*, Volume 52, November 1990, pp. 1124–54.

or news story highlighting the widespread Latino dislike of bilingual programs helped reassure moderate and liberal whites that our measure was not anti-minority, while simultaneously persuading conservatives that Latinos and other immigrants shared their own basic values and assimilationist goals.[54]

Opponents of bilingual education in the public schools may well have exaggerated its harmful effects. After all, children from non-English-speaking homes do eventually learn English, even if studies show that they may learn it better or faster through English-immersion techniques rather than bilingual ones. Becoming competent in Spanish or some other non-English language, as well as in English, would certainly seem to be a worthwhile goal, and becoming bicultural does not seem to be such a bad idea either. Nevertheless, the supporters of English immersion over bilingualism – according to a 1998 Zogby International survey, they appear to represent three out of every four voters – seem to have grasped a fundamental truth of America's exceptionalism in integrating people from diverse lands: For both practical and symbolic reasons, a common language is indispensable in creating that minimal level of social cohesiveness and shared experience that a society as polyglot and as free as that of the United States requires to maintain itself as a unified nation. And in America that common language is English.

And English has the great advantage of being the preeminent international language as well. Unlike the Dutch-descendant South Africans trying to get black South Africans to learn Afrikaans – or Canadian bilingualists trying to convince English-speaking residents of Vancouver or the North-west Territory to develop a high level of second-language proficiency in French – convincing non-English speakers in America to learn English offers great advantages in the international arena. Thanks to the success of British imperialism in the eighteenth and nineteenth century, and the emergence of America since the Second World War as the world's leading military and economic power, English has become the language of world commerce, of international science and international aviation, and of much of world scholarship. Learning English allows immigrants to America not only to integrate into a large national community but also to acquire linguistic skills that may be of value to them anywhere in the world. Prioritizing English language acquisition, even if this means denying an equal status to other languages in the public school system, would seem to be a very wise policy for America to follow.

V. The Principle of Color-Blind Justice

In what would be celebrated in time as one of the most eloquent and momentous dissenting opinions ever handed down by a member of the U.S.

---

[54] Ron Unz, "California and the End of White America," *Commentary*, November 1999.

Supreme Court, the elder Justice Harlan explained his reasons for rejecting the "separate but equal" doctrine of racial segregation that the state of Louisiana had applied to all public conveyances in the early 1890s. "Our Constitution is color-blind," Harlan proclaimed in denouncing Louisiana's segregation law,

and neither knows nor tolerates classes among citizens. In respect of civil rights, all citizens are equal before the law. The humblest is the peer of the most powerful. The law regards man as man, and takes no account of his surroundings or of his color when his civil rights as guaranteed by the supreme law of the land are involved. ... The sure guarantee of the peace and security of each race is the clear, distinct, unconditional recognition by our governments, National and State, of every right that inheres in civil freedom, and of the equality before the law of all citizens of the United States without regard to race. (*Plessy v. Ferguson* 163 U.S. 537 [1896])

Even though the color-blind principle of equal justice has been honored throughout much of American history as much in the breach as in the observance, we list it here as a fourth factor responsible for America's exceptionalism in avoiding the curse of most other multiethnic societies because of the enormous influence it exerted during the civil rights era of the 1945 to 1970 period, and the substantial influence that we think it will continue to exert in the future in what we hope is the beginning of our post–affirmative action era. All the major civil rights victories of the early post–World War II years – President Truman's executive order integrating the military (1946); Jackie Robinson's breaking of the color barrier in major league baseball (1947); the *Brown* school desegregation decision (1954); the Montgomery bus boycott that catapulted Martin Luther King, Jr., to national prominence (1955); President Eisenhower's dispatch of troops to support school integration in Little Rock, Arkansas (1957); the 1964 federal Civil Rights Act; the 1965 federal Voting Rights Act; President Johnson's Executive Order 11246 outlawing discrimination by federal contractors (1965); the *Loving* decision striking down all state antimiscegenation laws (1967); and the federal Fair Housing Act (1968) – all were inspired in one way or another by the color-blind principle of equal justice that Justice Harlan had articulated so eloquently two generations previously in his ringing dissent in *Plessy*.

It is almost impossible to understate how powerfully the color-blind principle of justice resonated across racial, ethnic, and religious lines with the generation that had come of age during and immediately after the Second World War – the generation for whom Myrdal wrote his great treatise. Even where long-term practice, ingrained prejudice, and substantial self-interest worked against it – as it did throughout much of the white South – the color-blind principle was one that by the mid-1960s proved itself capable of mobilizing enormous energies throughout the American political system. Here was a principle that all Americans of good will, at least in their better moments, could readily accept as right and just. Here was a principle of generalized inclusion that all the diverse racial and ethnic groups in America could readily support.

The principle of color-blind justice would be written into the most important pieces of civil rights legislation that came out of the 1960s. Again and again the laws written in this period, whether at the national, state, or local level, proclaimed that all citizens of the United States were to enjoy the same legal rights regardless of their race, ethnicity, or religion. The federal Civil Rights Act of 1964 set the general pattern. Here, for instance, is a section from Title VII of that act dealing with employment discrimination:

It shall be an unlawful employment practice for an employer, (a) to fail or refuse to hire or to discharge any individual, or otherwise to discriminate against any individual with respect to his compensation, terms, conditions, or privileges of employment, because of such individual's race, color, religion, sex, or national origin; or, (b) to limit, segregate, or classify his employees or applicants for employment in any way which would deprive or tend to deprive any individual of employment opportunities or otherwise adversely affect his status as an employee, because of such individual's race, color, religion, sex, or national origin.

Similarly, Lyndon Johnson's Executive Order 11246, issued in September 1965, established the same kind of principle of equal justice for private contractors seeking to do business with the federal government:

Except in contracts exempted in accordance with Section 204, all government contracting agencies shall include in every government contract hereafter entered into the following provisions: (1) The contractor will not discriminate against any employee or applicant for employment because of race, creed, color or national origin. The contractor will take affirmative action to ensure that applicants are employed, and that employees are treated during employment, without regard to their race, creed, color, or national origin. . . . (2) The contractor will, in all solicitations or advertisements for employment placed by or on behalf of the contractor, state that all qualified applicants will receive consideration for employment without regard to race, creed, color, or national origin.

For reasons that are not entirely clear, Executive Order 11246 did not include gender along with race, ethnicity, and religion, as rejected categories for the making of employment decisions. Two years later, however, Lyndon Johnson sought to rectify this oversight by issuing another executive order – Number 11375 – that would add "sex" to the list of proscribed categories. The preamble to Executive Order 11375 is instructive for gauging the extent to which the color-blind, ethnicity-blind, and religion-blind ideal of equal justice had triumphed in American law by the late 1960s, at least at the national level. "It is the policy of the United States Government," the Executive Order began, to provide equal opportunity in federal employment and in employment by federal contractors on the basis of merit and without discrimination because of race, color, religion, sex or national origin. The Congress, by enacting Title VII of the Civil Rights Act of 1964, enunciated a national policy of equal employment opportunity in private employment, without discrimination because of race, color, religion, sex, or national origin. Executive Order 11246 of September 24, 1965, carried forward a program of equal employment opportunity in government employment, employment by federal contractors and subcontractors, and employment under federally assisted construction contracts regardless of race, creed, color, or national origin. It is desirable that the equal employment opportunity programs provided for in Executive Order 11246 expressly embrace discrimination on account of sex.

Whether seen as a generalized principle of political morality, or more narrowly as an appropriate construction of the Fourteenth Amendment's Equal Protection Clause, the color-blind theory of justice in America was one that had always had considerable appeal among the general public outside the white South, even if its practical implications were not always fully drawn or fully honored. The theory was, after all, only an adaptation of what Myrdal identified as America's binding creed, and its triumphal legislative victories throughout the 1960s came about not through innovative claims or novel arguments but by appeals to principles that were well known and widely shared throughout much of the American polity.

Dramatic changes, however, were to take place beginning in the early 1970s and continuing well into the next decade and beyond. During this period, the color-blind consensus broke down, at least among certain strategically placed elites in the federal bureaucracy and the federal courts, who were successfully able to transform their own views of compensatory racial and ethnic preferences into public policy. The catalyst for this dramatic change appears to have been the urban riots of the mid and late 1960s, which convinced many policy planners in Washington and elsewhere that something more had to be done to make up for the harmful effects of past racial and ethnic discrimination, particularly that against African Americans, than could be achieved under the color-blind ideal.[55] The official interpretation of the urban disturbances, which was presented in a report by a presidential advisory commission headed by Illinois Governor Otto Kerner, had struck a tone of grave urgency ("Our nation is moving toward two societies, one black, one white – separate and unequal"), and

[55] On the emergence of preferentialist policies for blacks and other minorities as a response of certain elites to the urban riots of the late 1960s, see John David Skrentny, *The Ironies of Affirmative Action* (The University of Chicago Press, Chicago, 1996). On the transformation from color-blind to color-consciousness in American law, see Nathan Glazer, *Affirmative Discrimination: Ethnic Inequality and Public Policy* (Harvard University Press, Cambridge, Mass., 1987); Hugh Davis Graham, *The Civil Rights Era* (Oxford University Press, New York, 1980); and Herman Belz, *Equality Transformed: A Quarter Century of Affirmative Action* (Transaction Publishers, New Brunswick, N.J., 1991).

convinced important segments of the intellectual and political elite of the nation that extraordinary measures were called for to deal with America's pressing racial problems.

Under the collective term "affirmative action," a host of policies were instituted, at first at the federal level, but later at the state and local levels as well, which offered an array of special protections and special privileges to people who were deemed to be members of certain historically disadvantaged minority groups. Although the major impetus to the switch from color-blind to color-conscious policies had come about as a result of the special plight of the black urban poor, such policies would eventually encompass special programs for members of all the Spanish-language national-origin groups, Native Americans, and often for members of Asian national-origin groups as well. Women, too, often qualified for affirmative action preferences regardless of their race or ethnicity – or of their economic status or class. The new reigning principle seemed to be no longer the color-blind principle of "No Allocation of Official Burdens or Benefits on the Basis of Race," but a new principle, "No Disadvantaging of Racial or Ethnic Minority Groups," that permitted discrimination in favor of minority group members, even if this inevitably entailed a breach of the color-blind principle, and the disadvantaging on the basis of their race and ethnicity of those classified as nonminorities. Affirmative action preferences would be extended to the areas of hiring, promotions, layoffs, set-asides, and the vast area of university and professional school admissions.

Two key Supreme Court decisions in the 1970s helped to legitimate the new scheme of racial and ethnic preferences. The 1971 decision in *Griggs v. Duke Power Company* (401 U.S. 424 [1971]), upheld the application of "disparate impact" theory to employment discrimination cases under Title VII of the 1964 Civil Rights Law. Under this novel legal theory, employment practices, such as the uniform requirement of a high school diploma, were to be considered suspect under racial discrimination statutes if the practice resulted in a disproportionate number of the members of specially protected minority groups failing to gain employment or promotion. As a result of *Griggs*, minority group impact, in the sense of the success or failure rate of the members of a specially protected minority group, became a major criterion of determining whether an employment practice was legally permitted or not. In effect, what *Griggs* did was to create a system of incentives and official oversight, which often made it wise for an employer who sought to avoid costly legal challenges to hire and promote on the basis of a group-proportionality or group quota principle. Instead of being color-blind, employment decisions in the aftermath of *Griggs* would have to be made with the utmost concern for color-impacts and color-outcomes.[56]

---

[56] See the discussion of *Griggs* and related matters in Herman Belz, ibid., Chapter 2.

The other Supreme Court case of great significance in the 1970s in this area was the case of *The Regents of the University of California v. Bakke* (435 U.S. 265 [1978]). This was a case dealing with preferential admission to a state-run medical school. The University of California at Davis medical school had a special admissions program in which it set aside sixteen of the school's 100 entering places exclusively for members of certain minority groups. Allan Bakke, a white male of Scandinavian background, had applied twice to the Davis medical school and each time just missed getting accepted even though he had much higher college grades and much higher test scores on all four parts of the Medical College Admissions Test (MCAT) than most of the minority applicants admitted under Davis's special admissions program. Bakke brought suit in federal court claiming among other things that his right to the equal protection of the laws under the Fourteenth Amendment had been violated. After winning at the lower court level, his case eventually made it to the Supreme Court, where he again won his case as the Davis medical school was ordered to admit him. Justice Lewis Powell, writing for a shifting five-vote majority, seemed at first to reaffirm the basic tenet of color-blind justice. "The guarantee of equal protection," Powell wrote, "cannot mean one thing when applied to one individual and something else when applied to a person of another color. If both are not accorded the same protection, then it is not equal."

However, while saying that Davis's rigid quota system violated the Equal Protection Clause, Powell declared that educational institutions have a First Amendment right of academic freedom, which grants them the option to take race and ethnicity into account as a means of enhancing the demographic diversity of their student body. Race could be used as a "plus-factor" in admissions decisions, he said, though dual-track admissions systems of the kind Davis used were not permissible. Powell, however, set no limit on how much of a plus-factor race and ethnicity might be counted in university and professional school admissions, and in practice the *Bakke* decision proved to be a green light for most elite universities and graduate schools to adopt highly race-conscious admissions policies. For many schools led by liberal administrators eager to increase their representation of black and Latino students, being black or being Latino would be considered as much of a plus-factor on one's application as being a highly recruited athlete. As a result, at many of the nation's top undergraduate institutions, minority and nonminority admits would often differ in their average SAT scores (adding the math and verbal scores together) by a gap of over 200 points.[57]

---

[57] See on this the chapter on "Affirmative Action in Higher Education," in Richard Herrnstein and Charles Murray, *The Bell Curve: Intelligence and Class Structure in American Life* (The Free Press, New York, 1994).

To those who had grown up under the older ideals and battle cries of "equal rights" and "color-blind justice," the shift from color-blindness to color-consciousness in public policy came as quite a shock. For many, it was seen as a great betrayal of the high ideals that had formed the backbone of the grand civil rights coalitions of the 1950s and 1960s. This latter attitude was well expressed by Nathan Glazer in his influential book, *Affirmative Discrimination*, first published in 1975. "In 1964," Glazer writes,

we declared that no account should be taken of race, color, national origin, or religion in the spheres of voting, jobs, and education (in 1968, we added housing). Yet no sooner had we made this national assertion than we entered into an unexampled enterprise of recording the color, race, and national origin of every individual in every significant sphere of his life. Having placed into law the dissenting opinion of *Plessy v. Ferguson* that our Constitution is color-blind, we entered into a period of color- and group-consciousness with a vengeance. Larger and larger areas of employment came under increasingly stringent controls so that each offer of a job, each promotion, each dismissal had to be considered in the light of its effects on group ratios in employment. Inevitably, this meant the ethnic group of each individual began to affect and, in many cases, to dominate consideration of whether that individual would be hired, promoted, or dismissed.[58]

Supporters of the new policy argued that race-based preferences were necessary to make up for the current disadvantages experienced by members of racial and ethnic minority groups as a result of systematic discrimination in the past. Blacks, in particular, it was argued, were never given their forty acres and a mule as was promised after the Civil War, and the few jobs and preferential admissions given to them under affirmative action programs, it was said, should be viewed as a very meager – and very late – attempt to compensate the descendants of former slaves for all the centuries of degradation and oppression visited upon them. Affirmative action supporters also defended the policies on the grounds that they would help to create a stable middle class among historically disadvantaged minority groups, and that the members of this class would provide needed role models to encourage higher aspirations among minority youth. Nonminority members would also be helped by such policies, it was claimed, as all people benefit from the sharing of differing perspectives and life experiences, and affirmative action was said to be an important means of furthering this kind of diversity both on the job and in the educational setting.

Critics of such policies, however, pointed out that race- and ethnicity-based preferences are contrary to widely shared concepts of fairness and justice in America, and largely because of this, they inevitably lead to increased racial hostility and racial polarization. Such hostility and polarization, it is added, are what multiracial, multiethnic societies like the United States can least afford. Critics also point out that affirmative action

---

[58] Glazer, *Affirmative Discrimination*, p. 31.

policies are improperly targeted, insofar as the better-off members of the beneficiary groups, who are usually the most likely to have achieved the requisite credentials, are those who benefit most from the policies, while the "truly disadvantaged" are left behind. The costs of the policies too, it is charged, are not equitably distributed, insofar as it is the worst-off members of the nonbeneficiary groups (i.e., the poor whites) who incur the greatest burdens when their life opportunities are diminished. Critics also point to a "stigma reinforcement" effect of such policies: policies of racial and ethnic preference, they charge, send out a message that members of the beneficiary groups are inferior or less capable than those in the nonbeneficiary groups and are only able to compete successfully with others if given a substantial degree of preference. Black critics also complain that although Latinos and white women often receive the bulk of affirmative action preferences, the policy is closely associated in the public eye with blacks, who inevitably become the focus of most of the public outrage over the policies.

While opinion polls continued to show large majorities of the general public to oppose most race- and ethnicity-based preferences, opponents of such policies generally remained poorly organized throughout the 1970s and 1980s and were able to effect little change in the legislative arena. Powerful clientele groups, including the black civil rights lobby, in conjunction with a generally pro–affirmative action news media, were able to thwart over this period most attempts at a legislative rollback of affirmative action programs. The 1990s, however, saw the emergence of considerable grass roots activism on the part of affirmative action opponents, and by the middle of the decade they could boast that the political momentum had shifted in their favor. Their most important victory was the passage in November 1996 of Proposition 209, a California ballot initiative that mandated the elimination of racial, ethnic, and gender preferences in all state-run employment, education, and contracting. Opponents of preferences in California also saw their views acted upon when the state Board of Regents, under pressure from the Republican governor, voted in July of 1995 to abolish racial and ethnic preferences at all nine campuses of the University of California system. By the late 1990s, California at least, with a reputation as a trend-setting state, was moving in the direction of dismantling many color-conscious programs of affirmative action and replacing them with programs predicated on the older ideal of color-blind justice.

The largest changes in public policy, however, have come about not by legislation or ballot initiatives but by changes in the decisions of the U.S. Supreme Court. Largely as a result of shifting personnel, the Court by the late 1980s began to take a second look at the wisdom and constitutional permissibility of race- and ethnicity-based affirmative action programs. In the case of *Wygant v. Jackson Board of Education* (476 U.S. 267 [1986]), the Court struck down the use of race-based preferences in layoff situations as being inconsistent with the Constitution's equal protection guarantees.

The case involved a white Michigan public school teacher (Wendy Wygant), who had been laid off from her job despite the retention of black teachers with lesser seniority because of a race-based layoff policy of the Jackson, Michigan, school board that granted employment-retention preferences to blacks and other minorities. An even more important case was that of the *City of Richmond, Virginia v. J. A. Croson Company* that was decided in 1989 (488 U.S. 469). The City of Richmond had previously instituted a contracting set-aside program that guaranteed that a fixed portion of city contracting dollars would go to firms owned by "Blacks, Spanish-speaking, Orientals, Indians, Eskimos, or Aleuts." In the majority opinion, the Court applied the demanding "strict scrutiny" standard of Equal Protection Clause review to Richmond's race classification scheme and found it to be lacking the compelling state purpose required under this standard. The Court held that while specific acts of discrimination against specific people might justify the use of race-conscious remedies of some kind, more amorphous "societal discrimination" was not sufficient to justify a racial classification.

Two important cases decided in the mid-1990s moved the Supreme Court further in the direction of invalidating race- and ethnicity-based schemes of differential treatment and reaffirming the older ideal of a color-blind constitution. In *Shaw v. Reno* (509 U.S. 630 [1993]), the Court struck down on equal protection grounds a racially gerrymandered districting scheme in the state of North Carolina that had produced two bizarrely shaped black-majority congressional voting districts with little relation to geographic coherence or continuity. Speaking for the Court majority, Justice Sandra Day O'Connor wrote:

[R]eapportionment legislation that cannot be understood as anything other than an effort to classify and separate voters by race injures voters [in more than one way]. It reinforces racial stereotypes and threatens to undermine our system of representative democracy by signaling to elected officials that they represent a particular racial group rather than their constituency as a whole. . . . Racial classifications of any sort pose the risk of lasting harm to our society. They reinforce the belief, held by too many for too much of our history, that individuals should be judged by the color of their skin. Racial classifications with respect to voting carry particular dangers. Racial gerrymandering, even for remedial purposes, may balkanize us into competing racial factions; it threatens to carry us further from the goal of a political system in which race no longer [matters]. It is for these reasons that race-based districting by our state legislatures demands close judicial scrutiny.

Of equal importance to *Shaw* in the movement to reaffirm the color-blind principle was the important decision concerning federal set-asides in *Adarand Constructors v. Pena* (515 U.S. 200 [1995]). In *Adarand* the Court in effect reversed an earlier 1980 decision that had upheld the constitutionality of a federal set-aside law that granted special rights in government contracting to the members of six specified racial and ethnic minority groups. The federal government under the theory developed in *Adarand* would be held to the same "strict scrutiny" standard of constitutional review when it sought to classify its citizens according to race as was applied to the City of Richmond in the *Croson* decision. Under *Adarand* and *Croson*, governments at all levels were prohibited from using racial and ethnic classifications in their official acts unless a truly compelling state interest were involved and the governmental objective could not be achieved through nonracial means. Justice Scalia delivered a particularly forceful concurring opinion in the *Adarand* case that went even further in the color-blind direction than the Court's majority:

> In my view, Government can never have a "compelling interest" in discriminating on the basis of race in order to "make up" for past racial discrimination in the opposite direction. Individuals who have been wronged by unlawful racial discrimination should be made whole; but under our Constitution there can be no such thing as either a creditor or a debtor race. That concept is alien to the Constitution's focus upon the individual, and its rejection of dispositions based on race or blood. To pursue the concept of racial entitlement – even for the most admirable and benign of purposes – is to reinforce and preserve for future mischief the way of thinking that produced race slavery, race privilege, and race hatred. In the eyes of government, we are just one race here. It is American.

Although Scalia is currently one of most conservative justices on the Court, the sentiments expressed here seem to be widely shared by large segments of the general public, including substantial portions of America's black and Latino population and many who would consider themselves politically liberal or middle-of-the-road. They also have an impressive pedigree among Supreme Court justices from across the ideological spectrum.[59]

---

[59] The color-blind theory of justice, as the most appropriate reading of the Fourteenth Amendment's Equal Protection Clause, has been held by the nineteenth century's only civil rights crusader on the Supreme Court (the elder John Marshall Harlan), by the most liberal justice of the twentieth century (William O. Douglas), by the Court's most brilliant conservative justice (Antonin Scalia) by the only black on the present Court (Clarence Thomas), and by several of the Court's quintessential centrists (Potter Stewart, Lewis Powell, and Sandra Day O'Connor). Potter Stewart's dissent in the *Fullilove* case, one of the early cases dealing with affirmative action ethnic preferences in contracting set-asides, reveals the continuity in thinking with Harlan's dissent in *Plessy*. While a majority on the Court approved a federal set-aside program that earmarked 10 percent of contracting dollars spent under the federal Public Works Employment Act to go exclusively to businesses owned by "citizens of the United States who are Negroes, Spanish-speaking, Orientals, Indians, Eskimos, and Aleuts," Stewart vigorously dissented: "'Our Constitution is color-blind, and neither knows nor tolerates classes among citizens. . . . The law regards man as man, and takes no account of his surroundings or of his color.' Those words were written by a member of this Court eighty-four years ago. His colleagues disagreed with him, and held that a statute that required the separation of people on the basis of their race was constitutionally valid because it was a 'reasonable' exercise of legislative power and had been 'enacted in good faith for the

The editors of this anthology agree with social philosopher Michael Walzer that, "in general, the struggle against a racist past is more likely to be won if it is fought in ways that build on, rather than challenge understandings of the social world shared by the great majority of Americans, black and white alike."[60] Ameliorating the dire plight of the inner city

promotion [of] public good.' Today, the Court upholds a statute that accords a preference to citizens who are 'Negroes, Spanish-speaking, Orientals, Indians, Eskimos, and Aleuts,' for much the same reasons. I think today's decision is wrong for the same reason that *Plessey v. Ferguson* was wrong, and I respectfully dissent. The equal protection standard of the Constitution has one clear and central meaning – it absolutely prohibits invidious discrimination by government. That standard must be met by every state under the Equal Protection Clause of the Fourteenth Amendment. And that standard must be met by the United States itself under the Due Process Clause of the Fifth Amendment. Under our Constitution, any official action that treats a person differently on account of his race or ethnic origin is inherently suspect and presumptively invalid" (*Fullilove v. Klutznick* 448U.S. 448 [1980]).

In a similar vein, William O. Douglas lashed out at an officially sponsored program of racial and ethnic preferences in admissions to a state-run professional school. The case, *DeFunis v. Odegaard* (416 U.S. 312 [1974]), was one of the first affirmative action disputes to come before the Supreme Court. It dealt with admission to the University of Washington law school, which in the early 1970s had a program of admissions that gave special weight to members of certain stipulated racial and ethnic minority groups. Marco DeFunis, a Sephardic Jew who for purposes of the University of Washington's admissions program was considered "white," claimed he was discriminated against because of his race when he was denied admission to the state's law school despite the fact that he had much higher college grades, and much higher test scores on the Law School Admissions Test (LSAT) than many of the Black, Mexican American, and other admitted students considered to be members of underrepresented or disadvantaged minority groups. Like Stewart and others who believe racial and ethnic classifications in public law should be subject to the strictest of strict scrutiny standards of constitutional review, Douglas found affirmative action preferences to violate the Fourteenth Amendment's Equal Protection Clause: "The Equal Protection Clause commands the elimination of racial barriers, not their creation in order to satisfy our theory as to how society ought to be organized. The purpose of the University of Washington cannot be to produce black lawyers for blacks, Polish lawyers for Poles, Jewish lawyers for Jews, Irish lawyers for the Irish. It should be to produce good lawyers for Americans and not to place First Amendment barriers against anyone. . . . If discrimination based on race is constitutionally permissible when those who hold the reins can come up with 'compelling' reasons to justify it, then constitutional guarantees acquire an accordion-like quality. It may well be that racial strains, racial susceptibility to certain diseases, racial sensitiveness to environmental conditions that other races do not experience may in an extreme situation justify differences in racial treatment that no fair-minded person would call 'invidious' discrimination. Mental ability is not in this category. All races can compete fairly at all professional levels. So far as race is concerned, any state-sponsored preference of one race over another in that competition is in my view 'invidious' and violative of the Equal Protection Clause."

[60] Michael Walzer, *Spheres of Justice: A Defense of Pluralism and Equality* (Basic Books, New York, 1983), p. 154. Walzer writes further on this: "[T]he difficulty with [the affirmative action remedy] is that it would require the denial of equal consideration to white candidates who are neither participants in, nor direct beneficiaries of, racist practices. An important and morally legitimate social purpose is to be served by violating the candidate rights

"estranged poor," we believe, is truly a compelling state interest, but it is not one that we think has been wisely or adequately addressed by the race-based affirmative action policies of the past three decades. We think it important in confronting these problems that public policy concern itself with alleviating the distress of those truly in need and that it do so in ways that can appeal to the good will of Americans of all races, ethnicities, and national-origin groups. Projects like Head Start and other need-based programs, we believe, should be the model for such ameliorative efforts rather than race-based affirmative action.[61] Both fairness and the general fragility of multiracial, multiethnic societies like the United States are factors we must always keep in mind. Although it is tempting, to cast aside the color-blind principle of justice, even to further what is believed to be a worthy goal, is something a society like the United States does, we believe, only at its peril.

VI. A Common Creator

We have now reviewed four key factors that we think have contributed to the relative success of the United States in avoiding the kind of communal strife that has torn apart so many other multiethnic societies: (1) the widespread acceptance of the American Creed, (2) the optimism and future-orientation of the American Dream, (3) the unifying force of the English language, and (4) the principle of color-blind justice. The final factor we must add to this list is (5) the transforming power of the dominant American religious beliefs.

America, it is often said, is one of the world's most religious countries, and there is certainly much evidence to support this view. Whether one looks at rates of church membership and weekly church attendance, the proportion of the population professing a strong belief in God, the frequency of prayer activity, the amount of money contributed to religious

of individuals. . . . In our culture . . . careers are supposed to be open to talents; and people chosen for an office will want to be assured that they were chosen because they really do possess, to a greater degree than other candidates, the talents that the search committee thinks necessary to the office. The other candidates will want to be assured that their talents were seriously considered. And all the rest of us will want to know that both assurances are true. That's why reserved offices in the United States today have been the subject not only of controversy but also of deception. Self-esteem and self-respect, mutual confidence and trust, are at stake as well as social and economic status. Rights are also at stake – not natural or human rights but rights derived from the social meaning of offices and careers and vindicated in the course of long political struggles. Just as we could not adopt a system of preventive detention without violating the rights of innocent people, even if we weighed fairly the costs and benefits of the system as a whole, so we can't adopt a quota system without violating the rights of candidates" (pp. 152–3).

[61] See Carol M. Swain, editor, *Race Versus Class: The New Affirmative Action Debate* (University Press of America, New York, 1996).

organizations – on all these and many other scales Americans consistently come out at or near the top in international comparisons, at least among the more economically developed countries. It is not immediately apparent, however, that this should bode well for social stability. Now as in the past, religion has often been the source of much of the intergroup bloodshed and secessionist violence one sees around the world. Lebanon and Northern Ireland, Sri Lanka and the Indian subcontinent, Israel and the Sudan – the mere mention of these places evokes vivid images of bloody confrontations and unresolved hostilities between ethnico-religious groups that never seem to be able to get along. Given the wide diversity of religious affiliations in the United States, and the seriousness with which so many Americans take their religious commitments, one might suppose that America would be a real hothouse of religious conflict. Yet this has not been the case. It is true that one can point to serious instances of religious discord in America: the persecution of Quakers in the early Colonial era; the persecution of the Mormons in the middle decades of the nineteenth century; the anti-Catholic agitation of nativitists before the Civil War; the acrimonious dispute over public funding of religious schools and later over the issue of organized prayer in the public schools; the anti-Semitic and anti-Catholic activities of the World War I era Ku Klux Klan; the clash between Jehovah's Witnesses and local school boards over the issue of saluting the flag. Religion, too, we should not forget, was used by the Southern slave-holding class to justify its brutal subordination and enslavement of America's black African population. Nevertheless, "on balance and in the long-run" religion in America has not only not been a divisive force but has served as one of the most powerful means of breaking down racial and ethnic walls of separation that in other countries have been the basis of bitter domestic strife.

Part of the reason for this can be located in the fact that at the national level America never had an established church, and all the state churches were disestablished within a generation following the adoption of the Constitution. The religion clauses of the First Amendment guaranteed that there would be no official national orthodoxy or official national church in the United States (Establishment Clause), while all Americans would be guaranteed the right to believe and worship as they freely chose without hindrance from Washington (Free Exercise Clause). The effect of the First Amendment's two religion clauses was to take the issue of the "true religion" – or the "true godly manner of worship" – out of the civic realm, where it had caused so much mischief in the Old World, into the realm of voluntary associations. The result, as Tocqueville and other foreign visitors would observe, was simultaneously a greater degree of religiosity and a lower level of religious strife in America than in most countries of Europe, where religion was usually a state establishment. Depoliticizing religious affiliation in America proved to be a way both to enhance domestic peace and to promote religious vigor.

Equally important was the adoption on the part of much of the leadership class in America during the founding era of critically pruned versions
of traditional Protestant religious orthodoxies. Influenced by eighteenth
century Deism and the Latitudinarian-style of Christianity of John Locke,
many of the members of the founding generation had come to believe that
all the major Christian denominations – or indeed all the major world
religions, Christian as well as non-Christian – contained important elements of moral and religious truth that were universally valid and worthy of
propagation. This positive and universal element in the differing religions,
however, was seen to be mixed up with many harmful, superstitious, or
absurd elements that needed to be deemphasized or ignored. Preeminent
among elements in this latter category were all tendencies toward the intolerance of other religions or the forceful imposition of one's own religion on
outsiders. The spirit of the leaders of the founding generation in this regard
can be well discerned from the following passage taken from Ben Franklin's
Autobiography:

I had been religiously educated as a Presbyterian; and tho' some of the dogmas of
that persuasion, such as the eternal decrees of God, election, reprobation, etc.,
appeared to me unintelligible, others doubtful, and I early absented myself from the
public assemblies of the sect, Sunday being my studying day, I never was without
some religious principles. I never doubted, for instance, the existence of the Deity;
that he made the world, and govern'd it by his Providence; that the most acceptable service of God was the doing good to man; that our souls are immortal; and
that all crime will be punished, and virtue rewarded, either here or hereafter. These
I esteem'd the essentials of every religion; and, being to be found in all the religions
we had in our country, I respected them all, tho' with different degrees of respect,
as I found them more or less mix'd with other articles, which, without any tendency
to inspire, promote, or confirm morality, serv'd principally to divide us, and make
us unfriendly to one another. This respect to all, with an opinion that the worst had
some good effects, induc'd me to avoid all discourse that might tend to lessen the
good opinion another might have of his own religion; and as our province increas'd
in people, and new places of worship were continually wanted, and generally erected
by voluntary contribution, my mite [monetary contribution] for such purpose, whatever might be the sect, was never refused.[62]

Deist and Latitudinarian ideas similar to those of Franklin were incorporated into the Declaration of Independence, where they were critically
linked to the natural rights ideas of universal human freedom, individual
as well as collective. The importance of this linkage can hardly be underestimated in adding depth and conviction to what would become the
American Creed. All men, the declaration proclaimed, are *created* equal: it

---

[62] Benjamin Franklin, *The Autobiography of Benjamin Franklin* (Dover Publications,
Mineola, N.Y., 1996), pp. 62–3.

is God, the God of Creation, the God common to all the major religious denominations in America despite their prior history of sectarian strife, who endows men with the unalienable rights to life, liberty, and the pursuit of happiness. Natural rights are theologically grounded in the Author of Nature, whose sweep is universal across all boundaries of race, sect, and class. Human rights are God given and normative for all. The "Laws of Nature and of Nature's God" also confer the collective rights of a people to civic independence, to a "separate and equal station" amongst the powers of the earth. Among other things, this latter provision involves a radical rejection of any claim to empire or to the manifest destiny of a master race. However imperfectly America may have conformed in practice to the principles of its founding document, it never ceased to provide a powerful standard of judgment when public actions deviated from the prescribed norm.

The universalist potential of religion in breaking down barriers of race and tribe in America was never more fully realized than in the abolitionist movement prior to the Civil War and in the black church-led civil rights movement in the decades following the Second World War. Indeed, the combined impact of these two movements has left an indelible stamp on the nature and character of America's political culture that persists to the present. It is in large measure because of these movements that America today possesses the philosophical and theological resources for integrating into a meaningful social order racially and ethnically diverse peoples that elsewhere in the world have not succeeded in forming a stable society. It pays, therefore, to look at these movements – and more specifically their use of religious teachings – more closely.

In their ideological combat with opponents, leaders of both the abolitionist movement and the civil rights movement drew liberally from the rhetoric of the Declaration, but they also drew much of their inspiration from the teachings of the Bible. Three Biblical themes in particular would be invoked again and again in propagating their message. First, there is the Divine Image theme of Genesis 1:26–7, where God is said to create man "in his own image" – "So God created man in his own image, in the image of God created he him, male and female created he them." Second, there is the "one blood" theme of Acts 17:26, where St. Paul, in speaking to the Athenians, invokes the common parentage motif of the Genesis creation story and declares men of all nations to be of "one blood" – "And [God] hath made of one blood all nations of men for to dwell on all the face of the earth." And finally, there is the theme of the unity of all Christians in Christ taken from Galatians 3:26–9, which proclaims all who follow Jesus to constitute one unified people regardless of caste, gender, or national origin – "There is neither Jew nor Greek, there is neither bond nor free, there is neither male nor female: for ye are all one in Christ Jesus." Though all of the three played a role in each of the movements, the one blood theme

from Acts was the most important for the abolitionist movement, while the
theme of man "created in the image of God" took center stage during the
civil rights struggles of the 1950s and 1960s.

These Biblical influences can be illustrated by select quotations from
prominent figures in each of the two movements. We might begin with
Samuel Sewall, a Puritan writer whose *The Selling of Joseph* (1700) was
one of the first antislavery tracts to be printed in America. "It is most
certain," Sewall wrote,

that all men, as they are the sons of Adam, are co-heirs, and have equal right unto
liberty, and all other outward comforts of life. God "hath given the earth . . . unto
the sons of Adam" (Psalm 115:16). "And hath made of one blood, all nations of
men, for to dwell on all the face of the earth . . . that they should seek the Lord.
Forasmuch then as we are the offspring of God" (Acts: 17:26–7). These Ethiopians, as black as they are, seeing they are Sons and Daughters of the First Adam, the
Brethren and sisters of the Last Adam, and the offspring of God. They ought to be
treated with a respect agreeable.[63]

In this statement Sewall has linked the idea that all human beings are of
"one blood," that they are all descended from common human ancestors
(Adam and Eve), and that ultimately they are all the creation of the same
supreme God – and hence equally children of that same God – with the
idea of universal human dignity and respect. All human beings, including
the black-skinned "Ethiopians" (a general term for black Africans) are seen
as "sons and daughters of the first Adam," and hence constitutive of a single
human race. However much physically they may differ form whites in color
and outward appearance ("as black as they are"), and however significant
this difference may appear to the whites, the Ethiopians are seen to be part
of the same extended human family as all other human beings. As both kin
and children of God, they possess a special status and dignity, Sewall
believed, that was not being sufficiently respected by the white Christians
of his day who oppressed and enslaved them.

Sewall's appeal to the spiritual universalism implicit in the Genesis
creation story, and his further chastisement of white Christians for their
hypocrisy and inhumanity in their treatment of blacks, set a pattern that
was later followed by subsequent abolitionists in the following century. It
is well illustrated, for instance, by Frederick Douglass in his famous speech,
"The Meaning of July Fourth for the Negro," delivered in Rochester, New
York, in 1852 on the day following America's Fourth of July celebration.
In the speech, Douglass charges America with hypocrisy for its racial double
standard in regard to its black slaves:

[63] Quoted in *Racial Thought in America*, Volume 1, edited by Louis Ruchames (University of
Massachusetts Press, Boston, 1969), pp. 47, 51.

Americans! Your republican politics, not less than your republican religion, are flagrantly inconsistent. . . . You invite to your shores fugitives of oppression from abroad, honor them with banquets, greet them with ovations, cheer them, toast them, salute them, protect them, and pour out your money to them like water; but the fugitives from your own land, you advertise, hunt, arrest, shoot, and kill. . . . You profess to believe "that, of one blood, God made all nations of men to dwell on the face of all the earth," and hath commanded all men, everywhere, to love one another; yet you notoriously hate (and glory in your hatred) all men whose skins are not colored like your own.[64]

Douglass may have been grossly overstating the degree of America's hospitality to immigrant white refugees, but he was hardly exaggerating the plight of freedom-seeking black slaves. Having not too long before been a slave himself, he no doubt knew what he was talking about. And having experienced firsthand the cruelty and hypocrisy of white Christian slaveholders, he had good reason to point out the gap between Biblical teaching and white Christian practice. "The Afro-American uses of Acts," writes Werner Sollors in referring to black abolitionists like Douglass, "are variations upon the pattern of challenging white exclusivism, of scolding as hypocrites people who make distinctions on the basis of skin color, and of persuading Christian audiences to be reborn in abolitionism."[65]

Abolitionist Wendell Phillips conjoined the spiritual universalism of the one blood doctrine with the equal rights doctrine of the Declaration of Independence. Writing in the middle of the Civil War, Phillips proclaimed a new mission for the future generation coming of age in America. Previous generations in America, he argued, had done great things, especially in bringing the promises of the American Revolution and of the Christian religion to the New World; however, the new generation had a new, but equally noble and equally challenging task before it. "This generation," he wrote, "has another work, which is to say: All races have equal rights. 'God hath made of one blood all nations to serve Him on the face of the earth.' That is the motto of this generation."[66]

William Lloyd Garrison, the most flamboyant and widely read of the white abolitionists, extended the reach of the one blood doctrine to include support for interracial marriage. In an era in which Africans were often seen as closer to beasts than humans, this was a radical thought, indeed. If the Creator, Garrison argued, has

"made of one blood all nations of men for to dwell on all the face of the earth," then they are one species, and stand on a perfect equality: their intermarriage is neither unnatural or repugnant to nature, but obviously proper and salutary, it being

---

[64] Quoted in Sollors, *Beyond Ethnicity*, p. 61.
[65] Ibid., pp. 62–3.
[66] From the May 29, 1863, issue of *The Liberator*. Cited in ibid., p. 63.

designed to unite people of different tribes and nations. As civilization, and knowl-edge, and republican feelings, and Christianity prevail in the world the wider will matrimonial connexions extend. . . . An unnatural alliance is not that which joins in wedlock an African descendant with an American, or an Indian with a European, who are equal in moral worth. . . . The standard of matrimony is erected by affec-tion and purity, and does not depend upon the height, or bulk, or color, or wealth, or poverty, of individuals.[67]

Garrison also called upon the Pauline teachings in Galatians, and the dynamic spiritualism of the Christian revivalist and Christian missionary traditions, to convince skeptics that people of different races and ethnici-ties could work together in one society and be united by a common spiri-tual bond:

I call upon the spirits of the just made perfect in heaven, upon all who have expe-rienced the love of God in their souls here below, upon the Christian converts in India and the islands of the sea, to sustain me in the assertion that there *is* power in the religion of Jesus Christ to melt down the most stubborn prejudice, to over-throw the highest walls of partition, to break the strongest caste, to improve and elevate the most degraded, to unite in fellowship the most hostile. . . . "In Christ Jesus, all are one: there is neither Jew nor Greek, there is neither bound nor free, there is neither male nor female" (Galatians 3:28).[68]

The one blood doctrine continued to inspire calls for racial inclusion and racial justice long after the victory against slavery had been won in the Civil War. W. E. B. DuBois, for instance, wrote in one of his autobiographical works shortly after the First World War: "I believe in God, who made of one blood all nations that on earth do dwell. I believe that all men, black and brown and white, are brothers, varying through time and opportunity,

---

[67] From *The Liberator*, May 7, 1831 (quoted in Ruchames, *Racial Thought in America*, pp. 308–9).

[68] Ibid., pp. 312–13. The Christian Identity movement didn't exist in America in Garrison's time (it was just beginning to get started in England), but if it had, he would no doubt have dismissed it with the same contempt with which he greeted the attempts of Southern slaveholders to use the Bible to justify slavery. Whatever else one may say about Pauline Christianity, the message of the Pauline epistles, and of Paul's heroic missionary activities throughout the Greco-Roman world, can hardly be seen as anything other than a radical break with the ethnically restrictive elements of the Hebrew Bible, which as a result of this break would acquire the status of an Old Testament in contrast to the universalist message of the Christians' New Testament. The idea that Paul sought to restrict the Good News he was proclaiming to the world only to those Gentiles who were descendants of the lost ten tribes of Israel is so fanciful, and so unsupported by the text of the Pauline epistles them-selves, that only those with the most powerful predisposition to believe it could ever take it seriously. The Christian Identity doctrine in this regard is like the teaching of certain Afrocentric writers who claim that Jesus, Moses, and Paul were all black Africans. It should be seen as a pitiable exercise in ethnic self-congratulation and self-delusion indicative of a sad loss of the true sustaining love that authentic Christians throughout the centuries have drawn from the Good News of Jesus.

in form and gift and feature, but differing in no essential particular, and alike in soul and the possibility of infinite development."[69]

The Divine Image doctrine came into its own in the 1950s and 1960s as black Baptist and black Methodist clergymen entered the public arena in their attempt to overthrow the brutal Southern system of caste subordination known as Jim Crow. Their appeal struck an enormously responsive chord in the hearts of many Americans of all faiths and all ethnic backgrounds. No figure was more successful in this endeavor than the Rev. Martin Luther King, Jr., whose booming baritone voice spoke from out of the depths to all who had the capacity to hear. In innumerable speeches, sermons, articles, and books, King spelled out his vision of the Beloved Community in which every human being was respected because every human being was created in the image of his Creator.

The Divine Image motif is developed with particular force and insight in the following passage from *Where Do We Go From Here: Chaos or Community?*, a book published just a year before King's tragic murder.

Deeply rooted in our religious heritage is the conviction that every man is an heir of dignity and worth. Our Judeo-Christian tradition refers to this inherent dignity of man in the Biblical term "the image of God." The image of God is universally shared in equal portions by all men. . . . Every human being has etched in his personality the indelible stamp of the Creator. Every man must be respected because God loves him. The worth of an individual does not lie in the measure of his intellect, his racial origin or his social position. Human worth lies in relatedness to God. An individual has value because he has value to God. Whenever this is recognized, "whiteness" and "blackness" pass away as determinants in a relationship and "son" and "brother" are substituted.[70]

The potential power of the Divine Image doctrine in breaking down racial, ethnic, and class barriers to human solidarity is equally well presented in the following King sermon "On Being a Good Neighbor." The sermon takes as its focus the Biblical story of the Good Samaritan:

Too seldom do we see people in their true *humanness*. A spiritual myopia limits our vision to external accidents. We see men as Jews or Gentiles, Catholics or Protestants, Chinese or American, Negroes or whites. We fail to think of them as fellow human beings made from the same basic stuff as we, molded in the same divine image. The priest and the Levite saw only a bleeding body, not a human being like themselves. But the good Samaritan will always remind us to remove the cataracts of provincialism from our spiritual eyes and see men as men. If the Samaritan had considered the wounded man as a Jew first, he would not have stopped, for the Jews and the Samaritans had no dealings. He saw him as a human being first, who

---

[69] Quoted in Sollors, *Beyond Ethnicity*, p. 64.
[70] From *Where Do We Go From Here: Chaos or Community?* (Beacon Press, Boston, 1967).

was a Jew only by accident. The good neighbor looks beyond the external accidents and discerns those inner qualities that make all men human, and therefore, brothers.[71]

Dr. King's religious teachings would perhaps reach their largest and most receptive audience during his famous 1963 "I Have A Dream" speech before the assembled multitude on the Washington mall. The speech is laced throughout with imagery drawn from both the Bible and the abolitionist movement, the two being welded together in its magnificent finale to a fever pitch of inspired oratory:

When we allow freedom to ring, when we let it ring from every village and every hamlet, from every state and every city, we will be able to speed up that day when all of God's children – black men and white men, Jews and Gentiles, Protestants and Catholics – will be able to join hands and sing in the words of the old Negro spiritual, "Free at last, free at last; thank God Almighty, we are free at last."

When we descend from the prophetic heights of King's inspired speeches to the more mundane world of public policy debate, we find the Divine Image doctrine, and the related Biblical teaching that all human beings are the offspring of the same Father-Creator, to have played a considerable role in the major legislative struggles over passage of civil rights legislation. In the U.S. Congress, for instance, during the debate over the 1964 Civil Rights Bill, Senator Joseph Clark, a leading supporter of the bill, went on record to explain why he personally was so strongly in favor of the bill's passage: "The primary reason why I support it," he announced to his colleagues on the Senate floor, "is that it raises as clearly as any piece of legislation which has come before the Senate since I have joined it . . . the clear issue of right and wrong." To support his view regarding the preeminence of the moral factor as reason for supporting the bill, Clark then read aloud a statement condemning racial segregation that had been made earlier before his committee by a group representing thirty church and synagogue organizations:

The religious conscience of America condemns racism as blasphemy against God. It recognizes that the racial segregation and discrimination that flow from it are a denial of the worth which God has given to all persons. We hold that God is the father of all men. Consequently in every person there is an innate dignity which is the basis of human rights. These rights constitute a moral claim which must be honored both by all persons and by the state. Denial of such rights is immoral. (110 *Cong. Rec.*, p. 7203)

Clark also read into the record a related remark made on behalf of a rabbinic organization:

---

[71] From *Strength to Love* (Simon and Schuster, New York, 1964), p. 23.

The major points of our statement, Mr. Chairman, have to do with [our] concern for the immorality of discrimination in the area of employment. . . . We believe that this kind of discrimination is blasphemous, it is an affront to our religious commitment and to our religious convictions, believing as we do that man is created in the image of God. (110 *Cong. Rec.*, pp. 7203–4)

Immediately after quoting this statement, Clark indicated the depth of his own commitment to the Civil Rights Bill's passage, which appears to have derived in equal amounts from both Biblical and Jeffersonian sources: "I speak only for myself," Clark explained, "when I say that if I opposed this bill, I would find it very difficult indeed at the next public meeting I attended to pledge allegiance to the flag of the United States of America and to the Republic for which it stands, one nation, under God, indivisible, with liberty and justice for all" (110 *Cong. Rec.*, p. 7204).

President Johnson, whose genius as a legislative mover and shaker proved indispensable to the Civil Rights Bill's passage, would offer a defense of the bill very similar to that of Clark. In a TV address shortly before signing the bill into law, Johnson explained to the nation the bill's true purpose and the rationale for passing it. "We believe," Johnson said,

that all men are created equal, yet many are denied equal treatment. We believe that all men have certain unalienable rights, yet many Americans do not enjoy these rights. We believe that all men are entitled to the blessings of liberty, yet millions are being deprived of those blessings, not because of their own failure but because of the color of their skin. . . . The purpose of this law is simple. . . . It does not give special treatment to any citizen. . . . It does say that those who are equal before God shall now also be equal in the polling booths, in the classrooms, in the factories, and in hotels and restaurants, and movie theaters, and other places that provide service to the public.

At the end of the TV address, Johnson made a plea for racial harmony in America, choosing as his main metaphor of reconciliation the Common Creator theme of the Genesis creation story:

Let us close the springs of racial poison. . . . Let us hasten that day when our unmeasured strength and our unbounded spirit will be free to do the great works ordained to this nation by the just and wise God who is the Father of us all.

Religion can bring out the worst in people; it can bring out the best in people. It can divide; it can unify. It can elevate to the heights of heroic charity and overflowing human love; it can degrade to the depths of human depravity and demonic cruelty. It can produce a Torquemada, a Grand Inquisitor, a Conquistador as easily – indeed much more easily – than a Francis of Assisi, a Father Zossima, or a Junipero Serra. In America, like most places, it has rarely produced at these extremes, though to return to what was stated earlier, we can say that "on balance and in the long run" its effects have been largely salutary. And it was perhaps nowhere more

salutary than in the black church-inspired civil rights movement of the
1950s and 1960s, where it brought together people of diverse racial, ethnic,
and religious backgrounds – Italian housewives, Jewish college students,
Irish priests – in a collective action that successfully called America to its
higher self. It is with good reason that we celebrate the Rev. Martin Luther
King, Jr., and the movement he headed not simply as a black treasure, or
a black Baptist treasure, but as a genuinely American treasure.

While we have been talking about "religion," the examples we
have given have been drawn almost exclusively from the Western Judeo-
Christian tradition. Since over 95 percent of Americans who have been
affiliated with an organized religious body have in the past been adherents
to some Jewish or Christian faith, this is quite appropriate. But what about
non-Western religions? As the number of adherents to non-Western religions
increases, driven largely by immigration from Asia, Africa, and the Mideast,
will their effect be as salutary in encouraging interracial, interethnic, and
interreligious peace and cooperation in America as biblically oriented
religion has been in the past? This is obviously an important question, and
any answer to it is by nature speculative. But for most of the Asian religions,
there seems to be little problem here since all the major religions that have
derived from India (Hinduism, Jainism, Buddhism) and China (Taoism,
Confucianism) contain traditions of mutual tolerance considerably better
developed than has been the case with Christianity throughout most of its
history. If the American milieu can transform Christianity into a powerful
force for tolerance and inclusion, it should have little difficulty doing this for
most Eastern religions.

But what about Islam? Will the increasing number of Muslim immigrants
to the United States pose a serious threat to social harmony? Will Islam be
an exception to the general rule that religion in America has generally served
more as a unifying force than a force of social division? This is a much harder
question to answer, and one that has taken on a particular salience in the
wake of the devastating attack upon the World Trade Center in New York
City by Muslim suicide bombers on September 11, 2001. Many Westerners
have come to view Islam as a largely negative force in the world, one that
encourages fundamentalist fanaticism, terrorism, and religiously intolerant
holy wars. There is certainly some factual basis for such belief, and the antiwhite racial ideology of certain leaders of the Black Muslim movement
in America has led some to conclude that Islam is a force contributing to
racial, ethnic, and religious intolerance in the world. But as President
Bush emphasized in his address to Congress after the World Trade
Center attack, the kind of Islam represented by terrorist organizations like
Al-Qaeda and Islamic Jihad is a "fringe form of Islamic extremism that has
been rejected by Muslim scholars and the vast majority of Muslim clerics."[72]

[72] *The New York Times*, September 21, 2001, p. B4.

In the United States itself, the Muslim community has overwhelmingly condemned terrorism, and following the World Trade Center bombing went out of its way to display American flags and assert its basic loyalty to America.[73] Since most Muslims who have come to the United States are voluntary immigrants who have come to America's shores for much the same reason as the adherents to other religious faiths (i.e., to realize the American Dream), such behavior should not be too surprising. Although there may be profound differences between Muslims and others in America regarding certain foreign policy issues, particularly America's steadfast support for Israel, Muslim parents, like Jewish, Christian, Hindu, and Buddhist parents, share certain common goals: all seek a better life for themselves and their children, and they do not want to live in a society where terrorism and religious intolerance stamp the character of national life.

It is of utmost importance in this regard to distinguish mainstream Islam from some of the distinctly nonmainstream and often fringe versions of the religion that have gained such notoriety in recent years. The racial chauvinism of certain leaders of the Nation of Islam like Louis Farrikhan and Khalid Muhammad is a case in point. In many ways, nothing could be more un-Islamic than the claims to racial or ethnic superiority that have sometimes been made by Black Muslim representatives. Islam is a religion that not only preaches equality across racial and ethnic lines but also has done more to put this preaching into practice than perhaps any other large religion. Indeed, Islam has been even more successful than either Christianity or Buddhism (the two other large proselytizing world religions) in integrating within its fold people of the most diverse racial, ethnic, regional, and socioeconomic backgrounds.

The effect of mainstream Islam on Malcolm X may be instructive here. Having been converted in prison in the early 1950s to the peculiar African-American version of Islam preached by Elijah Muhammad – one which taught that black men were the original humans and that white men were a bleached-out devil race originally created in a laboratory by the evil genius Yacub – Malcolm was both shocked and overwhelmed when he visited Mecca in 1964 and discovered how racially inclusive mainstream Islam really is. The letter he wrote home to his followers at this time is a classic of religious conversion literature and suggests something of the power that religious enthusiasm and religious ecumenism can have in breaking down racial, ethnic, and national-origin barriers that can otherwise divide people

---

[73] The attitude of most Muslims in America toward the suicide bombers was perhaps best summed up by boxing champ Muhammad Ali: "I am a Muslim. I am an American. If the culprits are Muslim, they have twisted the teachings of Islam. Whoever performed, or is behind, the terrorist attacks in the United States of America does not represent Islam. God is not behind assassins" (quoted in Ira Berkow, "Calm Needed During Time of Anger," *The New York Times*, September 19, 2001, p. D5).

into hostile camps. What he says about Islam closely parallels what Garrison preached about the power of missionary and revivalist Christianity. "Never have I witnessed such sincere hospitality and the overwhelming spirit of true brotherhood," he wrote, "as is practiced by people of all colors and races here in this Ancient Holy Land, the home of Abraham, Muhammad, and all the other prophets of the Holy Scriptures." He goes on:

Over the past week, I have been utterly speechless and spellbound by the gracious-ness I see displayed all around me by people *of all colors.* . . . There were tens of thousands of pilgrims, from all over the world. They were of all colors, from blue-eyed blonds to black-skinned Africans. But we were all participating in the same ritual, displaying a spirit of unity and brotherhood that my experiences in America had led me to believe never could exist between the white and the non-white. . . . I have never before seen *sincere* and *true* brotherhood practiced by all people together, irrespective of their color.

You may be shocked by these words coming from me. But on this pilgrimage, what I have seen, and experienced, has forced me to *re-arrange* much of my thought-patterns previously held, and to *toss aside* some of my previous conclusions. This was not too difficult for me. Despite my firm convictions, I have been always a man who tries to face facts, and to accept the reality of life as new experience and new knowledge unfolds it. I have always kept an open mind, which is necessary to the flexibility that must go hand in hand with every form of intelligent search for truth. During the past eleven days here in the Muslim world, I have eaten from the same plate, drunk from the same glass, and slept in the same bed (or on the same rug) – while praying to the *same* God – with fellow Muslims, whose eyes were the bluest of blue, whose hair was the blondest of blond, and whose skin was whitest of white. And in the *words* and in the *actions* and in the *deeds* of the "white" Muslims, I felt the same sincerity that I felt among the black African Muslims of Nigeria, Sudan, and Ghana. We were *truly* all the same (brothers) – because their belief in one God had removed the "white" from their *minds*, the "white" from their *behavior*, and the "white" from their *attitude*.

I could see from this, that perhaps if white America could accept the Oneness of God, then perhaps, too, they could accept *in reality* the Oneness of Man – and cease to measure, and hinder, and harm others in terms of their "differences" in color.[74]

Intellectually, "white America," like "black America," has clearly ac-cepted the "Oneness of God" from the very beginning. We would like to think that, in the more than thirty-five years since Malcolm X wrote this letter, Americans of all races and ethnicities have done a better job of trans-lating this widespread theological belief into the kind of moral practice and attitudinal change envisioned here. We think that on balance they have, and that part of the reason for this is the continued vibrancy of religious life in America. America has done better at resisting the eroding forces of secularism and religious indifferentism than most other technologically

---

[74] Malcolm X, *The Autobiography of Malcolm X* (Ballantine Books, New York, 1965), pp. 339–41.

advanced societies, and we think this has had an important payoff in terms of fostering respect for people of all races and colors.

Perhaps at no time was this better displayed than in the immediate aftermath of the World Trade Center catastrophe when Americans of all racial, ethnic, religious, and political backgrounds rallied around Irving Berlin's "God Bless America," which appeared for a time to replace "The Star-Spangled Banner" as America's official national anthem. In a time of grief, confusion, and profound national uncertainty, Americans of all backgrounds turned to public acknowledgment of their dependence on a Higher Authority as the source of their national unity and strength.[75] Few who watched the first gathering of the nation's political leadership in the National Cathedral three days after the terror attack on the Trade Center could fail to be moved by the great public display of unity in which prominent representatives of Muslim, Jewish, Catholic, Protestant, and Orthodox faiths offered prayers of condolence and reassurance to a traumatized nation. Whatever may have been the baleful effects of religious belief in other places in the world, or at other times in American history, the full potential of its salutary effect was on display in America in September of 2001. Even those who are not themselves personally religious were forced to acknowledge that religion can be a source of great national strength and one that can help break down barriers of race, class, ethnicity, region, and political ideology. In America at least, religion seems to be more of a force for national unity than a source of social fragmentation.

VII. Two Final Notes

Before concluding these introductory remarks we would like to say something about two features of the following interviews that we found most surprising – and most distressing. Both can be used to illustrate the point we have made earlier that when open consideration of controversial issues is effectively banned from mainstream forums and becomes the focus of narrow sectarian discussion, half-truths and one-sided distortions are the usual result.

The first of these features is the salience in the remarks of so many of our interviewees of genetic-based theories of racial differences. With the possible exceptions of Reno Wolfe and Dan Gayman (who do not express themselves explicitly on the matter), all the white nationalists interviewed for this volume simply accept as a matter of established fact that observed differences between blacks and whites in terms of school performance and

---

[75] See in this context the article by Gerald Seib, "After the Terror, God Reappears in Public Life," *The Wall Street Journal*, September 19, 2001, p. A22; and the article by Celestine Bohlen, "No. 1 Anthem: 'God Bless America,'" *The New York Times*, September 19, 2001, p. E1.

IQ scores is largely the product of innate and ineradicable genetic differences. Blacks will always lag far behind whites in terms of their educational
achievements, it is said, and as a result will always display much lower levels
of income, job status, and professional attainment than whites. It is futile
to think otherwise, they insist. Moreover, many other behavioral traits associated with IQ, such as family stability, future-orientation, and level of self-
control, it is said, will also continue to display huge racial disparities.

The belief in the innate intellectual superiority of whites over the darker
skinned peoples of the globe, or of northern Europeans over southern and
eastern Europeans (the Northerners variously referred to as Nordics,
Aryans, Teutons, or Germanic peoples), was, of course, a mainstay of
nineteenth- and early twentieth-century European imperialists and racist
writers. The works of the French aristocrat Arthur de Gobineau and his
Germanophilic British admirer Houston Stewart Chamberlain were particularly important in popularizing such views.[76] Today, however, when
looking for historical forbears, white nationalists in America generally show
less interest in these earlier European writers and turn instead to the
twentieth-century American racialists Madison Grant and Lothrop
Stoddard.[77] The ideas of these latter writers are particularly prized by many
contemporary white nationalists since they were instrumental in convincing
the American Congress in 1924 to severely restrict immigration to the United
States from nonwhite and non-Nordic nations – a policy that most of the
white nationalists interviewed in this volume would like to see reinstituted.[78]

Despite the many important continuities between the new white nationalists and the older style of race theorizing represented by thinkers like
Grant and Stoddard, what is perhaps most striking in the newer race theorizing is the centrality played by data drawn from contemporary psychological research. While the older racial theorizing of the Grant/Stoddard
variety relied primarily on historical and ethnographic data (much of it of
a most dubious kind[79]), the newer racial theorizing, by contrast, is much
more sophisticated in its use of quantitative evidence, much of it gleaned

---

[76] Arthur de Gobineau, _Gobineau: Selected Political Writings_, edited by Michael Biddiss
(Harper and Row, New York, 1970); Houston Stewart Chamberlain, _The Foundations of
the Nineteenth Century_ (John Lane, London, 1913).

[77] Madison Grant, _The Passing of the Great Race_ (Charles Scribner, New York, 1916);
Lothrop Stoddard, _The Rising Tide of Color Against White World Supremacy_ (Charles
Scribner, New York, 1920).

[78] Both Grant and Stoddard have been the subject of celebratory feature articles in Jared
Taylor's _American Renaissance_ magazine (see the December 1997 issue for Grant; the
January 2000 issue for Stoddard). Stoddard's _The Rising Tide of Color_ is made available
through William Pierce's National Vanguard Books and is also disseminated in a scanned
version over the Internet.

[79] The great British historian Arnold Toynbee, who knew something about the rise and fall
of civilizations in world history, once described the attempt of racialist writers like
Gobineau and Chamberlain to find the key to human history and culture in the concept of

from studies published in reputable professional journals.[80] The journals most frequently cited in this regard are *The Journal of Personality and Individual Differences, Intelligence, Mankind Quarterly, Behavioral and Brain Sciences, Behavior Genetics,* and the *Journal of Vocational Behavior.* Favorite authors of the white nationalists include the psychologists Arthur Jensen, Richard Lynn, Glayde Whitney, Edward Miller, Linda Gottfredson, and (most cherished of all) J. Phillippe Rushton.

The white nationalist presentation of the research data in this area, however, is extremely selective and gives a thoroughly distorted view of the very real controversies that divide researchers in the race/intelligence area.[81] While the topic can only be treated briefly here, a few words must be said about the current race/IQ controversy, which became the subject of heightened public interest in 1994 after the publication of Richard Herrnstein and Charles Murray's controversial book, *The Bell Curve: Intelligence and Class Structure in American Life.*[82]

Drawing upon decades of psychological research, white nationalists can accurately point out that ever since standard intelligence tests were first used on a mass scale during the First World War a black/white gap of approximately 15 points has usually been observed on tests normed so that the mean score is 100 and 15 points represents a full standard deviation of variance. This one standard deviation difference, they also correctly point out, appears on all kinds of intelligence tests whether they have a high level of cultural loading (like the Stanford-Binet IQ test which requires knowledge of English vocabulary words) or an absolute minimal level (like the Raven Progressive Matrices, which consists entirely of pattern-recognition problems and requires no knowledge of English or any other specific language). Socioeconomic and other environmental factors, they readily concede, account for some of this observed difference, but even when blacks and whites are matched on a number of socioeconomic background factors (like parents' income and education), a 10- to 12-point disparity continues to exist. Blacks whose parents are in high-income, white-collar professions, they point out, do no better on standardized IQ tests – and a number of other tests closely correlated with IQ scores such as the SATs – than whites

---

race as "either an ineptitude or a fraud" (Arnold Toynbee, *A Study of History*, Volume 1, Oxford University Press, New York, p. 245). See also the classic work of anthropologist Ruth Benedict, *Race: Science and Politics* (The V. King Press, New York, 1947).

[80] See, for instance, David Duke, *My Awakening* (Free Speech Press, Covington, La., 1998), Part II, Race and Reality, pp. 37–213; and Michael Levin, *Why Race Matters* (Praeger, Westport, Conn., 1997).

[81] The best introduction to the scholarly problems and debates in this area is the report commissioned by the American Psychological Association, *Intelligence: Knowns and Unknowns*, written by a task force headed by the distinguished psychologist Ulric Neisser (American Psychological Association, Washington, D.C., 1995).

[82] The Free Press, New York, 1994.

from low-income, working-class families (the disadvantaged whites may even do slightly better). Evidence of this kind, combined with many other considerations, lead many to conclude that genetics is more important in explaining black/white differences in IQ scores and other standardized test scores than any known environmental or nongenetic factors.[83]

Although there is some controversy over scores on the most recent versions of certain popular IQ tests (with some reputable scholars believing the black/white gap today has shrunk to about 10 IQ points),[84] the white nationalists are clearly correct when they state that a consensus exists among researchers that for most of the twentieth century a one-standard-deviation rule has reigned supreme: over many dozens of different studies, using many different types of tests going back to the earliest decades of the century, a black/white test score gap of between about 7 and 22 IQ points (approximately 0.5 to 1.5 standard deviations) has consistently been shown, with a 15-point difference (one standard deviation) being about the mean. One meta-analysis of 156 such studies showed a mean black/white difference of just about 16 points (1.08 standard deviations).[85]

Knowing that there has been a persistent black/white IQ score gap, however, tells us nothing about the relative weight of genetic and nongenetic factors in explaining the observed difference. And two sets of facts that white nationalists almost never mention offer strong support for nongenetic explanations for most of the black/white difference. The first of these deals with research going back to at least the 1930s that has looked into the correlation between the degree of white ancestry of African-American test-takers – as determined by either skin color, genealogical information, or blood-group testing – and their scores on standardized IQ tests. If genetic differences play a very large role in the black/white intelligence gap, as many believe, one would expect to find a strong positive correlation between the degree of white European genes in the African-American test-takers and their IQ scores (pure-blooded Africans, in other words, would be expected to score much lower than the lighter skinned mulattos and others of mixed

---

[83] The most thorough and competent treatment of the race/IQ issue from the standpoint of someone who believes in the genetic hypothesis is to be found in Arthur Jensen's *The g-Factor* (Praeger, Westport, Conn., 1998). A useful and well-written popular summary of "the case for genes" can be found in Daniel Seligman's *A Question of Intelligence* (Birch Lane, New York, 1992), as well as in Herrnstein and Murray's *The Bell Curve*, Chapters 13 and 14. On the beliefs of mainstream educational psychologists on this controversial issue, see the intriguing study by Mark Snyderman and Stanley Rothman, *The IQ Controversy* (Transaction, New Brunswick, N.J., 1988).

[84] See, for instance, the report of the American Psychological Association task force by Ulric Neisser and his colleagues, *Intelligence: Knowns and Unknowns*, p. 31. The task force members suggest that the current black/white IQ gap may have narrowed for older children to only 10 points.

[85] Herrnstein and Murray, *The Bell Curve*, pp. 276–8.

black/white ancestry since white genes on the genetic hypothesis are supposed to make black people smarter). Almost all the studies that have been done along these lines, however, show either a very weak correlation between degree of white ancestry among African Americans and IQ scores (typically a correlation of only 0.15 on a scale of 0 to 1) or no correlation at all.[86] The most sophisticated of these studies, which was carried out by psychologist Sandra Scarr and her colleagues in the mid-1970s, showed a correlation of virtually zero between degree of European ancestry among African Americans and IQ. The Scarr team used sophisticated genetic testing for blood groups designed to distinguish African and European ancestry among a sample of 144 pairs of black adolescent twins.[87]

In interpreting the Scarr team study, even Herrnstein and Murray, who are usually associated with the genetic hypothesis, acknowledge that its implications strongly support a nongenetic interpretation of black/white disparities in IQ. "If the whites who contributed this ancestry were a random sample of all whites," Herrnstein and Murray write, "then this would be strong evidence of no genetic influence on black-white differences."[88] Herrnstein and Murray add, however, that "there is no evidence one way or another about the nature of the white ancestors." This is true, of course, and adherents to the view that genetic differences are paramount in explaining racial IQ gaps will quickly invoke what one might call a "white trash hypothesis" and claim that the whites who have mated with blacks over the generations in America have been disproportionately drawn from the lower end of the white intelligence gradient. People seek their own kind, they would say, and through a process of "assortative mating" the less intelligent whites would be the ones to seek to mate with blacks. If this were the case, the European genes would whiten in a physical sense but not brighten the intellect.

While such a conjecture is impossible to disprove, it would seem to be inconsistent with certain known facts of the long period of slavery in America when much of the black/white interracial mating is known to have taken place. After all, it was the slave-holding class that probably had easiest access to young, fertile black women during the long period from

---

[86] See the discussion in Richard E. Nisbett's important article, "Race, Genetics, and IQ," in *The Black-White Test Score Gap*, edited by Christopher Jencks and Meredith Phillips (Brookings Institution Press, Washington, D.C., 1998), pp. 89–93. For the older literature, see the discussion in Audrey M. Shuey, *The Testing of Negro Intelligence*, Second Edition (Social Science Press, New York, 1966). Shuey's remarks on the lack of a substantial correlation between the degree of white blood in Negroes and their IQ carry added weight since, as she makes clear in the last pages of her comprehensive study, she clearly believes in a genetic-based explanation of black/white IQ score differences.

[87] Sandra Scarr et al., "Absence of a Relationship between Degree of White Ancestry and Intellectual Skills within a Black Population," *Human Genetics*, Volume 39, 1977, pp. 69–86.

[88] Herrnstein and Murray, *The Bell Curve*, p. 729.

1619 to 1865, and, if anything, one would suppose that the members of this class were disproportionately drawn from the more intelligent members of the white population.[89] Thomas Jefferson (or whoever else it was from the Jefferson clan who fathered Sally Hemmings's mulatto children) was one of innumerably large numbers of white Southern slave holders who engaged in illicit sexual relations with their black female slaves. A reasonable hypothesis on this matter would be that "master class" genes and "white trash" genes are both well represented in the contemporary African-American gene pool, and that neither predominates. If this is true, then the Scarr team study, and others of a similar nature, would seem to lend strong evidence to an environment-dominant view of current black/white IQ differences.

The second set of facts conveniently ignored in most white nationalist discourse on this topic is what has become known as "the Flynn effect." In two important articles published in the mid-1980s,[90] social scientist James Flynn produced extensive data showing that in many advanced industrial nations IQ test scores have been persistently rising each decade since the time such tests were first administered on a large scale in the early decades of the twentieth century. The increase has often been three or more IQ points per decade. The upward trend in IQ scores, Flynn explained, has been generally obscured because the IQ tests in question have been periodically reconfigured or renormed so that the mean always comes out to be 100.

In many cases, the IQ gains over the forty- or fifty-year period from the time IQ tests were first administered on a large scale in the 1920s and 1930s amounts to 15 to 20 points or more, which would be almost the same as, or somewhat more than, the current black/white IQ gap. To state Flynn's findings in a somewhat different manner: if one administered the type of IQ tests given to Americans in the 1920s, blacks today will do slightly *better* on average than the whites of the earlier era. The typical African American today probably has a slightly higher IQ than the grandparents of today's average white American.

Since it is agreed by virtually all who have looked at Flynn's data (and related data from other researchers stimulated by Flynn's findings) that IQ differences of the magnitude discovered could not possibly be explained by the genetic changes that have occurred over this period, the conclusion is inescapable that environmental factors can boost IQ and boost it very substantially. This is something that genetic-based theorists like Arthur Jensen and his followers have long denied.

---

[89] See the discussion in Nisbett, "Race, Genetics, and IQ," pp. 92–3.
[90] James R. Flynn, "The Mean IQ of Americans: Massive Gains 1932 to 1978," *Psychological Bulletin*, Volume 95, 1984, pp. 29–51; "Massive Gains in 14 Nations: What IQ Tests Really Measure," *Psychological Bulletin*, Volume 101, 1987, pp. 171–91.

While it is not clear just what environmental change is responsible for the increasing IQ scores in the twentieth century, a fair guess would be that it is the product of a combination of factors including improved intrauterine nutrition and improved neonatal care (babies have been born bigger and healthier over the decades); better childhood nutrition and fewer debilitating childhood diseases (this also explains the increasing height of the population over the same time period); fewer toxic environmental pollutants (which can reduce brain efficiency); increased cognitive stimulation in the home and school environment; and smaller family size (the fewer the number of children per family, the greater the amount of one-on-one adult interaction with children).

The facts illuminated by Flynn and others have obvious implications for the race/IQ debate. The steady rise in IQ scores throughout most of the twentieth century, writes psychologist Richard E. Nisbett, lends "substantial weight to the possibility that the IQ difference between blacks and whites might be entirely due to environmental factors, since the gene pool of Western countries is not changing at a rate remotely rapid enough to produce a genotypic difference in intelligence of one standard deviation." It seems entirely plausible, Nisbett argues, "that, with respect to factors relevant to IQ, the environments of blacks today more nearly resemble the environments of whites a generation ago than they do the present environments of whites."[91]

Once again, even Herrnstein and Murray acknowledge the possibility of the kind of environmentally driven account of black/white intelligence differences suggested by someone like Nisbett. On this they write:

Indirect support for the proposition that the observed B/W difference could be the result of environmental factors is provided by the worldwide phenomenon of rising test scores. We call it "the Flynn effect" because of psychologist James Flynn's pivotal role in focusing attention on it, but the phenomenon itself was identified in the 1930s when testers began to notice that IQ scores often rose with every successive year after a test was first standardized. . . . The average person could answer more items on the old test than the new test. The tendencies for IQ scores to drift upward as a function of years since standardization has now been substantiated, primarily by Flynn, in many countries and on many IQ tests besides the Stanford-Binet. In some countries, the upward drift since World War II has been as much as a point a year for some spans of years. The national averages have in fact changed by amounts that are comparable to the fifteen or so IQ points separating whites and blacks in America. To put it another way, on average, whites today may differ in IQ from whites, say, two generations ago as much as whites today differ from blacks today. Given their size and speed, the shifts in time necessarily have been due more to changes in the environment than to changes in the genes. . . . The instability of test scores across generations should caution against taking the current ethnic

---

[91] Nisbett, "Race, Genetics, and IQ," p. 99.

differences as etched in stone. There are things we do not yet understand about the relation between IQ and intelligence, which may be relevant for comparisons not just across times but also across cultures and races.[92]

In pointing out the implications of the facts illuminated by researchers like James Flynn and Sandra Scarr and her colleagues, we do not mean to suggest that it is a proven fact that genes are inconsequential in explaining racial differences in IQ. What we are saying is that important data and evidence is available that is more supportive of an environment-dominant view of black/white racial differences than of any genetic-based theory, and that this evidence is rarely if ever given its due in white nationalist discourse on these matters. Like-minded sectarians reinforce their own one-sided views with highly selective data, and the distortions in the resulting picture are never brought to light.

The second feature of these interviews which we found so surprising was the passionate hatred that so many of our respondents showed toward Jews. Given the fact that most Jews in America are as white as any of the other European ethnic groups, and that in recent years young Jews have been intermarrying with the members of these other groups at an astounding rate, this finding was quite startling. White nationalists, we found, are often considerably more hostile toward Jews than toward blacks or other people of color, and the hostility is not confined to the neo-Nazi fringe of the movement. Jews are often portrayed in white nationalist discourse in classic anti-Semitic fashion as the real power brokers around the world who wield immense influence both nationally and internationally, and from ancient Biblical and Talmudic times until the present have been bent upon worldwide domination and the weakening of the racial and ethnic solidarity of

---

[92] Herrnstein and Murray, *The Bell Curve*, pp. 307–8. Even Arthur Jensen, who has done more than anyone else in the psychological research community to convince people of the importance of genes in explaining black/white IQ differences, readily acknowledges that the facts of upward IQ shift over time that have been highlighted by James Flynn may call into question many currently popular notions about the development of mental ability: "One of the most puzzling phenomena [in IQ research]," Jensen writes, "is the increase in raw scores on various IQ tests in many populations over the last sixty years or so. This phenomenon has been under investigation since the mid-1980s. . . . This upward trend in the population's mean test scores has been aptly dubbed the 'Flynn effect,' after James R. Flynn, a professor of political science at the Otago University in New Zealand, who was responsible for amassing most of the evidence for what he has referred to as 'massive IQ gains.' The bulk of this evidence comes from the period between 1930 and 1980. . . . The secular trend in IQ raw scores . . . has been a decidedly upward trend in all economically advanced countries for which data are available. The overall average gain is impressive. . . . On average, it amounts to about one standard deviation (fifteen IQ points) per generation (thirty years). . . . Whatever its cause(s), the Flynn Effect is important because it does not seem to 'fit' in neatly with any existing environmental or genetic theories of mental ability. In science generally, it is such novel facts, when fully investigated, that lead to an increased level of understanding" (Jensen, *The g-Factor*, pp. 318, 328, 330).

their host peoples. Jews, it is said, were the real power behind the international communist movement that caused so much misery in the world during most of the twentieth century; they were ultimately the cause of the devastation of two world wars; and they are the current source of racial chaos in America and Europe. In comparison, blacks, Mexicans, and other people of color are depicted as weak and feeble agents of a destructive racial process that they themselves may not fully understand but that is always fully understood by – and fully controlled and orchestrated by – the perfidious Jews. While blacks and other dark-skinned people are depicted as animal-like and dangerous, the Jew is seen as calculating, fiendish, and diabolical.

Don Black, David Duke, William Pierce, Matthew Hale, and Lisa Turner each in very similar fashion adhere to this basic complex of anti-Semitic feelings and beliefs. The salient features of this complex are well captured in the following remarks from David Duke's *My Awakening*. Explaining that the black-led civil rights movement of the 1950s and 1960s was really not what it appeared to be, Duke writes:

Most [white] Americans who fought against the civil rights movement, believing correctly that it would lead to the destruction of the fabric of society, never recognized the source of its power. In the South some blamed the "Yankees," some the politicians, and some the media. Few understood that the civil rights movement was an outgrowth of the same power that propelled the Russian revolution, that influenced the participation of America in the First World War, that helped bring about the Second World War, and that finally created the nation of Israel. How ironic that the civil rights movement had its roots in [Jewish] racism, that it was simply a weapon wielded by the most ethnocentric people on Earth against their ancient enemies [i.e., white Gentiles]. Blacks were simply pawns in a much larger political game. Most of the non-Jewish Whites who were enlisted in the cause never realized that the struggle was not really about civil rights. These participants, like the Blacks themselves, were being manipulated in the much bigger contest of the Jewish struggle for power.[93]

This alleged Jewish ethnocentrism, power-lust, and hatred of Gentiles is often traced back by white nationalists to the Talmud and other Jewish religious writings, from which select passages are often highlighted on the basis of their anti-Gentile content. America is currently in peril, they proclaim, because of the leftist Jews who run Hollywood, who dominate the mass media of television and newspapers, who orchestrate much of what goes on in Washington, and who run our banks, our universities, our publishing houses, and our legal profession. Jewish leftists – both political leftists and cultural leftists – are seen as responsible for the current moral decline

---

[93] *My Awakening* (Free Speech Press, Covington, La., 1999), p. 291.

of America, and Jews are closely identified in the white nationalist mind with communism and racial egalitarian posturing, with the explosive growth in pornography and the general decline in Christian family values, with the widespread acceptance of homosexuality, and with the sleazier aspects of the Hollywood entertainment industry.[94]

Anyone knowledgeable of the history of anti-Semitism in Europe and America will be struck by the similarity in both style and content of current white nationalist discussion of the Jews and the rhetoric of anti-Semites in the 1920s and 1930s. Indeed, unlike the newer racialist speculation about genes and IQ scores, which differs significantly from the much less sophisticated speculation of the Grant/Stoddard era, almost nothing has changed on the anti-Semitic front in recent years – a very old story has been updated and embellished with little change in its basic content or structure. Those familiar with some of the classics of early twentieth-century European and American anti-Semitism – with works such as Hitler's *Mein Kampf*, Alfred Rosenberg's *The Myth of the 20th Century*, or the essays on the Jews published by Henry Ford in his *Dearborn Independent* – will feel that they have entered a time warp.[95]

The white nationalist treatment of Jewish influences in America, however, is similar to its treatment of the race/IQ issue in one crucial respect: both display a penchant for half-truths and selection bias in the choice of facts to illuminate. While the matter can once again only be taken up briefly, we would like to say at least a few words about two of the charges made by white nationalists: that Jews were the leaders of the communist movement in this century, and that the Talmud and other Jewish writings command Jews to hate Gentiles. Both of these claims play a central role in the anti-Jewish propaganda of the anti-Semitic elements among white nationalist writers, as the reader of several of the interviews in this volume will readily discern.

Let us take up the Jews-hate-Gentiles issue first. It cannot be denied that great bitterness and hatred toward non-Jews can be found expressed in

---

[94] All the ideas in this paragraph are developed at great length and with extensive examples and supporting material in David Duke's *My Awakening*. This book contains a 250-page section on "The Jewish Question," which, taken as a whole, is perhaps the most sophisticated and complete indictment of the pernicious influence allegedly exercised by Jews around the world to be found in any publication of the contemporary racist right. According to Duke's website, this section has been translated into Russian for publication in Russia as a free-standing volume.

[95] Important historical treatments of anti-Semitism can be found in Hannah Arendt, *Antisemitism* (Harcourt, Brace, and World, New York, 1968); Arthur Hertzberg, *The Jews in America: Four Centuries of an Uneasy Encounter* (Simon and Schuster, New York, 1989); Leonard Dinnerstein, *Anti-Semitism in America* (Oxford University Press, New York, 1999); and Frederic Jaher, *A Scapegoat in the New Wilderness: The Origins and Rise of Anti-Semitism in America* (Harvard University Press, Cambridge, Mass., 1994).

certain passages of the Talmud and other Jewish writings,[96] and that certain influential religious Jews during certain times in Jewish history have taken an elitist attitude concerning the Jewish people and the Jewish religion, and a correspondingly condescending or contemptuous attitude toward the *goyim* and their various "pagan" or "heretical" beliefs. In the latter case, the attitude was much like that of the ancient Greeks toward the non-Greeks ("the barbarians").[97] Several reasons can be given for this. In part it reflects the usual kinds of antagonisms that one finds among representatives of rival religions. (One could certainly match the anti-Gentile vehemence of certain rabbinic writers with select anti-Jewish passages taken from remarks of Martin Luther or several Roman Catholic popes.) It also reflects the bitterness of a persecuted people toward the persons and beliefs of those who persecuted them. And finally, it also probably reflects something of the ease with which the Chosen People doctrine, so central to Judaism, can degenerate into tribal chauvinism and baseless self-congratulation, as a number of the great prophets in the Jewish tradition in biblical times would constantly have to remind the Jewish people.[98]

But it is wrong to conceive the Jewish religious tradition primarily in terms of Gentile scorn or derision. While intolerant and chauvinistic elements can readily be found in certain Jewish writings, one can also find the opposite. Mention has already been made of the Genesis creation story, whose spiritual universalism and teaching that all men are created in the image of God has played such an important role in Jewish and Christian reflection on the human condition throughout the ages. One could also cite in this context many of the Psalms, whose spiritual depth and beauty have long been a treasure to all mankind, not just to Jews. Similarly with many of the teachings of the prophets. Amos 9:7, for instance, specifically repudiates the notion that Yahweh is a narrowly national God and attributes divine guidance to the historical path even of some of Israel's fiercest national rivals:

[96] A large selection of anti-Gentile passages from Jewish writings is given in David Duke's *My Awakening*, pp. 263–73.

[97] One Jewish scholar explains the situation as follows: "The attitude of the [Talmudic] sages toward other religions was antagonistic. As monotheists, who maintained that God is universal – the God of the entire human race – they opposed idol worship. They forbade the partaking of bread and wine with pagans.... Their attitude toward non-Jews was analogous to that of the Hellenes toward non-Hellenes, but it was based not on belief in racial superiority but on religion, and the sages welcomed proselytes – one who accepted Judaism was regarded more highly than a native Jew. No laws were directed against gentile Christians, but certain strictures were passed upon Jewish Christians, who were regarded as heretics and apostates and suspected besides of being informers to the Romans. The rabbis, since they considered the Jewish Christians to be the destroyers of Judaism, showed great animosity toward them." Solomon Zeitlin, "Talmud," *Encyclopedia Britannica*, Volume 21 (Encyclopedia Britannica, Chicago, 1969), p. 624.

[98] See Martin Buber, *The Prophetic Faith* (Harper and Row, New York, 1949); and Eric Voegelin, *Israel and Revelation* (Louisiana State University Press, Baton Rouge, 1958).

"Are you not like the Ethiopians to me,
   O People of Israel?" says Yahweh.
"Did I not bring up Israel from the land of Egypt,
   and the Philistines from Caphtor and the Syrians from Kir?"[99]

Even in the Talmud, the most frequently cited Jewish source used by white nationalists to impute anti-Gentile race hatred to Jews, the record shows a much more complex picture than that usually drawn. The historian Robert Pois makes a useful comment in this context in responding to similar attacks on the Talmud by the Nazi race theorist Alfred Rosenberg:

It cannot be denied that various [Talmudic] writers indicated that there was a qualitative difference between Jews and non-Jews. However, [the] assertion that Jewish law *as a whole* did not view non-Jews as human beings is absolutely false. Maimonides, for example, says that any form of cheating or theft is forbidden, whether directed against Jew or non-Jew, and the Talmud, in various places, exhorts Jews to be loyal to the state (Aboth 3, 2); to help heathen poor and sick; even to assist in burying heathen dead (Gittin 61a), and supporting their aged (Kiddushin 32b); and to deal honestly and fairly with non-Jews "for sanctification of the name." . . . A great deal of anti-Gentile bitterness can be found in Jewish writings. Sectarian bitterness and recrimination is always especially ferocious and painful. But in Judaism, as in Christianity, the obverse of this can always be found as well.[100]

Citing anti-Gentile passages in traditional Jewish religious writings, however, suffers from another defect in the contemporary American context even greater than one-sidedness. For even if the Talmud and other traditional Jewish authorities propagated an unequivocal message of Gentile scorn and derision, this fact would have little bearing on the attitudes and practices of most contemporary Jews. It is here perhaps that white nationalists show their greatest ignorance. As anyone with the least bit of acquaintance with contemporary American Jewry should know, the vast majority of Jews in America, insofar as they are observant at all (and large portions of the approximately six million Jews in America are nonobservant), adhere to non-Orthodox varieties of Judaism. The vast majority of practicing American Jews today adhere to either Reform, Conservative, or Reconstructionist versions of Judaism, which do not accept uncritically anything and everything within the Orthodox tradition. And even among the 15 percent or so of American Jews who could be classified as Orthodox, many consider them-

---

[99] On this passage, the biblical scholar Bernhard Anderson writes: "Two of the peoples referred to, the Syrians and the Philistines, had been Israel's worst enemies; and yet, says the prophet, Yahweh – the lord of all the nations – has brought these peoples to their national homelands, just as he brought Israel out of Egypt into Canaan. In this instance, the prophet repudiated Israel's notion that Yahweh was a national god, to be mobilized for the service of Israel's interest." Bernhard Anderson, *Understanding the Old Testament* (Prentice-Hall, Englewood Cliffs, N.J., 1966), p. 237. See also the related remark on this passage in Buber, *The Prophetic Faith*, p. 45.

[100] From the Introduction to *Race and Race History and Other Essays*, by Alfred Rosenberg, edited by Robert Pois (Harper and Row, New York, 1970), p. 26.

selves Modern Orthodox and willingly modify certain ancient practices and ideas in an attempt to engage the non-Jewish world in a loving, creative, and productive manner. (The career of Connecticut Senator Joseph Lieberman would be a prime example of this style of Modern Orthodoxy.) Most American Jews, in other words, pick and choose from the long and complex Jewish religious tradition just what aspects of Judaism they wish to embrace.[101] To cite anti-Gentile sayings in the Talmud or other ancient Jewish writings as an indication of what most American Jews today believe is to display base ignorance of contemporary Jewry. Most American Jews never read the Talmud (an encyclopedic work of over sixty volumes) and are unlikely even to be acquainted with the passages and sayings that white nationalists find so offensive. At best, citing anti-Gentile passages in the Talmud or other ancient Jewish writings may have some relevance for understanding the thoughts and behavior of a small number of ultra-orthodox or ultra-nationalist Jews, such as the followers of the late Rabbi Meir Kahane, but it has little relevance outside this very narrow sphere.

The communism-is-Jewish claim of white nationalists has somewhat more substance behind it than the ludicrous claims made about the Talmud. Karl Marx was, after all, the descendant of a long line of Jewish rabbis (though he harbored a generalized hatred of Jews that was the equal of any Gentile anti-Semite),[102] and many of the leaders of the Communist Revolution in Russia, including Leon Trotsky, Karl Radek, Grigori Zinoviev, and Lev Kamenev were Jews, as were many of the Marxist leaders in Germany,

---

[101] Alan Dershowitz speaks for legions of second-, third-, and fourth-generation American-born Jews who came of age in the second half of the twentieth century, when he describes the "pick-and-choose" imperative that they found necessary to assume toward the more Orthodox views of their Eastern European forbears: "I was a terrible student in elementary school and at Yeshiva University High School, especially in the religious subjects. I simply couldn't pay attention to the rote manner by which we were 'taught' to memorize and recite portions of the Torah, prophets, and Talmud. . . . I recall proudly announcing to a high school teacher that I had become an *apikoros*. In the Hebrew–Yiddish idiom, *apikoros* – a Hebrew variant of the Greek term for a follower of Epicurus – means 'disbeliever' or 'heretic.' . . . I do . . . precisely what orthodox religions say you can't do: I pick and choose – hopefully on some principled basis – among the religious practices and select those with which I wish to comply. It's my religion, after all, and I don't see why I can't be the final arbiter when it comes to its content. In this respect, at least, my attitudes are similar to those of many in my generation who are struggling to adapt traditional religious values and practices to contemporary views. . . . It is a journey that many men and women of my generation have taken. I suspect that a considerable number of Jews and non-Jews as well have shared similar reflections and analogous experiences. They struggle with some of the same conflicts, conundrums, and inconsistencies that I have encountered since departing from the path – the Halakah [Orthodox Jewish religious law] – that was so well traveled by the Jews who came before me." Alan Dershowitz, *Chutzpah* (Little, Brown and Company, Boston, 1991), pp. 41, 12–13.

[102] For Marx, Jews were the great carriers of a loathsome capitalist/commercial spirit (which he sees as the Jews' real religion) that had spread to the Gentile world as well. In his 1843 article "On the Jewish Question," he wrote: "Let us consider the real Jew: not the *sabbath Jew*, whom [Bruno] Bauer considers, but the *everyday Jew*. Let us not seek the secret of

Hungary, and several other nations of Europe. The situation was similar in the United States where Jews were vastly overrepresented among the ranks of the American Communist Party and formed the backbone of the communist movement in many strategically key cities including New York, Hollywood, and Los Angeles.[103] Julius and Ethel Rosenberg, convicted of passing nuclear secrets along to the Russians in the early Cold War years (an action for which they were later executed), were also Jews.

The Jewish penchant for radical left-wing politics in the twentieth century could also be seen in the student rebellions of the late 1960s in a number of countries, including France and the United States. Jews were among many of the top leaders in the 1960s-era New Left movement in America, which became ever more extreme as the sixties progressed, culminating in the apocalyptic terrorism of the Weather Underground. Many American New Left leaders – particularly the Jews – were "red diaper babies" whose parents had been active in the communist and radical socialist movements of the previous generation.[104] It is also true, as white nationalists point out, that leftist Jews are currently a powerful presence within many leading universities and law schools in America, and that many top Hollywood producers and directors are Jews, most of whom have a strong affinity for the cultural left.

The Jewish penchant for left-wing politics is one of those conundrums that many find difficult to explain. How could a people, for whom trade and commercial activity served as such a lifeline throughout much of their history when other areas of making a living (such as agriculture and government service) were closed to them, turn out offspring in such large numbers who rejected the system that sustained their forbears for so long to pursue an unrealizable utopian dream? Such is the question often asked about Jewish radicalism in the twentieth century, and there are at least three considerations relevant to an answer. First, being underdogs themselves for

---

the Jew in his religion, but let us seek the secret of the religion in the real Jew. What is the profane basis of Judaism? *Practical* need, *self-interest*. What is the worldly cult of the Jews? *Huckstering*. What is his worldly god? *Money*. Very well: then in emancipating itself from *huckstering* and *money*, and thus from real and practical Judaism, our age would emancipate itself. An organization of society which would abolish the preconditions and thus the very possibility of huckstering, would make the Jew impossible. . . . In the final analysis, the *emancipation* of the Jews is the emancipation of mankind from *Judaism*. . . . The Jew has emancipated himself in a Jewish manner, not only by acquiring the power of money, but also because *money* has become, through him and also apart from him, a world power. . . . The Jews have emancipated themselves in so far as the Christians have become Jews." From *The Marx/Engels Reader*, Second Edition, edited by Robert C. Tucker (W. W. Norton, New York, 1978), pp. 48–9.

[103] On the involvement of Jews in American Communism, see Nathan Glazer, *The Social Basis of American Communism* (Harcourt, Brace, New York, 1961).

[104] See Peter Collier and David Horowitz, *Destructive Generation: Second Thoughts About the '60s* (Summit Books, New York, 1989); see especially Chapter 9.

centuries, Jews have had a natural tendency to identify with the down-trodden and dispossessed perhaps no more so than when they themselves are experiencing a rising standard of living and have the leisure time to reflect on the plight of the less fortunate. However illusory the vision of proletarian universalism and communist abundance may appear to us now in the post-Soviet world, it was not always so clear in earlier decades. Second, the most virulently anti-Semitic regimes in eastern and central Europe were traditionalist monarchies or right-wing autocracies and the association of anti-Semitism with the political right is one that was seared into Jewish memory by the late nineteenth- and early twentieth-century pogroms. For much of the twentieth century, identifying with the radical left was a way for Jews to acknowledge that they knew who their true enemy was.[105] Finally, left-wing radicalism served for many Jews as a substitute religion. As many young Jews who came of age in a post-Enlightenment world redirected the traditional Jewish passion for learning away from the sacred books of the Orthodox tradition to the new world of secular learning, they experienced the same kind of intellectual excitement coupled with spiritual ferment and spiritual yearning that made revolutionary politics so attractive for many Gentiles. Jewish intellectuals, for reasons that have not been entirely explained, have tended to lose their traditional religion much more rapidly than their Gentile counterparts, and throughout much of the twentieth century many would find in the cause of revolutionary socialism a focus and direction to their life's energies that Orthodox religion once served.[106]

---

[105] Political analyst Michael Barone traces the continued tendency among Jewish voters to support left-of-center politicians even when their own financial interests might better be represented by more conservative candidates to the continuing effect of the Eastern European experience with anti-Semitism. "One could almost say," Barone wrties, "that American Jews are still voting against the tsar" (*The New Americans: How the Melting Pot Can Work Again*, Regnery, Washington, D.C., 2001, p. 240).

[106] What Nathan Glazer says about the Jewish attraction to psychoanalysis can be said mutatis mutandis with equal validity about the Jewish attraction to left-wing political radicalism: "For the East Europeans who made up the greatest part of New York Jewry, and for the bourgeois German Jews of the nineteenth century and their descendants who made up a smaller part of the community, nothing could have been on the face of it more foreign than psychoanalysis. . . . Why then do large numbers of psychoanalysts and patients come from this group in the United States? The explanation probably lies in the effects of secularism on Jews, who have been so rapidly divorced from traditional religion and who have accepted the possibilities of science and intellect so completely that a movement like psychoanalysis – even had its founder been a German anti-Semite – would have been irresistibly attractive. For here was a scientific form of soul-rebuilding to make them whole and hardy, and it was divorced, at least on the surface, from mysticism, will, religion, and all those other romantic and obscure trends that their rational minds rejected. And then, too, it was also a new field with room for new people, which fact may explain why so many Jews became analysts. But it is primarily the complete secularization of the second-generation East European Jew in America that explains why so many became patients"

The association of Jews with left-wing radicalism, while there is clearly some basis for the association, nevertheless grossly distorts the much more complex picture of Jewish participation in American (and European) political and social life. To begin with, it is important to keep in mind that only a small portion of Jews were ever sympathetic to the communist movement or supported communist candidates for office. The reality of the situation is well captured by author Ernest van den Haag: "Out of one hundred Jews, five may be radicals. Out of ten radicals, five are likely to be Jewish."[107] Even among those Jews who identified actively with socialism and other left-wing causes, the vast majority gravitated more toward the Jewish trade union movement and a social-democratic style of thinking that supported political democracy and a mixed economy rather than toward Soviet-style communism. From the 1920s through the 1980s, many Jewish socialists and social democrats were decidedly anticommunist and saw in the Soviet Union a form of tyranny little different from that of the tsars.

Anticommunism among Jews was not confined to those on the social democratic left. Indeed, much of the Cold War–era conservative and libertarian defenses of free market capitalism against the ideological challenge of Marxism was conducted by Jews. Jews, for instance, were an important component of those New York City–based intellectuals who wrote for *National Review* magazine, the flagship journal of American conservatism in the 1950s and 1960s. Will Herberg, the magazine's religion editor, was a Jew, as was its leading in-house political theorist (Frank Meyer) and its leading champion of free markets and the limited state (Frank Chodorov).

Jews were even more prominent in the post–World War II libertarian movement than in the contemporaneous conservative movement. The novelist/philosopher Ayn Rand, who defended radical individualism and free market capitalism against any and all freedom-denying social schemes, was a Russian-born Jew, who migrated to the United States as a young woman in the 1920s. Her novels, especially *Atlas Shrugged* and *The Fountainhead*, have continued to inspire young people in the values of the libertarian philosophy even decades after her death. The economists Murray Rothbard and Milton Friedman played a similar role in the defense of laissez-faire capitalism, with the latter's influence on mainstream thinking in America over the past several decades arguably exceeding that of any other economist, whether of the left or right. Richard Epstein, another Jew, has been the most influential laissez faire legal philosopher in recent years, and

(Glazer and Moynihan, *Beyond the Melting Pot*, p. 175). The attractions of Marxist–Leninism as a substitute religious faith are described with matchless power in the foreword to Whittaker Chambers' *Witness* (Regnery, Chicago, 1952). See also the classic work of Norman Cohn, *The Pursuit of the Millennium* (Harper and Row, New York, 1961).
[107] Ernest van den Haag, *The Jewish Mystique* (Stein and Day, New York, 1969), p. 118.

Robert Nozick, author of *Anarchy, State, and Utopia*, the most influential theorist of the libertarian "minimal state."

If Jews were influential in the conservative and libertarian movements of the early Cold War era, they would virtually dominate what became known in the mid-1970s as the "neo-conservatve" movement, whose major goal was to defend the values of American-style "democratic capitalism" against the assaults of the ideological left, whether new or old. Centered around the journals *Commentary*, *The Public Interest*, and *The National Interest*, neo-conservatism would bring to the world of conservative ideas a new sophistication and high octane brain power that greatly enhanced the ability of the conservative anticommunist message to compete with the voices of socialism and communism. Irving Kristol, Norman Podhoretz, Midge Decter, Gertrude Himmelfarb, Nathan Glazer, and Adam Wolfson – all Jews – played a central role in the movement.

Jewish academics, many of them refugees from a Nazi-dominated Europe, also played a key role in developing the philosophical and moral case against totalitarian ideologies, both communist and fascist. Political theorists Hannah Arendt, Hans Morgenthau, Carl Friedrich, and Leo Strauss – all German-Jewish émigrés – had an enormous impact on the character of American academic discourse in the area of philosophy and politics that still casts its net over the present. Strauss effectively established an entire school of scholars dedicated to challenging key assumptions of modern political philosophy from the standpoint of the ancient political philosophy of Plato, Aristotle, and Xenophon. The conservatively tinged thinking of the "Straussians," under the leadership of a host of energetic scholars, including the Jews Allan Bloom, Harry Jaffa, Martin Diamond, Stanley Rosen, and Nathan Tarcov, continued to influence important segments of academic thinking into the 1970s, 1980s, and beyond. Mention should also be made in this context of the National Association of Scholars, an organization founded in the 1980s by a determined Brooklyn-born Jew, Stephen Balch, to combat what was seen as the pernicious influence exerted on many college campuses by various far-left professors and administrators (many of the latter tenured radicals from the 1960s). Balch's group has been the most effective academic organization in standing up for the free speech rights of those on college campuses who find themselves outside the reigning left-liberal political and cultural mainstream.

Even in the case of the "treacherous Rosenbergs" and the other Jewish members of the Manhattan Project espionage ring, the total picture looks very different from that painted by white nationalists[108] when one looks at the role influential Jews played in combating Soviet espionage during the early Cold War years. The chief prosecutor in the government's case against

---

[108] See the chapter "Jews, Communism and Civil Rights," in David Duke's *My Awakening*, pp. 274–92.

the Rosenbergs was a Jew, Irving Saypol, as was the federal judge in the case, Irving Kaufman, who sentenced the Rosenbergs to death. Another federal prosecutor in the case, Roy Cohn, became a chief counsel to Senator Joseph McCarthy's Government Operations Committee and went on to become a hero to many of the members of the 1950s and 1960s era anticommunist right in America.

The response of the U.S. government to Soviet expansionism during the Cold War was also influenced by a number of prominent Jews. Edward Teller, the "father of the H-bomb," was a Hungarian-born Jewish emigre, who throughout the Cold War was the leading anticommunist "hawk" among the community of atomic scientists. Hyman Rickover, the "father of the nuclear navy," was an American-born Jew, who did more than anyone else of his generation to modernize U.S. naval forces and make them more than a match for their Soviet competitors. Jewish strategic planners, including Herman Kahn and Henry Kissinger, greatly stimulated the policy-making community in the 1960s and beyond to think seriously about nuclear weapons and their role in diplomatic and defense policy. And throughout the latter decades of the Cold War, Jews would go on to play an increasingly important role as presidential advisors and cabinet members dealing with foreign policy issues. Besides Kissinger, who served as secretary of state and national security advisor in the Nixon Administration, Jews who have helped to develop and implement America's anticommunist foreign policy included Walt Rostow, Caspar Weinberger, Richard Pipes, and Elliot Abrams. All were dedicated opponents of communism and Soviet expansionism and had little in common with the Jewish radical tradition.

With the collapse of the Soviet Union and the end of the Cold War, Jews would continue to play important roles in the development of an articulate opposition, not only to political leftism, but to the general leftist cultural drift in America as well. So-called social conservatism (or family values conservatism) is a movement usually associated with the Christian Coalition and other Christian groups in America, with Jews usually cast in the role of vehement opponents. While there is some truth in this generalization, it is equally true that individual Jews have been among the most outspoken and effective opponents of the cultural drift to the left in recent years of anyone in America. For example, no prominent national politician over the last ten years has spoken out more forcefully against what is perceived to be the degrading entertainment often displayed on television and in the movies than Senator Joseph Lieberman. Few radio or TV talk show hosts have been as effective in making the case for traditional, religiously grounded family values as Laura Schlesinger or Dennis Praeger. No ethical philosopher has spoken out more eloquently – or more thoughtfully – about the decline in courtship and the coarsening of sexual relations in recent years than University of Chicago professor Leon Kass. And no movie critic has offered more intelligent and informed commentary upon – and more trenchant criticism of – Hollywood's leftist cultural agenda than Michael Medved. One could also mention in this context the *Wall Street Journal* – no publication targeted at a general audience has been as influential and effective over the past two decades in promoting social conservatism and free market economics as the *Journal*'s op-ed page. The *Journal* is published by a Jew (Peter R. Kann) and has many Jewish editors. Even on the hot-button issue of abortion, which many see as the issue most clearly dividing Jewish and Gentile opinion, Jewish individuals have been prominent in defending the right-of-center position. Few activists on the right-to-life side of the abortion controversy have been as able in making the moral case against abortion as the physician Bernard Nathanson, the journalist Nat Hentoff, or the philosopher Hadley Arkes – all of them Jews.

In presenting this long list of Jews who do not fit the Jews-as-communists or Jews-as-cultural-leftists model, we do not seek to deny that Jews have been in the past, and continue to be in the present, much more likely to be associated with leftist and left-liberal causes than members of most other American ethnic groups. One could certainly compile a much longer list than the present one of prominent Jewish-American leftists and cultural radicals, both living and dead. What we do deny is that the picture of Jewish political participation is anything like the monochromatic version one finds in white nationalist publications. The imbalance and one-sidedness that one gets from these sources is in need of the kind of correction we offer here. No more than the members of any other ethnic group do Jews speak in a single voice.

PART I

WHITE RIGHTS ADVOCACY

I

Jared Taylor

It is fitting to begin our interviews with Jared Taylor, the founder and chief editor of *American Renaissance* magazine. For Taylor, more than any other figure over the past decade and a half, has succeeded through his magazine and his periodic national conferences in creating an intellectual forum in which white rights advocacy, white nationalism, and white ethnic assertiveness could be shifted from the redneck margins of society to a position, if not of mainstream respectability, at least of cultured urbanity and general intellectual seriousness. Taylor is in many ways a most unlikely figure to have carried out this project. Raised in Japan by Christian missionary parents, Taylor attended Japanese schools throughout his childhood and adolescence where he learned to speak fluent Japanese. He went on to attend Yale University and later worked and traveled extensively in West Africa. He also studied in France, where he received a graduate degree in international economics from the Paris Institute of Political Studies. His cosmopolitan and peripatetic background, however, did not prevent him from moving gradually in the early 1980s to adopt a white-centered view of American nationality and to develop the conviction that cosmopolitan and multiethnic societies are much less successful than those consisting of a single dominant ethnic group. While viewed by many as a highbrow racist, Taylor himself strenuously rejects the racist label and claims that his views on race and nationality are moderate, commonsensical, and fully consistent with the views of most of the great statesmen and presidents of America's past. All human beings are by nature tribal, Taylor contends, tribal in the sense that they all have a special affinity for – and a natural loyalty toward – the members of their own race. White people, he says, have their own legitimate racial interests, just as the members of all other racial and ethnic groups do, though white people, he adds, have been slow to realize this.

The interview of Jared Taylor on December 21, 1999, by Russell K. Nieli is printed with kind permission of the interviewee.

White people have allowed other groups to organize and defend their racial interests while doing nothing to defend their own. This situation, Taylor believes, is akin to unilateral disarmament. Like many of the other interviewees in this volume, Taylor believes that the high incidence of various social pathologies among non-Asian minorities in America is at least partially the result of differing genetic endowments, though he also believes that bad social policies and the reigning liberal agenda on race have made these problems much worse. Taylor offers no concrete vision for the future racial landscape of America, though it is clear from his remarks here that he vigorously opposes affirmative action policies that preference racial minorities, antidiscrimination laws that restrict private associational rights, and immigration policies that are shifting the racial demographics of America away from the previous white majority.

Interview with Jared Taylor

INTERVIEWER: Could you explain the nature of *American Renaissance* magazine? What is its underlying philosophy, its stated mission, and the sorts of people who write for it?

TAYLOR: The purpose of *American Renaissance* is to discuss issues that are of interest to whites. After all, every other racial group in the country has groups and media organs that speak for them, and the purpose of *American Renaissance* is to speak for whites. Its subsidiary purpose is to convince a larger number of whites that it is legitimate for an organization or for a publication to in fact speak for them. Most whites are not convinced that they have legitimate group interests, so another purpose of *American Renaissance* is to convince a larger number of whites that it's entirely legitimate for them to have group interests that may sometimes be in conflict with the interests of other groups.

As far as *American Renaissance*'s philosophy is concerned, that's a very long subject, and I think we might have to go about that in a somewhat more piecemeal manner. I think perhaps you could summarize it in the most economical terms by saying that the position of *American Renaissance* is that race is not a trivial matter of either individual or group identity, and that it is a mistake to try to build a society – as the United States has been trying for perhaps the last forty or fifty years – to build a society in which race can be made not to matter. I think that the architects of the civil rights movement, both white and black, those who were most enthusiastic about it in the 1950s and 1960s, would never have anticipated the end of the century in which race is still an extremely salient characteristic in the social life of the United States. I think they would be surprised because at that time they misread human nature. They seemed to be working on the assumption that race was in fact something that was ultimately trivial. The stylish way to look at it these days, of course, is to say that race is not biological, that it is merely a social construct. I don't know anyone who was putting it in those terms at that time, but that was the thinking. What we find today is that people still do sort themselves out quite reliably on the basis of race. In elections, they very frequently vote for candidates of the same race. The United States is scarcely more integrated racially today than it was in the 1950s and the 1960s, and I think that's because once again race is a salient and significant biological and social fact. I suppose you could say that that is the major assumption that underlies the positions *American Renaissance* takes – that race is important and race matters, and it's folly to try to build a society on the assumption that it can be made not to matter.

INTERVIEWER: And the magazine is specifically geared towards white people and towards the interests of white people?

TAYLOR: It's not geared towards white people in that sense. We have a surprisingly large number of black subscribers.

INTERVIEWER: What would interest a black subscriber in your magazine?

TAYLOR: I think there are many black subscribers who share our view that race is a significant matter. In fact, when I talk to Americans about racial consciousness and about the legitimacy of racial consciousness, blacks understand this much more readily than whites because they themselves *have* racial consciousness, and they have group interests that they make no bones about expressing and advancing. It's whites for whom the idea of racial consciousness has been turned into something that is, if not irrelevant, then even loathsome. Because blacks understand their own racial interests, they find it much more straightforward to imagine that whites can have racial interests, and I think that gives them an interest in what racially conscious whites may be thinking. For my own part, I find it interesting to read the black press – for example, *The Final Call*, Louis Farrakhan's magazine, or the *Amsterdam News*. The black press expresses black interests more explicitly than any other press, which is exactly what you would expect, and I think for anyone who has a consciousness of race and is conscious of the kinds of group conflicts that race can give rise to, it's very interesting to see how other groups in their organs that are directed to their own group approach these same questions. And I think for that reason blacks would be interested in *American Renaissance*.

INTERVIEWER: Besides your black readership, which, one would imagine, is only a small portion of the total readership, could you tell us something about your readership in terms of demographic categories. What sorts of people are attracted to the magazine and what are their reasons for wanting to read it?

TAYLOR: We did a reader survey some years ago. My recollection is that, oh, something on the order of about 75 percent of the readers or subscribers were men, they tended to be of an average age of about forty to forty-five, they are overwhelmingly college educated, and they have above-average household income. Also, they tend to be conservative in their political views, and my recollection is that about half of them pronounce themselves to be Christians. The other half expressed no particular religious orientation.

INTERVIEWER: Do you have any strategies for increasing your circulation? Do you advertise, for instance, in like-minded magazines, in college newspapers, or over the Internet?

TAYLOR: We have a web page on the Internet that sometimes brings in new readers. There are two primary ways we increase readership. One is through radio and television appearances by myself. Sometimes they bring in quite large numbers of new subscribers. The other is through direct mail, the way every publication tends to increase readership. I don't doubt that you get solicitations in the mail all the time for various kinds of publications. We do the same thing. We rent mailing lists and we send pitch letters out to people who read other magazines that we think would suggest that they have a view of the world that would be compatible with ours.

INTERVIEWER: Have you been successful in recent years in increasing your circulation?

TAYLOR: Oh, no editor or publisher would ever tell you that he's been successful . . . never sufficiently successful . . . but sure, it's growing all the time. This is about our tenth year of publication, and we are growing steadily.

INTERVIEWER: It's a monthly magazine, now isn't it?

TAYLOR: Yes, it's always been a monthly.

INTERVIEWER: How many people read your magazine each month?

TAYLOR: Well, this is a figure we release only to advertisers if you wish to advertise. I wish I could tell you that it was hundreds of thousands, but I can tell you only that it is thousands.

INTERVIEWER: How would you characterize the current state of race relations in America?

TAYLOR: I think race relations are essentially unchanged for the last forty or fifty years. I think that the greatest set of problems having to do with race is simply inherent to multiracialism. There has never been a multiracial society on the face of the earth in which there was *not* racial friction, and in fact the most stable multiethnic or multiethnic societies that I can think of have been ones in which there was some kind of quite firm hierarchy of different groups, whether it be in the United

States – if you're just speaking of blacks and whites, for example – or South Africa. Whatever one may think of apartheid, it was a stable situation, as was slavery, if you will. These things can continue for years whether one considers them just or unjust. In the past also, say in the Austro-Hungarian Empire, generally there was a group that was considered dominant . . . when you have multiethnic groups, you have a kind of overclass and an underclass. You'll find the same thing elsewhere. The Tutsis tended to be the aristocratic class and dominated the Hutu in Rwanda and Burundi. The Sinhalese and the Tamils in what is now Sri Lanka, they were in a hierarchical relationship at one time, too, but now once that hierarchical relationship disappears, you find them in conflict. This is a fairly reliable pattern that you see around the world.

Race, of course, isn't the only source of group conflict. Probably language may be the most fertile source of conflict after that, but any kind of group identification, be it religion, language, race, culture, tribe, all of these things are sources of friction – far from being the kind of source of strength that we have been encouraged to take them to be. But as far as the United States is concerned, I think, well, there are many, many subsidiary aspects of this problem, but, as I say, the great source – the original problem, the original sin, if you will – is the attempt to try to construct a society of such disparate racial elements. Any society that attempts this will encounter the very problems we have always been wrestling with, and I think for that reason, race relations have always been America's greatest challenge. And, in fact, you can describe them as America's greatest failure, but I think that they are inevitably a failure, given the way human nature is.

If you want to be more specific about race problems and what causes them, that was an aspect that I think I explored pretty thoroughly in my book *Paved with Good Intentions*. At the heart of our race problems is the assumption in the United States today that when nonwhite groups – specifically blacks but also including Hispanics – when nonwhite groups are less successful in America, their differences in achievement when compared to whites must be attributed to white racism and white wickedness. I think that, by and large, this is a mistake. I think that the different racial groups are different biologically, and they differ on average in their intelligence, and that's, of course, why we never have this problem with Asians. Wherever you look, Asians outperform whites academically and financially, and so you would suspect that this nonwhite group that is doing better than whites would somehow cause a little bit more widespread skepticism about the white-racism-as-the-cause-of-nonwhite-failure theory. We don't find that this Asian anomaly is much of a reason to doubt the prevailing view that all the problems of nonwhites can be attributed to whites.

In any case, in my view the differences in achievement are largely due to differences in inherent ability, and it is the unwillingness of America at large to recognize these differences in ability that I think are the cause of a certain very specific set of problems you see in the United States today. I think that most people, for example, accept the fact that blacks are, for biological reasons, the better athletes, certainly in many sports. And no one therefore assumes that the fact that the National Basketball Association is 80 percent black is a result of some kind of systematic antiwhite or anti-Asian or anti-Hispanic racism. On the other hand, if we discover that most of the mathematicians and physicists and research scientists in the United States are white or, in fact, Asian, then we insist on assuming that some kind of institutional racism is throwing up vicious barriers to advancement for blacks and Hispanics. I think the analogy is, whether one likes it or not, an almost perfect one, between basketball and, for example, nuclear physics. People who do nuclear physics do it because they're good at it, and people who play professional basketball likewise do it because they're good at it. To assume that we have to have some kind of perfect, mathematical-geometrical equality of representation in all these fields I think is to overlook the significance of race and the biological aspects of race.

Another aspect of this problem is that by constantly blaming whites for the failures and shortcomings of nonwhites, our society is, despite I think the best intentions, teaching nonwhites to hate whites. After all, we are constantly telling blacks that it's those racist bankers who won't give you loans, it's those racist policemen who arrest you despite your innocence, it's those racist teachers who expect you to fail, it's those racist television producers who portray you in a bad light – racist this, racist that, white society is just seething with racists. How can blacks help but grow up disliking or even hating whites? I think that if we have a real problem of outright, visceral racial hatred in this country today, it's not a problem of whites hating blacks, it's more a problem of blacks hating whites. And you find this in the overwhelmingly lop-sided crime statistics when it comes to the different races committing crimes against other races. You also find it, I think, in the kinds of statements that you see publicly made by blacks about whites, the equivalent of which would be very, very difficult to find in any kind of public figure . . . public white figure speaking about blacks. So this notion that the failure of blacks specifically – and now Hispanics have been brought into this game to a large degree – this idea that the failures of blacks and Hispanics can be attributed directly to white racism, past or present, is first of all wrong. Second of all, it creates hostility toward whites in the minds of blacks and Hispanics, and I think it creates a whole set of unnecessary guilt-related problems for whites. So aside from the great racial problem that inevitably arises simply from having different races in the same territory, I would put this first and foremost in characterizing America's current racial problem, namely, this assumption that the failures of blacks and Hispanics can be attributed to white maliciousness or white wickedness.

INTERVIEWER: It seems as if your views on some of the underlying causes of racial problems have changed in recent years. Today you stress innate biological differences, but in your book, *Paved with Good Intentions* – which was published in 1992 – the main message seems to be that the real problem with blacks is that they don't act enough like Asians, and that if they did, they would be able to integrate successfully into American society. Clearly, you want to suggest in your book that blacks need to become more responsible parents, that they have to stop blaming whites for all their problems, that they have to learn to work hard and save money, and it would seem as if your message is a hopeful one that looks forward to some kind of future integration of African Americans into American society. Yet now, in your more recent writings, you seem to have abandoned the integrationist vision for some kind of not-too-well-defined separationist one, and see black problems rooted not in bad habits which are correctable, but in bad genes which cannot be changed. Could you explain the transition of your thinking on these matters?

TAYLOR: I wouldn't say that I have completely abandoned one point of view and adopted another. In *Paved with Good Intentions*, I simply made no attempt to expound on the biological point of view. I think it is certainly the case that blacks are likely to be psychologically handicapped to some degree by the conviction that they live in a racist society full of racist white people. I think that if I were a racial minority in some other country and I were convinced that the majority was constantly sharpening its knives trying to think of new and exotic ways to skin me alive, if I were convinced that at every turn, there were racist people trying to block my progress, I think that I would find that very dispiriting and discouraging. I think that to the extent that blacks do believe that, I think that it can be a psychological obstacle for them. I think that blacks, instead of constantly blaming whites for their shortcomings, if they did try to take more individual responsibility for their success and their failure, I think there could be a not insignificant improvement in the circumstances of blacks. I think one of the most telling social statistics in the United States today is the fact that approximately 70 percent of black children are illegitimate. It is very, very difficult to argue that somehow white people are responsible for this, although many blacks and a number of whites have come up with Rube Goldberg-type explanations to try to pin this on racism. But just that one statistic alone, I think, is symptomatic of a whole terrible set of obstacles that blacks are setting up for themselves.

Now, this said, I think that the kind of improvement that dismantling psychological barriers would result in is nevertheless limited by differences in average intelligence. Ever since the First World War, we have this very, very well-established difference in average IQ of one standard deviation, and no one, *no one* has come up with some kind of environmental intervention that will narrow that gap. At the same time, we have a considerably less than one standard deviation difference between Asian IQ – North Asian IQ – and white IQ. I think that, too, is a result of genetics, and I think that that is what explains the dominance of Asians in certain fields, and their lower rates of illegitimacy compared to whites, their lower crime rates, their better achievement in school, their higher average incomes. I think that we are living in a time that has willfully blinded itself to biological differences that every previous generation took for granted. The differences between men and women, for heaven's sake! Now it has become somewhat more possible to talk about the differences in the natures of men and women, but there was certainly a time a great many people would have agreed with the proposition that, for example, the sexual appetites of men and women were inherently no different from each other, and they would have explained the fact that there is a great deal of female prostitution and very little male prostitution as simply a result of social training. Well, I think now most people would concede that these are the result of inherent biological differences. And so I see a certain amount of progress in recognizing biology in that respect, but the resistance to recognizing the reality of biology as far as race is concerned is still tremendous, and I think that this unwillingness to recognize it is going to hamper any kind of attempt to try to minimize differences, which, although attributed to environment, I believe are caused by genetics.

INTERVIEWER: Is this a recent conviction on your part, or was this also a view that you held when you wrote *Paved with Good Intentions*, but for whatever reason, didn't emphasize or mention at the time of writing it?

TAYLOR: My views were similar to those I hold today, but they weren't as well elaborated. I wasn't as well informed about the research on IQ as I am today, but generally I had those same views. One of the reasons I didn't write about IQ differences in *Paved With Good Intentions* is because it probably would have been impossible to get the book published if it had made a point of trying to explain these racial differences in terms of inherent abilities. It's still very much a radioactive subject and was probably, if anything, even more radioactive then than it is now. I thought I had a great many things to say about race that were worth considering aside from that, and if I had to, if I had to keep that in the background, or suggest it only by implication in order for these other ideas to be considered . . . I didn't like doing it, but there was kind of a compromise there.

INTERVIEWER: *Paved with Good Intentions* devotes two whole chapters and part of a third to criticizing our current policies of racial preferences. For a book that's only eight chapters long, this is a considerable emphasis. Could you explain the function of current racial preference policy in the evolution of your views on black/white relations?

TAYLOR: You mean whether or not my views are affected by the existence of these policies?

INTERVIEWER: Yes.

TAYLOR: Not a great deal. Of course, preference policies are based on this assumption that it's white racism that keeps blacks and Hispanics from achieving at the white level. The idea seems to be that, oh, evaluation methods for job applicants, for applicants for university places, all of these are somehow biased. By weighting the scales in favor of these disadvantaged groups, we can somehow get them into environments where their real abilities will flower and that they will eventually find themselves achieving at the levels of whites, and perhaps of Asians. I think it's a well-intentioned policy, but it results in the kind of discrimination which, if practiced to the benefit of whites and to the detriment of blacks, would be instantly denounced as unconscionable racism. I think affirmative action racial policies of this kind are an inevitable outgrowth of this will to universal equality, be it the male–female, be it racial, be it social classes, this tremendous desire that everything and everyone be equal, coupled with a willful blindness towards the biological effects of race.

In a way, although I would never have guessed it at the time, I think that racial preference policies are an inevitable result once you pass a law like the Civil Rights Act of 1964. That law forbids racial discrimination in employment, for example, and in a number of other things as well, but the only way that you can demonstrate lack of discrimination satisfactorily to those who will suspect you of it is to show that you have people of all different races equally represented in every level in every function. In order to achieve this, you're going to have to have racial preference policies. In other words, you have to engage in racial discrimination in order to convince a suspicious third party that you are *not* engaging in racial discrimination. We have an absolutely absurd situation in the United States, and anyway things are changing now, and I foresee the eventual demise of official racial preferences of this kind, but for the past couple of decades, we had a situation in which whites who were opposed to racial discrimination directed at themselves were, of course, accused of racism. It's really a topsy-turvy, Alice-in-Wonderland state of affairs, but once again, I think it derives almost inevitably from this overwhelming desire for equality of outcome, coupled with an absolute unwillingness to investigate biology. But if you're asking whether I was ever a victim of racial preferences of this kind and that this somehow fueled my interest in this, the answer is no. I may have been a victim of some kind, but I've never been particularly conscious of it.

INTERVIEWER: How did you get interested in black/white issues? A number of years ago you wrote a book about Japanese culture but didn't indicate at that time that you had any special interest in American racial issues. How did your interest in this area come about?

TAYLOR: Well, that's a good question, and I don't have a satisfactory answer for it. I was born in Japan. I lived there until I was sixteen years old. I was for that reason a racial minority, I suppose. I attended all-Japanese schools, and children are very conscious of differences. To some degree, I was picked on because I was different, but, believe it or not – and most people refuse to believe this – I say it with as much conviction as I can muster, I don't think that experience had any effect whatsoever on my current racial views. When I left Japan at age sixteen to come to the United States to go to college, I was very much a conventional liberal as far as race is concerned. My views on race didn't change . . . well, they certainly didn't change while I was in college, and it was only gradually as I studied history and as I did a fair amount of traveling – I spent several years in West Africa – it was a process of time and various experiences. There are very few particular discrete events that I can point to. I realize that may seem unsatisfactory to you, but I just don't have a good answer for that question.

INTERVIEWER: Is there any particular time period that you could point to where your interests in this subject began to grow?

TAYLOR: I suppose in my thirties, I would guess. It was – let's see, I attended graduate school from 1976 to 1978. I took my graduate degree in France after having lived in Africa for awhile.

INTERVIEWER: What was your degree in?

TAYLOR: It was in international economics. And, then, I suppose, gosh . . . it was a very gradual process. I would say from maybe the late seventies on, I began to be interested in racial questions and also to become increasingly struck by the racial double standards that prevailed in our country. But, as I say, I'm just not able to point to many particular specific instances that changed my mind.

INTERVIEWER: What are some of the specific instances of the racial double standards that bothered you?

TAYLOR: For one, the way crime is reported. I remember . . . what was that famous crime in New York City? It was before the Bensonhurst killing. I've forgotten now what it was called, but it was a case in which there had been a racial confrontation between blacks and whites in Brooklyn, if I'm not mistaken. The whites came back and chased one of the blacks. . . .

INTERVIEWER: Howard Beach?

TAYLOR: Yes, Howard Beach, that's exactly right. That was a huge, huge, huge media hullabaloo, and I remember thinking, well, wait a minute, wait a minute, if America is this horrible racist country, this sort of thing should be happening all the time. Why is this such an enormous media event? Why are we wringing our hands so dismally over this particular crime? I remember that that was one that struck me as very strange, whereas you would read about killings of whites by blacks with no particular investigation into their racial motives, and even if racial motives were uncovered, there was no national hand-wringing that went along with it . . . that's a double standard many people are aware of, and it's one that probably nudged me in the directions I was already moving in.

I think perhaps living in Africa made me more open to the possibility of biological differences between the races. There you see Africans in Africa, and you encounter a certain inertness of mind and spirit among many Africans. It's not universal, of course, and partly it has to do with endemic diseases, but I think that that began to open my mind to the possibility of there being biological differences that were mental as well as physical. Of course, as soon as you start looking into at least the race and IQ question, there's just a tremendous amount of literature out there, and I ended up finding it quite convincing. The attempts to refute the geneticist point of view on these differences, although they get a lot of popular acclaim – books like *The Mismeasure of Man* by Stephen J. Gould, for example – they're not even very honest, but they're just not convincing. I think science and the facts all line up in a very, very persuasive way to support the view that there are these biological differences.

INTERVIEWER: You say in *Paved with Good Intentions* that there is no other subject about which public pronouncements diverge so sharply from private opinions as in the area of race. Do white people, in your experience, say things in private about race that they don't say in public?

TAYLOR: Well, I suppose that in the circle of white people that I move in, it tends to be somewhat unusual in this respect. They say in private the very things they say in public, but I think that's unusual. Well, let me just give you an example. I think actions, after all, speak louder than words. Take our beloved "Great White Father" William Clinton. He has been praising racial diversity for a long time, and he looks forward to the day when differential birthrates and increasing nonwhite immigration will reduce whites to a minority, and yet I suspect he couldn't name a single, nonwhite neighborhood that he'd like to live in. I think that there's a tremendous hypocrisy about this. If I'm feeling mean, I'll sometimes ask a racial liberal, I'll ask him is integration something worth striving for? Is it important for blacks and whites or Hispanics, people of different races, to be together more often than they are? And almost invariably they'll say that it is important, and yet I know of no one who has for that reason decided to buy a house in a Mexican neighborhood, or a Haitian neighborhood. Here is a profoundly significant and important act of integration that each one of us could perform. I know of no one who has done that, and I think that in that sense, people's actions do speak quite loudly. Whites don't want to live among large numbers of nonwhites. They don't like it, and although very few of them will say so, they certainly act upon those impulses when their neighborhood or their school or their church becomes nonwhite. I think that it's pure hypocrisy to pretend otherwise. I forgot what your question was.

INTERVIEWER: Well, that pretty much answered it. I asked you whether whites often say things about race in private which they don't say in public.

TAYLOR: That's right. Well, the New Century Foundation, of which I am president, just conducted a poll. We hired one of these polling firms to do this, and we asked the question two different ways. One of the questions was: Would you prefer to live in a neighborhood where your race is the majority or your race is a minority? We offered three different replies. One was, I prefer that it be the majority, the other is that I prefer it to be a minority, and the other is that it makes no difference. Well, what would you guess were the sorts of answers we got from whites? Given the choice of I'd rather "be a majority," rather "be a minority," or "makes no difference," what percent . . . think about it for a moment, and tell me what sort of answers we are likely to get from a representative sample of whites.

INTERVIEWER: I would assume you'd get a vast majority saying they would rather be with their own group as the majority.

TAYLOR: Well, the overwhelming majority *claimed* that it makes no difference. [Laughter]

INTERVIEWER: And you interpreted that to mean that they weren't being honest with the pollsters?

TAYLOR: Well, who am I to impute dishonesty to my fellow Americans, but 70 percent said that it makes no difference [laughter]. *No*, I don't think they're being honest.

INTERVIEWER: Judging from where they actually move, you're saying that they're not telling even an anonymous pollster in public what they actually believe privately?

TAYLOR: Nope, I don't think they do. About 25 percent said they'd rather be the majority, and then 1 percent said they'd like to be a minority. I think the idea that it makes no difference, that's a joke! I mean, for a very small number of whites, perhaps it does make no difference, but for 70 percent to claim that it makes no difference, I just don't think they're being honest, and this, of course, is because attitudes toward race today have become a kind of touchstone of morality. The overwhelming view in this country, at least *publicly*, at least officially, is that people who take my view on race are moral inferiors. My views are loathsome, retrograde, hate-filled, and very few people, even if in their bones they believe as I do, are prepared to face that kind of condemnation.

INTERVIEWER: Many a reader of *Paved with Good Intentions* who would agree with many of the things you say in the book regarding the behavior of blacks and the attitudes of blacks and whites toward each other would nevertheless criticize you for lacking a certain compassion or fellow-feeling with the underclass blacks whose often self-destructive and socially destructive behavior you described in very vivid terms. How would you respond to that kind of a criticism?

TAYLOR: Of insufficient sympathy?

INTERVIEWER: Yes.

TAYLOR: Well, perhaps I would only dig myself further into a hole if I were to say that I'm not sure I have any less sympathy for black degenerates than I do for white degenerates. I think that by and large we can't blame the factors outside ourselves for what we do. And I think that part of the problem in the United States has to do with an unwillingness to tell people that it is their own fault. Blaming the victim is almost a cliché phrase these days, but I think there is a real hesitancy among any kind of public person, certainly a politician or journalist, to say, "Well, yes, these people are poor because they're lazy," or, "These people are in jail because they're just bad." And I'm not restricting these observations to any particular racial group. I think there are plenty of whites who are a very bad lot, and they deserve to be in jail, and they deserve to be poor. Now that may sound like a very heartless thing; on the other hand, I think that charity – and I make this case pretty strongly in *Paved with Good Intentions* – I think charity should be voluntary, and not engineered by the government, but that's more a principled classic libertarian position than one that has anything to do with race. I think that if you were to criticize my attitudes toward the black underclass, I think you would probably have to make the same criticism of any libertarian view of social or economic differences.

INTERVIEWER: To what extent have government policies and programs, in your view, either increased or decreased racial tensions in America?

What government policies or programs would you like to see changed
and which ones retained?

TAYLOR: Well, I think the obvious culprit in terms of increasing racial
tension is our immigration policy. Up until 1965, we had an immigration policy that was designed, I think, to keep the country white. I see
absolutely nothing wrong with that. In fact, I think that's a healthy,
normal, and natural position for a country to take. I think Japan
should stay Japanese. I think Mexico should stay Mexican. Some think
somehow that it's virtuous of the United States, after having been
founded and built by Europeans, according to European institutions,
to reinvent itself or transform itself into a nonwhite country with a
Third World population. I think that's a kind of cultural and racial
national suicide.

We never had a tremendous amount of, say, black–Hispanic hostility in this country, because there weren't any Hispanics . . . or only a
very small number of Hispanics. But now there are jails in Bridgeport,
Connecticut, and certainly lots in many parts of Texas and California,
that are sometimes in a virtually constant state of lockdown because
Hispanic and black prisoners will be at each others' throats if you let
them mingle in the day rooms. Or when prisoners riot, one of their first
demands is almost invariably that they be separated by race. They don't
like to be mixed up together, and, after all, prison is a kind of forced
intimacy with strangers that many of us can't even imagine, and to
share that forced intimacy with people who are of different races and
who often have quite a strong racial consciousness, this is an extremely
disagreeable experience. But, once again, this kind of experience, which
has become increasingly common, of having to deal with some kind
of racial tensions or racial barrier, this problem has been terribly exacerbated by our immigration policies. We now have, oh, groups of
Haitians in Florida, many of whom don't get along well with
American blacks, for heaven's sake, much less with Hispanics. Asians
have by and large done very well in contact with whites, but I'm sure
you are familiar with the conflicts between Koreans and blacks. In
Detroit, we have the conflicts between what are called the Chaldeans
– my recollection is that they are Christian Iraqis – between Chaldeans
and blacks. Wherever you go, wherever you mix racial groups, you're
going to have tensions, you're going to have friction, and to have an
immigration policy that imports millions of people of all sorts of different racial and ethnic groups, I think it's bound to cause racial tension.

I know that some people take what is to me an absolutely absurd
view, namely that, well, okay, yes, there's racism in this country . . .
well, we'll *solve* racism or we'll try to improve the situation by getting
more and more different kinds of people. Well, that just makes things
worse. And to me, the notion that somehow America is going to be

improved by gradually swapping out the founding stock and replacing it with people from the four corners of the earth, people who are as unlike each other as it's possible to be, that that's somehow going to be an improvement and a source of strength and goodness, truth, and beauty, it's just absurd. It's absurd. It's absurd on the face of it. And to me it's just astonishing that grown people can even pretend that it's true. Of course, a great many people do, but I think it's because they've essentially been brainwashed. It's like pretending that the racial composition of your neighborhood doesn't matter. We're all now more or less obligated to say, "Oh! Diversity is a wonderful thing for the country," whereas, practically every example of tension, bloodshed, civil unrest around the world is due to precisely the kind of thing we're importing – diversity. So that to me is the one government policy that I think is ultimately suicidal, and I would certainly change that. I would completely revamp the immigration law.

Frankly, I don't see the point of having more people. Why should the United States be increasing its population at Third World rates. When was the last time you were out driving on the highway and you thought to yourself, "My gosh! There's just not enough cars on the highway – I wish there were more!" Or when's the last time you went up to a checkout counter in a supermarket and there was no line, and you thought, "Oh, my gosh! I wish there were more people. I wish there were people to stand behind!" Or, when were you out in the countryside, and you saw green hills and forest, and you thought, "My gosh! How ugly! I wish there were a strip mall there. I wish there were more people here." The idea that somehow 270 million people isn't enough, the whole business is cuckoo as far as I am concerned. Why do we import more people? Do we need more people? I certainly don't think so.

In any case, government policies – what would I change? Well, gosh, you see, I think the federal government has no business passing race-related laws at all. I think, if you read the Constitution, you would find absolutely no federal authority for passing antidiscrimination laws of any kind, and I would certainly repeal every one of the antidiscrimination laws that the United States Congress has passed. There's nothing in the Constitution that prevents states from passing antidiscrimination laws, or, for that matter – depending on how you read the Reconstruction amendments – from passing discriminatory laws. But I think everything, everything from the Civil Rights Act of 1964 onward in terms of antidiscrimination – including laws against sexual discrimination – I think all of that is an unconscionable invasion of federal government power into what should be private decision making. I mean, after all, there is no real qualitative difference in the government telling you that you must not discriminate on the basis of race when you hire someone and the very same government telling you that you must not discriminate on the basis of race when you marry someone.

INTERVIEWER: Are those two cases comparable in terms of the level of intimacy and privacy that is involved?

TAYLOR: Well, some people spend more time with their employees than they do with their wives. No, I think most people would say that obviously marriage is the more intimate relationship, but at what degree of intimacy are we allowed to discriminate and at what degree are we forbidden to discriminate. I think that it's clear that, oh, when people choose their church congregations, it's often lamented that 11:00 a.m., Sunday morning, is the most segregated hour in America. That reflects natural, unfettered preferences, and I don't think that it's the government's right to interfere with those natural, unfettered preferences. After all, what's known technically as a refusal to deal – that is to say, if I refuse to hire you or if I refuse to sell you something, refuse to do business with you, I've not actually harmed you because you are no worse off than you were before our encounter and my refusal. But I think the refusal to deal or the refusal to associate is one of the absolutely fundamental human rights – or should be. It certainly was one of the essential rights of an Englishman, the freedom of association, and I think to have given that up as nonchalantly as we did has led to all manner of mischief . . . that was the camel's nose under the tent. Now, we are obliged to at least pretend not to discriminate on the basis of all kinds of other things.

INTERVIEWER: Where do Asians fit in here. You suggest that Asians, unlike Hispanics and blacks, integrate well with whites. How would you describe your vision of the future for America in regard to Asians?

TAYLOR: Well, let's see . . . I think Asians are objectively superior to whites by just about any measure that you can come up with in terms of what are the ingredients for a successful society. This doesn't mean that I want America to become Asian. I think every people has the right to be itself, and this becomes clear whether we're talking about Irian Jaya or Tibet, for that matter. No one would defend the wholesale incursion of non–New Guineans into Irian Jaya, changing their way of life, even though we might think that objectively the standards of civilization on New Guinea are extremely low and the level of culture is abysmal. We might accept that cultural differences objectively exist and yet be completely opposed to the displacement of that culture and those people by those with a culture that we might describe as superior. By the same token, even if Asians build societies superior to those built by white people, I think white people are perfectly legitimate in preferring the kinds of societies that they build. And I think they have the right to build those societies.

INTERVIEWER: What about Jews? Where do Jews fit into your picture? Many of the white nationalist or white pride publications have a deep hostility toward Jews. Your organization though, or at least your magazine, has had a number of Jews who have written articles for it. What are your views regarding the Jews? Are they considered "white"?

TAYLOR: Oh, I think European Jews are Europeans, sure.

INTERVIEWER: So you don't see any problem with Jews integrating into American society?

TAYLOR: I think if they – if European Jews wish to assimilate – I think many of them have and do. I don't see any particular problem there. I think it's unquestionably the fact that, by and large, Jews tend to be more liberal on the kinds of questions that we've been talking about. I think there are all sorts of historical reasons for that, but I don't think Jews, simply because they are Jews, are necessarily going to be not part of a European nation.

But if I could back up and make another point about this issue of displacement. People can work up a certain amount of sympathy for the Tibetans, for example, because Han Chinese are coming in and displacing them and their culture, and yet we're not supposed to feel sympathy for whites in the United States, despite the fact that they are being displaced. Ultimately, what I'm concerned about is the survival of my people. And I have the bad taste to be earnest about that question, and if you were to imagine a situation . . . if you were to imagine the reverse situation in which, say, hundreds of thousands of whites were pouring across the border into Mexico, insisting on school instruction in English, ballot papers in English, celebrating the Fourth of July rather than Cinco de Mayo, and buying up radio and television stations and broadcasting in English, and some of them perhaps even muttering darkly about breaking off chunks of northern Mexico and turning it into an all-white nation, it would be *impossible* to trick the Mexicans into thinking that this was some sort of cultural enrichment. It's only whites that have been brainwashed and bamboozled into thinking that somehow it's a virtue to be displaced by people unlike themselves.

Now since you raised the question of Jews, I might quote to you Yitzhak Rabin. Not long before he was assassinated, he told *U.S. News & World Report* that he had done many things as a leader of Israel of which he was proud, but the thing that he cared most about was that Israel remain at least 80 percent Jewish. Well, what he's saying is that the character of Israel is dependent on its people. Israel, in order to be Israel, must be Jewish, and to the extent that Israel ceases to be Jewish, it will not be Israeli in the sense that's meaningful for him. By the same token, in my view, the United States of America as founded by my ancestors is a white nation, and as it ceases to be white, it will change

in ways that are as unacceptable to me as it would be unacceptable to
Yitzhak Rabin should Israel cease to be Jewish.

INTERVIEWER: America was settled primarily by people from northern and
    western Europe, but in the last years of the nineteenth century there
    was an influx of Southern and Eastern Europeans, who, over time, inte-
    grated well into America. I am thinking particularly of Italians, Poles,
    Romanians, Jews, Russians, and so on. Why can't the same process
    proceed and expand the circle of who is considered American to include
    Hispanics and people of African ancestry?

TAYLOR: Well, I think you know what my answer to that question will be.
    Yes, it's frequently pointed out that there was nativist sentiment, oh,
    against Germans, for heaven sakes, and certainly against Southern
    Europeans, and that, yes, Italians, Poles, Hungarians, many of them
    have integrated very nicely in the United States. The analogy, of course,
    is that the people who were nativist then are just as wrong as today's
    nativists – that Haitians and Guatemalans and everyone else will inte-
    grate just as the Italians and the Poles did. That overlooks a number
    of things. First of all, it overlooks race, which is a subject most people
    don't wish to talk about. We have a bubbling successful melting pot in
    this country so long as the ingredients are essentially European. It over-
    looks the fact also that there are two racial groups in this country that
    have been here for far longer than the Hungarians and Poles, namely,
    blacks and American Indians, who are still in some respects on the
    margins of society. The white ethnics integrated because they're white.
    They assimilated because they are white, whereas blacks and American
    Indians, who have been here far longer, *didn't* assimilate because they're
    not white. Race is this great biological barrier, and so long as you have
    that biological barrier, it's one that will always, in my view, be an obsta-
    cle to assimilation and to building up any kind of strong, national unity
    or national consciousness. So, really, the obstacle once again is race. It
    would be as if language were an immutable characteristic, then the
    Germans, the Poles, the Hungarians would *not* have assimilated. Well,
    race is by and large an immutable characteristic, and for that reason it
    becomes a barrier, whereas language and culture, and to some extent
    religion, are not.

INTERVIEWER: What about intermarriage? When people of different races
    intermarry and they produce mixed-race offspring, the racial lines are
    blurred. Many people think that intermarriage on a large scale is the
    ultimate answer to racial cleavages and racial divisions.

TAYLOR: Well, even if it were to take place, it would not bring about the
    end of racial conflict. As I'm sure you know, even among blacks there
    is a considerable amount of conflict just based on the skin tone – lighter-
    skinned blacks and darker-skinned blacks. I think that if we were all

of mixed race, I don't think that would bring about an end to racial conflict. At the same time, I think that would be a biological disaster. It's interesting to me that the people who talk about celebrating diversity are sometimes the ones who wish to destroy biological diversity or racial diversity. I think that it is entirely natural for people to want their children to be like their ancestors. I think there's something basic and fundamental about that desire, and that is of course why there is as little interracial marriage as there is. People are loyal to their language, to their culture, to their race, to their own appearance, to the appearance of their ancestors. And I think to mix everything up into a kind of stew, I think that would be a biological and social and cultural disaster. In effect, though, what is being proposed is not the elimination of races, because no one proposes that as a solution for any sort of problems you might find in Asia or Africa. It's the solution that one proposes only for the United States or perhaps for Europe. So in effect what is proposed by this massive miscegenation scheme is not the elimination of race, it's the elimination of whites. Why should I be in favor of this so-called solution that results in the elimination of my race?

INTERVIEWER: Many people would characterize *American Renaissance* as a racist publication. How do you respond to charges of that kind, and if "racist" is an inappropriate label to describe your views, what sort of label do you prefer?

TAYLOR: Well, "racist" is inappropriate because it's pejorative, and I think that my views on race are perfectly natural, normal, and healthy, and I wish everyone had them. So it's not acceptable to me that my views be labeled with this emotional and morally charged term. Unfortunately, having rejected that and just about any other label you'd propose, I don't have one to offer in its place, because the way I view race is something that has been the way Americans viewed race up until just a few decades ago, and so there was never really any term to describe it. I think my views on race are by and large quite similar to those of Thomas Jefferson or Abraham Lincoln, to those of practically every American president clear up until John Kennedy, and because those were the views that were taken for granted by virtually every American, there's no word to describe them. It's only after those views became a moral failing that we had to cook up terms to describe those views. It would be a little like, say, if we were living in a kibbutzim society and the theory was that all children were to be reared in common, and yet there were a few odd holdouts who insisted on loving their own children more than the children of people that were not their own. And suddenly you came up with a derogatory term for them – let's call them, I don't know, "familial-centrists" and that became a terrible pejorative term. How would the people who thought that it was entirely legitimate to love their children more than the children of others, how would they reply if asked to come up with a word to describe themselves. I just don't know, but that is the situation I find myself in. In other words, my views on race are those that have always been the mainstream. There was no word to describe them because it was the mainstream, just as there is no word to describe people who love their own children more than they love the children of strangers. When someone suddenly demands that I come up with a term to describe those views, I am at a loss.

INTERVIEWER: You think that a certain type of racial/ethnic pride is not only natural but healthy and good and you don't begrudge other people their racial and ethnic pride. Would that be an accurate description of your views here?

TAYLOR: Yes, certainly. I think not only is it healthy and good, ultimately it's necessary. If whites have no sense of racial consciousness, they will simply disappear. They will either disappear through miscegenation, or they will disappear through displacement. And, you see the crazy thing about the United States today is that for someone to be conscious of being white and happy to be white, this is equated with hatred, and yet if someone is conscious of being Asian or happy to be black or proud to be Hispanic, that's considered normal, healthy ethnic pride. Only for whites is this essential sense of group consciousness forbidden and considered to be some form of moral failing. As I say, ultimately, any group has to have some form of group cohesiveness or group consciousness in order to survive. General Motors, the people who work for General Motors, *have* to put the interests of General Motors before those of Ford or Chrysler. If they don't, General Motors will disappear and collapse. It's the same for *any group,* any team, any family. If I don't put the interests of my family before the interest of strangers, my family disappears. It will collapse. It's the same with a race. All other races take this absolutely for granted, and the odd thing is even whites who would disallow racial solidarity for whites are happy to permit it and encourage it among nonwhites. But, yes, I have no animosity whatsoever for people of different races, people of different groups. I think that, in fact, when illiterate Mexicans cross the border into the United States, it's impossible for me to fault them. They're looking for a better life for their children, and they are coming from a society that has made a mess of a lot of things to a society that has done a better job on many of those things. It is an entirely natural thing for them to do, and it is difficult for me to fault them for it. The people that I fault are the people who run *this* society, who in effect want to open up their own society, open up their own house, and let a bunch of strangers move into it. Or, they want to open up my house and let strangers move into *my* house. That's what is insane. What the nonwhites are doing is perfectly understandable.

INTERVIEWER: Haven't immigrants, though, contributed greatly to America in terms of their energy, their enthusiasm, their willingness to work harder than Americans?

TAYLOR: Which immigrants?

INTERVIEWER: Well, immigrants from all over. For instance, the Mexican immigrants certainly work at jobs that most whites won't take and will do it with a great deal of enthusiasm and a sense of satisfaction.

TAYLOR: Well, picking tomatoes, for example. Sure, people who are desperately poor, who come from a society where the average wage is about one-sixth of the American minimum wage are *certainly* going to accept jobs that white Americans are going to be reluctant to take. And it is *certainly* going to make it easier for people running companies that depend on labor to manufacture products less expensively. There's an economic argument made for importing people who are willing to work for next to nothing. Of course there is. Is that kind of argument going to be the basis for building a successful nation? I think the answer to that question is obviously no. I just read a newspaper article today about Los Angeles. It said that if they were to apply real academic standards for graduating students in the L.A. public school system from one grade to another, they would have to flunk half the students there. That's *half* the students. In other words, you don't get cheap labor all in a vacuum all by itself. At the same time, you get racial problems, you get language problems, you get Hispanic solidarity, you get Hispanic groups, you get the second generation of Hispanics who are not willing to work in the fields the way their parents did. It is a very, very shortsighted and short-term solution to a problem that I think in a healthy society would be solved domestically. No, the answer obviously is that white people are capable of picking tomatoes, white people have picked tomatoes for centuries. Perhaps the price of tomatoes would go up, but the price of law enforcement, the price of schools, the price of social stability, the price of the integrity of our culture, all of these things would be much less, even if the price of tomatoes were higher.

INTERVIEWER: The kind of white pride or white nationalist viewpoint that you articulate in *American Renaissance* is often identified in America with the less educated and poorer elements of the white population. You, obviously, don't fit into this group. You are educated, you are articulate, and people who know you say you have all the refinement and manners of a courtly gentleman. Do you see white nationalist or white pride-type of thinking – or whatever we want to label the sort of thinking represented by *American Renaissance* – do you see this type of thinking as gaining ground among the better-educated middle and upper-middle classes in America?

TAYLOR: Oh, I think it's certainly gaining ground, and I think it's inevitable that it will gain ground. I think that as whites become more beleaguered, more criticized, as their influence and numbers dwindle, they will resist. It's amazing to me that they have resisted as little as they have, but I think that an increase of resistance is inevitable, absolutely inevitable. I just don't think white people – there is maybe what? 175 million white people in this country – I don't think they're going to smilingly and gladly walk off the stage of history and say, okay, fine, our culture and our institutions can be taken over by others, and we will gladly step aside. No people in the history of the world has ever done that, and whites are in the process of doing it, but I think there is gradually a certain firming of resistance to this process of dispossession.

INTERVIEWER: We celebrate in America annually the birthday of Dr. Martin Luther King, Jr. What is your opinion of Dr. King and the black-led civil rights movement of the 1950s and 1960s in which he played so prominent a role?

TAYLOR: I think, well, Martin Luther King is as close to a secular saint as the United States has ever produced. I think that there is no . . . probably no person about whom criticism is . . . well, so frowned upon. I don't know if you recall when it was learned that he had plagiarized his Ph.D. thesis and in fact plagiarized quite a few things that he had written. This fact was sedulously kept from the public, and even when the press learned of this, American newspapers refused to publish it. It was a British newspaper that first broke this story. Now contrast that, if you will, with the ill-concealed glee with which the press reported on the DNA analysis that reported that Thomas Jefferson could well have been the father of Sally Hemmings's third son. I think the contrast here is astonishing. We are perfectly prepared to catch the third president in hypocrisy and in a lie, and yet we are very, very hesitant to call to public attention anything that could be considered unfortunate about Martin Luther King's character. The fact that he was an inveterate womanizer is something that we're not supposed to consider, the fact that he had communist sympathies and a number of very, very left-leaning advisors, these are things that we are supposed to leave completely out of the equation when it's time to determine what sort of monument we're to build to Martin Luther King on the Mall.

Now, as far as Martin Luther King's own interests are concerned, I don't blame him for that at all. I think he was a black man who was interested in the welfare of black people, and I think he struggled his entire life for the good of black people. That's exactly what black people are supposed to do. I don't fault him for that in the slightest. What's aberrant here is that what he was demanding for black people came by and large at the expense of whites and whites are supposed to be grateful for this. That is what is so entirely strange. Now, I do not defend the hierarchical arrangement that prevailed in the United States before the civil rights movement. I think it was an inevitable consequence of trying to build a society that was multiracial and a society in which this biologically salient fact had to be dealt with. Slavery was unjust, apartheid was unjust, Jim Crow was also unjust, but I think our prevailing situation is likewise unjust. If it's not unjust, it's untenable and ultimately will lead to a United States in which whites lose their majority and lose their culture. So as far as the civil rights movement is concerned, as I say, I don't at all fault the blacks who wished to destroy white freedom of association. I do fault whites who worked to destroy white freedom of association, and I do fault whites for having given it up so easily. There was a famous debate, I believe, between James Farmer and some rather thoughtful black spokesman in the early 1960s who realized that by forcing whites to give up freedom of association, blacks, too, were theoretically giving up freedom of association, and if a black congressman, for example, or a black newspaper editor wishes to hire only black employees, that of course should be his right, and these days that kind of racial preference is almost never criticized. But theoretically it should be criticized just as loudly as the preferences of whites to hire only whites. In any case, this is a long and roundabout answer to your question. I don't think that Martin Luther King is by any stretch of the imagination a national hero. You could consider him a black hero. He was very successful at making whites feel guilty about exercising their freedom of association, and he was instrumental in destroying the right to freedom of association, but to then make him a national hero for this I think is part of the insanity that prevails on virtually all questions of race in the country today.

INTERVIEWER: Martin Luther King attracted to the civil rights movement a great number of supporters who were not black because he articulated a religiously based vision of universal human dignity that transcended race. His vision is well represented in the following quotation from his book, *Where Do We Go From Here: Chaos or Community*. Let me read this and have you comment on it: "Deeply rooted in our religious heritage is the conviction that every man is an heir to a legacy of dignity and worth. Our Judeo-Christian tradition refers to this inherent dignity of man in the Biblical term 'the image of God'. The image of God is universally shared in equal proportion by all men. . . . Every human being has etched in his personality the indelible stamp of the creator. Every man must be respected because God loves him. The worth of an individual does not lie in the measure of his intellect, his racial origin or his social position. . . . An individual has value because he has value to God. Whenever this is recognized, 'whiteness' and 'blackness' pass away as determinants in a relationship and 'son' and 'brother' are substituted." What is your view of King's vision here? Isn't it powerful enough, and inspiring enough, to serve as the basis for a harmonious, multiracial society in America?

TAYLOR: What he is proposing here is that race be transcended. And you are right to point out that this vision of brotherhood was one that attracted whites as well as blacks. It is very appealing to think of America as a place where racial and other divisions are beneath us and that we can all live in happy unity, but I am convinced this is a vision that runs counter to human nature. You know what it reminds me of? Communism. The idea of communism was to build a society in which people would live "from each according to his ability to each according to his need." The idea was to transcend selfishness, and this also was a vision that inspired many people. But what was the result? Forced collectivization, endless purges, the Great Leap Forward, the Cultural Revolution, slaughter in Cambodia – not to mention economic systems that were terrible failures. Communism was a high, inspiring ideal, but it was a misreading of human nature that produced one calamity after another. The Soviet Union staggered on for more than seventy years under this impossible system and will be paying the price of communist folly for years to come.

My view is that the attempt to transcend race is just as much a misreading of human nature as the attempt to transcend self-interest. We now have precisely the kind of ideological orthodoxy, hypocrisy, and refusal to acknowledge the obvious that characterizes the Soviet Union – except that we suffer from racial delusions rather than economic delusions. Sure, the idea of transcending an age-old source of conflict appeals to people. But I think the American experience clearly shows it is not possible to transcend race, and I think we should acknowledge the importance of race rather than keep pursuing an ideal that each new generation finds impossible to achieve.

INTERVIEWER: What would you do regarding the black people who live in the United States today? You don't believe that members of different races get along very well, but it's not clear that you support a more radical separationist policy either. What would the racial landscape of America look like if your vision for the future were realized, whatever that vision might be?

TAYLOR: That's a good question. No, I don't believe in forcibly driving people out of the country, for goodness sake! I don't believe in antimiscegenation laws, for example. They were very common in the United States. I believe twenty-four states had them on the books up until 1963 or 1964 or thereabouts when the Supreme Court struck them down. I don't believe in forcible separation any more than I do in forcible integration, but I do think that there comes a point at which the United States has to ask itself what sort of nation does it wish to be. I think the majority of whites do not want to leave to their grandchildren a Third World nation, which is what we will do if current immigration policies continue. What I would do is to stop immigration, and I would overturn all antidiscrimination laws. At that point, what one might do after that I'm really not certain. Of course, if we were to get to the point where the United States were to stop immigration, even if only in part for racial reasons, or if we were to overthrow antidiscrimination laws for racial reasons, it's possible that the sentiments that resulted in those change of policies might result in other policies, too, but I wouldn't go any further than that myself.

INTERVIEWER: Is there anything we haven't asked you about that you would like to address, any issues or any problems that haven't been mentioned that you'd like to discuss?

TAYLOR: Well, I probably should have been keeping a checklist of essentials here. But if I can elaborate on an analogy I was hitting on earlier . . . when people criticize my views of race, I think it really is no different from the way people feel about their own children. They do love their children more than they love the children of strangers. That doesn't mean they have the slightest ill will toward the children of other people, and that's the way I feel about race. I think race is one's extended family. In fact, the word "nation" comes from the Latin that means to be born – *nascare*, I believe is the past participle, meaning to be born. And a nation is, I think, the largest group of people to which one can feel a kind of familial association – and it is perfectly natural, normal, and healthy to want one's people to prosper and, certainly, to survive. And in that sense it's an extension of the legitimate feelings that we have for our family, and once again legitimate feelings that do not require or even imply any ill will to those not of our family.

INTERVIEWER: But you don't believe that either blacks or Hispanics can become part of that family and that commonality of feeling that constitutes the national relationship?

TAYLOR: I think in certain very unusual cases it can happen, but I think that once a language group, for example, or a racial group, reaches a certain critical mass, then the natural gravitational pull of that critical mass begins to compete inevitably with the larger loyalty to a nation, and so, no, you cannot have a multiracial nation in any kind of healthy sense. I think it's impossible.

INTERVIEWER: What about Switzerland? You have French speakers, German speakers, and Italian speakers, yet they consider themselves all to be Swiss?

TAYLOR: Yes, I think that's an example where the natural centripetal forces of language seem to be pretty well under control. It's not exactly a frictionless environment either though.

As you know, it has very strong cantonal government. Nobody can name the president of Switzerland because the federal government has very little power. There's lots of local autonomy, which is the kind of thing that's required in a situation like that. At the same time, in Belgium you have the Flemish speakers and the French speakers, who are practically prepared to break the country apart on the strength of language. Quebec, of course, came very, very close to voting itself right out of Canada. All of these divisions are very important ones, and I think language is not as salient a social fault line as race, and I think, by and large, when you do have linguistic blocs in a country, wherever you look, you'll find that there's tension – the Czechs and the Slovaks decided they were better off going their separate ways. Was that such a bad thing? No, I don't think so. I think they're happier that way, and more power to them. The Slovenians and the Croatians and the Bosnians, they're all happier living separately from each other. The Jews and the Arabs, they're happier living apart. It's almost impossible to think of any visibly or culturally or linguistically or religiously distinguishable groups coming together, embracing each other and saying, Yes! We want to live cheek by jowl with these people.

You know, the Navaho and the Hopi have long lived next door to each other. They have shared some of the same hunting grounds, and when their major reservation – I forget in which state it is – when their major reservation was established, the federal government was not going to draw any line and say this side is Hopi and this side is Navaho. The Hopi and the Navaho insisted it be drawn, however. *They* wanted separate reservations, and I think that's just the natural state of humanity. You can call it a fallen state, if you will, but that is the way we are, and I think to try to drive nature out through sheer ideology can only fail and only lead to suffering. In this case, of course, in the case of the United States, it's whites who have essentially disarmed unilaterally in the face of the racial consciousness of others. It's whites who are saying, "Yes, race doesn't matter." "White people don't have any legitimate racial interests." "Oh, it'll be wonderful when we become a minority." And, of course, they don't really believe it. To me, it's a kind of collective insanity.

INTERVIEWER: And you think, though, that it won't last very long, that whites will come to recognize what you are talking about and will adopt views more similar to your own?

TAYLOR: Well, do you read *Commentary*?

INTERVIEWER: Yes, actually I do.

TAYLOR: Did you read Ron Unz's article about – oh, I forget what it was called – it's the latest issue.

INTERVIEWER: I haven't seen that yet.

TAYLOR: He was writing about the fact that whites are now a minority in California, and he described white racial consciousness as the most potentially nation-breaking or nation-destroying phenomenon on the horizon. That's a very ironic thing. In effect, he is trying to come up with ways to shepherd whites gently into dispossession, and he's hoping for ways to persuade whites to accept minority status without developing any kind of racial consciousness. Well, I mean why should whites put up with that? Why should whites be happy to see their country transformed in the ways that demographic transformation will inevitably transform it? Why?! Why?! This is just crazy. He's asking whites to quietly commit suicide, and I think that's completely illegitimate and unfair.

INTEVIEWER: Thank you.

2

Reno Wolfe

If Jared Taylor's *American Renaissance* group represents a distinctly highbrow style of white rights advocacy and white protest, Reno Wolfe's National Association for the Advancement of White People is a much more middlebrow affair. Founded in January, 1998, Wolfe's NAAWP, National, Inc., is an Internet-centered protest organization that focuses on opposition to race-based affirmative action programs throughout American society. Like Taylor's group, Wolfe's organization believes that white people in America have distinct individual and group interests that need to be protected through vigorous advocacy, but the appeal of his organization is much broader and more grass roots oriented than Taylor's. At the heart of the NAAWP's white rights activism is its electronic news commentary, which delivers to the computer screens of all subscribers regular information and editorial comment on a variety of race-related topics. The NAAWP routinely denounces what it sees as racial double standards in the areas of education, employment, government service provision, and the reporting of interracial crime. White people in America, Wolfe charges, have often been accorded a subordinate status to blacks and members of other minorities in these areas, as the minorities, in effect, have been granted special rights and privileges rather than equal treatment. In the following interview Wolfe goes out of his way to disassociate his own organization from an earlier organization by the same name founded in the early 1980s by ex–Ku Klux Klansman David Duke. The new NAAWP, Wolfe contends, is not a white supremacist or white nationalist organization, but seeks only to advance the legitimate civil rights of white people in the same way that the National Association for the Advancement of Colored People (NAACP) and the older civil rights movement sought to advance the civil rights of blacks. Striking a distinctly moderate pose, Wolfe is the only figure among the ten persons

The interview of Reno Wolfe on December 22, 1999, by Russell K. Nieli is printed with kind permission of the interviewee.

interviewed in this volume to express continued support for the integrationist and civil rights ideals of the sixties-era civil rights movement. What is most needed today, Wolfe contends, is constructive public dialogue on issues of race in which white people can express their legitimate fears and concerns candidly and openly. He sees his own organization as helping to further this kind of public dialogue. The goal of his organization, he says, is not to establish white supremacy or white separatism but to get back to the ideal where everyone is treated equally regardless of race. The NAAWP, Wolfe explains, has been particularly active in support of anti–affirmative action initiatives, and in drawing attention to the true scope of black-on-white crime in America. The latter issue, he says, is often ignored by the mainstream news media, though it is a major reason why whites move away from neighborhoods with large black populations. Unless race-based programs of special privilege are eliminated, and a more open climate of discussion is created where white people are permitted to voice what is really on their mind, there will be no improvement in race relations, Wolfe insists.

Interview with Reno Wolfe

INTERVIEWER: Could you explain for us the nature of the organization you founded in 1998, the National Association for the Advancement of White People?

WOLFE: The NAAWP was set up to get us back to the point where everyone is seen as created equal, where everyone has equal opportunity, and where everybody is judged under the same guidelines and the same set of standards. The NAAWP does not wish to convey the idea that we are a white supremacist-type of organization or that we want to advance whites beyond other groups. We just want to return to the ideal in which racially based policies of affirmative action and special privileges and special programs of any kind, which are given to anybody, no matter what their race, are viewed as contrary to the best interests of race relations here in America. As far as promoting this end, we are very active in anti–affirmative action initiatives, such as what's been brought up in California under Proposition 209 and in Washington under Proposition 200. We were very active in those two states, and we're very active in the state of Florida, and we'll be very active wherever such initiatives pop up next, which, as I understand it, is going to be Michigan or Illinois. And we educate the American people as well as our own members about these special programs, and we will continue doing so in spite of the fact that the media accuses us of being very politically incorrect – and that goes all the way from the national media to local medias throughout the country. That's basically what we're doing, and because of that we have grown at a phenomenal, phenomenal pace in the last two years.

INTERVIEWER: Have you gotten a lot of people to join your organization over this two-year period?

WOLFE: Oh, yes, yes! Let me explain. People in the media don't like our name. They would hope that we would probably use another name instead of NAAWP – the National Association for the Advancement of White People. If we just called ourselves the National Association for the Advancement of European Americans, then that would be more politically correct, and probably more advantageous for us in terms of media relations. Just the word "white" scares the hell out of 'em. However, once people read and learn about our organization and learn about our goals and our concepts, about what we wish to accomplish, well then they understand where we're coming from. And we attract many educated people, well-educated people, and independent-minded people who wish to seek knowledge on their own – people who don't rely upon others to tell them what they should think. And we get people from all races in the organization and from all religious backgrounds, even though we're not a religious organization. We have members of the Jewish faith in the organization. Some of 'em even wrote ads in our newsletter. When people get past the word "white" and start understanding the whole concept and goals and principles of the organization, well then they join; then they understand what we're doing. We are the only organization out there that fights at the grass roots level throughout this country against affirmative action and all these special programs, special minority set-asides, special scholarships. The list just goes on and on, and there's probably at least a hundred different programs out there – actually we're probably talking about a thousand if you go through all the states that have these special programs. Instead of bringing people together, all these programs, we believe, are really racially divisive. As long as we have these programs, this country will be forever racially divided.

INTERVIEWER: So the main purpose of your organization, then, seems to be opposition to affirmative action. Your main goal in life seems to be opposing what you see as the special advantages and special privileges that are given to people because of their minority racial status. Is that an accurate description of the goals of the NAAWP?

WOLFE: Yes, that would be the main objective, though our objectives encompass much more. When you talk about programs that we oppose, we oppose all special privilege programs. These include programs that are offered at the time that a child is born to all the special programs that are given after that time. We have now special programs for how to take care of the young and how to raise them – special this and special that. There are special before-school programs when minority children get in elementary school, and then special tutors in the school, and then special programs for that child after school. And all the way up to high school they make special dispensation for minority students who for some reason are unable to graduate when judged by the same standards applied to others. Now that's not affirmative action itself, but those are just some of the programs that are out there that we think are unfair and that we oppose.

INTERVIEWER: And you oppose these programs because white people are not able to benefit from them under the same terms that people of other races or ethnic groups are able to benefit?

WOLFE: That is correct. The programs are not equal. If you go to any Head Start program, for instance, those in them are very predominantly of minority races. Caucasians aren't being treated equally in them.

INTERVIEWER: But don't Caucasians, if they are poor, qualify for Head Start under the same terms that a poor person who is black or Hispanic qualifies?

WOLFE: Yes, in theory that is so. However, when you have X amount of slots – let's say that you have a Head Start program in a certain city or a certain section of a city and there's thirty openings allocated for that age group, let's say, for the age groups encompassing two- and three-year olds – what happens there is that those slots are predominantly filled by nonwhites. In fact, I can't recall going into a Head Start program myself over the last few years that wasn't . . . I was going to say 95 percent, but it's usually 100 percent black or Latino. For some reason, the program directors are predominantly minority themselves, so they're the ones who pick and choose who gets into these programs. And they choose minority children.

INTERVIEWER: And you think that they discriminate against poor white people?

WOLFE: Well, they discriminate against whites. I'm not saying they discriminate against *poor* whites because they may not even have knowledge that a family is economically disadvantaged. But they discriminate against white people.

INTERVIEWER: Perhaps they don't know of the existence of poor whites who would qualify . . .

WOLFE: And they could care less because they're more interested in making sure that their people or their relatives are accepted over the white child. And that's discrimination. But it's covered up, it's covered up real good. And Head Start is only one program. I mean there's many programs out there that grant special privileges to minorities. I know here in the state of Florida, there are six school districts – I think they're in the major cities, like Tampa, Miami, Duvall County (which is Jacksonville), probably Tallahassee, and a couple of others – where if a minority student from the seventh grade to the twelfth grade maintains a 2.0

GPA, then they are automatically guaranteed, *guaranteed* by the state of Florida, a scholarship in one of the state universities. Now you need a 2.0 in this state to even graduate. Every minority who achieves a 2.0, which he has to do anyway just to pass, is guaranteed a scholarship. With whites, there's no such privilege. A white child could pull a 4.0 average from the seventh grade to the twelfth grade and not be guaranteed a college scholarship by the state of Florida. We don't think that's fair.

INTERVIEWER: Whites have to meet tougher standards to get a college scholarship?

WOLFE: Well, they have to look other places for the scholarship. It's not one that's guaranteed by the state of Florida. They'll have to go to many of the different funding programs, like Pell grants, and go out there and search for different scholarships that are offered. Whites in Florida, no matter what their grades, are not guaranteed scholarships, whereas minority students get such guarantees. And Florida is not the only state that does this. There's quite a few other states that have similar programs. Even some private corporations offer scholarships that are only meant for minority students. They'll spend hundreds of millions of dollars on setting up scholarship funding to ensure money just for the African American. But with whites, they will not subsidize or send one dollar for scholarships or educational-type grants of any kind. They have no scholarships specifically for whites or Caucasians, no matter what their economic status is. However, for blacks, they have many such scholarships.

Now in this day and age there is absolutely no reason whatsoever for a black student not to be able to get a college education. Blacks even have the choice of going to any of the historically black universities, which have much lower entrance requirements in terms of test scores than many other universities. A school like Edwards College, for instance, is less demanding than LSU or Ohio State. So there's no reason why a minority student shouldn't be able to achieve the goal of a college education. If the minority student stays in school and studies and is dealt with and judged equally and on the same basis as all the other students, there is no reason he can't get into college. Getting into college is even easier today than it was thirty years ago, as test standards have continually dropped and dropped, until even many white students now seem like they're coming out of high school as idiots. The educational input into these students now is just not anything like what it was before. Yet blacks will holler and scream and they'll say that they're being discriminated against, that they're not receiving the same chances as the white student. But many black students today, unlike earlier times, sit in the same classroom with whites. I know my own children have gone to school all their lives in mixed-race classes with blacks and whites and Asians and everything else.

INTERVIEWER: Your own children attended integrated public schools in Florida?

WOLFE: Yes, surely. In fact, my last one, he's sixteen years old now, ever since day one all of his classes have always been integrated, and he receives the same instruction as the others do, the same teachers. They don't separate them. They get the same instruction; they get the same guidelines; they get the same tests. So why, why shouldn't they both be treated equally when it comes to applying for a state scholarship to get into college?

INTERVIEWER: You think it is fundamentally unfair to have race-based scholarships that whites are excluded from?

WOLFE: That's correct, yes. It's discrimination – I don't know another word for it, it's flat-out discrimination. There was a similar case regarding white-only scholarships at Alabama State University – I think it was broadcast on 20/20. They wanted to integrate the university, bring more white people into the university, and the state of Alabama offered ten scholarships – full paid scholarships for white students because they were considered a minority on that campus. And the black students on the campus hollered and screamed about that, saying that it was not fair that these students were given scholarships, free scholarships to their university, just because they were white. But they could not see the exact same thing that's happening in the reverse all over America when blacks receive special scholarships. They were really upset that the state of Alabama had opened up these scholarships for these white students, a full paid scholarship, but they didn't think it unfair that blacks receive the exact same privilege when going to other universities on scholarships reserved just for them. I found that kind of amazing. It's like you want your cake and eat it too. But you can't have it both ways.

INTERVIEWER: The view of your organization, then, is that race-targeted scholarships of any kind, whether they exclude whites or exclude blacks, should be eliminated?

WOLFE: That's correct, that's correct. They should all have an equal playing field. Our position is: stop the discrimination, no matter what it is, and treat everybody equally, treat everybody fairly, have everybody take the same test, have everyone judged on the same standards in order to achieve whatever it is that they want to be. It should all be based on a principle of equality. You can't have separate standards for some groups of people. That will never, ever work, and if corporations and politicians and others think that that's the way to go, that we should have all these different racial guidelines and everything is going to turn out just fine, and everybody's just going to learn to live together with each other real well because of all this, well, I don't know where they're coming from. That kind of thinking makes no sense.

INTERVIEWER: Do you think there's going to be increasing racial polarization and racial hostility in America because of these special race-based scholarship programs?

WOLFE: Yes, naturally! How can it be any other way? Many blacks don't even like them. The blacks who are educated and know what it is leading to, they don't like it because when you have a well-qualified black that scored high on his tests, got himself a real nice scholarship, graduated from the university of his choice, and went on to become a successful person in life, whether it was in business or whatever, and he did that on his own, the way it is now, his achievement is undermined. When he meets or comes across white companions out there in the workforce or on the university level or wherever it is, in the back of their mind, they're going to be saying that the only reason why he's a professor at this university or the president of this company or owns this company is because he has received special privileges that were denied to others. And his reputation is always going to be tainted. Whites are going to label him saying that he really didn't earn his position. Even though he did, they're going to say that he was just given his position because of the color of his skin, and that to get to where he is he had to have all these special programs, and all this special help, and everything else down the line. This has to affect blacks negatively, which is probably why we have blacks in the organization, because they realize that policies like this hurt them as much as it does whites.

INTERVIEWER: You have black people in your organization?

WOLFE: Sure we do.

INTERVIEWER: Why would any black person want to join an organization like the NAAWP?

WOLFE: Because of affirmative action. They don't like affirmative action. The issue of crime reporting is also important. We have one member out there – a woman who converses with me quite often – and her main thing is the astronomical amount of black-on-white crime that is not reported by the media. However, it does show up in FBI statistics, and every person in America out there in any city knows that there's a tremendous amount of black-on-white crime that is actually really a hate crime that goes unreported as a hate crime.

INTERVIEWER: What does your organization do about this?

WOLFE: Well, when we run across a situation like that, we bring it to the people's attention across the nation by using e-mail and faxes. We locate the jurisdiction that the crime took place in from a member, contact the state's attorney, the district attorney, or whoever is the prosecutor who handles cases such as that, and we let them know that we're watching what's going on and that if something is a hate crime, we address it. And we have been very successful at this. While five or six years ago it could not be perceived that blacks could be charged with a hate crime, they're now being charged with hate crimes. Take a case right here in Jacksonville, Florida, the case of Gerald Griffin. You had a group of six blacks that waited in the dark near a sidewalk behind some trees and stated that the next white person to come down the street they were going to attack, and sure enough, when Gerald Griffin was the next white person coming down the street, they killed him. He was a fifty-year-old mentally disabled person, and they killed him.

And the story came out in the *Florida Times-Union* that after they arrested these guys, they openly admitted to the state's attorney that it was their goal to attack the next white person to come down the street. It made no difference whether it was a man, whether it was a woman, or whatever, they were just going to attack the next white person that came down the street. And that met the guidelines for the hate crime penalty to be added to their sentence or for the charges to be increased. But initially the state's attorney here, he was very hesitant about calling it a hate crime. He said that the hate crime law didn't really apply to this case, which was just a crock, just a crock! If it had been six white people out there that killed a black, you better believe that everyone of them would have been charged with a hate crime, and probably within three minutes of being arrested. And so I got on the Internet right away and contacted all my members nationwide, and we flooded their office down there with messages on this. And about two days later, the state's attorney came out and said that they had revised their opinion and determined that it was a hate crime after all. Well, naturally it was a hate crime.

For some reason, though, the American public thinks that a hate crime can only be white on black. You take Mr. Byrd up there in Texas that grabbed national headlines, and for weeks we had TV stations there, we had newspapers, all the way from the *The New York Times* to the San Francisco *Chronicle*, all reporting on this white-on-black hate crime. That situation out there made national headlines, but when you have a black-on-white hate crime done, it's never ever reported. It's always hidden. If I didn't have the network of people that I have out there reporting to me regularly, it would be real hard for the average person to read and find out about the tremendous amount of black-on-white crime that goes on in America. And it's tremendous, but it's never reported.

The *Florida Times-Union*, for instance, they'll only print the news that they want their public to hear, or their readers to hear, and if it's two women being shot in the back of the head in a gang ritual in North

Carolina by a gang of blacks, they won't report that because they believe it's best for race relations if things like that are not put in the newspaper. But stuff like that *needs* to be reported, and it *needs* the readership of everyone in the community. The community needs to find out about the total extent of all this. Only when it becomes known, when you have public awareness of black-on-white as well as white-on-black crime in America, can you sit down and begin to discuss the problems of race in America, the differences that divide the races, and the future of this country along racial lines. If we want to stay divided, well, we're doing real good the way it is now. But if the American people want to be all-inclusive, if this is our hope and our goal, then there's a lot of things that have to be put out on the table. You can't just take them off the table just because you don't like the cards that are out there. You don't take them out of the deck just because you don't like looking at them.

INTERVIEWER: So your organization seeks to encourage both a greater honesty about interracial crime and also wants to encourage interracial dialogue about some of these problems. Is that correct?

WOLFE: Yes, surely, because only when we can sit across the table from each other, or speak to our neighbors out there, and be able to discuss these issues openly and honestly can there ever be any positive result. If the government tries to force people to keep silent about these things, if it tries to become a thought police and say that there's certain things you can't say or you can't do, we can never have a productive dialogue that addresses people's real concerns like the concerns over black-on-white crime.

Take the case of black people moving into your community: if you don't like it, if you are concerned about crime, you can't say, "You know, I really wouldn't like blacks living in my neighborhood right now." Well, oh boy, you say that, you utter those words, let me tell you, you're in big trouble. You can't say those things. But that would be open and honest dialogue. So what usually happens is that the white puts his property up for sale, and then he moves someplace else. And the media and the government call that white flight, and they can't understand white flight. They say whenever something like that happens, it's white flight. Well, there's a reason for whites acting as they do, and the reason is that people will not sit down and discuss all the real differences that divide the races, and discuss everything that makes that white person not want to live next to the black and makes that white person want to leave the area. Whites are not permitted to discuss openly their real fears and concerns. And there's so many other examples that could be given. I mean there's hundreds and hundreds more out there. It's like New York City, there's eight million stories, and that's only one of them.

INTERVIEWER: Why do people join your organization and what are the demographics of your membership?

WOLFE: The main reason people join our organization is because they want a better future for their children or for their grandchildren. They don't like the way everything has been developing over the last twenty or thirty years, and they want positive change in the future. They say that if positive change is not made, it's going to just continue further deteriorating.

Now, as far as the demographics, in terms of age probably 50 percent of the organization is made up of people between thirty-five and sixty-five, and then it's probably pretty well split either side of that for the other 50 percent. We have them as young as eighteen, which is the youngest that you can join this organization. I won't let anyone under the age of eighteen join. In terms of occupations, we have a lot of professionals. There are many doctors, for instance, and they come from all specialties, whether its pediatricians, skin doctors, nose-ears-eyes-and-throat specialists, chiropractors, we have a lot of professionals like that. We have military people in there, and that too cuts across the line, all the way from high-ranking officers down to the enlisted-men ranks. And we have our share of truck drivers and business owners and everything else.

Many people perceive us to be just a bunch of low-income redneck-type people out there, backwoods types from Georgia, where the family tree goes up and down, straight up and down – you have no branches. I think that is how the media tries to portray us. You watch Jerry Springer. Jerry Springer just loves to get somebody up there, you know, with all of his front teeth missing, who has only an eighth grade education, and slam bash him all over the stage for entertainment purposes. And it's that mentality that people probably perceive organizations like ours to embody. I'm not saying that there aren't some organizations out there that are made up like that, but definitely not the NAAWP.

INTERVIEWER: So you get a range of people in terms of their socioeconomic and occupational status?

WOLFE: Yes, that's right. I would say that probably 70 percent of them are in the middle- to high-income group. I'd say 30 percent would encompass the low-income-type people, where they'd have a hard time, you know, coming up with the $25 yearly membership fee, people along those lines, where they live from week to week or payday to payday. They probably make up 30 percent of the total overall membership. Although I don't have exact figures, from my personal knowledge of talking with people, I would say that about 15 percent of our members are poverty level or below – the low-lowers – then you got the other 15 percent that is just barely scraping by, but are just above the poverty line, and then the other 70 percent do not have to worry about whether or not they miss a payday and can take a month's vacation time.

INTERVIEWER: Do you have any specific strategies for recruiting new members? For instance, do you recruit on college campuses, in churches, or over the Internet?

WOLFE: We're just beginning to recruit on college campuses now. We don't recruit in churches, however. It must be emphasized that were not a religious organization. We're founded on Christian principles, but we're not a religious-based organization such as a lot of the others are. It's not up to us to tell you how you should worship your God. That's between you and your pastor, or your priest, or your rabbi, or whatever. That's just not our thing. Our thing is civil rights, and our message is that everybody's got to be treated equally. If we started preaching the Bible, you would have over 300 different religions contesting how to interpret the Bible, and we just don't want to get into that. That's not what we're about.

Although we haven't made the strongest effort to recruit on college campuses in past years, we've had some moderate success recently in this regard. We have had individuals from some universities – in Indiana, for instance – that have requested guidelines and the like on how to start an NAAWP club or faction on campus, and we just tell them to go down to their administration office and get the paperwork and follow the exact same procedure that the NAACP has done and the Nation of Islam has done to establish clubs or a unit on their campus, and forward the required forms over to me, and we'll fill them out and get them back. It's got to be the exact same forms; it can't be anything different. We fill them out the same way, and we have to meet the same criteria as other groups. What is right for one is right for the other. We're still waiting to hear back from a couple of universities right now.

INTERVIEWER: What about recruitment over the Internet?

WOLFE: The Internet has been great for us; it's great. We get a lot of members off the Internet. When they go to our page, they click on the page – NAAWP.com – and they read what we're about. You'd be surprised . . . probably one out of ten who visits our website apply for an application right there. In fact, we figured out that in the last couple of months, about 12 percent of those who visit our website really follow through and join the organization. People can mail in their membership or join online. We just instituted the possibility of signing up online about three weeks ago, and that's taking off real well.

INTERVIEWER: Do people give you a credit card number to pay your $25 a year membership fee?

WOLFE: Well, they get a subscription to our publications and announcements, and then you get free membership. You can't sell memberships on the Internet, but we do sell subscriptions for $25 a year – membership is $25 a year, so you get both.

INTERVIEWER: Could you describe your vision for the future of America? What would the racial landscape of America look like if your vision for the future were to be realized? What would be changed and what would be retained?

WOLFE: What would be changed? Well, the government would have to realize that affirmative action programs and all the special privileges given to some people just aren't working, and they *will* not work. If they perceive that it will work, they have to step back and reevaluate their position and at least be able to read the writing on the wall. And the people who have taken advantage of all these programs, they have to sit back themselves at some point and reevaluate their position. At some point, you have to be responsible for yourself. You have to be responsible if you're a parent; you have to be responsible for sending your kid to school. You have to be responsible to make sure that your kid does his homework. You have to be responsible about what he does after school. Whether he's out standing on the corner trying to figure out some way to carjack someone, or whether he's on the debate team, you have to know what he's doing. You can't always wait for the government to come by and help you out.

And even now if minorities get busted, they get sent to jail, and this program is in there for them, government boot camps that help them set them straight. I mean how many chances do people need! At some point in time, someone's going to have to take responsibility. That's the way it was back in the twenties, and thirties, and forties; people were responsible. And that's just not the way it is any more, and that has to be recognized and changed. If you're going to bring a child into the world, it's a lifelong responsibility, or at least for eighteen years. It's not a part-time thing. And parents just have to pay more attention to what's going on, and you can't blame the school board or the school district or the schools or whatever it is because of the failure of your particular child to graduate. If your child is not able to graduate, there's got to be a reason for it. Maybe the reason is that the child is not doing his homework or the child is too busy doing other things in school instead of doing his schoolwork and his classwork. But you can't sit there and expect the school board or the government to lower the standards – the minimum scores for your child to be able to pass and to be promoted to the next grade. It's the damnedest thing I have ever seen, but that's what's going on now. And it's going to continue that way, and will continue that way, as long as you've got affirmative action and you got people out there hollering and screaming that it's racist at every turn in life. These problems have nothing to do with race; they have to do with being responsible.

INTERVIEWER: Some people would characterize your organization as racist. What do you say to such charges?

WOLFE: Well, just educate yourself! If blacks can be proud to be black, proud of their heritage and culture, why should it be considered racist for a white to feel the same way about his race and his culture and his heritage. What is racist about that? "Racist" is in the eyes of the beholder. You can probably ask ten different people what a racist is and you're going to get ten different answers. But everybody hates to be called a racist, and minorities know this. They have become real good at using this fear, and whenever they perceive anything that is not advantageous to them, well, they call it racist. And the person, or the company, or whoever is accused just can't stand it, they don't want to be called a racist, so they cave into the minority demands, and that's the way it goes.

INTERVIEWER: In America, we celebrate annually the birthday of Dr. Martin Luther King, Jr. What is your opinion of Dr. King and the black-led civil rights movement of the 1950s and 1960s in which he played so prominent a role? Is America a better place or worse place because of that movement and the philosophy of nonviolent multiracialism that it supported?

WOLFE: Well, in the fifties and forties, it seems like everybody was getting along pretty well. There were no big problems. I mean the G.I.s had come home from the Second World War, and then from Korea, and they had made their mark. And the black soldiers were recognized for their wartime service in the same manner that whites were. Maybe some of the blacks weren't treated as fairly and weren't as successful in going back to college as some of the whites, so it was a good thing that we had civil rights legislation as it was initially drawn up. I supported the Civil Rights Act of 1964. I thought that was great. But today, wow! The scope of the law has expanded beyond anything imagined then and touches everything today.

As far as Dr. King is concerned, I'll say this . . . he meant well. But sometimes the way he went about his life was questionable; it's kind of hard to say whether it was bad or good or whatever. When it came out that he plagiarized most of his writing, and then cheated to get his diploma, things along those lines, that's not a very good way to present yourself as a role model for the young. But many look at King's legacy in terms of his "I Have a Dream" speech. And, of course, that speech was very dynamic. It was a good speech; we all have that dream. But that dream did not encompass giving special privileges to anyone, yet blacks use that now, and the legacy of the civil rights movement, to try to gain special privileges. It's not the same now as what it was back then. Back then the civil rights movement served its purpose. It was a wake-up call for America, and America woke up, and probably 90 percent of the people out there at the time in 1964 realized that things had to be done to change things, had to be modified to make blacks and everybody else all-inclusive in America.

But then black leaders, they just took that to another level so that now it's "let not be equal here." Special privileges are now demanded. They all have their own perception of what equal is, and equal, again, if you have ten different black leaders out there and ask them what equal is, you're going to get ten different answers. It all depends on who's leading the parade at the time, whether it's Louis Farrakhan or Jesse Jackson. Jackson in my opinion is a joke. I have no respect for that man.

INTERVIEWER: Why not?

WOLFE: He's a media hog. All he wants is publicity. You take the instance up there in Decatur, Illinois, where you had those six students who were just running wild all over in the football stands, just beating each other and trying to hurt people. If you have seen the tape, and I'm sure you have because they played it so many times on TV . . . for him to come into Decatur and to chastise the school board for their actions, that was just unbelievable. He should have been a reverend, he should have gone to those kids right there, and those kids' parents, and told *them* that when you break the rules, when you break the laws, you're going to suffer the consequences. He should have talked to those kids about trying to reform their lives, about getting their stuff together so they can become productive citizens, instead of going to the school board and calling the school board racist because they expelled these kids for their violent conduct. This guy's a reverend? Come on now!

I'm not quite sure where he's coming from, but how he thinks that he is going to help these delinquents – and that's exactly what they were – I don't understand. If one of those kids had a gun that night in the school stand at that football game at Eisenhower High, you better believe you'd have had a situation on your hands far worse than Columbine because they would not have hesitated to use it. It was just by the grace of God that there were no firearms available, and for Jesse Jackson to go into Decatur and chastise that school board and call them racist because of their actions in expelling these kids, that is just totally outrageous. I just cannot believe that he has any following at all, and people who follow him and followed that line of reasoning, they must have fallen off the roof somewhere.

INTERVIEWER: You say the use of the word "white" in the name of your organization turns some people away from the organization. If that's the case, why don't you use a less offensive title like the "European-American Anti-discrimination League," or something comparable to that?

WOLFE: Well, for two reasons. I can see where it would be more politically correct to use the term "European American" rather than the word "white," even though they mean the same thing. Some people are afraid of the word "white" because they attach a supremacist connotation to it. The reason why I don't use another term, however, is that we are politically incorrect anyway. Using the word "white" stimulates many people's curiosity. If we were the European-American Anti-discrimination League or something along those lines, it wouldn't have the same visual grab that the NAAWP does. The title we use gets people thinking about what we are, and they begin reading and finding out about the organization. They may initially look for racism and supremacist thinking, or things along those lines, or they may initially identify us with radicalism, extremism, hate, and the like, and see if we conform to their expectations. But it's not there, none of it, and when they find this out, it kind of upsets them, and then they start reading more about what we are about, what we stand for, and what our goals are, and then that's usually all it takes. They sometimes then become our supporters and join our organization.

INTERVIEWER: So you like the fact that there's a certain shock value to the title of your organization?

WOLFE: Yes, "shock value" – that's the word I was hunting for. It is the shock value, and I don't see any reason at all why we should change the name to something else. There's no reason for it. We just want to get back to the point where everybody is treated equally and considered equally. And if people get upset about the word "white," they have to look within themselves about what's wrong with the word "white." I don't see anything wrong with the word "white." My grandparents were white. As far as I know, the whole family has been white, so, I mean, I have a white heritage, a white past. Why should I be ashamed to use the word "white"? Our adversaries have tried to make the word "white" a dirty word. But there's nothing dirty about it. There's nothing bad about being a white.

INTERVIEWER: Would "white pride group" accurately describe your organization, or at least one of the goals of your organization?

WOLFE: Well, you know, you mentioned that [in a preliminary communication]. White pride and white nationalism, that type of organizations – I don't think either one of these terms really fits us well if you were trying to put an accurate label on us. I don't think either one of those would really fit. We're a white organization, and we're proud to be a white organization. If that is your definition of white pride, then we would be a white pride organization. White nationalist organization, now there's other organizations out there who adhere to that line of thinking. They have the right to put out their message just like we do;

it's guaranteed to them by the Constitution, and I know personally many of them. We just have a different philosophy, a different view, and different goals. And that's not knocking them or anything else, they have a right to express their opinion just as we do, and we have a mutual respect for each other.

INTERVIEWER: I see on your website, you say – "We are a civil rights organization specifically founded for white people to counter reverse discrimination. We welcome all people who want to learn about us." So you consider yourself a white civil rights organization?

WOLFE: That's what we are, a white civil rights organization, that's exactly it. That's how we are incorporated, as a white civil rights organization. We're incorporated in the state of Florida as a white civil rights organization, that's exactly it. And many people inquire about us, and it's not just whites. We don't just reach out to whites. We reach out to people who want to make America a better place, and who realize that just because you're white does not mean that you are antiblack, or that your are anti-Asian, or that you are anti-Latino, or anti-anything.

INTERVIEWER: So you are a pro-white organization that seeks harmonious relations with members of other racial groups?

WOLFE: Right. We're whites that want to protect the rights of our race and our people to ensure that our children and our grandchildren are not discriminated against because they are white, which is what is happening now in the late 1990s.

INTERVIEWER: Could you tell us something about the history of the organization, how it originally got started?

WOLFE: Yes. This organization, the NAAWP, National, Inc., was founded in January 1998. A lot of people confuse us with an organization that originated out of Louisiana that went defunct quite a few years ago called the NAAWP. It's not the same organization. We are the National Association for the Advancement of White People, National, Inc., out of Florida. People like to refer to us saying that a former congressperson from the state of Louisiana, David Duke, founded this organization. He did nothing of the sort. Whenever the NAAWP gets mentioned, they always love to throw in the name of Mr. Duke, I guess to shock people, and throw in, you know, that he's a KKK grand dragon or whatever. I've never met David Duke; I've never seen the man; if I passed him on the street, I wouldn't know him. That philosophy that he espoused years ago, which I have read about – that he was an extremist and a radical and white supremacist – well, if that's all fact, I have no firsthand knowledge of that. I've never personally read any of his books. I've never followed or read anything about his life or anything else about him. But I can tell you that if anyone thinks that what Mr. Duke is said to stand for is the same thing as what the

NAAWP, National, Inc., here stands for, they're just totally misguided. But that's not going to stop people from writing about us in this way, though. You know, you got certain writers who, just no matter what, will always bring up Duke in talking about us.

INTERVIEWER: If your organization has nothing to do with the organization that David Duke founded, why do you use the same name? Aren't you encouraging confusion?

WOLFE: Well, I'll tell you. You know, the original NAAWP is defunct and has been for a long time. It was dead when I came on the scene. I guess I was naïve enough to believe that people wouldn't keep trying to connect the two organizations, but I see nothing wrong with it. I have had a lot of people join the organization just because of the organization's title. They wanted to start an NAAWP themselves, and they got online to try and suddenly realized that there actually *was* an NAAWP – and then they contact me and want to join. Well, I guess, I did basically the same thing back in '96–'97. As I say, I had heard about David Duke, through the newspapers. And I talked with a journalist, Mr. Bridges, of the Miami *Herald*, who evidently wrote a big book, or something along those lines, on Mr. Duke, and he told me a few things about Duke. However, this organization has nothing at all to do with David Duke, or his philosophy, or his goals – whatever they may be. It has nothing at all to do with Duke.

INTERVIEWER: Are the majority of your members from the South?

WOLFE: I'd say, 30, about 30 to 35 percent, would probably be what you would call from the Old South.

INTERVIEWER: And the other 70 percent are from outside the South?

WOLFE: Yes. We have members in Illinois and Michigan, in Indiana, Iowa – we're real strong up there. We picked up many members in the West, all the way to the states of Washington, California, and Nevada. We have quite a few in California and Washington, and that's what really helped in the passage of those two propositions, that we were able to mobilize our members and get them happy about the prospect of changing things.

INTERVIEWER: Do you have local chapters where people come together for regular meetings?

WOLFE: Yes, we do. But only certain chapters do this. They have regular meetings, and others communicate and have meetings by chat room on the Internet. That's an important point that you bring up. I require that all meetings held by any chapter, or by any leaders, or by any members, always be held in an open public area, such as a public library, and never, never held in private or in a secluded spot, because you do stuff like that, and people may think you're out there concocting up something illegal. Our organization, as a civil rights organization, is open to the public. The public can attend any one of our meetings. We don't care if you're a member. The meetings are always open to the public, and the best way to do this we feel is to hold our meetings in public facilities, such as local public libraries.

INTERVIEWER: Could you give us any estimate of the size of your membership?

WOLFE: Well, it's a mid four-digit range right now. Members and supporters together will exceed ten thousand. We have a small number of people who send donations and donate to the organization that are not members because of the adverse effects that would follow if people found out that they were a member of the NAAWP. People in job-sensitive places sometimes contribute without joining because open membership could jeopardize their livelihood.

INTERVIEWER: But these nonmembers offer financial support?

WOLFE: Yes, yes. It's amazing the support we get. When we went up to Decatur, Illinois, to support the school board up there after Jesse Jackson left town, it took just a couple of hours on the Internet to get enough funds in order to pay for our expenses. We don't get funding from any other sources but private contributions – we don't get government grants, nor does the United Way support our programs. Our scholarship program is funded entirely by private donations from members or supporters. Our food drive is totally supported by members and supporters.

INTERVIEWER: What is the purpose of your food drive?

WOLFE: Well, the purpose of the food drive is to give people a helping hand, not a handout. If you go down to your local welfare office just to get that little helping hand, chances are, because of the bureaucracy, you'll probably have to wait a month, or more to get anything – if you get anything – and usually when people need a helping hand, they need it right away. They don't need it a month and a half down the road. And that's what we do. We will help out a family twice, but then that's all, no more. And this last year, just in this area here, north Florida, we were able to give that helping hand to over 100 individuals and families.

INTERVIEWER: That's the end of our formal questions. Is there anything else that you haven't said that you would like to tell us about your organization?

WOLFE: Well, the only thing I would like to tell the people out there is this. Don't let the government, don't let the newspapers, don't let the TV or anyone else tell you what you should know about our organization. If you want to find out about the NAAWP, it's very easy to find out about us. You can either go on the Internet or you can just write me direct, and we'll send you our information packet. We also have a hotline number. People should make their own decisions and their own choices, and should decide for themselves if they perceive us to be a supremacist organization, or an extremist organization, or a radical organization. Think for yourself, don't let other people tell you what we are. Find out for yourself.

INTERVIEWER: Thank you.

3

Michael Levin

Unlike Reno Wolfe and Jared Taylor, Michael Levin heads no white protest or white racial advocacy organization. Even though he is loosely affiliated with Taylor's group and has attended *American Renaissance* conferences, Levin is by profession a full-time academic who teaches philosophy courses at the City University of New York Graduate Center and City College. He is included in this anthology primarily on the basis of the controversial and well-publicized positions he has taken in recent years on a number of contemporary black/white issues, as well as because of his even more controversial book, *Why Race Matters: Race Differences and What They Mean* (Praeger, Westport, Conn., 1998). As Levin explains in this interview, he became interested in issues of race largely as a result of the national controversy that first emerged in the 1970s over affirmative action policy and the issue of compensatory justice for the victims of past racial oppression. In the following interview as well as in his book, Levin argues that black people today are owed no compensation or special regard by whites for their current distress, because that distress – real though it may be – has little to do with the wrongs of the past. The main reason that black people today have such difficulty establishing stable families, succeeding in school, and controlling their socially destructive impulses toward violence, criminality, and sexual license, Levin contends, is rooted in their differential genetic endowment. The evolutionary process, he says, has produced a racial hierarchy in terms of abstract reasoning ability, the ability to control emotions, to delay gratification, and to plan for the future, with Jews and North Asians at the top of the hierarchy, white Europeans somewhere below them, and sub-Saharan Africans and their recent descendants at the very bottom. Drawing upon the work of psychologists Arthur Jensen, J. Phillipe Rushton, and Richard Lynn, Levin claims that in terms of group

The interview of Michael Levin on January 5, 2000, by Russell K. Nieli is printed with kind permission of the interviewee.

averages black people are innately less intelligent than whites and will always be underrepresented in the higher IQ-requisite jobs in America as long as there is fair competition and race-neutrality in determining who gets these jobs. Levin concludes from this that differential racial performance is always to be expected, that it is no prima facie case for the existence of racial discrimination and that we had better get used to the fact that in a free society such differential performance will continue to exist. Levin offers no special policy prescriptions, however, beyond the standard libertarian call for the elimination of racial preference policies on the part of government and the restoration of associational rights where private parties, including private businesses, will once again be allowed to associate or not associate with whomever they choose. Levin's ideas are of particular value as representative of the more extreme version of biogenetic theorizing about race, and while many find his views incendiary, they always have the great value of being stated with precision and clarity.

Interview with Michael Levin

INTERVIEWER: You started out your professional career as a fairly conventional academic philosopher interested in such perennial philosophical topics as the mind–body problem, freedom of the will, and the like. How did you become interested in such a contentious topic as race relations in America?

LEVIN: Well, I suppose it was a convergence of two philosophical interests. First, there were questions concerning affirmative action. When I began my career, the affirmative action issue was also bubbling up, raising questions about compensatory justice, which is a standard philosophical issue, so I was thinking about that. That got me into the racial area, and a lot of questions in philosophy of science are raised by the issue of the reality and testability of intelligence, so it's perhaps not that surprising that I ended up where I did.

INTERVIEWER: So it was the public policy issue of affirmative action that was central in initially directing your interest toward race?

LEVIN: Yes.

INTERVIEWER: In the afterword to your book, *Why Race Matters,* summing up some of the book's major conclusions, you imagine a future president of the United States saying something like the following: "The race problem is the friction produced when two populations differing in intelligence, emotional intensity, and concern for the future occupy the same geographical territory." You also say in this section: "The difficulty blacks have in competing in a white world are not the legacy of past wrongs, however regrettable those wrongs may have been, but are a result of biology for which whites are not to blame." Could you explain what you mean by these summary remarks?

LEVIN: Well, the first one is a statement of the facts. We are in the situation I describe, and nothing is going to change this fact. We have to look at the situation honestly. That particular remark I put there because somebody asked me, "Well, what in a nutshell is 'the race problem'?" and that is as well as I can summarize it. The second point is the gist of the whole book and what is at the core of the entire controversy about race over the last thirty years. There's the fact of discrepancy in outcome between the races. Whites do better than blacks in virtually any field of endeavor – whether it's education, making money, life span, you name it, except perhaps in athletics – and this difference in outcome is consistently blamed on white racism and white discrimination. Since the shortfall in black achievement is supposed to be the fault of whites – this is where the compensation issue enters – whites are deemed to owe blacks some sort of compensation, for instance, by lowering standards for blacks so they can compete better, or by giving them jobs for which they are not the best qualified, and the like. My central contention, which I think is pretty well documented by science, is that the reason whites do better than blacks, and all such judgments are comparative, is simply that whites are more intelligent and have certain traits of temperament which conduce to long-run success, and these differences are genetic in origin. These differences are not the fault of whites, they're not something that whites did to blacks, and they are not something for which whites owe blacks compensation.

INTERVIEWER: Could you explain these differences in greater detail?

LEVIN: The biggest one, the one that's most studied, the one that everybody is aware of, of course, is the race difference in intelligence. Volumes could be written – volumes have been written – on this. The usual place to begin is the scientific literature, and I'll get to that in a moment. But the idea that the races differ in intelligence is not really surprising if you just look at the world around us. You see the way black and white children perform in school, the way blacks and whites perform in any area, and the first hypothesis that would occur to you is that there is a difference in cognitive ability here. The differences are not such as to seem due to racism or anything similar. While most people put the burden of proof on those who say there is a race difference in intelligence, the burden of proof actually falls on those who deny it. The facts we ordinarily see seem to speak for themselves. Of course, some will describe these facts as the result of prior discrimination, of blacks bearing the burden of past discrimination, and so for that reason you do have to turn to the scientific literature, and here there are, so to speak, two levels of analysis. The first level of analysis disregards the question of genetics. Never mind where the race difference in intelligence came from, Is there a difference? And on that issue, there doesn't seem to be any doubt. On hundreds of tests given over the last eighty years, blacks consistently perform about one standard deviation below whites. This is true on culturally weighted tests that involve questions about general knowledge, and it's even more true on supposedly culture-fairer tests that pose questions involving ability to recognize abstract patterns and to reason numerically, where familiarity with white culture should presumably not make a difference. These differences in intelligence are found as early as the fourth year of life, pretty much the same size. So that there is a difference in intelligence no one really denies, although they will dance around the topic if asked in so many words.

The next level of analysis is the crucial one from the public policy point of view. Why does this difference in intelligence exist? You could argue that if it exists because of what whites have done to blacks, this still leaves whites with some sort of compensatory burden they must discharge. But the scientific evidence that exists suggests that the difference is due to biological factors having nothing to do with whites. Probably the weightiest piece of evidence is transracial adoption, which indicates that when black children are raised from infancy by whites in a white middle-class environment, their IQ doesn't depart very much from the average IQ of blacks in American society generally. This indicates that it's not that blacks have been denied something that whites have been given, or that blacks have been suppressed. Rather it is something in which blacks and whites differ when the environments are made equal. So it can't be environment, it has to be genetic differences. Then there is the supporting evidence from IQ tests given to Africans in Africa. You might question the validity of these tests because it's an entirely different culture, but nonetheless to the extent that such tests can be designed, African blacks score *much* lower than whites, even lower than American blacks. And since American blacks have an 80 to 85 percent black African ancestry, this dovetails with a genetic difference in intelligence. Most recently, some new statistical work has come out separating environmental and genetic factors in something as complicated as group academic performance. And, without going into a lot of detail, although I'll go into detail if necessary, that, too, would suggest that the difference in performance academically and in IQ tests is genetic.

INTERVIEWER: In the African case, might tropical diseases and nutritional differences account for some – or even all – of the black–white difference?

LEVIN: Well, as far as I know, disease and nutrition, despite what one hears, are not that important for intelligence, as long as the nutrition exceeds a minimal level and as long as the disease has not had a debilitating effect in childhood. In some of the African cases I've described, the children tested have been from students in middle schools and colleges that are as comparable as possible to white schools in Europe. In fact, often in Africa the educational system has been created by whites, and these students have been selected to be in white schools, so the educational environment does pretty much correspond to that of middle-class European children.

INTERVIEWER: But still, the pathogen environment would be different, and wouldn't also the nutritional environment be different?

LEVIN: Well, I must confess that in the studies I've seen no mention is made of controlling for that factor one way or another, so I suppose that that's always possible. But still, there's been no case in which blacks do as well as whites, and you'd think that if the differentiator was something like nutrition and health, you'd occasionally get a black population that scores as high as whites, and this never happens.

INTERVIEWER: Didn't Hans Eysenck, the distinguished British psychologist, toward the end of his life show that even small improvement in vitamin supplements and nutritional supplements for a certain portion of the population could substantially raise IQ? And wasn't he persuaded, contrary to his previous beliefs, that there might be a lot more to IQ differences here than genes?

LEVIN: Yes, that's right. I think that the jury is still out on Eysenck, but my sense is that, yes, there is a recognition that some part of the intelligence difference between individuals and perhaps between groups can be explained by these nutritional factors. But again in terms of public policy, even assuming this is true, it's not as if whites have kept blacks from eating nutritious food. So even if this factor proves to be more important than I myself tend to think it is, it won't support the conventional explanation of racial differences in achievement – namely, white racism.

INTERVIEWER: So much of your concern for explaining black–white differences then is driven by your desire to refute the compensatory justice argument for affirmative action. Is that correct?

LEVIN: Absolutely.

INTERVIEWER: Cultural and historical explanations for different levels of economic achievement among nations and national origin groups are generally dismissed in your writings as circular, or ad hoc, or unscientific. Critics would surely say that you tend to reduce culture to genes and that you are blind to such obvious facts as that societies that are similar genetically but different culturally have shown vastly different levels of social and economic progress. Think, for instance, of northern Italy in comparison to southern Italy, of Barbados in

comparison to Haiti, of the white South compared to the white North
in America, of Australia compared to Argentina. How do you respond
to those who would accuse you of ignoring historical and cultural patterns, and the way these are passed on from generation to generation,
and ignoring the impact of such patterns upon social and economic
development?

LEVIN: How would I account for the fact that genetically similar groups
can give rise to very different societies? You mentioned northern and
southern Italy, Argentina and Australia. For one thing, these societies
are *not nearly* as different from each other as black and white societies
are. Granted, say, northern Italy is more industrialized, richer, more
productive than southern Italy, but you still have in southern Italy the
basic institutions characteristic of Caucasian civilization. You have
schools, laws, paved roads, multistoried buildings, a written language,
numbers, and so on. When you take these base similarities into account,
the difference between north and south is not that great. You similarly
find the same factors in both Australia and Argentina. But if you look,
for example, at European and indigenous African societies, they differ
to a much greater extent. Africa didn't develop a written language,
didn't develop arithmetic, multistory buildings, codes of law, monothe-
istic religion, the calendar, or any other similar indicia of civilization.
The comparative difference, the comparative difference between northern and southern Italy, Australia and Argentina, is much less than that
between, say, northern or southern Italy and Africa. As to the general
question of the transmission of cultural traits, you must always return
to the question, "Where do these cultural traits come from?" Granted
environmental and accidental factors can play a role in history, so if
there is no metal for smelting in a part of the world, the people there
are not going to develop metal material culture. But beyond that I do
think that those who cite culture are begging the question.

INTERVIEWER: What about Barbados and Haiti? Now, Haiti is, as I think
you mention at one point in your book, the poorest country in the
western hemisphere. It's been run over the years by a series of ruthless
dictators, and it's certainly not a place where most people would want
to live. Barbados, on the other hand, which is also a former slave
colony, drawing its people from the same sections of West Africa as
Haiti, is among the most affluent of the middle-income countries, and
it has certainly made impressive gains in health and education. Because
of their decency and good manners, its people are sometimes referred
to as black Englishmen, and there is a tradition of democracy and
moderation in its government. Barbados is, I believe, the wealthiest of
the Caribbean countries, and in fact is slightly wealthier than Costa
Rica, which was settled entirely by white Europeans. Wouldn't this

be an example here of culture overwhelming any putative genetic differences?

LEVIN: Well, I know the argument from, I guess you could call it, Caribbean exceptionalism. I don't know enough about Barbados to be able to form a judgment. I agree that it is curious and seemingly a counterexample to the genetic determination of everything, including levels of wealth, but I don't know enough to guess, nor do I know anybody else that can explain it either.

INTERVIEWER: Well, those people who have tried to explain it have usually suggested that it's due to the fact that Barbados was led in its later colonial phase by very enlightened British rulers who tried to bring various British institutions to Barbados – including gentlemanly games such as cricket – and that this explains much of the difference between it, and, say, Haiti, which was settled by the French and wasn't ruled in as enlightened a manner. It is the difference, cultural interpreters would say, between British mores, on the one hand, and a combination of seventeenth-century French-Catholic and African mores on the other.

LEVIN: How long have the English been gone from Barbados?

INTERVIEWER: I believe it was the mid-sixties when it became independent. It had a sort of a semiindependent status for a number of years previous to this.

LEVIN: That's what I thought. Well, as I say, I really don't know enough about what goes on there. It's worth remarking that even if it's doing well because of this British ethos, this is an exogenous ethos that was created by Europeans, which seems to have taken reasonably well, rather than one that any black society ever developed for itself.

INTERVIEWER: In your book, you often refer to white Europeans and Asians together under the single term "Eurasian." At other times, however, you distinguish Asians from whites, usually to the detriment of the latter. How do Asian populations fit into your view of the human race and its intellectual potentials?

LEVIN: Well, looking at the data, it would appear that northern Asians are slightly more intelligent than whites. If the white average IQ is stipulated to be 100, the IQ of Japanese and Chinese would be 102 to 106, somewhere in there, so they're probably a little bit smarter than whites on average. This may well have great significance for the human future in the next few hundred years, although I am not in the habit of looking into crystal balls. The important point remains the gap between sub-Sahara Africa and the rest of the old world.

INTERVIEWER: Does the greater intelligence of Asians have something to do with their genes?

LEVIN: Yes, I would think it's also genetic for many of the reasons that I outlined before. There was an interesting natural experiment in which

Korean children were adopted by, I think, Belgian families. These children grew up to have IQs two or three points higher than the average Belgian, so there, too, the difference seems to be genetic.

INTERVIEWER: So the genes win out in the end over any cultural advantages?

LEVIN: Right, culture is the tail; genes, the dog that's wagging them.

INTERVIEWER: Okay, but if culture is the tail and genes are the dog wagging them, and if northern Asians, as you say in your writings, have higher intelligence than whites and blacks, why did most of the northern Asians who occupied the northern part of North America for the twenty-thousand-year period before Columbus arrived remain in a hunter–gatherer state of development? Why did they never progress beyond this level? Don't facts like these suggest that there's a lot more than genes to explain why some cultures are technologically and economically more progressive than others?

INTERVIEWER: Well, there's obviously something here to be explained, but it doesn't follow that the explanation is going to be culture. I'm not an anthropologist, but my own guess is that the evolution to the degree of intelligence presently exhibited by contemporary northern Asians happened in the last fifteen or so thousand years, after their descendants crossed over into America, so those who crossed over into America probably had IQs of about – I'm guessing here – say, 95, and were not subject to the same environmental rigors that affected those who stayed behind in Asia, namely the extreme Ice Ages.

INTERVIEWER: Could you explain what you mean by environmental rigors and how these impact upon intelligence?

LEVIN: Here we're getting into very speculative matters, but you have to bear in mind that there is a bedrock of data that does need explaining. The question that's obviously going to arise is what created this race difference in genetic intelligence – assuming there is one – and the natural speculation is – I'm certainly not the only one that says this – the natural speculation is that the environment of northern Europe and northern Asia placed a premium on intelligence. It made intelligence fitness-enhancing in a way that the African environment did not. It was colder in northern Europe and northern Asia than in Africa, so the technology of fire had to be mastered, in addition to the technology of making clothing, the technology of making buttons and hooks and eyes to keep clothing together, the technology to preserve fire, and the techniques of hunting for large animals. There aren't comparable large animals to hunt in Africa, and in any case it was evidently not necessary to bring any down to get an adequate food supply because gathering did the trick. These pressures differentially selected for intelligence in the northern part of the northern hemisphere.

INTERVIEWER: Gathering, you're saying, is a less cognitively demanding type of activity than hunting?

LEVIN: Right. You don't have to keep track of animals. There's also an important social dimension to hunting; namely, killing a large animal requires social cooperation, which in turn requires the emergence of norms of fairness and sharing and equity for dividing the kill, so any human mutation, which produced tendencies in that direction would be strongly selected for.

INTERVIEWER: So hunting societies, you are saying, are going to have both more intelligent people – or people with genes that tend to promote intelligence – as well as people with genes that tend to promote co-operativeness? Is that correct?

LEVIN: Yes, that's my guess.

INTERVIEWER: Daniel Patrick Moynihan once said in response to a questioner that the reason he understood before most other observers the destructive processes that were going on in the inner city black ghettos of America was because he had seen it all before in his studies of the Irish experience in the urban slums of the nineteenth and early twentieth century. In his 1965 report on *The Negro Family*, he explained the black predicament in the following terms, which we would like you to comment upon, since they provide a powerful alternative to your own biogenetic speculations concerning current black problems: "Country life and city life are profoundly different," Moynihan wrote. "The gradual shift of American society from a rural to an urban basis over the past century and a half has caused abundant strains, many of which are still much in evidence. When this shift occurs suddenly, drastically, in one or two generations, the effect is immensely disruptive of traditional social patterns. It was this abrupt transition that produced the wild Irish slums of the 19th century northeast. Drunkenness, crime, corruption, discrimination, family disorganization, juvenile delinquency were the routine of that era. In our own time, the same sudden transition has produced the Negro slum, different from but hardly better than its predecessors and fundamentally the result of the same process."

LEVIN: Well, I'll give the Moynihan analysis this: speaking of the human race generally, we did evolve to belong to small groups of hunter–gatherers who all know each other, and the urban environment is therefore not one, you might say, for which evolution prepared us. All of us living in big cities are to some extent in that same boat. But there are differences between even the Irish and the African experience in big cities. One is that the levels of crime and disorder, even in the Irish or Italian or Jewish slums in the early part of the century, never approached the level that's been experienced in the black slums. The same patterns of difference apply to illegitimacy. Third, if you look at mating patterns throughout the world, the pattern that's characteristic of American blacks, namely, high degrees of illegitimacy, father absence, children being raised by mothers and grandmothers, is found throughout Africa and in the Caribbean as well. It does appear to be something that goes beyond American urbanization, whereas in other countries, even in Ireland, the incidence of illegitimacy and father-absence are much lower.

INTERVIEWER: And you think black people are more prone to illegitimacy for genetic reasons?

LEVIN: Yes, I'm inclined to think so. Again, it's a guess, but it's not pure, blue-sky speculation. You do have this data about illegitimacy in different parts of the world, the baseline fact that illegitimacy rates differ tremendously and differ tremendously by race. The speculation which occurs to one is that in the African environment it was easier for a mother by herself to survive and support a child than it was in the environments of northern Europe and Asia, and, consequently, there was less intense natural selection for a tendency to look for those qualities in a mate which predict permanence and loyalty.

INTERVIEWER: To what extent have recent government policies in your view contributed to racial tensions in America?

LEVIN: Well, welfare obviously has had a very bad effect. Blacks, you might say, having evolved shorter time horizons than Asians or whites because of their evolutionary history, are going to be much more opportunistic. They are going to take to the existence of external provisions of resources much more readily than whites will. And welfare, by making it possible, as it did for many generations, and ultimately still does, to live off the efforts of others, is going to appeal to blacks much more than to whites and is going to reinforce – very strongly reinforce – the tendency to illegitimacy. I don't think there's much argument that black illegitimacy rose sharply when welfare was instituted. Black illegitimacy was always many times the illegitimacy rate of whites. What was it? About 16 percent in 1940, while the white rate was way below 1 percent. Now it's about 70 percent. You could say that is due to a combination of genes and environment – the changed environment working on this underlying genetic predisposition.

INTERVIEWER: Are there other public policy areas that you have strong opinions on? You mentioned affirmative action. Could you perhaps sketch your views here in greater detail?

LEVIN: Well, I'm not so much interested in the consequences of affirmative action – whether they've been good or bad. I think they are unjust for the reasons I've mentioned. Let's change gears from the impact of the policies to what affirmative action is all about. It's always said, look, there are 12 percent blacks in the population but only 3 percent of the doctors are black, as if this must be the result of discrimination, because how else could blacks be so underrepresented. From that it is argued that blacks should be admitted to medical schools with lower MCAT scores than whites to make up for this discrimination they've suffered. There's lots wrong with that argument even if you don't accept the racial difference in intelligence. The whites penalized did not harm the blacks being set ahead of them. The blacks, in fact, may not have been harmed by anyone. But quite apart from all of this, the so-called under-representation of blacks in medicine is exactly what's predicted by the difference in IQ. It takes a certain amount of brains to be a doctor. You need an IQ about a standard deviation above the average to make it successfully through medical school and get your medical degree, and there are proportionally many, many fewer blacks than whites with that intelligence. So instead of seeing this underrepresentation in medicine as something that has to be corrected because it represents a wrong and malfeasance, the proper attitude is that that is exactly what we should expect, given the difference in ability on the part of the two races.

Well, let's move to another area that I don't discuss much in the book. Everybody complains about education – our children are failing – and then they point out virtually every day in the newspaper, say, that only 25 percent of the children in a school are black, yet 80 percent of those disciplined or expelled are black. Or that blacks are 40 percent of the school system, but only 5 percent of those in accelerated or enriched programs. Never once in any of these discussions is the pos-sibility even raised that maybe these differences are due to the talents of the children. It's always the teachers who are blamed, or the insti-tutions, and then the principals get fired, or somebody gets fired, and a *new* study is commissioned, and new techniques undertaken to help the blacks. People are even gun-shy of asking, "Could not at least *some* of this be due to a difference in talent?" That's what happens when people stick their head in the sand about the race differences.

INTERVIEWER: Why do people stick their heads in the sand about race differences?

LEVIN: That's something I really don't know, and I've talked this over with a lot of people, and nobody really knows what people are afraid of. They're obviously afraid of being called racists and bigots. But that just pushes the question back, why are they so afraid of that? It's very easy to get fired if you say any of these things, but again why are the elite and the intelligentsia so hostile to them? I really don't know, and have no testable hypotheses about it.

INTERVIEWER: Might the reason here be simply the historical experience of the Holocaust and the fact that genetic-based explanations for human behavior are identified in the public mind with genocide and the brutality of the Hitler regime?

LEVIN: Well, there's no doubt that any time anybody says anything about genes, up comes the Holocaust like something in a carnival game. But that doesn't seem the right explanation to me because, realistically speaking, the possibility of death camps being set up and blacks being herded into them is so remote that . . . I just don't think this can be what anybody is afraid of. That explanation rings false. . . . I suppose to some extent people are afraid of blacks' violence, but that can't be all of it either.

INTERVIEWER: Could you describe your vision for the future of America. What would the racial landscape of America look like if your vision for the future were to be realized?

LEVIN: It would be a whole lot less radical than you might think. What I would go for – you mentioned Moynihan – I would go for a very *serious* benign neglect. Get rid of all affirmative action; get rid of all civil rights laws. Let people associate freely as they please and simply face the fact that – in a free society where people can associate as they please, in which outcomes depend pretty much on your ability – there are always going to be statistical gaps between black and white achievement, that the high-status, high-prestige positions are going to be occupied disproportionately by northern European whites, Jews, and northern Asians and the less desirable positions which have lower status and require lower cognitive skills are going to be occupied disproportionately by blacks. We just have to get used to it.

INTERVIEWER: So essentially you want a laissez-faire or libertarian-type regime where the government doesn't try to interfere either to prevent discrimination or to make sure that a certain number of places are set aside for underrepresented groups in education and business?

LEVIN: I should distinguish the two bases for saying that. On one hand, it arises from a kind of libertarian outlook, which is a *moral* position, having nothing to do with any genetic facts. People shouldn't be forced to associate with those with whom they don't want to associate. But quite apart from that, even if you have laws against discrimination, we cannot use an effect test to judge when it is present. We have to accept the fact that if blacks are earning less than whites, being expelled from schools at higher rates than whites, making it into special enriched programs less than whites, and being accepted for loans less frequently than whites, that's not even prima facie evidence of discrimination. In fact, if blacks were doing as well as whites, *that* would be the evidence of discrimination – against whites.

INTERVIEWER: Because blacks, on average, you are suggesting, are not as talented or gifted in the areas that require high levels of intelligence?

LEVIN: Right. So if you see an engineering school where 10 percent of the student enrollment is black, you can be sure that the playing field is not level.

INTERVIEWER: What about immigration policy? Do you have any suggestions as to how future immigration policy should be formed?

LEVIN: Well, there I don't have much to recommend because that's a separate issue. I would, however, say it is a mistake to think that every group of people entering the United States is as talented and as intelligent as every other group. Immigration policy based on an egalitarian assumption is going to leave us in for some very rude surprises. Were immigration restricted to descendants of Scotsmen and Englishmen and Germans, you'd get much more intelligent immigrants than you're getting now. And, as the population changes under the present immigration policy, which includes failure to stop illegal immigration, you're getting groups with lower intelligence. Eventually this will mean a change in the nature of the country.

INTERVIEWER: What are these groups with lower intelligence?

LEVIN: I think it's pretty clear that Mexicans have lower average intelligence than European whites.

INTERVIEWER: And you think this is due not to nutrition or culture or disease or any nongenetic factor but to basic genetic factors that are explained through evolutionary biology?

LEVIN: Yes. When you take mestizo children who are raised in the United States and have eaten well – the Department of Agriculture has got plenty of statistics on what kids of all races eat, and the diets of these kids meet all the requirements – they still drop out from high school more.

INTERVIEWER: In *Why Race Matters*, you write the following: "The suffering in the Civil War of hundreds of thousands of white northerners for the benefit of blacks would seem to have discharged part of whatever obligation whites as a group may have to reduce their net advantage over blacks. When the Civil War, black crime, and black destruction of property are added in, blacks may turn out to owe whites." Many people would find this statement perverse. Could you explain your reasoning here?

LEVIN: I should think it is self-evident. After all, the argument for reparation to blacks is that whites have done such horrible things to so many generations of blacks that blacks living today labor under various handicaps and deprivations. It is as if, to make it concrete, in every one of the last ten generations whites have stolen things from blacks, so blacks living today have much less than they would have had if these things hadn't been stolen from their ancestors and passed down to whites. So the legal theory is whites must compensate blacks for the amount by which they've been worsened by these crimes. But if you're going to compensate blacks for the amount by which their lot has been worsened, and that means asking whites to transfer all the benefits that whites have reaped from crimes against blacks, you must also look at the sacrifices whites have already made for blacks. If I steal $1,000 from you, and have already sacrificed $500 for your sake, my debt is reduced. The Civil War certainly counts as an enormous sacrifice – 300,000 northern men died in order that blacks be freed. It's hard to calculate how much wealthier northern whites would be today had their great-great-great grandfathers not died fighting in a war to emancipate blacks. But if you say to a white, "You owe it to a black to step aside so he can have a job for which you're better qualified because of all the things your ancestors did to his ancestors," it is appropriate for him to reply, "Yes, but one of my ancestors died in the Civil War for his ancestors." Isn't that already enough to balance the books? You've got to ask the same question about crime. Grant, for the sake of argument, that blacks don't do as well as whites because of the bad things whites did to them (I deny this, of course). Blacks have also done enormous damage to whites. Black crime is close to ten times per capita the rate of white crime, so whites have given up a lot or at least been materially reduced in their circumstances by black crime. That also tends to even the books.

INTERVIEWER: What is your opinion of Martin Luther King, Jr., and the black-led civil rights movement in the 1950s and 1960s in which he played so prominent a role? We celebrate his birthday every year. Do you believe that America is a better place or a worse place because of that movement and the nonviolent philosophy of Dr. King?

LEVIN: I think on balance it's a worse place. One doesn't like to get into personalities, but his character is of a much less respectable order than is usual of national heroes. He was an adulterer, and more important a plagiarist. A lot of the things he is credited with he didn't write, so he is a fraud. It's well known that he plagiarized his doctoral dissertation, which would normally result in the university canceling his degree, but somehow . . . talk about Teflon. To the extent that the civil rights movement was a movement against the right of private individuals to discriminate, it's been destructive. Take those famous sit-ins in restaurants: the restaurant owner owns his restaurant and it's his business who he wants to serve. To the extent that that principle was weakened, that has been nothing but bad. I have no objection to whites and blacks mixing, but don't like it being forced.

INTERVIEWER: In your book, you defend what you call negative discrimination by whites and Asians against blacks. Could you explain what you mean by this?

LEVIN: People have a right to avoid those whom they don't like, and a right to refuse to deal with people they don't want to deal with. Refusal to deal imposes no harm. That is not the same thing as actively hunting out and harming blacks, or otherwise interfering with their lives.

INTERVIEWER: This would be, though, in their private associations?

LEVIN: Right.

INTERVIEWER: What about government employment and government services? Wouldn't you support a legal regime which enforces a non-discrimination principle on government in the conduct of its own business?

LEVIN: Absolutely! I wish the government were nondiscriminatory in the conduct of business. That would mean the elimination of the Section 8 small-business loans and all the government programs in which blacks are given all kinds of benefits. It would mean the return of the merit system.

INTERVIEWER: So public employment should come under nondiscriminatory civil rights laws, but not private employment. You would support a private employer's right to discriminate but not a government's? Is that your basic view here?

LEVIN: Right, and so, for example, there would be no more bonus points on civil service exams, no more targets and goals for hiring black police.

INTERVIEWER: Critics have labeled your ideas "racist" and "white supremacist." How do you respond to such criticism? Do you accept or reject such terms as appropriate labels to describe your views?

LEVIN: Well, no academic likes labels much, but these are particularly bad. I don't know what "racist" means anymore, but if a racist is anybody who thinks that there are innate race differences in important abilities, okay, I'm a racist, and there's nothing wrong with being a racist. On the other hand, the word has negative connotations so that anything racist is automatically bad and evil, making me want to shun the label. The best thing is just to pack the label away. "White supremacist," well, I don't think that whites *ought* to rule, that they've got some sort of God-given or gene-given right to rule, but in any situation in which a modicum of freedom is permitted, they are going to rule, they are going to do better, they are going to exceed blacks. And Asians will probably exceed whites by a little. There is nothing wrong with that.

INTERVIEWER: And Jews will exceed them all?

LEVIN: Apparently so, yes.

INTERVIEWER: In many people's minds your name is associated with the black scholar Leonard Jeffries, whose views are said to be as extreme and as erroneous in a black nationalist direction as yours are in a white nationalist one. What do you say to those who equate you with Jeffries in this manner?

LEVIN: I would invite them to examine his writing (what there is of it) and mine, look at the relative quality of the data. All he's got is this mish-mash about melanin. Supposedly, if I get this right, melanin at the base of the brain is supposed to affect the brain. This has got absolutely no medical credibility whatever. My stuff is based on standard genetic and psychometric tests and data.

INTERVIEWER: The liberal writer Andrew Hacker is cited in your book no less than forty times, and you seem to have a special contempt for his ideas. Is there any personal animus or blood feud between you and Hacker?

LEVIN: No, his book just seemed to be an absolutely perfect distillation of liberal egalitarian thinking.

INTERVIEWER: And this is the type of thinking that you set out to combat or refute in your own book *Why Race Matters?*

LEVIN: Right.

INTERVIEWER: Okay. You are a Jew, and the views you express on race are most usually expressed by whites who dislike Jews as much as they dislike blacks. Does this make you uncomfortable?

LEVIN: No, no. I get a little impatient with Jews myself. After all, egalitarianism has been mostly an idea associated with Jews in the twentieth century, and if you look at those who attack the current data on race and try to pooh-pooh it and dismiss it, it tends to be almost entirely Jewish.

INTERVIEWER: But those who hold your view that whites are in some sense genetically superior to blacks are most likely to be anti-Semitic whites. Doesn't that make you uncomfortable?

LEVIN: Well, you have to ask what anti-Semitism here means. People who think that whites are genetically more intelligent than blacks don't think that whites are genetically more intelligent than Jews. They don't dislike blacks and Jews in the same way. If anything, they think Jews are too clever, they're too tricky, they take over everything. They're always plotting and planning together. Obviously, that's not an attitude I have toward Jews, but the beliefs behind anti-Semitism are very different than the beliefs behind any kind of antiblack feeling. Actually, I do get pretty disgusted sometimes with the anti-Semitism of many racialists. It disgusts me because it is so stupid. It's as if the IQs of these people drops thirty points when they hear Jews mentioned. Suddenly it all becomes Jewish conspiracies – Jews in the media, Jews inventing the Holocaust, that sort of thing. Still, their stupidity doesn't change the facts about race.

INTERVIEWER: You teach at the City University of New York Graduate Center as well as City College, an institution with many black students and several black faculty members. How have you been received by your black students and the black members of the school faculty?

LEVIN: Well, I'm not sure a lot of these students have any idea of what I've been up to. They're not au courant with current events. There are not that many black members of the faculty at City, as in universities in general, except for the members of the Black Studies Department, who I assume regard me as evil. For the most part, the rest of the faculty is white.

INTERVIEWER: And the small number of faculty members who are black, though, how have you gotten along with them?

LEVIN: I don't interact with them one way or another.

INTERVIEWER: A colleague of yours once described you as an "intellectual provocateur" and suggested that you have an infantile penchant for expressing your ideas in ways designed to maximally shock and infuriate many of your listeners. Is this an accurate description of you?

LEVIN: I don't think so. I think that's a pretty cheap shot. At the same time, one is not the best judge of one's own motives.

INTERVIEWER: Upon reading your writings on race, many people, including some who would agree with much of what you say, would get the clear impression that this guy Levin really doesn't like black people very much, that he has little or no use for them, and that he has no compassion or sympathy for their current suffering and distress. In a word, they would say he lacks what in German and Yiddish is called *menschlichkeit*. Is this a fair assessment of your attitude towards blacks?

LEVIN: No, I don't think so. When you write about something like this, you try to adopt the most neutral tone possible, and that means neither ranting and raving like Holocaust deniers nor does it mean weeping crocodile tears. It means trying to be as objective as you can.

INTERVIEWER: And you're saying that your quest for objectivity shouldn't be confused with a lack of compassion or concern for the suffering and distress of the black community?

LEVIN: Right, although I would say I think that the black community has advertised its suffering and distress sufficiently that any catering to it at this point is pandering. To use an analogy I use in the book, if somebody comes into court with a broken leg and accuses me of breaking his leg and wants me to pay him $5 million in compensation and I try to demonstrate that it wasn't my fault that his leg was broken and that his leg problem is a congenital condition, it is absurd for anybody to say that I'm not showing enough sensitivity. Look at the poor man; the poor man has a broken leg. Well, it's ludicrous for me to commiserate. He's accused me of a wrong, and I'm defending myself on the facts. That's not insensitivity. It shouldn't be obligatory on me to preface everything by saying, Oh, it's terrible to have a broken leg.

INTERVIEWER: So the whole thrust of your work then is to try to show that in the case of blacks, the broken leg was not something that whites did to blacks but something resulting from inherent biological causes?

LEVIN: Right.

INTERVIEWER: But you don't lack sympathy or compassion for someone who has the broken leg?

LEVIN: Right, but it's neither here nor there. Just speaking personally, I think the suffering of blacks has been much, much overplayed. Occasionally one goes to academic talks given by blacks, and the only example that anybody can come up with anymore of how blacks suffer is the Danny Glover phenomenon of taxicabs not picking them up. I must say, just speaking personally and subjectively, this seems a very, very trivial sort of thing. It cannot justify all the breast-beating about all the suffering that whites cause blacks, if that's the extent of it, and it is all that I ever hear.

INTERVIEWER: Shelby Steele has said that it's harmful for black people to focus so much of their energy on their past victimization. Would you agree with that? His term is a "victim-focused personal and collective identity," and he says that it's harmful for black people to continue with that identity as the heart and soul of their self-understanding. Do you have sympathy with that line of criticism?

LEVIN: Yes, yes, naturally I do. It's unhealthy for anybody to dwell on the past overmuch. I have occasionally had blacks say to me, We can't forget history, and my reaction has been like Steele's. Well, at a certain point you have to forget history. You sometimes meet people who try to explain their failure in life by something their mothers did to them, and they're fifty years of age. At some point you're going to grow up, and even if your mother did do something to you, what you make of your life past that is in your own hands. But I'm not as confident as Steele is that if blacks did put aside this grievance accumulation and blame-casting, they would then turn around and do as well as whites. It's harboring false hopes to think that, too.

INTERVIEWER: Thank you.

PART II

WHITE NATIONALISM AND WHITE SEPARATISM

4

Don Black

Nothing has contributed more in recent years to the growing influence of the whole range of white nationalist, white supremacist, and white protest groups in America than the exponential growth in the use of the Internet. And no one has been more successful in exploiting the potentials of this new development than Don Black, the publisher of the *Stormfront* website. *Stormfront* is really a web junction box that provides the web surfer with links to literally hundreds of other white racialist websites ranging from fairly mainstream European heritage organizations to the outer fringes of neo-Nazi and white militia groups. *Stormfront* reportedly receives many tens of thousands of visitors each month. Black himself is certainly no newcomer to the world of white racial activism and white supremacy. While still a high school student at Athens, Alabama, in the early 1970s, Black joined a white supremacist group called the National Socialist White People's Party, and later, while a student at the University of Alabama, he joined forces with David Duke in revitalizing the Knights of the Ku Klux Klan. Black's career as a white nationalist and white separatist leader, however, came to a sudden halt in the spring of 1981 when he and several other Klan members were arrested in a bizarre plot to invade the tiny Caribbean nation of Dominica in support of anticommunist forces on the island who were dissatisfied with the prime minister. Black spent three years in a Texas federal prison for his participation in the foiled coup, but he made good use of his time there – Black first learned how to program computers in federal prison. Not long after his release from prison, Black left the Klan and decided to focus on less violent means of propagating his racial views. In 1991 he was active in the David Duke for Senate campaign, and he began to put his computer skills to use in furthering the white nationalist cause at this time. Black began the present *Stormfront* website out of

The interview of Don Black on April 20, 2000, by Russell K. Nieli is printed with kind permission of the interviewee.

his West Palm Beach, Florida, residence in March of 1995. In the following interview, Black explains what the white nationalist movement stands for and the role of the new computer technology in furthering its mission and goals. White people in America, Black argues, have a right to preserve their heritage and culture just like all other peoples of the globe, and under present conditions, he believes, this will almost certainly require the formation of a separate white state. A major function of *Stormfront* and similar websites, Black explains, is to provide an alternative news media to the current news media in America, which is dominated, he says, by white-disparaging liberals, many of them Jews, who try to instill guilt and shame in white people for what is seen as a shameful white past. White European Americans, Black believes, have a right to pursue their own national and cultural destiny and to do so in their own separate state. Black says that his views on white nationalism and white separatism, while they are presented as extreme by the mainstream news media, are really little different than the views of Thomas Jefferson and other Founding Fathers, who did not believe that an integrated black and white society was possible in America. Even if such an integrated society were possible, Black argues, it would not be desirable because there is something of great value in races maintaining their distinct and separate cultures uncontaminated by the influences of alien peoples. Far from being a form of white domination or white supremacy, white nationalism and white separatism, Black insists, reflect a true respect for the integrity and autonomy of the world's diverse peoples.

Interview with Don Black

INTERVIEWER: Five years ago, in March 1995, you launched the *Stormfront* website. Could you explain what *Stormfront* is and what you hope to accomplish by it?

BLACK: *Stormfront* is a resource for a movement which we call white nationalism. Our purpose is to provide an alternative news media with news and information and online forums for those who are part of our movement or for those who are interested in learning more about white nationalism. And we believe that the basis for our movement is the fact that white people throughout the world have the right to organize and to promote their heritage and their cultural values, just as every other race and ethnic group has been doing for years. *Stormfront* began in 1991 as an online bulletin board, a dial-in bulletin board, during one of the David Duke campaigns – the David Duke for U.S. Senate campaign. The purpose of the bulletin board system, or BBS, was simply to provide those participants in that campaign who had their own computers and modems and knew how to use them with the ability to exchange messages and files. At that time, we had very few users because there were very few people who had the equipment or were savvy enough to understand how to use it.

It was with the exponential growth of the Internet, which began, I think, in '94 or '95, that we first had the opportunity to reach potentially millions of people with our point of view. These are people who for the most part have never attended one of our meetings or have never subscribed to any of our publications. We were for the first time able to reach a broad audience. And *Stormfront*, being the first white nationalist website, was able immediately to draw a very large number of visitors. The response has continued to grow until this day. And in the future, with the advent of broadband technology for consumers, we hope to be able to compete with television networks themselves by providing an alternative video – video both on demand and in real time – with full motion and full resolution. So the Net has certainly provided our movement, and other movements like ours with only limited resources, with the ability for the first time to compete with what we consider to be a very biased and controlled news media.

INTERVIEWER: Who controls the news media and how would you characterize its bias?

BLACK: Well, the bias is certainly directed against the white majority in this country and toward white culture throughout the world, where white people are typically characterized as being oppressors and exploiters of other races. We're supposed to feel guilty for being white. There's an attempt to instill guilt in our people because of our history and our heritage, whereas, on the other side, racial minorities in this country who are nonwhites are typically portrayed as being intelligent, sensitive, and often the victims of white oppression. So there is a liberal bias.

And this liberal bias in the media, I think, is caused by several things, not the least of which is the disproportionate Jewish influence. This influence is particularly prominent in television – and particularly television in Hollywood – but it is also present in newspapers, magazines, and other print publications. The Jewish culture has typically taken a very liberal point of view, and throughout most of its history, it has assumed an aloof attitude toward white Western civilization and frequently a very hostile attitude. In the twentieth century, Jews gained control of much of the mass media beginning with the motion picture industry. Motion picture technology was originally invented by Thomas Edison. To escape Edison's control of the new technology, Jews left the Northeast and migrated west to Hollywood. Originally all the major motion picture studios were run by Jews of eastern European origin after they left the Northeast to escape Edison's control. So beginning with Hollywood, and then with the broadcast media later, we've seen a very disproportionate Jewish influence, and I think that has resulted

in a very biased attitude toward white Western civilization. It is an attitude which does not reflect America's vision of itself, or at least its original vision of itself.

INTERVIEWER: Why did you choose the name "Stormfront"? To many, the
term conjures up images of Nazi stormtroopers. Is that the image you
want to convey?

BLACK: Well, it could convey a number of things. It could convey any kind
of political front – especially a somewhat militant one. But there's also
the weather analogy. We believe that the idea of a storm can evoke
images of cleansing. Even though tumultuous, a storm ultimately results
in a cleansing. So I wouldn't read too much into the name. It's basically just a neat name that has the projected kind of aura that we would
like to surround our movement with.

INTERVIEWER: You have web links to neo-Nazi and anti-Semitic websites. Many people hearing the name "Stormfront" and looking at some
of the groups that you associate with would assume that you were a
neo-Nazi and rabidly anti-Semitic group. Would that be a correct
perception?

BLACK: Well, the term "anti-Semitic," like "Nazi," is one of those words
that really is a term of abuse and intended to stifle discussion. We're
certainly going to talk about Jewish influence over our media, over our
government, and over our foreign policy, and we are certainly going to
discuss the real history of World War II. That doesn't mean that we are
Nazis, but we are certainly going to be called that among other things
as a matter of course by our opposition. As for our links, I'm not sure
which specific links you would consider neo-Nazi, but certainly we link
to a number of sites that take a differing approach than ours. But we
feel that they are all, all the ones we link to, are of value and are of
interest to those who might visit *Stormfront*. To answer your question,
no, I don't consider myself a Nazi, but that's a term that's frequently
applied to us and it's not entirely accurate. It's like calling every liberal
a communist. No one gets away with that in the mainstream media
today, but they routinely get away with it when referring to us.

INTERVIEWER: Would you also reject the term "white supremacist"?

BLACK: I think that's an inaccurate description of most of the people
that are part of our movement because white supremacy implies a
system, such as we had throughout most of this country through the
fifties and early sixties, in which there was legally enforced segregation
and in which whites were in a position of domination. We did have a
supremacist-type government in most states, but today the people who
are attracted to the white nationalist movement want separation. And
so supremacy really isn't descriptive of what we want, the changes we
want to see.

INTERVIEWER: What sort of changes then do you want?

BLACK: We are separatists. We believe that we as white people, as European Americans, have the right to pursue our destiny without interference from other races. And we feel that other races have that right as well – the right to develop a nation with a government which reflects their interest and their values without domination or any other interference from whites. We believe segregation certainly didn't work, and the only long-term solution to racial conflict is separation. As long as races are forced together by government, there will continue to be racial hatred and mutual animosity caused by one side or the other feeling that they are being discriminated against. As Thomas Jefferson said, "Nothing is more certainly written in the book of faith than that these people are to be free, nor is it less certain that equally free, they cannot live under the same government. Nature has an opinion. It's drawn indelible lines of distinction between them."

INTERVIEWER: "These people" were the slaves, the black slaves?

BLACK: That's right. That was the context of his writing, and that was in his autobiography. The first half of that statement, the first sentence, is what is inscribed on the Jefferson Memorial to deliberately misrepresent what Jefferson believed. Apparently, the memorial commission shortly after World War II didn't think that anybody would have access to the original autobiography . . . but they didn't bank on the Internet, so now anybody can find it.

INTERVIEWER: Jefferson, you are saying, basically believed what you now believe, namely, that an integrated society in America that includes both blacks and whites is impossible?

BLACK: Right. Almost all of the founding fathers believed that. They even founded an organization called the American Colonization Society whose purpose was to free black slaves and repatriate them to Africa. And, of course, the nation of Liberia, with its capital named after James Monroe, Monrovia, was a result of that, too. But this part of our history is now hidden from most students going through our school systems today because it's not politically fashionable. People like Thomas Jefferson, George Washington, and James Monroe spoke out forcefully on the issue of race, but that part of their philosophy is simply ignored. And, of course, in the case of Jefferson, he is being vilified with the Sally Hemmings accusations, which have not been proven despite what's been said in the press. You know, I firmly believe that the television, the television dramatization and all of the earlier media frenzy over the Sally Hemmings affair is a result of what Thomas Jefferson said about race. What he said about race is unacceptable to many. *Stormfront*, in particular, has done its best to bring to the attention of the American people the truth about Jefferson's beliefs on race. And I really believe that this vilification of Thomas Jefferson is a direct result of that awareness. I may be a little bit paranoid on this. But I really believe that that's a big part of it.

INTERVIEWER: You describe yourself as a racial separatist. Could you explain your vision for the future of America in terms of race?

BLACK: I think part of America . . . part of this continent will be a white nation. That's what we want to see ultimately. In the short run, we want to see the government get out of the business of race mixing, get out of the business of forcing races together, and of telling employers who they can hire, who they must hire, and who they must promote, telling schools how they have to run their business, and telling people where they have to live or who they have to live with. And I think left to their own devices, members of most races will separate naturally. I think most people of whatever race prefer to live and work and go to school with people who share their background and their values.

INTERVIEWER: So you oppose antidiscrimination laws?

BLACK: Yes, I do. Not only do we oppose antidiscrimination laws, we also oppose affirmative action, which are prodiscrimination laws, in which white people are the people who are discriminated against. But we don't think that government has any business telling businesses who they have to hire. We don't think that they have any business telling neighborhoods, or real estate people, who they have to sell to, and we believe that if people want to go to a school that's all white or all black, they have that right as well.

INTERVIEWER: What sort of racial separation would you want to see in the distant future? Would you want to see America broken up into different ethnic enclaves?

BLACK: Well, you know, I think that's going to happen. Yes, I want to see separation. That's the whole fundamental premise of white nationalism. We want a separate white nation. But regardless of what I want, I think it's going to happen. In some areas, specifically in the Southwest, there are many nonwhite Hispanics, mestizos, and Indian Hispanics who are loyal to Mexico rather than the United States and who want to take the southwestern United States back and rejoin Mexico. This is a serious movement, and I think it will continue to grow and gain influence, and at some point in the next twenty years, I believe that we will actually see a physical seizure of that part of the United States. And I don't think that the government in Washington, which is becoming an imperial government, is going to be able to do much about it. So at that point, there will likely be other races who will decide they want to do the same thing, and at some point, European Americans will have to realize that they must defend their own interests as well.

INTERVIEWER: If the Southwest became an Hispanic state, where geographically would the European American state be located?

BLACK: Well, that remains to be seen. I don't know just how this is going to work out, but the broadest expanse of predominantly white populated area in this country, of course, is in the Northwest. But I don't know that that is where we will end up.

INTERVIEWER: Where would Asians fit into this picture? And Arabs?

BLACK: Well, our purpose is to see the development of an all-white nation. I don't know where Asians are going to go or where Arabs are going to go, but our purpose is simply to provide white people with their own territory with defensible borders. The history of the world is one of migration and conquest, and I'm sure that is going to continue. But I don't have a plan for everybody in the world. We only have a plan for ourselves, the white people, and at some point we believe that it will become obvious to most of our fellow whites that an all-white nation is necessary somewhere on this continent.

INTERVIEWER: Most Jews in the United States are Ashkenazic Jews from Europe. Would they be part of that white nation?

BLACK: No.

INTERVIEWER: Why not?

BLACK: Well, most Jews aren't going to want to be a part of that white nation, for one thing. Probably 90 percent of Jews have a very liberal attitude toward race and have been very much a part of the multicultural movement to turn everybody into one homogenized brown mass. But the Jews are a distinct racial and cultural group – many Jews themselves stress their separateness.

INTERVIEWER: How does that differ from Italian Americans who have a high level of ethnic identity?

BLACK: The Italians and Irishmen and other European nationalities have shared the same general culture, and they are assimilable from the cultural and racial standpoint, whereas Jews are not. Jews have not assimilated over the last few thousand years despite living among a variety of nations.

INTERVIEWER: What about the high level of intermarriage? The intermarriage rates – the out-marriage rate – among Jews is estimated to be about 50 percent. Wouldn't that suggest a willingness to assimilate?

BLACK: Well, if that's true, why do we have the state of Israel? The only real, truly nationalist state – a religious and race-based national state – is Israel, and obviously the Jewish leadership, which supports Israel, doesn't feel that assimilation is very desirable. And that 50 percent assimilation rate, I question the accuracy of that because I don't think Jews are in any danger of disappearing from the planet, as they well would be if the rate truly were 50 percent, given the fact that Jews have about the same birthrate as whites, which is below the level needed to maintain the existing population. Jewish nationalism is a major force, and while the assimilation movement is probably going to have some effect on Jewish numbers, it's by no means going to result in the assimilation of the race.

INTERVIEWER: Is your aversion primarily to Jewish liberalism or to all Jews? Many Jews certainly are not liberal – important segments of the Jewish population are anything but liberal.

BLACK: But most Jews are liberal, and there is a racial and religious cohesiveness which extends beyond their particular politics. I've certainly known many Jews who agree with most of what we have to say, but they are a very small minority, and they are not part of the Jewish mainstream. They are not the people who control the TV networks and the banking system, and they are really not calling the shots.

INTERVIEWER: You were quoted in an article in the February 1998 issue of *New Times* magazine as saying, and here I quote: "A multicultural Yugoslav nation can't hold up for too long. Whites won't have any choice but to take military action. It's our children whose interests we have to defend." This sounds like a violent, bloody picture. Do you envision violence on the horizon here and military actions?

BLACK: I think that is certainly possible. There's a lot of violence right now. There is a lot of racial crime now, and, contrary to the media's portrayal of hate crimes, more hate crimes are committed against whites by nonwhites than the other way around. And I think we are going to see that kind of thing continue. I think there will be more racial strife, and I would much prefer that it not reach the point of what's happened in the Balkans, but that could happen. That's a possibility if the current policy of our government to set itself up as some sort of imperial government in which it controls these diverse racial and cultural groups continues.

INTERVIEWER: What sort of people visit the *Stormfront* website and why do they visit it?

BLACK: All kinds of people come to our site. Some people are just curious. Some people hate us. But the majority, I think, judging from our e-mail, have some positive interest. They may not agree with most of what they read, what we say at this time, but they nevertheless find some things to agree with, and they visited our site because they are looking for answers. My guess would be that a third of our visitors are full supporters, who more or less completely support what we do, who agree with our stand on the issues, and of those, a certain percentage continue to participate in our on-line forums.

INTERVIEWER: You don't have any membership dues? People just visit your site to get free information, is that correct?

BLACK: Right. There's no formal membership and no dues.

INTERVIEWER: Do you have any plans for the future on your website in terms of expanding its scope or adding additional features?

BLACK: We have lots of plans [laughing].

INTERVIEWER: Like what?

BLACK: The most ambitious is, of course, more video programming, and that will at some point include live video, live talk shows, and taped documentaries. And, of course, that capability is pretty much there now, but most people don't have broadband connections to the Net, and the Internet infrastructure isn't really able to handle that kind of traffic right now. But it is coming within a couple of years, and that would be the next giant leap for us.

INTERVIEWER: In the 1980s you were active along with David Duke in the Knights of the Ku Klux Klan, and you eventually rose to the rank of Grand Wizard. Have your views on race changed at all since your Klan days?

BLACK: Well, everybody's views change somewhat, but, no, my basic ideology and philosophy is pretty much the same. My views are essentially the same as they were in the seventies. The tactics, however, are different.

INTERVIEWER: How have your tactics changed?

BLACK: Well, our purpose in the Klan was different. The David Duke Klan was not an organization which advocated violence or illegal activities, so our purpose there was to build a political movement, but that really turned out to be impossible. The Klan has a reputation for random and senseless violence that it can never really overcome, and we could never on any large scale attract the kind of people that we wanted. So, my tactics now are different. The Net itself is, as I have mentioned, an alternative news media. My work now is centered around that, of bringing our point of view to as many people as we can who otherwise would never have come to a Klan rally, or never have subscribed to one of our publications, but who will be very important to us in the future. We are particularly interested in those people who feel that because of their jobs, or their plans for the future, they can't be in any way associated with us, can't be publicly associated that is, cannot let their true feelings be known. But they do feel comfortable visiting a website and sometimes even participating in our discussion forums with a pseudonym. But most of them don't go that far. They just visit and the information is there, and we feel that we are planting the seeds with these people which later will grow and later may be the basis for a more viable political movement. These are people who frequently are in government or corporations, the military, or even the news media. These are people who are really important to us. I don't think we're going to have any kind of revolution strictly from the outside. Any kind of major change will necessarily have to involve people who are part of the system as well.

INTERVIEWER: How would you characterize your current relationship with David Duke and his new organization for European-American rights?

BLACK: We work closely with David. I saw him two weeks ago and participated in a demonstration with him in Richmond, Virginia, so we certainly can work together. We at *Stormfront* support all organizations which reflect our point of view and our objectives. But we're not, we're not linked to any particular group, that is, to any one group.

INTERVIEWER: You have expressed strong disapproval of both antidiscrimination policies on the part of the state, as well as affirmative action policies – policies of racial and ethnic preferences. Are these the government policies that you find most galling and most destructive, or are there other government policies which you find harmful . . . harmful to race relations, anyway?

BLACK: The government policy we find most detrimental in the long term, of course, is the government's immigration policy, in which Third World immigrants are allowed to come to this country, either legally or illegally. Of course, these millions of people who come here every year have resulted in many parts of the United States coming to resemble a Third World country. Of course, this is the kind of thing that's much more difficult to reverse than just a set of laws, such as affirmative action and other laws of that type. So immigration would be the single most destructive policy that's implemented by the government.

Of course, there are other issues that concern us – the domination of our foreign policy by un-American interests is of concern to us. The recent bombing of Serbia, which was a sovereign nation which had done nothing to the United States, was unprecedented and morally outrageous and will likely result in many people throughout the world hating the United States even more than in the past. The subjugation of our foreign policy to the state of Israel is another example of an issue that would be of concern to us. Half of our foreign aid budget goes to either Israel or to Egypt to keep peace with Israel. Our military and all of our policies in the Middle East are oriented toward protecting Israel, and that's something else that's probably unprecedented in the history of the world – where such a small nation has managed to dominate the foreign policy of a world superpower.

Obviously there are many issues that concern us. The tax system we have and the welfare system we have in this country concerns us. A tax system designed to support a welfare system which encourages the welfare underclass to continue to grow is obviously wrong. But these are all policies that can be changed very quickly. The immigration policy is something whose consequences are much more long lasting.

INTERVIEWER: What sort of immigration reform would you like to see passed?

BLACK: Well, in the 1920s the United States passed its first broad immigration laws, which favored Europeans based on the fact that most Americans considered this to be a country whose heritage was European. Ensuring that immigration was limited to Europeans was a very logical thing. And, of course, we believe the same thing as the immigration reformers of the 1920s. This is not a melting pot, except for European nationalities, who are able to melt because they share a general culture. This isn't a country in which every race from every continent with every culture can just assimilate without serious problems. We believe that we have the right to maintain a nation which reflects its original European values and culture.

INTERVIEWER: Surely there are great differences between many of the European ethnic groups in terms of their own national cultures. The Irish peasant culture, the French urban culture, the Polish rural cultures – these are very different cultures, and yet people have been able to form some kind of common core American values coming from these disparate backgrounds. Why can't this process of assimilation be expanded to include African Americans and Japanese and Jews and Chinese and so on?

BLACK: Because the gulf with those groups is simply too great, particularly with Africans and with the mestizo and Amerindian Hispanic cultures, and with Asians as well, but to a lesser degree. But certainly there are some profound differences between European nationalities and between economic classes within those nationalities, but those differences are dwarfed when compared with the differences between races. The question is why is this so desirable anyway? It's really not diversity, it's antidiversity when one promotes the mixing and homogenation of every race. From that standpoint, we at *Stormfront* are the true promoters of diversity because we want to see our race preserved, as well as every other race, as a distinct cultural entity. Why is there such an imperative to bring everybody together into one society where they are all going to somehow assimilate, where they are going to be equal and the same. It simply doesn't work, but even if it did, what's the point? Why do we have to do this?

INTERVIEWER: What are your views on interracial marriage? I mentioned already the Jews. With the Japanese, the story is similar. About half of Japanese men, it has been estimated, marry non-Asian women, usually Caucasians.

BLACK: Well, we're obviously opposed to interracial marriage since it further threatens the integrity of our race and culture. Many members of other races are probably even more opposed to it than we are. I'm not familiar with the figures regarding Japanese men, but I know that many members of, many members of other races also would like to maintain the integrity of their race as well, and see interracial marriage as being very harmful. Yeah, there's a lot of intermixture between Asians and whites because aesthetically they see themselves as somewhat similar, and mentally they are pretty close, whereas these same people would never consider marrying a black person because they see the blacks as being different than them. They see their mental abilities as being less than theirs. But Caucasians and Asians – northern Asians, at least – evolved somewhat along the same lines, and they developed somewhat similar social mores, culture, and mental abilities.

INTERVIEWER: So northern Asians and whites, you are suggesting, have a great deal more in common than whites do with blacks, and for that reason you think they intermarry more often?

BLACK: Right. I don't agree with intermarriage, but that's clearly the reason that it's much more common between Asians and whites than between blacks and whites or Hispanics and whites.

INTERVIEWER: *Stormfront* is routinely characterized by its critics, including the Southern Poverty Law Center, the Anti-Defamation League of the B'nai B'rith, and HateWatch, as racist. What do you say to such characterizations?

BLACK: Well, "racist" is another one of these scare words that doesn't have any real meaning. I certainly believe in race. I am a racialist, but I reject the term "racist" because it is a word that was invented by our opposition. In fact, it was first used by Leon Trotsky in a speech in the early twenties, but really didn't become popular until the fifties and sixties. So I reject the term "racist" simply because of the connotations that have been ascribed to it by our opposition. But I believe in racial differences, and from that standpoint maybe you could call me a racist, but that's not a term that I accept.

INTERVIEWER: What term do you prefer to use to describe your philosophy?

BLACK: Well, the traditional word was "racialist" for anyone who believed in racial differences. That's the traditional construction. I know this sounds a little pedantic to some people; in fact, I just responded to a threat on our message board about this very subject – racialist vs. racist – but the thing is, words are important, and the impression they carry is very important. I think "racist" became popular among our opposition instead of the word "racialist" simply because it's got this hiss to it. It actually sounds evil, and I really believe that these kinds of things in a propaganda war are very important. And, of course, we are losing the propaganda war, and that's one of the reasons – because we have these words ascribed to us which carry connotations which are not true but nevertheless sound very offensive to the kinds of people whom we would like to attract to our cause. So racialist is a legitimate word, and it's a traditional word for those who believe in racial differences. We go a little beyond that because we are also white nationalists in that we want a separate white nation.

INTERVIEWER: Thank you.

5

David Duke

David Duke is perhaps the only person interviewed in this volume who needs no introduction. For an American audience, at least, he has what political scientists call "high name recognition," which is attributable largely to his controversial incursions into electoral politics. Duke stunned the Republican political establishment when he was elected a State Representative from Louisiana in 1989 despite intense opposition to his candidacy from virtually all mainstream Republican figures from President George Bush and Republican National Chairman Lee Atwater on down. He also caused tremors among more mainstream Republicans by his subsequent statewide bids for the U.S. Senate and Louisiana governor's office, which, though they did not succeed, resulted in Duke's winning the support of a clear majority of Louisiana's white voters. What shocked the Republican establishment was not so much Duke's spirited opposition to racial preference policies, widespread welfare dependency, and Louisiana's rising crime rate, but the focus on such race-sensitive issues by someone with Duke's extensive and well-publicized background as an activist for various white nationalist and white racist causes. Duke began his involvement with racial issues as a student at Louisiana State University in the late 1960s. At LSU he founded a white protest group called the White Youth Alliance and published a newspaper called *The Racialist*. Duke's activities at this time were largely concerned with celebrating the heritage and achievement of white people, drawing attention to black/white racial differences, and exposing what he believed to be the Jewish domination of American government and the news media and the vast Jewish involvement in domestic and international communism. After college, Duke became a leader in the Ku Klux Klan and went on to become a mainstay of the national radio and TV talk-show circuit. In the following interview, Duke explains the purpose and underlying philosophy of his new group, the National Organization

The interview of David Duke on February 15, 2000, by Russell K. Nieli is printed with kind permission of the interviewee.

for European-American Rights,* which was founded in January 2000. NOFEAR, Duke explains, was established to defend the rights of European Americans against what he sees as the multileveled discrimination against them that occurs through various affirmative-action-type policies that favor minorities. His organization also seeks to preserve the heritage and values of European Americans, he says, which are threatened by multiculturalism and the massive influx of non-European immigrants into the United States. Duke has harsh words for Jewish organizations in America, which he takes to task for what he says is their double standard in supporting the state of Israel as a nation specifically dedicated to preserving Jewish religious, ethnic, and cultural values while denying to European Americans their right to preserve America as a nation reflecting specifically European religious, ethnic, and cultural values. Duke also charges that there is a bias in the way American history is presented to children in textbooks and other media. Whites, he says, are often collectively presented as exploiters or oppressors of blacks and other minorities, but such collective condemnation of an entire people would never be tolerated were the group involved a nonwhite minority. Duke concludes the interview by holding open the possibility that he might someday reenter electoral politics.

Interview with David Duke

INTERVIEWER: You have recently formed a new organization, the National Organization for European-American Rights, whose acronym is NOFEAR. Could you explain the overall purpose and mission of this new group?

DUKE: Well, the purpose of NOFEAR is obviously to secure European-American rights in this country, and to defend those rights – civil rights, human rights, political rights. We believe specifically that European Americans face a pernicious racial discrimination on a multilevel basis in this country. There's discrimination going on in hiring and promotions, in college admissions, in scholarship programs, in university admittance, in contracting, and in many other areas of American life. It's our contention that if discrimination is indeed morally wrong when exercised against minorities, then it's just as morally reprehensible when exercised against members of the European-American majority.

INTERVIEWER: So basically you see your organization as an antidiscrimination league?

DUKE: As a civil rights group. But beyond that, it's also a group about preserving the heritage and way of life of European Americans in this country, just as the NAACP works for quote "the Advancement of

---

* Several months after the following interview the name of Duke's organization was changed to the European-American Unity and Rights Organization (EURO).

Colored People," or La Raza Unita works for Mexican interests, or the Anti-Defamation League or the American Jewish Congress work for what they perceive to be Jewish interests and Jewish heritage. This organization works for what we perceive to be the overall interests of European Americans and the preservation of our heritage and way of life in this country. So it's about civil rights, but it's also about preservation of our entity as an ethnic people, our existence, our values, our culture, our traditions, and the things that really go to make up traditional America.

INTERVIEWER: How does the National Organization for European-American Rights differ from the organization you founded in 1978, the National Association for the Advancement of White People?

DUKE: Well, it's very similar. That organization went on its own way a number of years ago, and this organization, I think, is more broad based and it's really based more on the principles of the survival and the heritage of European-Americans, rather than purely a civil rights organization.

INTERVIEWER: What has been the response to your new organization as far as membership is concerned?

DUKE: Well, the organization has only been in existence for less than thirty days, but the response has been extremely pleasing. We now have members in almost every state, I think maybe every state but one or so. Right now, we have chapters forming all over the United States, and we've had really literally tens of thousands of inquiries and expressions of interest, and letters of support from people all over the United States. We did C-Span the other day, a speech that I had in Philadelphia which launched the organization, and the C-Span speech has resulted in about ten thousand e-mails. We've had a tremendous outpouring of support from around the country.

INTERVIEWER: What sort of people join NOFEAR and what are their reasons for joining?

DUKE: Well, I think we have members and supporters at this point who range everywhere from students to college professors, from truck drivers to people in politics, from housewives to corporate executives. We have a very wide range of members, and they join for the same reasons that others join the American Jewish Committee or the NAACP. They join because they want to act to preserve their rights and their heritage in this country.

INTERVIEWER: Do you have any specific strategies for recruiting new members. For instance, do you recruit on college campuses or over the Internet?

DUKE: Well, we recruit members wherever we can find them. I think the Internet is a tremendous alternative source of information, and it's really a media bypass, which is excellent. It allows people of differing opinions to express those opinions more freely than heretofore possible. In this country, we have had very little political debate on a lot of very critical and important issues. The Internet allows that debate to go on. For instance, we have had an immigration policy in America since 1965 that is literally transforming America from a European-descended society to a Third World society. Present immigration rates discriminate specifically against people of European descent in terms of immigration rates to America, and this is resulting in a widespread demographic change in America – a tremendous change. We have gone literally from a nation almost 90 percent European American in 1960 to one where we are less than 75 percent European American today, and probably less than 50 percent by the middle of the twenty-first century. This will have a tremendous impact on American life. It will impact on politics dramatically and will certainly be a very dangerous policy for American conservatism. It will have a tremendous impact on culture, on heritage, on taxes, on many different areas of American life, and this issue has not been thoroughly debated on a national scale, even though it's one of the most profound changes that can take place in any nation's history.

INTERVIEWER: And it's these concerns that induce people to join your organization?

DUKE: Well, I think so. I think that there's a natural desire of all living things to continue themselves, and to want to see their descendents be something like themselves, and have the same values that their fathers and mothers and their ancestors had. And I think that that's a natural drive, it's common to every people of the earth. That's why Israel was founded – it was founded as a place for the Jewish people to preserve their heritage and preserve their culture, and for them to flourish. All people have these same basic desires and concerns. It's surely true of the European people.

The only countries in the world that have serious population decline and where you have massive introduction of numerous alien elements is in Europe and America. There's no really mass immigration into Kampala, Uganda. There's no mass immigration into Beijing, China, but there is mass immigration into New York City and Chicago and Los Angeles and New Orleans – and London and Paris and Berlin and Rome and many of the major European and American cities of the world. What's happening is that this demographic onslaught, this immigration onslaught, will change the genetic and cultural stamp of the societies that are affected by it. It will have a dramatic impact on many aspects of life in these particular areas. It has already had an impact on many aspects of American life.

INTERVIEWER: Isn't America, though, already irreversibly multiethnic and multiracial?

DUKE: Well, I think we have been multiethnic for a long, long time, but we've always had a great predominance of European Americans who have set the basic standards, the basic values, you know, the cultural mores, the traditions of our society. As non-European members increase, we are beginning to see a direct attack on our European traditions, institutions, and values. For instance, in the city of New Orleans where I grew up, where I went to school, the black element of the city has basically taken over the city politically, including the school board. The New Orleans school board recently voted to remove the name of George Washington after black militants accused Washington of being quote "an immoral example" for children. Obviously, George Washington is the father of our country, and if a school board of a major city can remove George Washington's name and put him in disgrace, the same thing can happen on the national level when the nation's demographics change dramatically.

But we see many other aspects of this. Just twenty-five or thirty years ago, the people of this country would not have thought it possible that children would not be allowed to sing Christmas carols in public schools. Whether or not you are religious or whether or not you are a Christian, Christmas carols are certainly a part of the traditions and values of Western civilization, something which was intrinsic in our educational system, and the communities of our society. Now the courts have ruled in many areas that children cannot even sing Christmas carols in their own schools. Again, it is a direct attack on the traditions and culture of the American majority so we are seeing how multiculturalism is making an impact. It is not simply adding to the cultural mix of our society, but literally denying the cultural rights of the American majority.

INTERVIEWER: Could you describe your vision for the future of America? What would the racial landscape of America look like if your vision of the future were to be realized?

DUKE: Well, a vision must be based on reality. The reality is that unless the immigration policies in this country change and unless the government ceases to pursue policies which will make the minority elements of our society dramatically grow in number from higher birthrates and immigration rates, and unless our government begins enforcing our border laws, whites will become a minority in America. I believe it will come more and more to resemble that of a Third World society, more like a Haiti, or a Mexico, or some other Third World society, rather than a Western Christian society. And that's the vision I see of reality unless things are changed. My hopeful vision would be that if we were to protect our borders, and have an immigration policy that would protect the heritage of this country, that we could still be an overwhelmingly European nation with European values. The rights of the minorities would still be protected.

INTERVIEWER: Weren't many of the immigrants who came to this country around the turn of the century essentially coming from Third World countries? The Italian peasants, Polish peasants, and earlier Irish peasants – weren't they from the Third World of their day, yet they seem to have Americanized quite well?

DUKE: Well, there have certainly been areas of the world that have been poor, but nothing similar to the Third World now. An Italian, or an eastern European is part of Western civilization and culture. Look at the Italian, look at the art of the Italian Renaissance. There certainly was a transition era and a difficult period of assimilation for some Europeans. In some ways, it took place actually rather rapidly in terms of national time periods. But when you're talking about dealing with different races, from entirely different civilizations and cultures, you're talking about a much more difficult process. And I think that it is also important that we had great periods of time-out in terms of immigration, which gave America a chance to assimilate these new arrivals from different parts of Europe, and we haven't had that in America.

INTERVIEWER: By "time-out" you mean there's a kind of respite period that is required to assimilate the immigrants who have already come without adding to the burden of taking in more people, and you think that America needs this kind of period now?

DUKE: Well, there was that period in the past, but the problems today are much greater. Previously assimilation was really of people that had some language barriers and some individual cultural differences in terms of European culture. But they had the same underlying Western Christian culture. Whether a person was English or Irish or German or French, they still had the same kind of appreciation of Leonardo da Vinci or Michelangelo or Rembrandt. In whatever school they attended anywhere in Europe, they studied these painters as the icons of our civilization. Whereas when you talk about people coming from Africa, you're talking about people that did not in any way have that kind of education, that kind of cultural underpinning.

INTERVIEWER: You say both in your book, *My Awakening,* and in articles on your website that American society, particularly the mass media and the government, vilifies white history, white character, white values, and white traditions. Many would say that it's black history, Hispanic history, and Asian history that's vilified. How would you respond to such claims?

DUKE: First off, I think it's easy to respond to it. In the years past the vilification that blacks talk about, their version of vilification, is that they were left out. The textbooks didn't certainly portray black people as an evil force in terms of American history. And in fact, even in the movies, blacks were often portrayed, even if they weren't portrayed as space scientists and doctors, generally speaking they were portrayed in a friendly manner, in a decent manner – as loving people, and decent people, often humorous. Maybe that's not exactly the portrayal that black people would want, but it wasn't of a sinister nature. Today, European Americans are portrayed continually in a sinister way in regard to nonwhites and Third World peoples, and there is a collective guilt assigned against the people of white descent. Now, when slavery is talked about, they talk about the *"white* people" that enslaved blacks, or the "white people" did this, or the "white people" did that. It wouldn't be tolerated if the textbooks talked about the black people in this manner – how the black people, for instance, commit great waves of crime in urban cities, or how black people do this or that. You see what I'm saying? White people are talked about collectively in a negative way. And whether it be in a movie or a modern play or a textbook, whenever there's a conflict between whites and blacks, or whites and any other minority, the whites are always portrayed as the evil forces and the minorities are portrayed as the forces of goodness and light.

We've all seen the movies, and there's many hundreds of movies I can give you as examples of this, as well as many examples from student textbooks. I'll give you an example this way. When a textbook, say, uses the word "African Americans" or "black Americans," it's always in a positive way. African Americans contributed "such and such" to America. Black Americans did "such and such." George Washington Carver was "a great black American," or Martin Luther King was "a great black American," or this type of rendition. Whenever the term "white race" or "white people" is used in our modern textbooks, it's always in a negative fashion. White people exploited blacks in slavery, white people stole the land from the Indians, whatever, and it's always a negative connotation. So there is always a double standard, and it's apparent just by picking up any textbook. Any perceptive person can begin to see this very antiwhite racist attitude present.

INTERVIEWER: Why do you think this state of affairs exists, given the fact that white people have generally been the politically and numerically dominant force in America?

DUKE: What we're talking about here is the primacy of an ideology – an anti-European ideology. And the fact that people happen to be white or happen to be black doesn't necessarily determine their thinking. There are many white people who have ideologies which obviously are anti-European, and it's these people who seem to dominate the media today.

INTERVIEWER: In another article, also on your website, you suggest that there is a coming worldwide white revolution that's destined to sweep the world with the same speed with which Islam swept the Arab world in ancient times. You say: "Centuries ago, in a single generation Islam swept the Arab world. The Arabs were suited to it and ready for it and it exploded across history. Now there is a new racial consciousness, growing in our people that will sweep the West even more dramatically than Islam swept the Arabs." Could you explain what you mean by this, this new white racial consciousness, and why you believe that it is going to sweep the world?

DUKE: Well, there are a lot of factors. Let's talk about what this racial consciousness is first. I think that Europeans, people of European descent, wherever they live on the globe, are beginning to realize that our people are truly the real minority of the earth. We've had a great and rich history – art, literature, music, architecture. We have a unique character – to our aesthetic appearance and to our artistic and cultural achievements, as well as to our technological and philosophic achievements. Our people are coming to the realization that unless we begin to defend our borders and our way of life, all of this will be swept away, that we are facing really a destruction of our very kind of life on the planet. In a real sense, it is a genocide, and of course genocide means destruction of the genes or destruction of the genotype. And you know, it's said that the great evil of the Holocaust was an attempt to destroy the Jewish people in Europe. I would suggest that if that would be evil or wrong, then it would also be very evil or wrong to destroy the European genotype. We do have a genotype, we do have a unique genetic flavor and makeup of our people. We've got to learn to live, we've got to learn to preserve our heritage, and I think that as the perceptive and courageous people of our race begin to understand this, and devote themselves to our survival, I think that this renaissance among our people will sweep over our people very rapidly. And I believe one of the reasons why this will happen is because there is a new orthodoxy today of egalitarianism, and it's draconian in its ways, just as repressive as anything they used in the Middle Ages.

But there will be a reaction against this. The truth is that there are dramatic racial differences. Science has been uncovering these differences dramatically over the last few decades. They exist in physiological areas, psychological areas, cultural areas, and in actual physical areas. We have these great differences between the races, and knowledge of these differences has been suppressed. And knowledge of what's happening to the European people has been suppressed. I think that as people begin to find out the racial reality of the world – it's not racism, but racial realism – when they begin to realize this, I think it's going to unleash just a tremendous power, a tremendous force. Truth has a way of doing that. When truth is bottled up – as truth was bottled up for a long time in the eastern European countries under the heel of an aggressive and despotic communism – I think when the truth about racial matters and the perilous position of European mankind, when that is finally discovered, and finally understood, I think there will be a tremendous reaction. The Internet and modern communication means that ideas can travel faster, farther today than ever before. I think what it will mean is that history in effect speeds up, and that great ideas will grow and spread much faster than ever before and can achieve victory more quickly than ever before. So I do think that within a generation a lot of these egalitarian falsehoods will be swept away, and a new truth and a new understanding will come about in Western civilization.

INTERVIEWER: In your autobiographical work *My Awakening* you describe the formative influence upon your thinking about race of Carlton Putnam's book *Race and Reason*. It was under Putnam's influence, you say, that you first came to believe that blacks and whites differed by much more than skin color – and that blacks were intellectually less capable than whites, that this intellectual inferiority was rooted in biology and genetics, and that as a result of this black people would never be able to attain to the high level of civilization characteristic of whites. Do you still adhere to these ideas of Putnam or have your ideas on black/white differences evolved over the years?

DUKE: Well, in that book, I'm very careful to say that I don't endorse the principle of inferiority. I think that human beings, if you talk about our differences in terms of talents or intelligence or any other area, that does not necessarily make an individual human being inferior or a race inferior. There may be two people, one may have a high IQ and create all sorts of scientific advancement. One may have a low IQ but still be a good person and still be a productive member of society. He's not necessarily inferior as a human being. He may be inferior in terms of one aspect of human talents. I may be inferior to someone who has a Gold Medal in the Olympics in terms of my ability to travel 100 meters in a certain amount of time or lift a certain amount of weights in a gymnasium. So there are differences but I don't get into the game of speaking of inferior or superior human beings.

But I do think there are dramatic differences between racial groups, and I think that these differences have come about through evolutionary processes that have gone on obviously for hundreds of thousands of years. I think that most scientists would agree that there's at least a 140,000-year split between Europeans and Africans, and I think these differences – the differences of climate in Europe – affected our evolutionary development different than it did in Africa, and I think that this had a tremendous impact and a tremendous influence on culture. I also believe that not only are physical characteristics such as eye color or skin color or hair color or height or body structure affected by genetics, but also that such things as intelligence, and even personality traits, have a very powerful genetic component. I think science is uncovering this more and more. Just recently – I read in the paper today in fact – there's an article about how criminals have, on average, 11 percent less gray matter in the prefrontal areas of the human brain. This is a recent study. I'm trying to think of the university where the study took place, but I thought maybe it was Princeton. I'm not quite sure, but it was in the papers this morning, and so that's a physical difference. Now obviously the difference in the amount of gray matter of the brain is not something that came about through physical forces or educational forces. That came about through genetics of the brain, and to think that some people may be predisposed to violence more than others, I think, is an important reality, and it's a reality that has been ignored and really suppressed by a lot of the establishment and a lot of the mass media in America.

INTERVIEWER: What are some of the specific black/white differences that you think might be genetically influenced?

DUKE: Well, we could talk about a number of them. I think propensity to crime for one. I think that blacks on average have a higher propensity to crime than whites, and I think it has to do with a number of factors, including brain differences and also including testosterone levels. We know that men have a much higher violent crime rate than women, and we know that even among white men or among black men that men with higher testosterone levels have higher rates of violent crime, and we know that on average blacks have a higher testosterone level than whites. I mean, this is a fact. This testosterone level also influences, for instance, their greater problems with prostate cancer and other areas of cancer in their lives. So that's a perfect example there of intrinsic racial differences.

We know that there is – and this has been confirmed by literally thousands of studies – that there's almost an entire standard deviation of difference in IQ between whites and blacks, and obviously IQ has a tremendous impact on society. IQ in fact is a better predictor of success in life, or socioeconomic success in life, than a person's family income. One of the great revelations of *The Bell Curve* was that when they studied massive numbers of people, even among one race, they found that a higher IQ, being born with a higher IQ, was more important to a person's later socioeconomic success than being born with a silver spoon in one's mouth. IQ has a tremendous impact, moreover, not only in terms of educational levels and achievements but upon everything from marriage rates to illegitimacy to crime rates. It has an impact in many, many areas of life, even that go beyond simply academic study.

INTERVIEWER: And you think these IQ differences are basically of bio-genetic origin?

DUKE: Well, first of all, there's no argument that these differences do in fact exist. I mean, whether or not they are biological in origin . . . there's no argument that they exist. Thousands of studies have confirmed it. Now the question is – and that is the big question – whether they are biological or whether they are cultural – and there's been tremendous numbers of studies I think that show beyond any reasonable doubt that they are certainly of genetic origin, the genetics overwhelmingly over-riding the environment. Which is not to say that environment can't affect scores to a degree. They can. But there are many ways to deter-mine the mix of environment and hereditary in terms of intelligence. For instance, you can compare the IQs of identical twins who have been separated from birth and raised in different households and see how close their IQs are compared to siblings raised in the same household. And you can also look at the differences, say, between fraternal twins and identical twins when the twins are reared together in the same household. When reared in the same household, identical twins have much closer IQ scores than fraternal twins, yet they're born at the same time, they're brothers and sisters or brothers and brothers, and they can match them for sex and family and everything else. So there are a lot of ways we can get a handle on whether intelligence is basically a product of environment or heredity, and if there would be a ratio of genetic influence to environmental influence, I think it would be between two-to-one and three-to-one – of genetics over environment. Genetics accounts for between two-thirds and three-quarters of the observed difference.

INTERVIEWER: In *My Awakening*, you devote over 250 pages to a highly unflattering discussion of the Jews and their influence in America. You quote in this context Mark Twain, who once remarked, and here I quote: "Every nation hates each other but they all hate the Jews." The clear implication of your observation is that the Jews have been hated by so many people over the centuries because they display many hate-able qualities. Is this an accurate reading of your views here? If so, what is it about Jews that provokes your hostility?

DUKE: [laughing] No, I don't think that's an accurate reading, but I think that we're all familiar with Mark Twain's quotation. In fact – and I say this in the book – Mark Twain's essay about the Jews was quite favor-able. But he did point out that the Jews have obviously had a lot of opposition and a lot of hatred exercised against them around the world. So the question arises if you're going to understand this phenomenon of anti-Semitism, it's important to understand all aspects of it. I point out in my book, for instance, that if you go to the encyclopedia *Encarta*, or *Funk & Wagnall's Encyclopedia*, and you read an article on anti-Semitism, the article itself is written by a Jewish Zionist, who I would call a Jewish supremacist because I think Zionism is a supremacist doctrine, and I document that quite well in my book. And almost all the books recommended for further study to the readers of this article on anti-Semitism are also written by Jewish advocates. That's kind of like an article on anticommunism being written by a full-fledged communist, and all the recommended readings on anticommunism would be by communists. Of course, we'd think we couldn't get a good judgment about those issues.

However, I don't think my book is necessarily unflattering about the Jews. In fact, I really flatter them in some ways because I point out that they have fought very hard for their interests, they've banded together, they've promoted education in their families, they have worked untiringly for what they believe to be their particular interests. What I point out is that sometimes the Jewish interests and gentile interests conflict, and that today we seem to have a foreign policy, such as in the Middle East, that is really not in the interest of the American majority but is truly rooted in the interest of the Jewish minority. And I can't understand why, but some of these policies that Jews have specifically advocated, I think, are very pernicious to the well-being of the European-American majority (for instance, the immigration issue). In my book, in the chapter I have about the European-led immigration, I point out that there's no organized groups that have fought harder to break down American immigration policy, in other words, to make America minority European, than the American Jewish Congress and other Jewish organizations. And I point out in my book Jewish scholars and leaders and organizations that bragged about the fact that they've changed America from a majority European nation to a minority European one. And I also point out in there the Jewish interpretation of why they think they'll have an advantage in that kind of society.

Obviously Jews have every right to pursue their interests. They have every right to pursue what they think to be their best interests. If they think their best interests are taking Christmas carols out of schools because it offends them, they have that right. But European Americans also have the right to work for our interests in our own country, and what I really object to, and what I say would be the most objectionable part of what I think about Jewish suprematism is the fact that it has a hypocritical nature about it. At the same time that Jews want to make Europeans a minority in America, the Jewish community supports very strongly the nation of Israel, which is a nation based on the preservation of the Jewish people with very restrictive immigration laws. In fact, while Jews anywhere in the world can emigrate to Israel, the Palestinians who were born in the country, whose families were forced out during the Israeli formation of Israel, they're not even allowed back into the country where they were born. Israel is a nation which segregates Jewish settlements from Palestinian settlements, segregates schools; it has laws that don't even recognize marriage between Jews and Palestinians because they don't recognize civil marriage. It is a nation where they allow Jewish settlers to carry machine guns if they desire, whereas the Jewish elite in this country, which has so much power in our media and government, is trying to break down American immigration laws. They're trying to break down Christian traditions in America. But they're certainly not trying to break down Jewish traditions in Jewish schools in Israel. They're trying to break down Christian traditions in America, while they support Israel at the same time. So there's a double standard there, which I object to.

And I really have discovered in my readings and research of many Jewish authors and Jewish leaders that there is a Jewish supremacy that exists that is not condemned by our media because the media often is led by these same supremacists. I'll give you an example. In my book, I point out that David Ben Gurion – who is often called the George Washington of Israel, and was certainly the leading individual figure in the formation of the state of Israel, and the first, of course, the first great prime minister of that country – Ben Gurion made a statement which I reprint from *Reform Judaism* where he says that he sees the Jews as intellectually and morally superior. You can imagine what would occur if a president of the United States, say, Mr. Clinton, came out and said he saw the white race as morally and intellectually superior. There'd be no end to the attacks upon him. But someone like Ben Gurion can say this, and there's no objection, there's no challenge, there's no horror. So I think there's a double standard on these questions. I think you can't understand American politics, American foreign policy, and many aspects of our American dilemma today without understanding the dynamics between the Jewish supremacist elements and their conflict with the European element in America.

INTERVIEWER: But aren't most American Jews European? The vast majority of American Jews are Ashkenazic Jews whose ancestors stem from eastern and central Europe.

DUKE: Yeah, but they basically say that they came from migrations from outside of Europe, and if you read the Jewish publications, they clearly do not consider themselves to be quote European. In fact they bristle at the idea when they are called Europeans. I can give you a lot of Jewish sources on that. I think certainly there are Jews who respect European culture and heritage, and I respect those who do and those that don't. I mean everyone's got a right to advocate whatever they desire, but there are certainly many Jews who feel quite alienated by

America, and they tend to want to overthrow our traditional systems and society, such as the AJC [American Jewish Congress] trying to eliminate Christmas carols from our schools.

INTERVIEWER: Aren't there also though many socially conservative Jews who share many traditional Christian values? One thinks, for instance, of *Commentary* magazine, which over the last few decades at least has been one of the leading voices of intellectual opinion defending socially conservative values. One can certainly name many Jews who are prominent in the neoconservative movement – Irving Kristol and Gertrude Himmelfarb, for instance.

DUKE: Well, I think they've certainly been influential in certain aspects of the conservative movement, primarily in terms of economic conservatism, but I think this influence has also been pernicious because even so-called neoconservatism supports open immigration, so it's again supporting the minoritization of European Americans in this country. It's been slavishly pro-Israel, which again is I think a big mistake for American conservatism as well because I think the traditional conservative would put American interests first, and I think American interests have been sacrificed for that of a foreign country. The most powerful lobby in this country today is the Israeli lobby, a lobby for a foreign nation, and that's quite a sad state of affairs when the most powerful lobby on our U.S. government works for the interest of a foreign government. So I think that, yes, you know, the Jews are a very smart people, and they've been involved in many different areas of American life, but I don't think neoconservatism overall has really been a positive element for America. In fact, I think they've co-opted the more traditional elements of American conservatism, so I think even in that field, they've been a destructive force.

INTERVIEWER: You've spoken at length on immigration policy. What other policies of the federal government do you speak out against? I see in your promotional literature, you often highlight the issue of racial preferences and affirmative action.

DUKE: Well, yes, I mean there is an institutionalized racial discrimination going on against white Americans today. There have been some recent studies at major universities, for instance, at the University of Virginia, where they found that white students were one hundred times more unlikely to get the admission or the scholarship than minorities. I mean, it's an amazing ratio. These are better qualified whites – let's make sure that this is understood. These are better qualified whites who face racial discrimination in college admissions, in scholarship programs, in hiring for major companies, in promotions in major companies, and also in the public sphere, such as police departments, fire departments, city government, the federal government, the United States Post Office.

There's a pernicious discrimination going on against white Americans today, and I believe, as I said earlier, that civil rights must be for everyone in this country *including* white Americans.

But there are other areas of policy that have been very detrimental to European Americans, such as this massive forced integration policy. I think forced integration has been a terrible destructive element in public education. In fact, we can trace the decline of American public education almost directly to forced integration in our major cities. Where it's occurred, test scores have fallen precipitously, violence has increased, and problems have increased in these schools dramatically. We've gotten to a point in fact where many European Americans in many areas of our major cities, such as my city of New Orleans, they've actually had to flee the public schools. In fact, we've had to flee our public cities. I mean, we really fit into the modern United Nations' definition of an internal refugee [laughing]. We, for reasons of personal safety and other reasons, we've actually had to flee many areas, and we've had to flee our major cities for the suburbs, and there are many European-American refugees in that sense.

INTERVIEWER: You are frequently referred to in the press as a racist and a white supremacist. What do you have to say about such labels? Do you accept such labels?

DUKE: I don't accept either label. I'm certainly not a supremacist. I don't believe that one race should rule over another, I don't believe in that. I think equal opportunity should exist. I'm not trying to go around to some other country and control their politics and control their way of life. I simply want to have my own country reflect my own values as a member of the majority. So I'm not a supremacist. But, as far as racism is concerned, I'm not a racist. A racist today is defined as someone who hates other people or wants to oppress other races, and that's not my opinion of the race problem. If anything, I'm a race realist, and that simply means to recognize and understand the fact that there are racial differences and that these differences have an impact on society, education, crime, and many other aspects of life. It is not being a racist. It's simply being a realist and a person who's in search of solutions, rather than simply allowing these problems to continue to escalate.

INTERVIEWER: You were once a high official in a Ku Klux Klan organization, but in recent years you have downplayed your involvement with that group. Do you regret having joined the Klan in your younger years?

DUKE: I regret it in the sense that it lessens my ability to reach some people because they become closed-minded, but I think there's a double standard here. Robert Byrd was a former Klansman, and then he later became Senate Majority Leader. In fact, he was called the "conscience of the Senate." When he's introduced, it's not former Klansman Robert Byrd; it's former Senate Majority Leader Robert Byrd, or Senate Minority Leader Robert Byrd. And Bobby Rush was a former Black Panther who has now served in the United States Congress, and he's not introduced as "former Black Panther Bobby Rush," but I'm always referred to as former Klansman David Duke, even though I have served in the House of Representatives in Louisiana, and I've been a Republican official for a number of years as well, an elected official. So I think there's a very major double standard and it's really indicative of the kind of discrimination that goes on against those who represent the European-American people, as compared for instance to the African-American people. Mr. Barak, who is the present leader of Israel, was a violent terrorist who physically murdered with his own hands a poet in Lebanon after a guerrilla raid into Lebanon years ago. But he's not referred to as "terrorist Barak." And so I mean there's a lot of double standards that exist in these areas of life in this country.

INTERVIEWER: You often speak of the importance of preserving the values that you say white Europeans brought to America. And you apparently see these in conflict with the values of black culture. Black people, however, are wedded to many traditional conservative values, and polls often indicate that however difficult black people may find it to realize these values in their own life, they adhere to them in many cases with much greater zeal than white Europeans. For instance, a greater proportion of blacks than whites support return of prayer to the public schools. Blacks are less likely to support homosexual marriage and the normalization of homosexual conduct than are whites, and blacks hold views on welfare and work that are remarkably similar to those of whites. Why do you see black people as a threat to traditional American white values?

DUKE: Well, let's take a look at it. I don't necessarily see all blacks as a threat, but I see the black political process as a threat. We have something called the black bloc vote in this country, and in Louisiana about a third of the electorate is black, and 70 percent is white. I received 65 percent of the white vote for the United States Senate, and whites who voted for me were called racists, because 65 percent voted for me in the state of Louisiana. Yet, blacks voted 97 percent against me. They act very strongly in support of the candidates they like, and usually it's the Democratic candidates. There are very few Republicans who have cracked even the 6 to 7 percent barrier. I even received 3 percent of the black vote myself, but if you take a look at black organizations and the leading black groups in this country, they're consistently on the liberal side of almost every issue, whether it be for welfare or advocating gun control – the NAACP right now is suing gun manufacturers. Whether it be taxation, whether it be being easier on criminals – I mean we see a consistent record of black organizations taking these positions, and we also see a consistent voting pattern of blacks for candidates they *perceive* as supporting the black position, and those black positions are obviously not traditional conservative positions.

Now, as far as other aspects of this, we have a situation in Washington, D.C., where we have over 50 percent of all young, black males between the ages 18 and 35 being in jail, on parole, or probation, or being involved in the criminal justice system at any one moment. You're talking about a vast majority of black males who are felons or criminals. That certainly has a big impact on our society, and it has an undeniably harmful impact, and that affects our society tremendously in terms of crime rates and safety on our streets and the quality of life that we have in our society. So I think the races do have a big impact on the way a society is constructed and the kind of lifestyle that the society might have.

INTERVIEWER: In America, we celebrate annually the birthday of Dr. Martin Luther King, Jr. What is your opinion of Dr. King and the non-violent civil rights movement which he led?

DUKE: Well, first off, I'm not quite sure I agree with your description. I'm not sure that it was so nonviolent. It seemed like everywhere he went, there occurred a lot of violence, and I think that King was a reprehensible individual, who, for instance, had plagiarized his thesis. In fact, Boston University in doing a study on his thesis found that about 40 percent of his thesis was actually copied from other sources. They didn't revoke his degree because of the fact that he had a stature in America due to the so-called civil rights movement. He had a record of being with literally hundreds of prostitutes and acting, I think, in a manner that really wasn't reflective of a great, honored American. And I think it's very unfortunate that we have a national holiday for King, and it's terribly unfortunate that we in fact place his holiday in more esteem than any other American because there's no other American, whether you're talking about Washington or Jefferson or Lincoln, that we give a single holiday to in this country. We lump the other presidents together as Presidents' Day, so we give him an honor we haven't given any other American. He was never elected, and I don't think he was that popular, and really the media and government institutions have forced this recognition on King against the wishes of most of the people of this country.

INTERVIEWER: Is your career in electoral politics now over or do you have any future political ambitions?

DUKE: I really can't answer that at this point. I mean, I'm still in my forties, I've got certainly some time left, and we'll have to wait and see. I don't know. I've got another book I'm working on, and I'm going to continue to advance my principles as best I can. I wouldn't be surprised to see the federal government take actions against me because I think this government and this country are becoming very repressive, and I think they're very worried about our kind of organization, and they should be because I think there's many millions of Americans that want to see a change in the way our government is going and the way the process is occurring, and so I don't know what to expect. I expect government action to try to suppress the Internet, to suppress free speech there, because they know the power of these ideas and these ideas represent a threat to their power, and I don't know whether to expect political persecution, I don't know whether to expect criminal persecution by the government. I've heard the government's planning all sorts of things against me, and I wouldn't be surprised if anything came down. I think this government wrongly burned to death many children at Waco. This government has a policy in terms of Iraq that's starved about a half million children. That's the United Nations' own figures. The same United Nations that did sanctions against Iraq also showed that a half million children starved by our embargo policies. And so I think this government is unconscionable. I don't know what to expect from this government in terms of my own activities, but I know one thing, and that is that they do fear me in terms of my ability to reach people and to mobilize white Americans for our principles. All I know is that I'm sure that they'll try and suppress me any way they can.

INTERVIEWER: Thank you.

6

Michael H. Hart

Michael H. Hart is by training an astrophysicist (he received his Ph.D. from Princeton in 1972), but in recent years he has turned his interests to issues relating to race and nationality. An associate of Jared Taylor's *American Renaissance* group, Hart delivered a much-discussed paper at a 1996 *American Renaissance* conference that proposed the geographic partition of the United States along racial lines. In the following interview, Hart argues that the idea of partitioning the United States to accommodate the national aspirations of its differing racial groups is not as radical a proposal as it might at first appear. Blacks, whites, and Hispanics, Hart contends, constitute distinct nations in America, and despite all the rhetoric about integration and assimilation, members of each of these groups, he says, live essentially separate lives. The history of multiracial, multinational states is not encouraging, Hart contends, as one or more of the constituent groups inevitably feels stifled, either culturally or politically. Whether one looks to the example of the Austro-Hungarian Empire, of nineteenth-century Sweden, of colonial India, of Cyprus, of Yugoslavia, of Czechoslovakia, or of the former Soviet Union, the tendency for people living in multinational states, Hart insists, is eventually to seek an independent political existence. Members of diverse racial, linguistic, and religious groups rarely get along well in the same state, Hart observes, and in the case of blacks and Hispanics in the United States, the problem, he says, is greatly exacerbated because each group harbors a deeply ingrained and fully understandable sense of historical grievance. Policies of racial preference only magnify the racial tensions in the United States and lead to a justified sense of outrage on the part of whites, Hart contends, but while eliminating such policies would be the fairest thing to do, it would not solve America's racial problems, he believes, because differential performance in the acquisition of the higher

The interview of Michael H. Hart on April 14, 2000, by Russell K. Nieli is printed with kind permission of the interviewee.

status positions in the society will inevitably result from any fair competition in the job market. Hart is convinced that the races differ in their intelligence and their ability to acquire higher education, and he says that the lower achieving groups will always feel deep resentment over their poorer performance, which they will inevitably blame on racism and discrimination, rather than inadequate talent. Hart believes that there is simply no solution to this problem of resentment other than geographic partition. Hart's four-part partition of the United States envisions a black state, a white state, an Hispanic state, and an integrated/mixed-race state. Such a partition, Hart contends, would allow a choice suitable for everyone. While white separatism is often associated with anti-Semitism, Hart, who is a Jew, says Jews would have little to fear in a white separatist state since by and large white Americans have treated Jews fairly and would continue to do so in an ethnically based state in which whites are the majority. Anti-Semitism, he believes, is a more serious problem among blacks than among whites, so Jews are better off throwing in their lot with a white state than a black state or mixed-race state. Hart's remarks are of particular value as an illustration of the appeal that white nationalism and white separatism can have even among former liberals who once supported integration but who have become disillusioned over recent racial developments in America.

Interview with Michael H. Hart

INTERVIEWER: By training you are a physicist and an astronomer and you also hold a degree in computer science, yet in recent years you have become interested in issues of race, ethnicity, and nationality. How did you become interested in these issues, which seem so remote from your earlier academic training?

HART: There are several reasons. My interest in these issues was originally provoked by my resentment at having quotas being placed against me as a white man and as a male. I am Jewish, and in my earlier years I was frequently discriminated against. Some institutions had quotas against Jews; others did not hire Jews at all. But later, when I became older, I was told that in order to make up for the privileges I had in the past there should be a new set of quotas and preferences put in operation against me. Quite naturally, I grew to resent this. In addition, I resented the fact that although I had never personally discriminated in any way against blacks, Hispanics, or anyone else, and although I had always tried to treat people fairly, I – and the whole group to which I belonged – was nevertheless being attacked as being relentlessly racist.

Another thing that influenced me was that I started seeing that people were not talking honestly about race. Although it is apparent that there are large differences between the races – including differences in intelligence – everybody was scared to talk about them. After a while

I saw that because people were scared to talk about racial differences a type of censorship was falling over the country. As a scientist who is devoted to the idea of a free exchange of views, free inquiry, and an honest search for truth, this bothered me a lot.

In addition, I noticed that racist remarks, attitudes, and activities by blacks were passed over and ignored, while comparable actions by whites were highly publicized and denounced. There was an obvious double standard involved, and that bothered me. More recently, I became interested in immigration. I realized that the probable result of our current immigration policies (if they are not changed) will be the impoverishment of our country and the destruction of our culture. Yet there is no candid public discussion of our current immigration policies.

INTERVIEWER: So racial preferences, the immigration issue, and the fact that you believe that black racism was being ignored were the major factors responsible for your recent interest in issues of race and nationality.

HART: Yes, those three factors, and a fourth – the general dishonesty about race and the ongoing censorship turned my interest to these matters.

INTERVIEWER: Why do you think there is this dishonesty in talking about matters of race?

HART: Well, when I speak to people about racial differences in, say, IQ, they seem to understand that those differences exist. Sometimes they argue or quibble a bit, or make some excuses, but most of them seem to understand these differences exist, and that they are large. Nevertheless, they feel: "You mustn't talk about this. It will cause disharmony and anger and resentment and embarrassment, so you have to be quiet about it." In other words, most people are scared to talk about the subject. They don't want to rock the boat. They are scared of how blacks may react.

INTERVIEWER: You have said previously, and here I quote: "American blacks constitute a separate nation." What do you mean by this? Do you mean to imply that black Americans are somehow less American than members of other racial or ethnic groups?

HART: We are a multinational society now. When I initially made that remark, it was a more controversial statement, but now you frequently see comments like "we are a multinational society, we are multiracial, we are multinational." A *nation* is a group of people who are held together by some common language, some notion of common ancestry, above all by a notion of common history. A nation is not the same as a state or a country. A state or country is a political entity, but not necessarily a nation. The Soviet Union had many nations in it, although it was one country. Norway is a mononational state – a state encompassing just one nation. Almost everyone in Norway is Norwegian by nationality, and they all share a common heritage, common history, and common language. We are not, at this point, a mononational state. There are at least two or three different nationalities here. Now when I say that people are of different nationalities, that is not necessarily, in and of itself, to say something bad about them. To give an example: Czechoslovakia was basically a binational state, but this doesn't mean that the Czechs were better than the Slovaks or worse than the Slovaks. But Czechs and Slovaks are *different*, and there were two nations living in the same country, and they did not get along. So they separated into two countries. This pattern – in which members of different national-ities living in the same country cannot get along and must separate – seems to be very common.

INTERVIEWER: In an address that you delivered at one of Jared Taylor's *American Renaissance* conferences, you proposed a plan for the geo-graphical division of America along racial lines. You also described a liberal plan for dealing with race relations in America and a conserva-tive plan. You concluded, however, that neither the liberal plan nor the conservative plan will work very well in bolstering racial harmony in America, and that racial tensions and racial separatist feelings will continue to increase over the next few decades. Could you explain the weaknesses that you see in the contemporary liberal and conservative approaches to race?

HART: Well, one of the underlying factors, of course, is black resentment at past mistreatment by whites. That is very large because the mis-treatment was, in fact, very large, and because it lasted for a long period of time. The resentment has been partly ameliorated, but unfortunately not very much despite all the changes which have taken place. In many ways, black resentment is even larger now than it was thirty or forty years ago. While whites tend to think that things are getting better, blacks don't believe it. I have here a column by Clarence Page in the *Washington Post*. He is considered to be a moderate black, and in his column he discusses perceptions of what is going on in the military. The whites say, "Hey, things are pretty even here. Everything is okay. We get along fine." But when Page talks to black soldiers, he finds that "beneath our surface tranquility a cauldron of racial resentment boils."

INTERVIEWER: And you don't believe that either liberals or conservatives have adequately addressed this continuing resentment?

HART: They don't believe that this intense resentment is widespread. They choose to close their eyes and not see it. For example, Carl Rowan's book was simply ignored by whites. Carl Rowan is certainly not con-sidered to be one of the more radical blacks; if anything he is some-one who has been co-opted into the white establishment. (He was an ambassador for a while and a nationally syndicated columnist.) However, just a few years ago he wrote a book with the title: *The Coming Race War in America*. Certainly a striking title, but whites paid no attention to the book. "Oh, it's just rhetoric, that's all," was the white reaction. But Rowan was speaking from his heart about the magnitude of black resentment.

David Horowitz, in his book *Hating Whitey*, gives another example, an article by a professor at City University of New York. The article is titled "A Rage to Kill," and in it she says: "I am writing this essay sitting next to a white male that I long to murder." She then goes on to explain the rather trivial reason for her rage. And the author of this article is not some poor, downtrodden black, but rather a university professor earning a nice income. But comments like hers are simply ignored by whites, whether liberal or conservative. There is a tremendous amount of black resentment out there, and it will not go away by simply pretending it does not exist.

This resentment is partially fueled by the message that blacks receive from the mainstream communication media. What the blacks hear from the media is essentially this: "You are inherently equal to whites in ability; however, you are visibly much poorer. You have very few positions of power, and very few high-ranking jobs. This has been going on forever. It is completely unfair, and it is the result of white racism." And blacks have been hearing this message – over and over for decades – and every young black has this message drummed into his ears every single day. The message is repeated on television, in newspapers, and in the movies, and it goes on endlessly. (Politicians eager for black votes frequently repeat the same message.) How can blacks possibly overcome hostility and resentment for past injustices when they are told that these injustices are continuing and are harming them drastically all the time?

This relentless hatemongering by the media ensures that black rage will continue indefinitely. But the liberal view seems to be: "If only whites would get rid of their racism, then black resentment would end." We have, in fact, long since removed all the laws that once discriminated against blacks, and most private discrimination has also ended. However, as long as this hatemongering continues – and I see little prospect of it ending – then no matter *what* whites do, black resentment will persist.

In addition, even if there were no racism at all, blacks would still be poorer than whites. Part of the problem is that there is a substantial difference in the average intelligence of the two races, and that difference is partly genetic in origin. Even if blacks and whites had completely equal opportunity, the result would be that the higher incomes, the most prestigious professions and jobs, and the main positions of power will be disproportionately occupied by whites. Because genetic factors are involved, this will continue indefinitely, and cannot be overcome by laws against discrimination.

At this point, liberals often suggest: "Well, if nondiscrimination policies won't work, let's have quotas instead." (Sometimes these are called "goals" or "affirmative action" or "preferences," but in truth they are really quotas.) But even when these are only "preferences," the result is that significant numbers of better qualified whites do not get admitted to colleges, do not get the jobs they deserve, and do not receive the promotions they deserve, basically because they are white. Instead, these whites are being passed over in favor of blacks who are less qualified than they are for those college admissions, jobs, and promotions. It is a continuing injustice, and it will continue to arouse white resentment against blacks. It cannot help but do so.

Conservatives, on the other hand, say: "Just do away with the quotas." Well, yes, I would like to abolish all these quotas and preferences and goals, and go back to the idea of merit, an idea which Martin Luther King supported. But today's blacks strongly oppose the abolition of affirmative action. Occasionally, someone like Ward Connerly goes around trying to pass laws (or amendments to state constitutions) stating that there can be no quotas or preferences either for or against blacks, and that everyone must be treated equally. But the black establishment opposes these proposals vigorously, and Connerly is despised by the black establishment and is constantly getting death threats. It seems, therefore, that whether or not we have a system of racial quotas and preferences interracial resentment will continue. I do not see any way out of this quandary short of partitioning the country.

INTERVIEWER: Isn't there a difference here between the black establishment and the black rank and file? Some polls have shown that while there is very strong support for quotas and other forms of racial preferences and affirmative action policies among the black leadership, there is much less support among the black rank and file. Indeed, some polls show a majority of black people opposed to racial preferences.

HART: I suppose that if you ask individual blacks whether they want preferences or equal treatment, many of them will say that they oppose quotas and preferences. It is easy to tell a pollster, "Hey, I just want equal treatment." But most blacks *vote* for the leaders and politicians who demand preferences. This is plainly a matter in which actions speak louder than words. And if quotas were actually abolished, and the number of blacks in positions of high income and prestige then declined (as it would), then blacks would attribute the decline to white racism, and would demand that the quotas be reinstalled.

INTERVIEWER: Viewing the long-range prospects for a harmonious, multinational America as hopeless, you have proposed an elaborate three-way partition plan for dividing up the United States. Your plan, which seems to have generated considerable interest in *American Renaissance* circles, calls for a black separatist state, a white separatist state, and an integrated state. Could you explain the contours of this plan in greater detail and why you feel it would be preferable to the current arrangement in America?

HART: Well, let me answer the last question first. It is preferable to the present arrangement because a multiracial state hurts all of us, and hurts whites in particular. Whites have to put up with very high crime rates, approximately double what they would be without nonwhites – in fact, among non-Hispanic whites the crime rate would be a quarter or a fifth of what it is now. Because of the presence of so many non-whites, we have to put up with a high incidence of social problems – illegitimacy, for example, and many others. We have to put up with high taxes. We have to put up with declining schools and declining standards in schools. We have social promotions in schools because we don't want to leave blacks back. We are getting rid of SAT scores, not because they are inaccurate in assessing academic skills, but because they reveal the unwelcome truth that there are large differences in intelligence between racial groups. (If the news is unwelcome, shoot the messenger.)

Colleges, therefore, in deciding which students to admit, rely more on high school grades (which are a less objective measure of academic ability), and on other, even more subjective qualifications (such as "service"), which can always be adjusted so as to meet racial quotas. I recently read that some colleges are evaluating applicants by putting them in a room with Legos or building blocks and assessing the results. Anything to avoid admitting students on their academic merit!

Moreover, our multiracial condition is resulting in a progressive limitation of our civil liberties. For example, the right of free association – which was taken for granted throughout most of U.S. history – has been seriously eroded in recent decades. There are all sorts of ways in which that important right has been curtailed. Private schools and colleges can no longer freely decide which applicants to admit. Employers can no longer use their best judgment on who to hire, who to fire, and who to promote, but instead must comply with various quotas. Even purely recreational organizations have had their rights curtailed.

Our right not to be tried twice for the same offense – "double jeopardy" – which used to be a bedrock right in the United States and England, has been compromised in recent years. You remember the Rodney King case a few years ago. Even though the four policemen had been acquitted in a fair trial, they were tried over again in federal court. Now you can make up a legal justification for this, but the plain fact is that there has never been a double jeopardy prosecution in the United

States except in racial instances. We were able to protect that right for two centuries, but now it is being eroded. Similarly, it used to be that a defendant in a criminal trial could exercise a certain number of absolutely peremptory challenges against proposed jurors. That right, too, has now been curtailed. If a court thinks that a challenge is racially motivated, you cannot make it.

In an effort to decrease racial tensions (that is, to placate blacks) there has been a drastic increase in censorship within the United States in the last few decades. For example, most colleges have "speech codes" in force today. Even during the infamous "McCarthy era," few if any colleges had speech codes. These codes apply to both the students and the faculty and have a chilling effect on the free expression of ideas. However, the speech codes are only one part of the problem. Nowadays, student newspapers are sometimes destroyed by opponents if they include statements that are not politically correct, and those responsible for the mass destruction of an entire press run are never disciplined (even when their identity is known). Scholarly conferences are disrupted by militants if unpopular views on race are presented, and speakers who are politically incorrect are shouted down, prevented from talking, and sometimes attacked physically. In these cases, too, those who interfere with freedom of speech are almost never disciplined.

The combined effect of these various incidences and the speech codes is that there is far less freedom of speech on campuses today than there was in the worst days of the McCarthy era, and students (and faculty) are far less willing to express their true ideas. Incidentally, I was a college student during the McCarthy era (and I was a liberal at the time), so I speak from experience on this matter. These various restrictions on our liberties have become worse during my lifetime, and they are largely a consequence of the fact that we are a multinational country which is attempting to manage the resentments and hatreds that are endemic to multinational countries. We have tried to handle those problems by passing more and more restrictive laws. The laws have not eliminated racial resentments, but they are reducing our liberties.

It should be noted that the problems we are facing are not unique to the United States. The simple fact is that multinational states usually don't work well. For example, Norway was jointed to Sweden for most of the nineteenth century. Although the Swedish government tried to be fair to the Norwegians, the Norwegians were never satisfied with Swedish concessions and continued to push for complete independence. We see the same pattern in many other countries. Austria-Hungary fell apart; Cyprus fell apart; Yugoslavia fell apart; the Soviet Union fell apart. Again and again, we see that multinational states face continuing ethnic turmoil, and the only satisfactory solution is partition.

One reason for the turmoil is that multinational states are inherently unfair because they deny to the members of the minority group the right to control their own destiny. Fifty years ago, the problem arose of what should be done with Palestine, which was claimed by both Jews and Arabs. Many Arab spokesmen said, "Let's set up a single, binational state, including both Jews and Arabs." However, the Jews objected strongly to that proposal. The Arabs were a majority in Palestine, and the Jews realized that they would never receive fair treatment in an Arab-dominated state, and unless they had their own state they would not be safe (the Arabs, of course, feel that they will never have equal treatment in a Jewish state). Or consider the Kurds. How well off would the Kurds be even if Iraq had a democratic government? The Kurds would still be a small minority in Iraq and would still be mistreated. Or take Tibet: even if China were a democracy, the Tibetans would have only a fraction of one percent of the vote and would have no control of their own institutions and destiny. The Chinese would dominate the country, and the Tibetans' culture would be destroyed. Only independence can protect them.

The same thing applies to American blacks. Many of them feel, "It's the whites who run this country. We want to get whitey off our backs." And I sympathize with that viewpoint. It is entirely similar to the desire of the Tibetans to get the Chinese off their backs, or the desire of the Kurds not to be a permanent minority in Arab countries, and the Jews not wanting to be a tolerated but helpless minority in Arab countries. But if the United States continues as a multinational state in which blacks comprise only 13 percent of the population, then the blacks will never be able to make the main political decisions themselves about the problems facing them.

You asked about my proposal for partition. Many other people have suggested partition before I did. If there was something unique in my proposal, it was that it provided not just for separate white and black countries but also for a third country, a multinational country. The reason for this third country is that there are many Americans (of all races) who genuinely want to live in an integrated, multinational state, and I feel that their wishes must be respected. I might think that those people are foolish, but I do not wish to override their views. We would not force other people to live in accordance with *our* desires. I think that it would be very unfair to those people if we forced them to live in either an all-white or an all-black country.

But in the same way, I think that it is unfair for the integrationists to force their way on the separatists, and to tell blacks who wish to be independent, "No, you can't have independence. You will have to remain a small minority in a white country and hope for the best." And it is equally unfair of the integrationists to tell those whites who feel that they cannot sustain their culture in a large multiracial society, "No, you cannot have independence. You cannot go back to the older American culture which you revere so much, but instead must share power with blacks and Hispanics, even if eventually you will become a minority, and your traditions and culture will be overridden and destroyed." I would therefore like to see a peaceful partition of the United States. At the time I originally formulated my plan, I envisioned three countries; however, by now it is apparent that at least four independent states are needed: A separate Hispanic country (probably in the Southwest), a black state, a white state (perhaps including much of the Northwest), and the integrated country (which would probably be the largest of the four states).

INTERVIEWER: So you envision a four-part partition then?

HART: Yes. However, if any of the larger Indian reservations would like to constitute themselves as independent nations, I would have no objection. I think that it would be fair to give them that option. In various speeches and writings I have discussed how the boundaries of the four states might be decided upon, and how and when each individual would decide whether he wanted to live in a separatist state or in the integrated state, and what provisions might be made for compensation and for relocation costs. If and when the country is actually partitioned, those questions will be very important and will merit extended discussion. But until enough people are convinced that partition is necessary, it seems rather premature to discuss those other questions in detail.

INTERVIEWER: It is certainly true that multiethnic societies have often been fragile, and it's been very difficult to maintain harmony in many multiethnic states. Nevertheless, in the past America has done quite well it would seem in assimilating ethnically diverse elements, including, for instance, Irish Catholics and white Anglo-Saxon Protestants, Jews and Italians, Poles and Germans, Portuguese and Hungarians, Japanese and Swedes, and dozens of other national origin groups that in other parts of the world live in separate countries and consider themselves separate peoples. Why can't this assimilation process be expanded to include African Americans, Hispanics, and other non-European peoples?

HART: First, let's get our history straight. America was set up as a white, Anglo-Saxon, essentially British nation, and the Founding Fathers did not give citizenship to blacks and did not give citizenship to the Indians. They restricted citizenship and immigration to European whites; and far from trying to assimilate non-Europeans, they made no real effort to assimilate either blacks or Indians. For many years, we admitted only whites as immigrants, and nobody else. As for how well our assimilation worked, I might remind you that our Civil War – the bloodiest war in all of American history – was fought, more than anything else, over racial issues, in particular the issue of slavery. We also fought a whole series of Indian wars, of course. It is only recently – since 1965 – that we began to admit substantial numbers of nonwhite immigrants.

As for assimilation of white ethnics, that was made easier by the fact that they were, after all, white and that they looked pretty much the same as the persons who were already citizens. Furthermore, the European immigrants all came here voluntarily, and they were people who were willing to give up, to a large extent, their previous nationality. In addition, there were other factors that helped the European to assimilate. Generally, they learned English promptly (the children always did) and thus differences in language did not persist. In the second place, those who were unable to find jobs or who did not assimilate tended to return to their country of origin. (There was no welfare then to keep them here.) In the third place, we made a very large effort to assimilate them.

Let me elaborate on this last point. Throughout the nineteenth and early twentieth century, instruction in our public schools was entirely in English. The children of the immigrants had to learn English, and to learn it promptly. Under the policy existing then, there was no alternative. Furthermore, our public schools constantly propagandized children about the glories of America. They were constantly told that America was the greatest country in the world, that it was the land of freedom and opportunity, that we had been on the side of justice in all our wars, that we were a beacon to the entire world, that we were a wonderful, glorious country – not just in wealth but morally as well. They were told this constantly (and with virtually no contrary statements), and so they absorbed those views, and absorbed them readily. That's not what blacks are hearing in our schools today. It's not what native-born Hispanics are hearing either; and it's not what immigrants are hearing.

Today, the schools are playing up all the various misdeeds that our country and our civilization has been guilty of, and more emphasis is placed upon our misdeeds than upon our achievements. As a result, assimilation is not proceeding smoothly. Even in the past, assimilation was often a slow, difficult process. It took a hundred years for the Irish to be assimilated, during which time there was a lot of resentment felt, both by the Irish and against them. During that interval, Irish Americans were often treated very unfairly, and during that period, there was a high crime rate among the Irish Americans that the older citizens resented.

Another reason why Hispanic immigrants have not been assimilating is because of conflicting historical claims. It never occurred to the Italian immigrants settling in New York or Pennsylvania that those regions should rightly be part of Italy. They understood that they were guests coming here, and that we were doing them a favor by letting them in, and consequently they were willing to assimilate to our ways. Other European immigrants felt the same way. But Hispanics coming to the United States don't feel this way. They feel that the Southwest was stolen from Mexico a century and a half ago; and they believe, therefore, that it rightly belongs to them, not to us. In their view, *we* should be grateful that they don't kick *us* out, and maybe when they are strong enough they will. In similar fashion, since the ancestors of today's blacks were never guests, but were brought here against their will, today's blacks feel no obligation to assimilate to our ways.

INTERVIEWER: Many people believe that the ethnic diversity of the United States is one of America's great strengths, and they would say that ethnic diversity, when it's properly balanced by a common core of shared values, is a source of vitality and strength in a nation, and people would point to America's motto *e pluribus unum*, suggesting that unity can be forged out of diversity. What are your own views on this? Isn't an integrated, ethnically diverse state in some important ways superior to a single monoethnic state?

HART: Large numbers of German immigrants entered the United States during the nineteenth century, but the United States did not become half German and half English. Our culture remained Anglo-American, and the German immigrants assimilated to our culture. The same thing happened with the Norwegian and Danish, and Jewish and Swedish and French immigrants. While various groups retained some of their ethnic ways, they all assimilated to the dominant Anglo-American culture.

As for diversity being a strength, the truth is exactly opposite. When newcomers assimilate, it is the *unity* which provides the strength, not the diversity. If they do not assimilate, all that diversity leads to is quotas, preferences, and interracial hostility and violence. And diverse groups most often do not assimilate. Let me give you a personal example. Recently, I went to a birthday party of a friend of mine in New York, a person who is very liberal and very integrationist, and one who has never in his life said anything derogatory about blacks or Hispanics, and who feels no enmity against them in his heart. But I did a little counting. There were fifty-four people at the party, and all fifty-four were white! And that was in New York City, the very heartland of the melting pot. It is clear that socially there is very little integration going on. We Americans are living – to a large degree – as if we are two more or less separate nations.

Someone once asked me, "What about the common culture that we all share?" And my answer was, "Do you mean the Super Bowl? Is that what you are talking about? How many blacks do you see attending a ballet or an opera?" Whites and blacks in America generally live apart, generally marry persons of their own race; they go to different schools and, for the most part, watch different TV programs. There is some common culture, of course, but not much. If diversity is such a strength, I wonder why all those companies and universities need diversity managers? They don't seem to need unity managers. Diversity is a weakness, and it causes all sorts of problems and inefficiencies. In the old days, a graduating high school class would have one yearbook. Now, in many schools there are two yearbooks (one for white graduates, one for blacks).

We keep trying to "manage" diversity. We have all sorts of committees to do so and have adopted all sorts of rules in order to manage it. Nevertheless, most people avoid diversity whenever they can. Most whites – even those who claim to be liberals and integrationists — don't want to live in areas with too much "diversity." Just look at Bill and Hillary Clinton. They constantly talk about the glories of diversity. But when they moved to New York, they chose to move not to nice, diverse, Manhattan, but rather to Chappaqua, one of the most lily-white towns in the whole country. But it is unfair to say that the Clintons are different than other whites in this regard. Whites of all political persuasions tend to avoid living in areas with too much diversity. Instead they move into gated communities that have little diversity or into nice white suburbs. Blacks have complained about this for years.

Most whites avoid blacks, and blacks, for their part, avoid whites when they can. When blacks go to college, they usually form their own clubs, their own organizations. There is some contact between blacks and whites in college, but basically, the majority of blacks feel most comfortable among other blacks. You see that very plainly in lunchrooms.

INTERVIEWER: Why do you think people tend to associate primarily with the members of their own racial and ethnic group? Do you think there is a natural human tendency toward ethnocentrism?

HART: A combination of factors is involved. It is partly a result of our environment and our training. But I suspect that a certain amount of xenophobia is encoded in our genes. Moreover, there are practical reasons why whites stay away from blacks. The black crime rate is extremely high, and whites avoid areas with lots of blacks simply out of self-protection. That is a quite rational reaction.

INTERVIEWER: To what extent have government policies contributed to racial tensions?

HART: Well, as I have indicated, I think the whole system of quotas and preferences is unjust and should be scrapped. But I am less optimistic about the outcome of that course than I once was. I used to think, Just scrap quotas and afterward everything will be okay. Then we will judge everybody "by the content of their character" and not by the color of their skin, as Martin Luther King said. I really like that idea; it sounded wonderful. But I can see now that it is not really going to happen. No other country has been able to make it happen. India has quotas, too. In fact, most multinational states have imposed some sort of quotas or preferences in an attempt to manage diversity without bloodshed.

So although I think that quotas and preferences should be abolished – that would be the fair thing, and it would ease white resentment – I don't think that it would solve our problems. The result is likely to be an increase in black resentment over the fact that fewer blacks will hold jobs in the higher paying and more prestigious occupations. Nothing short of partition into separate racial countries is going to change this fact.

INTERVIEWER: Aren't many blacks, though, committed to certain universal principles that transcend race? If you read the writings of Martin Luther King, for instance, you will find again and again the universal principle of the Declaration of Independence invoked – that all men are created equal. And just as often you will find Biblical passages cited proclaiming that all human beings are children of God and members of the same human family. Hasn't there been within the black tradition, a strong universalist thrust that at times has been as strong as any racial particularism?

HART: You can't judge the opinions of everybody by the opinions of a few saints. If you remember the movie *Gandhi*, there's this wonderful scene. India is going to get its independence from England at long last, but the Muslims, led by Ali Jinnah, want a separate Muslim state, and Gandhi confronts him and says, "Why do you want a separate Muslim state?" And Ali Jinnah said, "Moslems will not be treated fairly in a country with a Hindu majority. There is much too much resentment, and we will be discriminated against." Gandhi turns to him and says, "Ali Jinnah, you have known me for thirty years. Surely you don't think that I would discriminate against you or anyone else just because you are Moslems." And Ali Jinnah replies, "The world is not made up of Mahatma Gandhis." Well, the world is not made up of Martin Luther Kings either. I know, it is not just Martin Luther King; there are many other blacks who would like to be completely fair, who would like to live in a world with no racial resentment, and who are willing to cast aside their own. But unfortunately, there are too many blacks who do not feel that way. These angry blacks may compromise a majority; but even if they only make up 10 percent of the black population, that would be too many for the races to live together in peace and harmony.

INTERVIEWER: You have suggested a division of the United States into racial separatist states. But many whites who consider themselves white separatists or white nationalists also have an animus against Jews. As a Jew yourself, how do you feel identifying or affiliating with members of the white nationalist right here?

HART: In the first place, I am not a member of, nor do I affiliate with any anti-Jewish or anti-Semitic organization. I dislike them, and I assume that they dislike me. But I do realize that any white separatist state will inevitably include some people who feel: "It's good that we have a country in which there are no blacks, but it would be even better if there were no Jews here either." I believe, however, that such people are a minority, and that most white Americans are not anti-Semitic and are quite willing to accept Jews as equal citizens. That is what my experience has been.

When I was a child, my parents brought me up to believe that the *goyim* hate the Jews, and that they will never give the Jews a fair shake. Well, that might have been true at one time (and is probably true in most Arab countries today); but in my own lifetime I have not found it to be true here. On the contrary, I have generally been treated fairly by gentiles (there have been occasional exceptions), and it seems to me that most American whites are willing to judge me (and other Jews) on their individual merits (or faults), which is all I can ask.

However, suppose it turned out that within the white separatist state the prevailing opinion was different, and that the majority view there was, "No, we don't want Jews in our country," and that they therefore decided to partition the *white* state into a Christian country, a Jewish country, and an integrated (Christian and Jewish) country. I would, of course, choose to live in the integrated state and I don't think that I would be worse off because the hard-core anti-Semites were not in my country, but instead had a separate state of their own. (In fact, I would be better off.) But even if the white separatist state was only partitioned into two states, all that would mean is that American Jews like me would be forced into a small, separate, all-Jewish country. That is not what I want to happen, but it would not be an unbearable catastrophe. And it certainly bears little resemblance to Hitler's policies. Hitler did not want to give the Jews an independent state, he wanted to exterminate them, a very different policy indeed.

INTERVIEWER: There has been a great deal written about the ongoing relationship between Jews and blacks, which has not always been very harmonious. Do you envision increased hostility between these two groups?

HART: In the past, American Jews have tended to sympathize with blacks and black demands and to be in the forefront of those working to eliminate discrimination against blacks. The reason for this is that Jews have a long history of being persecuted, and they tended to sympathize with any group that was being discriminated against, and to think, "Hey, let's stick up for them, and then, hopefully, they will stick up for us." The plain fact, however, is that most blacks do not stick up for Jews, and don't care at all when Jews are persecuted or discriminated against. Many blacks even approve of such discrimination. Indeed, a few years ago, when the Anti-Defamation League of B'nai B'rith – commonly called the ADL – made a survey of anti-Semitic attitudes in America, they found that severe anti-Semitism was much *more* common among American blacks than among whites.

In view of this, I think that the attitudes of American Jews toward blacks are pointless and anachronistic (almost masochistic, in fact). American Jews, like all Americans, should strive to be fair to blacks; but they should – and, I believe, increasingly will – cease giving unthinking support to every demand that black leaders make. Since many blacks will react angrily to this change, I think that there is likely to be increased hostility between the two groups.

INTERVIEWER: Why has America been more successful in integrating Asians into the dominant white society than integrating blacks?

HART: Well, one reason, of course, is that in general the crime rate is very low among Asians. Another reason is that Asian immigrants are, on average, about as intelligent as white Americans are. They are therefore more successful economically than blacks are. As a result, Asians do not tend to feel (as blacks do) that "We are underrepresented in colleges and in good jobs. We are poor and exploited, and will never have a fair chance to better ourselves." They therefore rarely feel the same resentment toward whites that blacks do.

However, if the number of Asians entering the country rivaled the number of blacks who are here, I think that there would be a lot of trouble. Consider what would happen if twenty or thirty million Chinese were to emigrate to Norway. Assume that they were all intelligent, hard working, law-abiding people, everything that you could ask for. Would the Norwegians be better off? No, they wouldn't, because they would not have their own country anymore. Norway would be, in effect, just a province of China. The five million or so Norwegians would then be a minority in what used to be their own country. They might be tolerated by the Chinese (or maybe not), but in any event they would no longer have their own country. Similarly, if sufficiently large numbers of Asian immigrants entered the United States, we would lose our country.

INTERVIEWER: That ends our formal questions. Is there anything else that you would like to tell us that you haven't spoken of so far, or is there anything that you have spoken about that you would like to reinforce, clarify, or elaborate upon?

HART: Yes, there are two or three additional points that I would like to make. In the first place, many people think that partition is an impractical goal, an unrealistic policy that has never been tried before. However, there are many historical examples of successful partitions. For example, for most of the nineteenth century, Norway and Sweden were combined as a single country under the Swedish throne. To outsiders, Norwegians and Swedes seem pretty much alike. Differences in language, in race, and in religion were all small. But the Norwegians always resented the union with Sweden, and although they were granted a high degree of autonomy, they continued to yearn for a separate country of their own. In 1905, the Norwegians voted to secede, and the Swedish government (quite sensibly) did not try to fight them, but instead said, "OK, go your way in peace." Since then, the two countries have been good neighbors, and there have been no problems between them.

You may recall that, just a few years ago, Czechoslovakia split into two separate countries. Once again, few foreigners could tell the difference between Czechs and Slovaks, nor understand what the problems between them were. However, the Slovaks wanted independence, and the Czechs wisely granted it to them without a struggle. Another recent example is Cyprus. There, the two groups involved (Turks and Greeks) were not geographically separate, but were intertwined, which made the situation more difficult. For a few decades, there was constant violence between Greek Cypriots and Turkish Cypriots, and many people were killed. In 1974, Turkey sent its army into the northern half of the island and set up a separate state there. Most of the Greek Cypriots living in the north fled to the southern part of the island, while most of the Turkish Cypriots living in the south fled to the north. A brutal solution to the problem – and to those who lost their homes, very unfair. But the result of that forcible partition has been an end to the violence. Greek Cypriots – and the Greek government – have continued to complain about how unfair the Turkish action was, but nobody is getting killed anymore, and the Greeks and Turks, in their respective parts of the island, no longer suffer discrimination.

Another example, also involving Greeks and Turks, occurred in eastern Macedonia a few years after the end of World War I. The region was ethnically mixed, and there was constant fighting between Greeks and Turks. Finally, the Greek and Turkish governments got together, drew a partition line down the middle of eastern Macedonia, and declared that all the Greeks living there would have to move west of that line and that all the Turks would have to move east of the line. A harsh, arbitrary decree, but the result was that the killing stopped. It is now roughly eighty years later, and there is still peace there.

Another point I would like to make is that I (like most other white separatists) resent being called a white *supremacist*. It should be clear from what I have said that I have no desire to rule over blacks or to attempt to rule over blacks or have someone else rule over blacks in my behalf. Quite the contrary, I want them to have complete independence. All that I (and most white separatists) want is the opportunity to rule ourselves in our own independent country. Far from wishing to extend our rule, we are quite willing to give up much of the territory that American whites already control. All we want is to live in peace in our own country and to trade with foreign countries on mutually acceptable terms. (I particularly object to being compared to the Nazis. The Nazis wanted to rule other peoples, and to extend their rule forcibly. I do not want to rule, enslave, or exterminate anyone.)

One further comment about partition. People sometimes ask if such a drastic solution is necessary. To quote Rodney King, "Can't we all just get along?" The answer is, No, we all can't get along, not under a single government. It has been tried, and it doesn't work. Changing human nature to fit governments is what tyrants have been trying and failing to do over the course of history. Ethnonationalities will sometimes continue their quarrels and hostilities even across state boundaries. But within the same state things are much worse. Of course, there can be no guarantees, and partition may not be a panacea, but trying to squish different nationalities together in one country doesn't work.

INTERVIEWER: So basically, you see the continued existence of a multi-ethnic, multiracial state as an attempt to defy human nature and to thwart ethnonationalist forces that are so strong in the human soul that they simply can't be overcome through wise public policies, moral exhortation, or the like?

HART: Yes, although I would not claim that there are *no* historic examples of successful integration. Prospects for success are greatest when the groups involved are very similar in race, religion, and language – or in two of those features, or better yet in all three. Even then, success is not guaranteed, as the example of Norway and Sweden shows. Where the ethnic groups involved are very different, integration almost never works. And even if, by heroic measures, and with a lot of luck, we somehow could make integration work, it would still be far easier to make partition work, and much more likely to prove successful in the long run.

INTERVIEWER: But don't blacks and whites share at least two of those three things you mentioned – a common religion and a common language? Most blacks are Christians, as most Americans are, and blacks speak English – a dialect of English perhaps, but a dialect no farther removed from standard English than many Southern dialects or mountain dialects.

HART: Yes, they do have two of the three features in common, but it still hasn't worked out too well. The racial differences, the pent-up hostilities between the groups, the anger of the blacks in particular, and the differences in natural abilities have overpowered the similarity in religion and in language. In the long run, I don't think that black/white integration can work in the United States as it is presently constituted.

INTERVIEWER: Thank you.

PART III

WHITE CHRISTIANITY

7

Dan Gayman

Dan Gayman is one of the leading figures in what is variously called the Anglo-Israelite, Christian Identity, or Christian Israelite movement. At the time he was interviewed for this volume, he was pastor of the Church of Israel, a fundamentalist-oriented evangelical group based in Schell City, Missouri. Gayman has developed a reputation among scholars and other knowledgeable observers of white separatist Christian sects for his theological sophistication and his ability to explain the often arcane doctrines of Anglo-Israelitism in a manner comprehensible to outsiders. Originally a high school principal and a member of a schismatic Mormon group, Gayman eventually abandoned the teachings of *The Book of Mormon* to become a full-time advocate for a more fundamentalist style of evangelical Christianity. As he explains in the following interview, his evangelical theology differs from liberal Protestantism in its fundamentalist assertion of Biblical inerrancy, but it differs from most contemporary fundamentalism in the theological importance it places upon ethnicity and in its identification of the ten lost tribes of Israel with the Anglo-Saxons and certain other white European ethnic groups. God, he believes, has singled out the modern Anglo-Saxons and kindred races as a Chosen People who have a special mission to live a life in greater harmony with Biblical teaching. The Anglo-Saxons and other white European ethnic groups, he believes, have displayed historically a superiority over other races in science, technology, philanthropy, and economic organization, but this superiority, he contends, is not the product of their natural endowments, but the result of their greater adherence to Biblical morality and the special graciousness by virtue of which God allows them to meet the demands of Biblical faith. In this interview and elsewhere, Gayman goes out of his way to distance himself from those Christian Identity groups who espouse violence as a means of

The interview of Dan Gayman on May 24, 2000, by Russell K. Nieli is printed with kind permission of the interviewee.

ushering in the Divine Kingdom (this may be one reason he disdains the Christian Identity label), and while asserting the special chosenness of the Anglo-Saxon people and other white ethnic groups, he says his group harbors no enmity or ill-will toward members of any nonwhite or non-European groups. Gayman believes strongly, however, that different racial and ethnic groups should maintain separate worship services and should not socialize with each other or intermarry. He thus rejects the human-universalist interpretation of the Gospel and Pauline message, which almost all other evangelical churches espouse. Although he is aware that most evangelical theologians consider his beliefs about Israel's lost ten tribes to be fanciful, if not bizarre, Gayman insists that his reading of scriptural promises and prophesies is textually grounded and sound.

Interview with Dan Gayman

INTERVIEWER: You are pastor of the Church of Israel in Schell City, Missouri, and a leader of what is sometimes called the Christian Israelite movement. Could you explain what the Christian Israelite movement is, and how it differs from more mainline evangelical Christianity?

GAYMAN: Well, first of all, I am not sure just exactly what is meant by the Christian Israelite movement. We do not perceive the Church of Israel as being a movement per se. It certainly is not a political movement. It is not really even a religious movement. It is simply a means by which some people are seeking to express their Biblical and spiritual feelings, and I don't know that it really qualifies to be a movement.

INTERVIEWER: Then how would you describe the basic tenets of the Church of Israel?

GAYMAN: The basic tenets of the Church of Israel are pretty much main-stream in many areas, so I'm not sure if you want me to focus on those points of theological agreement with what we'll call the establishment Christian churches of this country, or whether you would want me to focus on those areas that make us different.

INTERVIEWER: Why don't you give us a little of both, some of the similar-ities and the differences.

GAYMAN: Okay, I think where we overlap . . . we are Trinitarian, histori-cally we embrace all of the historic Christian creeds, all of the creedal statements of Christianity. In addition to the creeds of a Trinitarian position on the Godhead, we are also, I think, very orthodox in our treatment of what we would call the basic, fundamental doctrines of the church. And I believe that it is only in the area of identifying the lost ten tribes of Israel that we would have a major divergence from the establishment religious belief system that is presently in place in most of the Christian churches of our country. Only in respect to the identification of the lost ten tribes of Israel and perhaps related issues do we have significant differences.

Now there is one other major difference that I think probably should be underscored. That difference would be the manner in which the standard of what we would call Bible morality is looked upon by many of the establishment churches of our generation. The Church of Israel holds to a more historic, Biblical definition of morality, and that would be interpreted by us as refusing to change our moral standards with the passing of time. One of the tenets of our belief holds that God is unchanging, that He speaks the infallible, unchanging word of truth. Therefore, we believe that the same moral standards that were, say, given to the Israelites of the Old Testament are as valid in our generation as they were at the time they were first given. So we would differ not only in terms of identifying the lost ten tribes of Israel, but also we would certainly differ with the establishment churches in terms of our upholding a moral standard of belief for the Bible.

INTERVIEWER: On the morality issue, then, you basically would take the view of the more fundamentalist or conservative evangelical churches, as opposed to some of the liberal Protestant mainline? Is that what you are saying?

GAYMAN: That is correct. We would certainly tend, without reservations, to be far more conservative than is currently the unfolding pattern in the moral belief system of establishment Christianity.

INTERVIEWER: Okay. Let's take up the issue of the identification of the lost ten tribes, since that's clearly what distinguishes you from the more typical fundamentalist church. Could you explain your views on that?

GAYMAN: Yes, we believe that the identification of the lost ten tribes of Israel is singularly a very important theological belief for the Church of Israel. Now, obviously the very name of the church, Church of Israel, would indicate that the word "Israel" holds a position of great prominence in our belief system, which is true. Eighty-five percent of the total Bible consists of the Old Testament scripture, which is a book written exclusively to, for, and about Israel. It only talks about other nations and/or peoples in the context of their relation to the Israelites of the Old Testament. We also believe that the other 15 percent of the Bible, the New Testament, is a book that simply confirms the pledges, covenants, and promises made to the Israelites of the Old Testament. Therefore, we look at the Bible as being an Israelitish book, believing that every author of all of the sixty-six books of the Bible descended from Abraham, Isaac, and Jacob, the father of the twelve tribes of Israel. In this sense, then, we very much believe that the Bible is a book that points out the covenants, both conditional and unconditional, that were made with the Israelites in the Old Testament.

What happened to ten of those tribes at the time of the Assyrian captivity seven hundred years before the birth of Christ becomes of paramount importance to us because we believe that God has not forgotten the unconditional covenants and pledges made to these people at a time when they were still residing in their separate kingdoms, that is, the kingdom of Judah, with its capital in Jerusalem, and the kingdom of Israel, with its capital in Samaria. So those covenants and promises to the Israelites, many of them made unconditionally to the whole house of Israel, to all twelve tribes – all of those prophecies hold a very prominent place in the total spectrum of the theology of the Church of Israel. It is very, very important for us to know what happened to ten of the twelve tribes after they were carried into captivity by the Assyrian armies. We know what happened to the southern kingdom, made up of Judah and Benjamin and portions of Levi. A remnant from those tribes returned at the end of the seventy-year Babylonian captivity. However, that does not satisfy the need to know what happened to the greater body of the Israelites, that is, the ten tribes of Israelites. We believe that those people can be identified in history and that their movement across the geographic locations on a map can be fairly well and accurately pinpointed.

INTERVIEWER: What happened to these ten tribes? Who are their current descendants?

GAYMAN: The ten tribes today are to be identified among the great mass or millions of people who are generally referred to as the Anglo-Saxon and kindred peoples of the earth. These nations comprise the British Commonwealth of Nations, the United States of America, the Dominion of Canada, Australia, New Zealand, all of Europe, portions and places in Africa, and other scattered places of the earth.

INTERVIEWER: So the descendants of these lost tribes today are not the present Jewish people, they are the white, northern European, Anglo-Saxon and Nordic people, is that correct?

GAYMAN: That is true with this exception. We believe that there are people in the world today who are called Jews who are descended from the southern kingdom of Judah. They are people mostly from the tribe of Judah, of the remnant that returned at the end of the seventy-year Babylonian captivity, together with maybe a small percentage of the tribe of Benjamin and the tribe of Levi. But we could not be persuaded that that small number of people constitutes the whole House of Israel. We believe the whole House – the main body of twelve-tribed Israel – that went into dispersion at the time of the Assyrian captivities, those tribes remain in dispersion today, and they comprise the greater body of the total Israelite population. The Jews make up a very small percentage of that total population.

INTERVIEWER: What evidence is there for believing that the white, Anglo-Saxon peoples around the globe are the descendants of these ten lost tribes? Is there any DNA evidence? What sort of facts do you base your conclusions upon?

GAYMAN: Our conclusions are based on a number of confirming points of evidence, the first of which might be a careful reading of the Bible to ascertain what it says about the potential future of the seed of Abraham, Isaac, and Jacob. What were these people to be famous for? What were they to do in history? How were they to multiply? What would be their spiritual influence upon the nations of the world? As you carefully chronicle all that the Bible has to say about the millions of people that were to descend from Abraham and the prophetic promises made to him, you find only one people on the face of the earth that are made up of a nation and a company of nations, as in Genesis 35:11 – a group of nations that are called a multitude of nations that were to rise up in the midst of the earth, as in Genesis 48. We believe that through a careful examination of all that the Bible states about the twelve tribes of Israel, we could certainly say that these people are really able to be identified only among the Anglo-Saxon nations of the world.

Now, may I hasten to say also that our conclusions are not just based entirely upon what we will say are applied interpretations of the Bible. We believe that in the field of heraldry – much of the same heraldry that was assigned to the twelve tribes of Israel in the book of Numbers in the Old Testament has found its way into the heraldry of the Anglo-Saxon nations of the world. We also believe that much of the kind of activity that the Israelites were famous for in the Old Testament can also be found present among the Anglo-Saxon peoples of the earth.

INTERVIEWER: Do you believe that the members of these ten tribes, or the descendants of these ten tribes, have some special religious mission today?

GAYMAN: Yes, we believe that historically the Israelites of the Old Testament were to be a light to the world. They were to be the people through whom God would bless all of the nations of the earth. And we believe that if, for example, you look at the last, say, five hundred years of history, or at least since the Protestant Reformation in the sixteenth century, it has been the nations of the Anglo-Saxon world that have brought advances in medicine. They have brought advances in scientific creativity and knowledge. They have opened up their storehouses of agricultural productivity to the world. They have endeavored to rescue and rush to the aid of victims of every kind of cataclysmic event on earth. If there is an earthquake somewhere or a major tidal wave, you can be sure that somewhere from the Anglo-Saxon world, help will be on its way to whatever other portion of the world is suffering from some major calamity. So we feel that the Anglo-Saxon population of the world has historically been very ready and willing to allocate their resources and their knowledge to the assistance of these various and sundry people that were in trouble in any given location on earth.

INTERVIEWER: Do you believe that Anglo-Saxons are in some sense morally, spiritually, or intellectually superior to other ethnic groups?

GAYMAN: We do not believe that the Anglo-Saxon people are necessarily superior to any other ethnic group, but do believe that their success, their greater prosperity, their higher standard of living are no mere accidents or products of chance. The fact that the Anglo-Saxon people have historically generated the highest standards of living on the planet, we believe, derives entirely from their willingness to apply the principles of the Bible. Perhaps any other nation that wanted to likewise apply biblical principles might find themselves being blessed also. But we believe it of central importance that the Anglo-Saxon people have embraced Christianity and the Bible as the standard for their spiritual and moral value system in this present world, in contrast to, say, the Muslims, who run with a different theological program, and in contrast to the Jews and Judaism, in contrast to the Oriental world or to just about any other segment of the world. We feel that if there is a tendency for the Anglo-Saxon world to be blessed, it is because they have followed the Bible far more closely than others and have endeavored to apply the Bible and Christianity to their national life.

INTERVIEWER: So basically you are saying that the Anglo-Saxons, while they have displayed superior achievements in many areas, their superior achievement is not due to genes, or to climate, or to geography, or to the accidents of history. It's due primarily to their biblical faith – they have been more faithful to the Bible and any possible superiority is due to this.

GAYMAN: Yes, and may I add to that the fact that the Anglo-Saxon people, being the descendants of the twelve tribes of Israel, have a special calling and election to become a blessing to all the other peoples of the earth. In other words, every people that God has created may have their unique calling, but the Israelites have a unique calling and blessing in the election of God to bring the blessings of God to the rest of the world. We believe that a cursory examination of history would confirm very quickly that most of the technological blessings and advances of the last 150 years have basically come from the Anglo-Saxon nations of the world, and we want to emphasize that when we say Anglo-Saxon, we use the word Anglo-Saxon *and* kindred peoples of the earth. Sometimes it may not be possible to be inclusive enough if you just say Anglo-Saxon because we believe that there's a family of people that can be brought together through the word "kindred," all of which are part of the Anglo-Saxon world.

INTERVIEWER: Who would be these kindred peoples? Would they include Germans? Swedes?

GAYMAN: Yes, they would include people like the Germans and the Swedes and the Danes and people that sometimes might not always be thought of as being part of the Anglo-Saxon world.

INTERVIEWER: What about southern and eastern Europeans – Italians, Turks, Poles, Romanians, etc.?

GAYMAN: I would say that there may be pockets of those people that would fit into the category of the Anglo-Saxon kindred peoples, but just to say that they all broadly fit there, I don't believe that that would be a true statement.

INTERVIEWER: You believe, though, that the Anglo-Saxons and kindred peoples have a special, God-ordained mission to be a light unto the nations . . .

GAYMAN: Yes, sir.

INTERVIEWER: . . . both in terms of morals and religiosity, but also in terms of scientific progress and technology?

GAYMAN: Yes, scientific progress and technology, I think that they would certainly be leaders and forerunners and trailblazers in all of those areas.

INTERVIEWER: What are your views of non–Anglo Saxon, nonwhite Christians? Where, for instance, do black Christians or Hispanic Christians or Korean Christians fit in? Do you believe that they are created in the image of God and that they can find salvation through faith in Jesus Christ?

GAYMAN: We believe that all of the nations, all of the separate and distinct races of the earth, are the creation of God. God has uniquely designed and placed His mark of ownership on all of those races. Each of those races has the ability and the proclivity to worship God in the manner and means by which He ordained that they would worship Him. We believe that each of those distinctive races can relate to God. They can all connect to God. How that happens we do not pretend to know. We do not speculate on that. We simply believe that all races bear the image that God created them to bear. They have their own unique, distinctive design and mark of ownership that God has placed upon them, and we believe that in every distinct race there is a difference in calling, there's a difference in their uniqueness. Some are gifted in some areas. Others are gifted in other areas, so we would say that there is a tendency for all of the created races to relate to God in a unique and different way. The Arab world, for example, does not relate to the God of Christianity in the same way that the Anglo-Saxon world would relate. The Moslem world would not relate to the Bible. They relate better to the Koran. They do not relate to Jesus Christ. They relate better to Allah and to Mohammed. The same would be true for Judaism. Modern Jewry would not relate to the Lord Jesus Christ. They relate to their under-standing of the God of the Old Testament, Jehovah or Yahweh, so they would certainly not relate to God or connect to God in the same way that the Anglo-Saxon world would.

By and large, the Oriental world has always connected to God through philosophers, various and sundry religious leaders, and people that have risen up in their history, such as Buddha and others of well-known fame in the Oriental world. So the Orientals have not related to God in the same fashion that the Anglo-Saxon world has. The Oriental world has not historically embraced Christianity; only individual Orientals have embraced Christianity. There has never been a national embracing of Christianity among Oriental peoples, in contrast to the Anglo-Saxons, where entire nations have proclaimed Christianity as being their predominant faith. In certain stages of European history, there was almost a conversion of entire nations as Christianity moved across Europe. There is a stark contrast between the way that the Anglo-Saxon world has related historically to Jesus Christ and the way of these other nations. We might summarize all of this by simply saying that all of the distinctive races have their unique way of connecting to God, and we believe that it is an erroneous assumption to believe that *all* of the distinctive created races are going to be able to connect to God in the very same way. We do not believe that the people of the Anglo-Saxon world are going to be able to historically link up with Buddhism and with other Oriental religions simply because it's not in the nature of the Anglo-Saxon to embrace Oriental gods and Oriental ideas about God. And the same is true with regard to the Orientals in relation to Christianity. Only individuals from the Oriental world have embraced Christianity, and only very sporadic individuals from the Anglo-Saxon world have moved into Buddhism or some other Oriental religion. It seems very evident that the Anglo-Saxons have historically embraced one religious faith – Christianity – that the Bible has been pretty much the exclusive book that they have followed, in contrast to the rest of the distinctive races of the earth, all of whom have a different way of approaching and knowing God.

INTERVIEWER: What about, though, nonwhite Christians? You mentioned examples of people who are non-Christian. What about the non–Anglo Saxon, nonwhites who see Christianity as their religion? I'm thinking particularly of African Americans and Hispanics.

GAYMAN: Would you mind clarifying that? I'm not sure that I know exactly what you are saying.

INTERVIEWER: My question is, can nonwhites be Christians in the same way that Anglo-Saxons can be Christians? And if there is a difference, what is the difference?

GAYMAN: Well, we believe that in order to be a qualifying believer in the Lord Jesus Christ, there is a covenantal standing. In Jeremiah, chapter 31, verse 31, the prophecy is given that, "behold, I will make a new covenant with the House of Israel and with the House of Judah, not according to the covenant that I made with their fathers when they were in the land of Egypt." Now in Jeremiah 31: 32–33, it goes on to elaborate that this new covenant, of which the New Testament is the sum and substance, was to be made with the House of Israel and with the House of Judah. We do not believe that the God of the Bible entered into all these special, unconditional covenants with the Israelites, and then all at once universalized these covenants. Nowhere in the Bible do we find where God universalized the unconditional covenants and made them suddenly universally applicable to all the peoples of the earth. So we believe that if there are individuals from the other races that seek to embrace Christianity, they will most assuredly be blessed to the degree and to the measure that they embrace the moral principles and values of Christianity, but insofar as to say that these individuals share in the same covenantal standing or blessing as the Anglo-Saxons and kindred races, we would not be able to say that.

INTERVIEWER: So you see Christianity as in some sense an ethnically exclusive religion, and not a universalist religion as most Christian evangelicals have in the past?

GAYMAN: Yes, I would say that we would view Christianity and its connection to the Anglo-Saxon world very much in the same sense that there's an ethnic link between the Arabs and the Muslim religion. There's an ethnic link between the Orientals and the various Oriental spiritual leaders that have risen up in history, Confucius, Buddha, etc. For these people and the religious philosophies that they embrace and espouse, there seems to be an ethnic tie that makes the Oriental have a proclivity to move in the direction of these Oriental philosophers. We believe that, by the same token, the Anglo-Saxon world has historically embraced the tenets of the Christian faith because they are the principal subjects of the Bible.

INTERVIEWER: Let me just ask you how you would interpret some of the Biblical passages critics of your view would obviously cite as incompatible with your biblical interpretation. Take the central text of Paul's Letter to the Galatians, the third chapter, the twenty-second to twenty-ninth verse. Let me read part of this passage. "But the Scripture hath concluded all under sin that the promise by faith of Jesus Christ might be given to them that believe. . . . For ye are all the children of God by faith in Christ Jesus. For as many of you as have been baptized into Christ, have put on Christ. There is neither Jew nor Greek, there is neither bond nor free, there is neither male nor female, for ye are all

one in Christ Jesus. And if ye be Christ's, then ye are of Abraham's seed
and heirs according to the promise." Now this would seem to imply
very clearly that if people have faith in Jesus Christ, they become one
Christian people, and they are then all made members of Abraham's
seed. In other words, they all become Israelites not by virtue of their
genealogy or common biological descent, but by virtue of their common
faith and common religious belief. How would you respond to that sort
of criticism?

GAYMAN: Well, we would respond to that by first of all confirming the fact
that every book in the Bible and every chapter and text used in the Bible
must be placed in the context of the whole Bible itself. We would
respond to the Pauline epistle in Galatians by saying, let's first look at
the Gospels and what Jesus says on these matters. Jesus said in Matthew
15:24, "I am not sent but unto the lost sheep of the House of Israel."
Now, since Jesus Christ is the founder of Christianity, we'll begin with
Him. "I am not sent but unto the lost sheep of the House of Israel."
This is a very important passage and it says that Jesus has come specifically to save the Israelites. In the conversion of Zacchaeus in St. Luke's
Gospel, chapter 19, Jesus makes the statement that, for as much as
Zacchaeus was a son of Abraham, that he had found salvation. So
Zacchaeus found salvation because he was the seed of Abraham, that
is, because he was an Israelite. Jesus said in John's Gospel, chapter 10,
verse 26: "My sheep hear my voice and know me." The sheep that
heard His voice and believed did not believe in order to become his
sheep; rather, they believed because they were His sheep. His sheep, of
course, are the Israelites. In Matthew 10:5–6 Jesus commissioned and
instructed His disciples, "Go not into the way of the Gentiles. Into any
city of the Samaritans, enter ye not, but go rather to the lost sheep of
the House of Israel." This means that the message of Jesus is directed
specifically to the House of Israel. Again, the emphasis that we place
on the lost ten tribes of Israel is there because we believe that the Bible
places great emphasis there . The founder of Christianity, the Lord Jesus
Christ Himself, instructed His disciples to go out and find the lost sheep
of the House of Israel.

Similarly, when James wrote his epistle, he begins, "James, a servant
of God and of the Lord Jesus Christ, to the twelve tribes which are
scattered abroad" (James 1:1). We are somewhere in the middle of the
first century of the Christian era, with James addressing his epistles to
all twelve tribes. When the apostle Peter, one of the original twelve
apostles, wrote his epistle, he goes on to say to the dispersed across
Asia, Bythnia, Cappadocia, and so forth, "Elect according to the foreknowledge of God the Father" (1 Peter 1:1). He is here talking to all
of the Israelites in the great dispersion – 1 and 2 Peter are written to
the Israelites. Similarly, when we come to the Gospel of Matthew,

Matthew was written originally in Hebrew. It was addressed to Hebrews, ethnic Hebrews who spoke Hebrew. This, we believe, is all very important.

When you come to the Pauline epistles, we have no problem there. We embrace all of the Pauline epistles. If you will notice in the last chapter of the book of Galatians, Paul makes it clear that peace is to be upon all the Israel of God. So when he is saying that there is neither male nor female, there's neither Jew nor Greek, the word "Jew" as you previously quoted from the book of Galatians 3, is an appellation that identifies an Israelite of the kingdom of Judah, perhaps of the tribe of Judah, so we would have no problem with the word "Jew" there. That would be a member of the House of Judah, or of the southern kingdom of Judah. The word "Greek" would have an application to the Israelites who were in dispersion that were Greek speaking. Seven hundred years after the Assyrian deportations of millions of these Israelite people into the very regions where mass conversions of Christians were taking place in the New Testament era of history, we would say that these people were indeed Greek speaking but they were also Israelites in dispersion. These were the Greeks Paul was referring to.

And I might say if I could, just to digress for a moment, if we go into the Bible, let's look at Ephesians 2. In Ephesians 2:11–12, where St. Paul talks about the Gentiles, he's talking to a group of people called Gentiles: "Wherefore, remember that ye being in time past Gentiles in the flesh, who are called uncircumcision by that which is called the circumcision in the flesh made by hands; that at that time ye were without Christ, being aliens from the Commonwealth of Israel, strangers from the covenants of promise, having no hope, and without God in the world." All right, now who were these Gentiles that at that time were estranged from the Commonwealth of Israel, were strangers from the covenants of promise, having no hope and without God in the world? Well, they were this great multitude of Israelites from the northern kingdom that some seven hundred years earlier had been divorced and sent into dispersion. But notice what the great apostle Paul says in Ephesians 2:13, he says that "now in Christ Jesus, ye who sometimes were far-off or made nigh by the blood of Christ," so he's now talking to that great body of divorced Israelites in dispersion. Now I hope that I am not overextending this discussion, but I'm trying to show that the chapter that you quoted from the book of Galatians has a very definite order and certainly needs to be addressed, but it has to be looked at in the greater context of the entire New Testament itself, and even beyond that, of the entire Bible. So now we are in verse 14 of Ephesians 2: "For he is our peace who hath made both one." Who does the word "both" refer to? Both Israel of the northern kingdom and Judah of the southern kingdom. But establishment Christianity makes no distinction between the houses of Israel, as carefully chronicled throughout the narrative of the Old Testament. They simply fail to distinguish between the kingdom of Israel and the kingdom of Judah, and in so doing, they miss the major thrust of the direction that God is taking in the words of the Old Testament Scripture.

So now we come to Ephesians 2, verse 16: "And that he might reconcile both unto God in one body by the cross, having slain the enmity thereby." Now who did God reconcile into one body by the cross of the Lord Jesus Christ, having slain the enmity thereby? Both Israel and Judah are the two separate divisions of people that are being joined together and brought into unity in one. Then he goes on to verse 17 and says: "And came and preached peace to you, which were a far-off, and to them that were nigh." Now who were the people that were a far-off? Well, these are those barbarian-speaking people that were called heathen by the Jews or Judeans – Israelites of the southern Kingdom of Judah, who are now being brought into the bond of the covenant of the Lord Jesus Christ and then to them that were nigh. The people that were nigh were the Israelites that were living right in the southern Kingdom of Judah, that were then known in New Testament times as simply Jews. Now where the establishment church has really erred, we believe, is that they have simply discounted the lost ten tribes of Israel. They have written them off as being irrelevant. All of the unconditional covenants and promises of the Old Testament have been essentially transferred by establishment clergy to simply the church. Well, we believe that Israel is the church, and the church is Israel.

INTERVIEWER: And this church has a definite ethnic base?
GAYMAN: Yes, we believe the church has an ethnic base. We believe that Israel is the church, and the church is Israel. May I digress for just a moment? If we turn to the epistle of 1 Peter, when Peter said: "Peter, an apostle to Jesus Christ and to strangers scattered throughout Pontus, Galatia, Cappadocia, Asia, Bythnia, *elect* according to the foreknowledge of God the Father." Who are the people in New Testament Scripture, 1 Peter 2, that are the elect according to the foreknowledge of God the Father? We don't need to look very far and deep into the Bible to find out that there's only one people that were ever given the status of being in the election of God the Father from before the foundation of the world, as in Ephesians 1, 4 and 5, and as found also in 2 Timothy 1:9. The elect according to the foreknowledge of God the Father are the Israelites. Notice carefully now, Peter comes along in chapter 2, same epistle, in verse 9, and says: "But ye are a *chosen* generation, a royal priesthood, a holy nation, a peculiar people, that ye should show forth the praises of him who have called ye out of darkness into his marvelous light." When Peter here is writing his epistles to the Israelites

in dispersion, he is paraphrasing in 1 Peter 2:9 a verse found in Exodus 19:6, which declared the Israelites to be the peculiar people, the treasure unto God that He had placed on the earth.

Now consider 1 Peter 2:10. This is *very* important because now I am going to show you how there is a direct *ethnic* correlation between the people that Peter is writing his epistle to and the promises made to the ethnic, physical, racial Israel of the Old Testament. 1 Peter 2:10 is a direct quote taken from the Old Testament prophet Hosea, chapter 1, verse 10. The prophet Hosea is talking about Israel of the northern kingdom, those people that are going to be divorced, going to be sent into dispersion. They will be the unpitied people, the people that are cut off, sent into dispersion, but at the very time that Hosea prophesies of their dispersion and being cut off, he also prophesies that "in the place where it was said unto them that ye are not a people, there will it be said, in that very place, that ye are the people of God" (Hosea 1:10). So Peter now, in 1 Peter 2:10, is going to give a direct quote from Hosea 1:10, reminding these people that he's writing to those who are ethnically the people to whom God has promised that even though they were not a people, sent into dispersion, cut off, and called Gentiles – meaning a nonpeople or a heathen people – that they would nevertheless become the children of the living God. Now these kinds of examples are laced throughout the New Testament Scripture.

I've been in Ephesians and I've been in 1 Peter, but let's turn to the book of Romans. This is important, I think, because I feel that when we look at the book of Galatians and those oft-quoted verses that you cited, which are probably the classic verses recited by most clergymen to universalize Christianity and take it from its ethnic Biblical setting and explode it into a universalist religion, Paul's remarks in Romans help to explain what Paul really meant. In Romans 2:14–15, Paul says: "For when the Gentiles which have not the law do by nature the things contained in the law, these, having not the law, are a law unto themselves." Now here is something very interesting. Here we have Paul speaking of "Gentiles which have not the law." These are heathen peoples outside the Commonwealth of Israel; they are estranged from the covenants God made to Israel. They are a nonpeople – that is, Gentiles. Now we believe that these so-called Gentiles, heathens, barbarians, Greek-speaking Hellenes, are indeed Israel of the lost ten tribes, who were then in the first century in dispersion in the very areas where New Testament evangelization was going on. By nature they were doing the things contained in the law (verse 15), which show the work of the law written in their hearts. Now here is something really unusual. Here are Gentiles, who though separate from the law, were by the very nature of the way they lived their lives living somewhat by the moral standards of the law, and Paul says they have the work of the law written in their hearts. One does not have to be a rocket scientist to go back into the Old Testament and find out who God said would have the law written into their hearts. The promise made to Israel and Judah, Jeremiah 31:31–34, was that God would write the law into the hearts of these people.

INTERVIEWER: So these Gentiles Paul speaks of were not just any non-Jews, but only those whose forbears had been part of the original tribal confederation of Israel described in the Old Testament?

GAYMAN: Yes, let me explain. When the Old Testament canon ends, the twelve tribes of Israel – except for a remnant of Judah and Benjamin and scattered individuals from the other tribes – had been carried away into the vast Assyrian wilderness. This event is chronicled in II Kings 17:5–6 and took place around the year 721 B.C. Conservative estimates place the number of Israelites that were carried into the Assyrian captivity to be about ten million people. None of them returned with the remnant that rebuilt the Temple. Only a small remnant numbering less than 50,000 people from the tribes of Judah and Benjamin returned from the land of Babylon where they had earlier been taken by the Chaldean armies under the leadership of Nebuchadrezzar.

The estimate of ten million people being captured and moved in mass is calculated upon the basis of I Chronicles 21:5 and related Scriptures. During the reign of King David, he commissioned Job to number Israel. I Chronicles 21:5 records an army of 1,100,000 men in arms among the tribes making up the Kingdom of Israel. Adding all the women, children, and older men and remembering that Israel was not carried away captive for almost three hundred years after the reign of David ended, the figure 10,000,000 would be a modest one. Later Jewish sources also confirm this. One of the most well-known historians and frequently quoted by subsequent historians was Flavius Josephus. Writing in the first century, this Jewish historian and contemporary of the Apostles confirms that the ten tribes of Israel were then in existence and that their numbers were immense: "there are but two tribes [of Israel] in Asia and Europe subject to the Romans, while the ten tribes are beyond the Euphrates till now, and are an immense multitude, and not to be estimated by numbers."

A more modern Jewish account appearing in the *Jewish Chronicle* for May 2, 1879, confirms the words of Josephus and further documents the existence of the ten lost tribes of Israel. I'll quote from that account: "There has always been, however, an unwillingness to admit that a fate which has befallen so many nations has overtaken the Ten Tribes. Why should they have been less tenacious of life than their brethren of Judah? Nay, the Scriptures speak of a future restoration of Israel, which is clearly to include both [the house of] Judah and

Ephraim [the house of Israel]. The problem, then, is reduced to the simplest form. The ten tribes are certainly still in existence. All that has to be done is to discover which people represents them."

The lost ten tribes ceased to be called Israelites in their captivity and appeared under a number of different names. These millions of "lost Israelites" occupied the geographical landscape of much of the Greek and Roman world in the first century of the Christian era. The early Christian churches at Rome, Corinth, the churches of Galatia, the churches at Ephesus, Philippi, and Colosse, were populated by the lost ten tribes of Israel, referred to as Gentiles in the New Testament. These Gentiles are one and the same with the lost ten tribes of Israel now settled by the millions into the regions where the Apostle Peter directed his epistle (1 Peter 1:1–2). When Peter was chosen of God to open the door into the Gentile world by bringing the Gospel to Cornelius, who was a Gentile from the lost ten tribes of Israel, he opened the Gospel up to divorced Israel, then in dispersion, and it was St. Paul who then spent the remainder of his life preaching to the Gentiles.

One of the principal names historically assigned to the lost ten tribes of Israel has been the name "Caucasian," derived from the Caucasus Mountains and always pertaining to the white race. It was in this very region that millions of Israelites belonging to the lost ten tribes of Israel dwelt as they made their way through and around the 750-mile-long range of the Caucasus Mountains from which the name "Caucasian" comes. Now establishment Christianity in our view has made two mistakes here. Number one, the Bible has been suddenly lifted from its ethnic perimeters and boundaries, and, secondly, all of the unconditional covenants, pledges, and promises made to the Israelites have been essentially transferred to the church. This church, by today's definition – modern Christianity's definition – is an international, multiracial body that is made up of whoever professes a belief in Jesus Christ. Whoever professes such a belief becomes the spiritual seed of Abraham. We believe this view of the church is inconsistent with the teachings of the Bible, which identifies the church with the ethnic, racial Israel.

INTERVIEWER: So the true church in your view is not any multiethnic, international organization, but the true body of the church is composed of the descendants of the ten tribes of Israel who you identify with the Anglo-Saxon and closely related races?

GAYMAN: Yes. But let me extend that definition to also include emphatically – now this is very important – that the church also incorporates the Israelites who historically were part of the southern kingdom of Judah, meaning that the portion of Judah, the portion of Benjamin, and Levi, that returned at the end of the seventy-year Babylonian captivity and returned to rebuild the Temple. All of those people certainly are incorporated into the ethnic body of what we call the twelve tribes of Israel, so we want to emphasize twelve tribes, and not ten.

INTERVIEWER: So besides the Anglo-Saxons, today's Jews would also be a part of that Israelite race, and hence part of the ethnic basis of the church?

GAYMAN: Yes. However, there is a discussion that would have to be held on what constitutes an ethnic Hebrew Jew versus those who say they are Jews and are not, as in Revelation 2:9 and 3:9.

INTERVIEWER: Who are the true Jews today?

GAYMAN: The true Jews today would be that body of people who are bringing forth the fruits of the children of Abraham, and we would conclude that there are many traditional historic Orthodox Jews who embrace the Old Testament Torah, and who, even if they deny the existence of the Messiah in the person of the Lord Jesus Christ, we believe that they are living in strict adherence and compliance with the Old Testament moral standards. These people, we believe, would constitute a part of the original tribe of Judah, portions of Benjamin or Levi that are ethnic Israelites, and all qualify in the ethnic setting of Scripture to be a part of the total plan of God for his people.

INTERVIEWER: Do these Jews have some special religious mission today, like the Anglo-Saxons?

GAYMAN: So far as having a mission, we believe that those who are true ethnic Jews, their primary mission in time and history has been to preserve the oracles of God. They have been the custodians and caretakers of the essential Old Testament Scripture. They have been the grand caretakers and keepers of the oracles of God that have been handed down through the centuries of time, and the Masoretic Old Testament canon probably would not be available today were it not for these people. At this point, I need to digress, however, and emphasize that there is a great part of what is called modern Jewry that is not ethnically related to that portion of the modern Jewish people that we believe are ethnic Israelites. For example, I am looking at a book entitled *The Thirteenth Tribe*, written by Arthur Koestler, one of the most well-known Jewish authors in the twentieth century. In *The Thirteenth Tribe*, which was a best-seller published, I believe, by Random House . . . what Mr. Koestler does in this book, that I think is rather remarkable, is that he traces an element of modern Jews who make up a rather significant portion of the total population of modern Jewry, and he very convincingly proves historically, archaeologically, and by other means that they have no relationship, no ethnic connection to Abraham, to Isaac, to Jacob, or to any of the Hebrew characters of the Old Testament. These Jews could be lumped – now this is not Mr. Koestler, this is Dan Gayman speaking – these Jews could be lumped with those spoken of in Revelation 2:9 and 3:9. We believe that all of those people who *claim* to be the true descendants of Abraham, Isaac, and Jacob and call themselves Jews but are not, fit into the category of Revelation 2:9 and 3:9, where Jesus Christ Himself said "I know the blasphemy of them which say they *are* Jews and are not." And then He goes on to say what He believes they should be rather known as.

INTERVIEWER: How can one tell the difference between the real Jews and the false claimants?

GAYMAN: How can one tell the difference? Well, by their fruits ye shall know them. In other words, let's suppose, for example, that we examine the fruit borne by the two classifications or groups of Jews in the world today. One group will be the very careful custodians of the Old Testament Scripture. They will be very, very faithful adherents to the idea of Judaism. They will be the caretakers of the synagogues, and they will be very devout in their faith. They will be very moral. They will be following the moral standards of the Torah in contrast to those others, who we'll call the pseudo or false group of Jews, who bring forth just the opposite. For example, let's just suppose that we look at the Bolshevik Revolution in 1917 inside of Russia. A great many of the leaders of the Bolshevik Revolution in 1917 in Russia were Jews, and they were not the kind of quiet, tranquil Jews that were carefully and meticulously following the Old Testament moral standards and attending to the needs of the synagogue and feeding the poor and doing all this sort of thing. The Jews operating in the Bolshevik Revolution in 1917 were out fomenting revolution.

INTERVIEWER: So the true Jews are the pious Orthodox Jews – the Hassidic Jews, for instance – rather than the more secularized Jews or Reform Jews?

GAYMAN: Yes. I would say that that is true, yes.

INTERVIEWER: Your views are very similar to those of the Christian Identity movement, yet in recent years you have tried to disassociate yourself from the label of Christian Identity, while still acknowledging important similarities between the Church of Israel and the Christian Identity religion. Could you explain what distinguishes your group from Christian Identity?

GAYMAN: Yes. First of all, Christian Identity, to the best of my knowledge, has no structured means by which they identify with historical Christianity. I know of *no* Christian Identity church that embraces creedal Christianity, as we do. We embrace the Apostles' Creed, the Nicene Creed, the Athanasian Creed. I do not find any known Christian Identity group in this country or abroad that embraces these historic creeds of Christianity. I would say also that there is an important difference in, for example, the doctrine of the Trinity. We have been long adherents to the doctrine of the Trinity, while in contrast Christian Identity groups vary in their position on the Godhead. Some of them believe in the Trinity; some of them do not.

You see, Christian Identity has a very loosely structured system of theology, and it almost defies anyone's ability to find out what they really believe because every individual Christian Identity church sort of has a different theological mold. It's very difficult to find a universal standard of belief system in Christian Identity. Very seldom would you ever even find a printed statement of what they believe because, in truth, many Christian Identity adherents do not know what they believe. They may have definite ideas in some areas of their belief system, but when it comes to theological formulas, they really have no systematized theological belief systems. Now, I would like to contrast that with the fact that the Church of Israel has a published theological belief system. It is well established; it has been printed up and is available for anyone to read.

I would also like to emphasize the fact that in the more than fifty years of the existence of the Church of Israel, there has never been a single racial incident whereby hostility toward other races has ever drawn the attention of law enforcement officers or agencies. So there is a *decided* difference, we believe, in the attitude that the Church of Israel has toward other races and that of certain Christian Identity groups. We believe God is the author and creator of *all* the distinctive races, that He placed His mark of ownership upon them all, that He has a unique plan and purpose for every race that He created, and that God relates to every race, and they relate to Him in a manner unique to their own special existence. This contrasts with Christian Identity, which might try to imagine that God is not the author of all races. I have read some pretty far out explanatory notes on where they believe some of the races came from. We believe that is a major contrast between us and Christian Identity. We count God as the author of all races, and we do not believe that there is any room whatsoever in our theology for hatred of any race. God says in Genesis 1:31: "He looked at everything that he made, and behold, it was very good." Therefore, if God called everything that He created very good, we're very happy to call it very good also. We believe this is one of the distinguishing differences between what the Church of Israel stands for and what Christian Identity has been doing – at least in the historical context that the media has placed it in over the last twenty years.

INTERVIEWER: So you don't believe in hatred toward any race and you don't believe in violence directed toward any race, but you do believe in ethnic separatism. In terms of worship, many Christian organizations in the twentieth century – Billy Graham's crusades being perhaps the most famous – have adopted interracial, interethnic worship services. Graham, I think, started multiracial crusades as early as the 1940s, and organizations like Promise Keepers in more recent times hold mass, mixed-race revivals. But you would strongly disapprove of this kind of multiracial worship service, is that correct?

GAYMAN: Yes. We have traditionally, throughout the entire history of the Church of Israel, held to a view of ethnic separatism in marriage, in worship, and in social settings. Like the Pilgrims who settled America in 1620 and the thousands of Puritans who followed them as Separatists from England, remnant Christians from the Church of Israel seek to live in marriage, worship, and social settings as *separatists*. We have no problem, however, with the diversity of races in the workplace. Our people have historically worked very well in racially diverse workplaces. In small businesses where there was racial diversity, our people have done very well, and they have also done well within larger corporate settings. Our people have done very well in the armed forces, and in college and university classroom settings, too.

But when it comes to the idea of marriage and worship and social settings, we practice ethnic separatism. It would be a violation of our religious conscience to bring the races together in a worship forum. Now there is a reason for this. We believe that there are a number of biblical injunctions that we would stress that are stated clearly in Scripture, and we would cite these as being the biblical grounds upon which we would want to practice ethnic separatism in respect to worship. This doctrine of ethnic separatism is as old as the Bible itself. The Book of Genesis calls Abraham and Sarah to separate themselves unto their God (Genesis 12) and move to a land where they had never lived before. Abraham and Sarah, followed by Isaac and Rebekah and then Jacob and his family, all practiced the basic law of ethnic separatism as they followed God's call. The twelve sons of Jacob blossomed into the twelve tribes of Israel, the very centerpiece of the entire Old Testament. God called for Israel to be a people separated unto Himself, saying, "I am the LORD your God, which have separated you from other people" (Leviticus 20:24).

Addressing Jehovah, the God of Israel, Moses made this core statement on the doctrine of ethnic separatism: "For wherein shall it be known here that I and thy people have found grace in thy sight? So shall we be *separated*, I and thy people, from all the people that are upon the face of the earth" (Exodus 33:16). When Solomon was dedicating the Temple unto the God of Israel, he declared this regarding ethnic separatism and Israel: "For thou didst separate them from among all the people of the earth, to be thine inheritance" (I Kings 8:53). The doctrine of ethnic separatism is as central to the Bible as apple pie is to most European Americans. The command of ethnic

224 *White Christianity*

separatism continues throughout the Bible, right into the New Testament. Moreover, if, as stated in chapter 7 of the Book of Revelation, 144,000 Israelite households are to be sealed at the end of the age – 12,000 from each of the twelve tribes – the doctrine of ethnic separatism is imperative to the very end of history.

Aside from specific scriptural problems, the idea that people can come together and worship God in the same building, sitting in the same pews, and not have interracial dating and marriage would be inconceivable. If we bring them together in the church and we are all going to become one family inside the walls of the sanctuary, certainly there will be no question that we will have interracial dating and then marriage, and all that goes with that. So we would be opposed to any kind of multiracial worship. Absolutely.

INTERVIEWER: Why do you oppose interracial marriage so strongly?
GAYMAN: We oppose interracial marriage so strongly because we believe that it is a violation of God's original design and the creation of every race. We believe that it basically undermines the whole concept of God's original design and creation. It erases God's mark of ownership upon the mixed children that come out of a union between two diverse race partners. So we feel that it is a direct threat to the very nature under which God originally separated and divided the races. In Deuteronomy 32, beginning at verse 7, in a well-known passage of Scripture, the Bible tells us very clearly: "Remember the former days. Consider the years of many generations. Ask thy Father, and He will show thee thine elders, and they will tell thee, when the most high divided to the nations their inheritance, He *separated* the sons of Adam according to the number of the children of Israel, for the Lord's portion is His people. Jacob is the lot of his inheritance." Now you see, we believe very clearly that the Bible teaches separatism in regards to certain areas of human conduct. One of those areas would be in worship because interracial marriage works against the very nature of all of the orderly design in the creation. Every form in the flora and fauna world that God has created follows the pattern of the law of kind after his kind, a law which is stated no less than ten times in the first chapter of Genesis. So interracial marriage is a violation of the law of kind after his kind. It breaks down the distinctive order of God's creation. And we believe that what interracial marriage really does is that it takes away from every race. We would want every race to retain the original creation design that God intended for that race, and we believe that interracial mixing or marriage tends to take away *from* every race what God intended.

Let me explain further what we mean by the law of kind after his kind and why we adhere to the principle of ethnic separatism in marriage, worship, and intimate social settings. All of nature surely does witness to the truth of mixing with your own kind. All the birds that fly in the heavens associate with their own kind, and have done so from the day of their creation. Black birds mix only with their kind. All the animals of the forest were programmed by the Creator God to mate among their own kind. Every individual species in the creation, and there are countless numbers of them, have maintained their own identity because of the inherent law of kind after kind.

God, we believe, has written the basic law of separatism into the very genetic code of all of His creation. The law of kind after kind is basic to the very genetic code of all created life. This basic law of God and creation is inherent in all of life, including the diverse and distinct races on earth. Within each distinctive race is a strong propensity to stay within the perimeters of their own kind. The proclivity for every distinctly created race to stay within its genetic borders is the very reason that the divergent racial stocks have persisted throughout history. The Caucasoid, Mongoloid, and Negroid races were created separate and distinct from one another. The Creator programmed within each race an instinctive drive to cohabit within their kind. The survival of every pure race is dependent upon the practice of ethnic separatism. It is only when these divergent races are brought together in the same landscape, places of worship, and educational settings that the law of kind after his kind is broken down. We believe that every race has the responsibility to preserve the original design of ethnic distinctions which the Creator God placed there, and that is why we practice ethnic separatism.

INTERVIEWER: In terms of demographics, what sort of people join the Church of Israel and what are their reasons for joining? Do you have any specific strategies for recruiting new members?

GAYMAN: We have no particular strategy for recruiting new members. We have no television programs, we have no radio programs, so our basic evangelistic presupposition is John 6:44: "No man can come unto me except the father which has sent me draw him, and I will raise him up to the last day." So we are totally dependent – dependent upon the power of the Holy Spirit to draw people to our religious persuasion. We really employ very minimal technological advances to achieve evangelical goals, and so the people that are drawn to this church are basically drawn by word of mouth. It's each one, teach one. The evangelists of this church are the people that come into contact with the theological menu of this church. They like what they find, and then they tell others. And the people that they talk to are generally, and always, people with an ethnic likeness – we're talking about Anglo-Saxon and kindred peoples who talk with Anglo-Saxon kindred peoples. We make no effort to evangelize other races. We make every effort to preach tolerance to the other races. We make every effort to advance a nonhostile position to the other races, to reemphasize that there has never been a single racial incident in the history of the church here. We have no problem getting along with the other races, and, in that sense, in the sense of our ethnic separatism, we're really no different than most of the synagogues that would be made up almost exclusively of Jews. They may have occasionally opened their doors to someone else, but it's kind of a rare thing. The Muslims are predominantly Arabs. So we don't think that there's anything really so extraordinarily different about our ethnic separatism. We feel that separatism is a part of nature. Nature itself segregates. The Amish have lived in segregation. The Mennonites live in segregation. A lot of the Jewish communities of the world live in segregation. There's segregation practiced all over the place. It's just unfortunate that if white people decide to do it, it suddenly becomes *extremely* bad.

INTERVIEWER: What is your opinion on the system of racial segregation that existed in the South under the Jim Crow era until the late 1960s?

GAYMAN: Well, first of all, I think if the Church of Israel had existed back in the earliest days of the formation of the southern United States, we would not have agreed to slavery in any form. We do not believe that slavery, as it existed in the South, has a Biblical foundation, so we would not have been in favor of any kind of slavery system. Indeed, we would have encouraged the southern plantation owners to have invited the multitudes of very needy and very poor people from Ireland and other places in the British Isles and Europe to have migrated to the United States to fill the role that had been placed upon the African people who were brought here as slaves. I think that we would, in general, have frowned upon the whole system that actually produced slavery and the Jim Crow laws that followed the basic Civil War–Reconstruction era of history.

But we do not feel that the post–Civil War, post–Reconstruction era history – from, let's say, 1865 to the present – has brought any great, significant blessings to the Negroid race. One merely has to drive through the ghettos of New York, Kansas City, St. Louis, Chicago, Cleveland, any one of those places, and one would have to greatly sympathize with the millions and millions of black people who find themselves living in such terrible conditions. We simply do not see where the great majority of the black people have been blessed by recent developments – let's say, for example, the termination of the separate but equal public school facilities. There's a strong indication that the blacks may have been better off with the pre-1954 separate but equal public school facilities than they are under full integration today because the test scores of both blacks and whites are not as good at the end of the twentieth century as they were at the midpoint in the twentieth century.

There is a failure in our public school system that came in with the termination of the separate but equal public school policies that had existed before 1954. So separate education may not have been harmful. But we certainly would want to emphasize that all the races should have equal access to the job markets of this country. We do no not support discrimination in job markets. But, by the same token, we do not believe that equal access to those jobs means that reverse discrimination should be in place against white people. We feel that what has happened now is that there has been a gradual evolution of the economic sector of this country such that it now practices reverse discrimination. In an effort to push affirmative action, Caucasians have been basically denied their fair stand in the workplace.

INTERVIEWER: So you would strongly oppose any government policy of affirmative action?

GAYMAN: Yes, we would oppose all forms of affirmative action as being discriminatory. In an effort to make things favorable for one race, we automatically discriminate against another one. We would be in favor of rescinding all affirmative action programs.

INTERVIEWER: How would you characterize the current state of race relations in the United States? What are the major problems dealing with race today?

GAYMAN: Well, it would seem that the major problem that we have in the racial programs of the twentieth century, moving into the twenty-first century, is that the whole concept of race in America has been one in which consistently the Caucasian – the majority race, the founding race – has been . . . gradually discriminated against as the government seeks to promote these minority races. The government has a pro-woman, pro-minority posturing in all of its economic philosophy, and we believe that that policy has become discriminatory against the Caucasian race in general.

Many of the institutions of American society, we believe, have come to share in this prejudice against whites. For instance, television and the movie industry simply are not neutral about white people. Instead, they use every opportunity to degrade and distort the culture, history, and self-worth of whites. The press and the camera are out to ridicule and intimidate any white American who would dare stand up in favor of his or her color, culture, or history. White people are finding that Hollywood and all major television networks are dedicated to elevating the stature of the nonwhite. The democratic one-person/one-vote formula for winning elections has endeared almost every American politician to favor Third World migration to America.

White people, moreover, have lost all control of their educational institutions. Public schools now cater to the growing, nonwhite majority on a colossal scale. Historical revisionism is removing every trace of white heroes from the pages of American textbooks. The culture and history of the whites is being stripped from the pages of history, while a new, fabricated history of America is being forced down our culturally impoverished school children. White people, too, face open discrimination in almost every college and university in America.

A generation of affirmative action programs have ushered in an era of white discrimination in the work place and elsewhere in American society. The disbursement of tax money, government entitlement, and a legion of other programs all favor the nonwhite majority in America. White people are becoming increasingly alienated from their government at every level. White people, it seems, are on their way to belonging nowhere! I might explain here, that we do not blame nonwhites for this situation. White people have no one to blame but themselves for their current plight. As I wrote in a recent article in our church magazine, "We have found the enemy, and he is us!"

INTERVIEWER: Evangelical Christians of a more mainstream cast would see your Biblical interpretation as highly strained, if not bizarre, and many would, I think, compare your ethnic claims about the ten lost tribes of Israel to Afro-centric writers who claim that Jesus and his disciples were all black. I think in both cases they would charge that you are motivated by some kind of ethnic self-congratulation or ethnic chauvinism. How would you respond to that kind of critique?

GAYMAN: I would respond to that critique by simply saying that until the turn of the twentieth century, until the year 1900, almost all of the philosophical and religious beliefs of the Church of Israel, as we practice them today, all the moral standards and the theology that the Church of Israel embraces today, were basically the moral standard of America. This was true, in fact, up to and including the year 1950. So our moral standards today are the moral standards that were in place throughout most of the history of America. Now with regard to our racial beliefs, we believe that the only difference between the way the Church of Israel understands and ministers to the racial issues of our day, the primary difference between the Church of Israel and mainstream Christianity, is that most of the white people – and certainly most of the white people in the rural sectors of the United States of America – believe in separation of the races in marriage and in worship, but they are reluctant to make that belief system public. The major difference that separates us from the vast majority of all Caucasians in America is that we do not hide our belief regarding racial separatism. Just look at America's white suburbs. White people have engaged in a white flight out of the inner cities and have congregated into the suburbs, and as the old suburbs fill up with a racial mix, we find a new white flight out of those suburbs into new all-white or nearly all-white areas. All of those people believe in their hearts what the Church of Israel practices, that is, the separation of the races.

And if I were to travel and visit the vast majority of all Anglo-Saxon religious services on a given Sunday morning in the rural villages and hamlets of this country, I would find ethnic separatism from beginning to end. Very seldom will I find a person of another race worshipping in these churches. I have personally visited any number of Protestant and Catholic churches on a Sunday morning in the villages and towns of southwest Missouri, and seldom do I find any person of another race other than Caucasian in those places of worship. In fact, I can go even to places where there is a distinctive nonwhite population and still can't find that racial mix in the churches. Now, the Church of Israel is out on the cutting edge of not hiding anything. We're trying to say what we want for ourselves, we want for all other races. We ask nothing for ourselves that we do not want for everyone else. Now some people would frown upon what we call good. We believe that racial, ethnic separatism by Biblical standards is what God ordained from the beginning of the creation, so we practice it. We have no problem with those who choose not to, but at the same time we feel that we are being deprived of *our* civil rights. We're being deprived of our First Amendment rights when the news media and even those not part of the news media want to point a discriminating finger at us because we have a right to practice our religious conscience just as everyone else does. Even though some people may call our belief system radically different from theirs, that's what America is all about. We're a nation of great religious and racial diversity. But we find it increasingly more and more difficult to practice *our* definition of ethnic separatism because in the very country of great religious, racial, and ethnic diversity, in the very country that promises such a democratic and liberal belief system to be practiced within its borders, there seems to be a growing unwillingness to allow Caucasian people to practice their religious differences and uniqueness.

INTERVIEWER: Well, that's the end of our formal questions. Is there anything else that you would like to tell us that we haven't discussed?

GAYMAN: Yes, there is. There is one other area that has not been touched upon that I think is extremely important.

INTERVIEWER: Please explain.

GAYMAN: The Church of Israel is not now, nor has it ever been, antigovernment, meaning that one of the cardinal principles of our belief system is that we are bounded by Scripture to offer daily prayers and supplication for all civil leaders and rulers, regardless of their political affiliation, that we are scripturally bound to be peaceful, law-abiding citizens. We endeavor to maintain close communion and relationships with all government levels of authority. We have open communion with all law-enforcement agencies in the county, state, and federal government. The church here makes no effort whatsoever to teach animosity or hostility toward civil government. We believe very strongly that good citizenship consists of obeying every ordinance of government at every level until government forbids us from doing something that God commands or commands us to do something that God forbids. So we are a very law-abiding church – and again, that, we believe, clearly separates us from what we'll call some of the radical behavior that has been exhibited in certain religious circles of this country in recent years. The people of the Church of Israel are hard-working, honest, law-abiding people, and they believe in complying with all ordinances of government. They have responded to the call of their country in every war of this century. They have paid their taxes. They comply with all state driving licensing requirements and registration. So we are not part of any so-called civil rebellion movement. The Church of Israel has never belonged to Operation Rescue. We have never picketed abortion clinics. We have never been part of any civil disobedience group in this country. In the entire history of the church, we have an impeccably clean record insofar as law enforcement is concerned.

There is also one final thing I would like to say by way of summary about the scriptural basis of our core beliefs. A mere cursory examination of the corpus of the Bible should quickly dispel any idea that the lost ten tribes of Israel are not a vital and imperative subject. From cover to cover, the Bible is a book about Israel and God's plan for them. At the end of the Bible, in the apocalyptic Book of Revelation, the people known as Israel remain its focus and grand theme of God's Kingdom on earth. From Genesis 12:1 through the remainder of the entire Old Testament Canon of Scripture, the Bible is written to, for, and about the twelve tribes of Israel. The New Testament itself is a confirmation of what God promised the twelve tribes of Israel in the pages of the Old Testament Scripture. The Bible is the family history of the Israelite people. Every author of the Divine Word of God, Genesis to Revelation, was an Israelite. The Law, Prophets, Psalms, History, Gospels, and Epistles are all about the twelve tribes of Israel.

The final eschatological view of Bible history targets the fulfillment of God's promise to Israel. The redemption of Israel was the first priority of Jesus Christ coming as the anointed Messiah. The return of Jesus Christ (the Greater David) to rule from the Throne of David, the future resurrection of the dead in Christ, the gathering of the twelve tribes onto the land of their fathers, and the subsequent restoration of the Kingdom of God are the central focus of eschatological history. Without a knowledge of who and where the lost ten tribes of Israel are, the subject of Bible prophecy is without a solution. When the international, multiracial church replaces physical Israel as those central to God's plan, the very heart and soul for which the Bible is written is lost. We believe that when the Bible is interpreted apart from the unconditional covenants made with the House of Israel, it is a false theology crafted by the mind of man apart from God and Scripture.

INTERVIEWER: Thank you.

PART IV

WHITE SUPREMACY AND NEO-NAZISM

8

Matthew Hale

Matthew Hale, who goes by the title of pontifex maximus of the World Church of the Creator, first came to national attention in late 1998 when a panel of the Illinois Bar Association's Committee on Character and Fitness voted to deny him a license to practice law in the state of Illinois. This action was taken by the panel despite the fact that Hale had received a law degree from the Southern Illinois University School of Law at Carbondale, had recently passed the Illinois Bar Exam, and had complied with most of the requirements usually associated with character and fitness. In denying Hale a license, the panel based its judgment on Hale's active advocacy of overtly racist and anti-Semitic views. "While Matthew Hale has not yet threatened to exterminate anyone," the panel wrote, "history tells us that extermination is not far behind when government power is held by persons of his racial views." Those seeking to deny Hale a law license became even more determined after Benjamin Smith, a friend of Hale's and former member of Hale's church, went on a racially motivated shooting rampage in July of 1999 that before it ended with Smith's suicide left nine people wounded and two dead. In the following interview, Hale explains some of the basic principles of the Creativity religion that are propagated by his organization. Creativity, Hale explains, is a religion that is not based on supernatural revelation as Christianity is but draws its inspiration from the eternal laws of nature itself. These laws, he says, can be determined through close observation and reasoning. Nature, says Hale, decrees that every species of living things must look out for its own kind or it will be eliminated in the struggle for existence. Conflict, competition, and struggle are ineradicable elements of human nature and life itself, Hale argues, and white people must wake up to the fact that the other races of the globe constitute their biological rivals and potential enemies. If white people don't

The interview of Matthew Hale on November 12, 1999, by Russell K. Nieli is printed with kind permission of the interviewee.

wake up to this hard fact of life, Hale claims, they will be dispossessed and eliminated by the nonwhite races from the territories they inhabit. Blacks and other nonwhite races, says Hale, claim to support equality, but in reality what they truly want is racial supremacy and racial privilege. Jews, too, Hale claims, seek domination and supremacy over other races, and it is because of this fact that they have universally provoked such hostility wherever they are encountered. Hale explains how his organization has been particularly successful in recent years in attracting young people and especially young college students. Although whites from many different demographic groups join his organization, the World Church of the Creator, Hale says, is particularly interested in appealing to "the best and the brightest" among the youth in order to form a racially conscious white leadership class for the future.

Interview with Matthew Hale

INTERVIEWER: You are the head of a white, racially based group called the World Church of the Creator. Could you explain the nature of this organization? We would like to know particularly what is its underlying philosophy, what are its goals, and what activities does it engage in to further these goals?

HALE: The World Church of the Creator is a prowhite, racial-religious organization which is dedicated to the survival, expansion, and advancement of the white race and the white race alone. We are not a Christian organization. Instead of basing our views, our ideology, our religion, on Christianity, we base it on the eternal laws of nature as revealed through science, logic, history, and commonsense. We believe that in a natural state each and every species looks out for its own kind. Each and every subspecies looks out for its own kind. This being the case, it follows that we as white people should look out for our own kind. We should not care about the other races – they can do what they will – but we should focus on our own. The World Church of the Creator in this respect is certainly a very radical organization, and we do not pay homage to Christianity or to the Constitution or even to America. We are an international organization in scope – we consider all white people, wherever they may be, to be our brothers and sisters.

The techniques we use for getting our message out for winning white people over include many things, such as the Internet. We have a large Internet presence, we have a website that is a general website, we have a website that's specifically for kids, we have a website specifically for teenagers, and we also have a website specifically for women. Also, the World Church of the Creator passes out a lot of literature around the country and around the world. I can safely say that at any moment in time there's a member somewhere passing out our literature. Another technique we use is using the mass media, or at least utilizing the media to reach our people. I do a lot of interviews myself. I'm on a lot of programs and I reach a lot of people that way. Also, we distribute our books, namely *The White Man's Bible* and *Nature's Eternal Religion* – those are the two main books of Creativity. We pass them out around the world, and people read of our religion that way, too. We really are the only religiously based racist organization that is not based on the Christian religion or based on an idea of a deity. I think that's one of the reasons why our church has experienced such growth these past few years. We have no real rivals, we have no real competitors. When people reject believe in Jewish Christianity or the idea of the supernatural, they naturally gravitate our way if they have racial beliefs.

INTERVIEWER: How would you characterize your membership in terms of its demographic characteristics? What sorts of people join your organization and what are their reasons for joining?

HALE: We particularly attract the youth. In fact, I can say that probably half of our members are younger than twenty-five years old – we are a very youth-based organization. As far as income is concerned, I would say that we attract a lot of people of higher financial status. We are considered by many in the white racial movement to be the elite. For example, we do not welcome people who are irresponsible, we do not welcome people who are prone to criminal activity. We encourage responsibility and knowledge in each and every member. Unlike other organizations, we have our own books, we expect our members to read these books, and to know them thoroughly, and certainly we have attracted a lot of college students. College students have been really the bulwark, I guess you could say, of our church, the vanguard of our church. I myself graduated from two colleges, so this is the type of person that we attract.

INTERVIEWER: Could you elaborate further on your strategies for recruiting college students. Do you actively recruit on college campuses? Do you have auxiliary college organizations? What sort of campuses do you go to? What sort of college students join the World Church of the Creator?

HALE: We attract college students mainly through the Internet. Many college students use the Internet, and they are attracted to us by that manner. We also have members that go on college campuses and distribute literature, members who will also simply talk to people on campuses. They will see a group of people, and they will walk up and say, "Hey, have you heard about Creativity?" And a lot of people have not heard of the name per se. They have heard of me, or perhaps even heard of the church, but when asked have you ever heard of Creativity, a lot of people still say no to that. And then the member will explain what our Creativity religion is all about. We generally reach out to the private colleges and universities, and indeed to the best schools, though not through any intentional design or disregard of the other schools. We find, however, that people at many of the best private schools . . . at schools such as yours, Princeton or Harvard or Yale or Northwestern . . . people at these schools seem to be a little more open-minded and able to grasp more thoroughly where we are coming from. This cause that we represent is by no means a cause for dummies or a cause for those who accept things blindly. We have a lot of evidence behind our views. We have a lot of history, a lot of facts, statistics and everything else to buttress our claims. Another reason why we go after the private schools is because we want to have the elite. We are striving for that, focusing on winning the best and the brightest of the young generation.

INTERVIEWER: What is the attraction of your organization to college students, and especially to "the best and the brightest"?

HALE: Well, oftentimes, they are very idealistic students, very idealistic people, and certainly they are not going to accept anything that they are told without some reason behind it. We find that college students in general are more receptive to new ideas, they're more open-minded, and they are willing to get involved in our church with less worry about peer pressure or what their parents may think. In a sense, it is an act of rebellion, and even students at Princeton or other prestigious universities still have the capacity to rebel.

INTERVIEWER: What exactly are they rebelling against?

HALE: Well, they're rebelling against the prevalent notions of our time, notions such as that all men are created equal, notions such as that we're simply all Americans, or that we all should just get along, things of this nature. These are really notions that no one ever tries to provide any proof of, or any evidence for. And when we question these assumptions and beliefs, it is often young bright college students who are most receptive to what we say.

INTERVIEWER: To what extent have government policies and programs in your view contributed to racial tensions in America? What government policies or programs would you like to see changed and which ones retained?

HALE: That is a very good question because oftentimes it is assumed, for example, that we are strongly opposed to affirmative action. Well, in a sense we are, and in a sense we aren't, because affirmative action brings more people into our cause. Blackness America pageants bring more people into our cause. Black Entertainment Television brings more people into our cause. The more that the other races obtain, the more white people feel that it's being obtained at their own expense. Take college scholarships . . . I've had so many students say, "Hey, wait a minute! Why can't I get a scholarship because I'm white . . . there are blacks that get them because they're black?" And, of course, my answer to that is, well, the blacks don't want equality. The other races don't really want equality – they talk about equality, but it's really just a smokescreen. What the blacks and other races really want is supremacy, and when I tell that to people who feel aggrieved, they are very interested and they take notice.

INTERVIEWER: And those who take notice are often college students?

HALE: Oh, yes! College students are the most upset about the governmental policies.

INTERVIEWER: How about your general views on race in America. Could you describe your vision for the racial future of America?

HALE: The Creativity religion holds, first and foremost, that multiculturalism breeds racial violence. We believe that as long as people are forced together in one big melting pot, as it is called, there will be all kinds of violence and tension. The only way to end the violence and the tension between the races is to have separation. Separation between the races – that's the first point. Second of all, we believe that as the white race becomes more of a minority in this country, this country will lose all stability and essentially it will become like a Yugoslavia. Hopefully there will not be the violence that we have seen in what was once Yugoslavia, but, in any case, there will be ethnic enclaves forming in America, and the country will essentially break apart. We believe this development is inevitable and should not be resisted or opposed.

INTERVIEWER: So you don't think that multiracial or multiethnic cultures can survive in any kind of peaceful manner? You don't believe that people of different races and ethnic groups can get together and form a multiracial, multiethnic society that's cohesive and stable?

HALE: No, not ultimately, and the history of the world has proven that. No multicultural society has ever survived for any length of time. Egypt, which had many cultures and races at one time, eventually fell. India fell. Certainly Central and South America, which are multicultural, have been stagnant as far as economic development is concerned. They have all kinds of natural resources, but they are way behind the more advanced nations economically. So yes, we do believe that no multicultural society can endure in peace and prosperity for very long.

INTERVIEWER: In America, we celebrate annually the birthday of Dr. Martin Luther King, Jr. What is your opinion of Dr. King and the black-led civil rights movement of the fifties and sixties in which he played so prominent a role? Is America a better place or a worse place because of that movement and the philosophy of nonviolent multiracialism that he supported?

HALE: Well, I think America is far worse than it was before he began his crusade. Certainly, it's worse for white people, and quite frankly, that's the only people we care about. It might be better for blacks in some ways, or it might not. I mean, I talk with blacks who feel that separation is good for their race, too, that they don't want to have schools that are integrated because black and white students have different needs. King's philosophy may have been a philosophy of nonviolence, but he used force to intimidate people. He used at least shows of force constantly. When you have people marching by the thousands down your street, if you're a homeowner, you feel a little intimidation. So he wasn't above using that kind of pressure, just as Jesse Jackson uses it today. As far as Martin Luther King himself, I think that one of the worst things that happened was that he was assassinated. I think that if he had not been assassinated, his statements and views concerning the Vietnam War would have led to his downfall and perhaps even the movement that he represented. I would much rather see a Malcolm X–type solution to the racial problem than a Martin Luther King–type solution.

INTERVIEWER: By a Malcolm X–type solution to the racial problem, do you mean a separatist solution rather than an integrationist one?

HALE: Yes, that's right.

INTERVIEWER: Many people would characterize your organization as a racist group or hate group. How do you respond to such characterizations?

HALE: Well, we certainly are racists, and we accept that label just fine, as a badge of honor. We believe that a racist is a person who loves his own race – and that is the epitome of good, as far as we're concerned. Now, as far as being a hate group, that's certainly some people's characterization of us, but we are no more of a hate group than the NAACP is a hate group or than the Republican and Democratic Parties are hate groups. What I'm getting at is that everybody basically hates, everybody has things that they love and things that they hate, and it's only natural to hate what is happening in this country to our white race.

INTERVIEWER: But can't people love one thing without hating something else? If a man loves his wife and children, it doesn't necessarily mean that he hates his neighbor's wife and children.

HALE: I'm glad you said that because that is an analogy I use quite often. If you love your wife, you would hate the rapist of your wife, and that's what's happening to white people today. The white race is being raped, pillaged around the world, and we therefore hate those who are engaging in this. We even hate those white people who are consciously doing this.

INTERVIEWER: But is it inevitable that people of differing races or ethnic groups are going to rape and pillage each other? Can't people respect each other's rights?

HALE: Well, I think we have to understand that war and struggle is a fundamental part of the human psyche, just as much as it is in animals, so we have to determine where and to whom we are going to divert our energy and our hostility. We submit that the other races are biological rivals, they are biological enemies. A shark is not our natural enemy, as long as we're not swimming in the water. A giraffe is not our natural enemy. A bear isn't even our natural enemy! But the other races are capable of dispossessing us of our territories, of our lives, and therefore they are our natural enemies.

INTERVIEWER: Could you explain how you came to your current views on race? Did you have any early experiences with white supremacist literature or white supremacist organizations?

HALE: I really didn't have any early experiences of this type. I wasn't raised in a racist household either – and racist is the term I would use here rather than white supremacist. White supremacy is not a label that I accept for the simple reason that it connotes an idea of holding others down or reigning over them, which we do not want. We want separatism. I guess you could say the first racial piece of literature I ever read was Adolf Hitler's *Mein Kampf*. I read it when I was twelve years old. I was interested in history and wanted to read about the man who had made such a mark on the Second World War. But I came to the views I hold today primarily by observation of the world around us. By observing the world, we can discover the laws that guide all life. Human beings, just because they may be more intelligent than other animals, or because they can wear fancy clothes, or drive nice automobiles, cannot divorce themselves from the laws of nature. If we follow the laws of nature and take care of our own kind, then our race will be secure, we'll be prosperous. But if we ignore the laws of nature, then our race will become extinct, and that's, unfortunately, what's happening today. The whole purpose of the World Church of the Creator is to straighten out the white man's thinking so that he can become the elite, as he was really destined by nature to be.

INTERVIEWER: You think that the white race is destined by nature to be an elite race?

HALE: Genetically, yes. I mean genetically we *are* the elite. If you look at any encyclopedia, 99.99 percent of the contributions listed within it are from white people. I don't think this is because whites wrote the history books or the encyclopedias. I think it's because white people have a genetic edge – intellectually anyway – over the other races.

INTERVIEWER: What was the late Benjamin Smith's relationship to your organization? What attracted him to the World Church of the Creator, and do you have any explanation for his descent into murder and mayhem?

HALE: Yes, Ben Smith joined the church . . . I think he was a member from May of 1998 until April of 1999. He joined the church, to my knowledge, because he believed in the racial struggle, and he did not believe in Christianity – that was something that attracted him, that we were not a Christian group. We feel that, as much as we respect our white racist Christian comrades, that it's simply a contradiction to believe in racism and believe in Christianity. The two do not go together. Ben Smith – it's hard to say exactly why he did what he did. I have surmised all along that it was because of the denial of my law license. I will never know probably the full reason why he did commit crimes. I'm concerned, though, that as white people feel more dispossessed, feel that they are without recourse, that violence will increase.

INTERVIEWER: Where do Asians and Asian Americans fit into your racial scheme of things? If high achievement in areas like science, technology, and economic organization confer upon white people some claim to preeminence or elite status, it would seem that Asians in recent years have an even greater claim. Asian Americans, for instance, have shown very high levels of academic achievement. They have higher scores than whites on many standardized tests. They are vastly overrepresented in such intellectually demanding fields as physics, engineering, and computer science, and they have much lower rates of many social pathologies, including out-of-wedlock births, crime, and welfare dependency. How would you assess the position of Asians in America and the world?

HALE: Well, I think that the Asians are a good example of hard work. They work very hard; there's no question about that. But I think if white people worked as hard, they would surpass the Asians without question. After all, most of the creative technological achievements of the world have come from our white race. The Asians are good at copying and expanding upon things that white people already created. If we were to go back 150 years, back before Commodore Matthew Perry sailed into Tokyo Bay, we would see that the Asian culture was extremely stagnant. There were almost no technological achievements there at all. So what we have seen is the Asians looking towards the Western white world and choosing to adopt a white culture, to adopt white technology and a white mode of achievement. And they have taken this white technology and run with it – there's no question about that. But if white people spend a little less attention drinking or partying, I think that they would be able to replicate, indeed surpass, what the Asians have been able to accomplish recently.

INTERVIEWER: And what about the Jews? Jews are white, and they have also made outstanding achievements in all sorts of intellectual fields. They are disproportionately represented among Nobel Prize winners, among prize winners in many sciences, and they are certainly vastly overrepresented in many academic fields. What are your attitudes on this? Why do you display such hostility towards Jews in your published literature?

HALE: Well, to your first question, I would answer very similarly to the situation with the Asians. The Jews work hard, and it's very much part of their religion to work hard. They work very late into the night, they see work as really being important for their ethic. As far as contributions, though, creatively the Jews once again are not a very creative people. I mean, they're good at some things. They are certainly found in large numbers in the science field, in medicine, and in law, but generally speaking they have not been a creative people. For example, if you were to look back into the classical period of time in Palestine, the Jews created almost nothing. There's a museum of ancient art, I believe it is at the University of Cairo, and when you walk by the exhibits, you find things from the Phoenicians, you find things from the Sumerians, etc. But when it comes to the Jews, you find nothing because the Jews did not create anything at that time.

As far as why we have antipathy towards the Jews, it is because of their religion largely. Their religion is extremely hostile to those not Jewish. The Talmud is replete with hostility towards non-Jews, calling us cattle, saying that we're created by God so that Jews would not have to be served by beasts. The Talmud condones the rape of three-year-old girls, for that matter. It says that a girl three years of age may be violated. This is a religion that has some serious problems with it, and it's because of their religion and because of their attitude towards non-Jews that Jews have been persecuted for so many years. They have not been hated for no reason at all, and that's one of the things that I thought about when I was eleven to twelve years old. "Why are the Jews hated so much?," I asked. I mean, why would people seek to exterminate them? Was it for no reason? And I found in my readings that the Jews have made themselves disliked, and that's the reason.

INTERVIEWER: Don't you think that jealousy is a big factor here since the Jews have been so economically successful?

HALE: That's just a cop-out. That's the Jews trying to erect a smokescreen over what they've been doing. I'm not jealous of Jews. I don't care how much money a Jew may have. I feel I have more character and more going for me than they do, and I think it's really another kick in the teeth from the Jews for them to say that the reason why anti-Semitism exists is because we're jealous of them. The reason why anti-Semitism exists is because Semitism exists, because of Jews trying to manipulate and control the finances, the government, the laws of the people. They have done this from time immemorial. They were kicked out of Egypt because of it. Of course, the Jewish version is that they wanted to go and the Egyptians wouldn't let them go, but that's not the Egyptian version of events. They caused problems in Germany and caused the rise of Adolf Hitler. They were a problem in ancient Rome; they've been a problem throughout Europe. And it was not because of jealousy.

INTERVIEWER: If your opposition to Jews has much to do with their religion, what is your attitude toward secularized Jews, particularly secularized Jews who don't identify with the Jewish religion, as many of them don't?

HALE: Well, it's certainly true that there have been some Jews that have taken that position, but what we call upon them to do is to repudiate publicly Judaism. And if they are unwilling to do this, we still consider them our enemies.

INTERVIEWER: You would consider them your friends if they would repudiate their religion? Let's say a Jew even married a Gentile and didn't identify with Judaism as a religion at all, that sort of person would be welcomed into your organization?

HALE: Well, I'm not saying that. I don't think it's an either/or. There is somewhat of a middle ground here, and what we're saying is that while we do not want the Jews as part of our white culture, part of the society that we are struggling to create, if Jews will repudiate the Talmud, repudiate the Jewish aim to control the world – the Jews have incredible control in the world – then we would not consider ourselves as much an enemy of those particular Jews as those who do not repudiate the Talmud.

INTERVIEWER: In the past, white racist and white supremacy groups have generally drawn both their leaders and followers from the ranks of the least educated and poorest of whites. You obviously don't fit this mold, and your organization doesn't seem to either. You are college educated and have now a law degree. Do you think racist and white supremacist thinking is gaining ground among the better educated middle classes? Is this a trend in the future that you see developing?

HALE: Yes, I do. I see the white middle and upper classes certainly seeing the handwriting on the wall, seeing that a multiethnic society is a mistake, that integration has not been a pie in the sky, that it has not been wonderful for white people. On the contrary, it has harmed us immensely – harmed our public schools and made our neighborhoods unsafe. I have talked to many white people who feel this way. In fact, in the nine and a half years that I have been a public activist, I've seen a great change for the better for our cause. I've seen a lot more people express interest, and I've seen the intellectual quality increase dramatically of those who express interest. Obviously, we have a lot of poor members, a number of them anyway, and we have members who are not very educated. We welcome all white brothers and sisters to our cause, but at the same time we realize that in order for our movement to succeed, we have to win the best, and that's what we are trying to do.

INTERVIEWER: Well, that's the end of the formal questions. Is there anything else that you would like to tell us that you haven't so far, either about your own views or about your organization?

HALE: Well, one thing I would like to say is that for me, the most powerful book I have ever read is *Nature's Eternal Religion*. This is a book available through our organization. I first read it in 1990. To all white men and women I offer this challenge: read this book cover to cover and see if you don't come to the same conclusions that we have. Read this book and judge for yourself the soundness of the principles we espouse. I invite anyone to do this.

INTERVIEWER: Thank you.

9

Lisa Turner

All of the people interviewed in the present volume up to this point have been males. This is no accident or selection bias, but reflects the simple fact that the most activist members of white protest, white nationalist, and white supremacy organizations have almost always been males, and despite important changes in recent years, the gender composition of such groups seems to have changed very little over time. Lisa Turner, the Women's Information Coordinator of the World Church of the Creator,* is clearly an exception to the general rule here. Ms. Turner is a dedicated and zealous adherent to the philosophy of Creativity described in the previous interview with Matthew Hale, and her views on white superiority and white supremacy are among the most extreme of any expressed by those profiled in this volume. Turner's views are of particular interest to students of the racist right in America as a prime illustration of how many of the ideas and ideals that motivated the Nazi regime in Germany during the 1930s can continue to exert a powerful fascination and attraction for certain disaffected Americans today. White humanity, Turner claims, represents the highest of nature's creations, and whites have both a right and a moral imperative to preserve themselves and to expand their influence around the globe. Drawing much of her inspiration from Adolf Hitler's *Mein Kampf* and from the classics of the Creativity religion, Turner adopts a Social Darwinian model of interethnic relations where stark choices are seen to exist for the white race between either domination or being dominated by others. Nonwhite people are effectively engaged in a state of war with whites, Turner contends, and the whites must learn how to assert themselves and how to win in this undeclared racial war. Turner dismisses nonwhite races

The interview of Lisa Turner on April 28, 2000, by Russell K. Nieli is printed with kind permission of the interviewee.
*More than two years after this interview was given Ms Turner informed the editors that, as of October 2001, she is no longer associated with the WCOTC.

contemptuously as "mud people" and sees these mud people as inferior to whites in their morality, their self-control, their law-abidingness, and their general capacity to create higher civilizations. As she explains in the following interview, she first started to think seriously about racial issues while living in California in a once white neighborhood that experienced an influx of illegal Mexican aliens. Her first personal experience with nonwhites led to a rapid transformation in her previous liberal views regarding race. Turner displays an even greater contempt for Jews than for nonwhites and claims that Jews have acquired an extraordinary degree of power in America and around the world and have used this power primarily for their own ethnic self-aggrandizement and parasitic ends. Wherever Jews migrate, Turner says, they destroy the civilization of their host peoples. The news media and the government in the United States, she believes, are dominated by Jewish influences, as well as by the interests of the "mud races." The Christian religion is also singled out by Turner as a destructive force in America that exacerbates its racial problems. By Christianity's pacifistic call to turn the other cheek and to love one's enemies, and by its principle of universal love to be extended to peoples of all races, the Christian religion, Turner charges, weakens the will of the white race to combat the onslaught of its racial enemies and to develop a proper racial consciousness. The Christian religion is seen by Turner as a series of fairy tales, but unlike the fairy tales of childhood, ones that have a lasting and pernicious effect in undermining white racial solidarity, white assertiveness, and white pride.

Interview with Lisa Turner

INTERVIEWER: You are the Women's Information Coordinator for the World Church of the Creator, an organization that espouses an atheistic and white supremacist religious philosophy known as Creativity. Could you explain what the Creativity religion is and how you first became interested in it?

TURNER: Well, basically Creativity states that the white race is nature's finest creation, that through looking at the lessons of history, through commonsense, and through our own powers of observation, we can see that the white race has accomplished the most, has invented the most, has been indeed the most productive and creative race on the face of the earth. The members of the World Church of the Creator are called Creators, because we believe that we have indeed brought forth the highest and finest creations.

My involvement with the World Church of the Creator came about through a contact with Rev. Matt Hale over the Internet. Prior to that time, I had not been a formal member of any prowhite organization, and when I came into contact with him, he introduced me to the racial religion of Creativity. The Creativity religion seemed to express more

clearly than anything else I had ever encountered before exactly what
I felt the white race should be following and should be adhering to –
which is getting away from the Jewish pollution of our race through
the Biblical fantasies of Christianity, which we believe have led our race
to destruction. The central tenets of Creativity really appealed to me.
I had never been very interested in being part of what they call the
Christian Identity movement, so I started reading the primary books of
Creativity, such as *Nature's Eternal Religion*, which is one of the main
books that was written by our founder, Ben Klassen, and I was very
impressed by what he had to say. I therefore joined the church formally
in March of 1998. Besides Klassen's work, I was extremely impressed
by Rev. Hale in terms of his leadership ability. I felt he was a very charis-
matic, magnetic person who really had the capacity to lead our people
to victory and make a real impact in today's prowhite scene.

INTERVIEWER: Your initial contact with Matt Hale, you say, came through
the Internet?

TURNER: Yes, it did.

INTERVIEWER: What was your interest previously in prowhite groups and
white supremacy groups?

TURNER: Well, I had been part of the movement for about ten years or so,
even though I had not joined a particular organization. I had had loose
affiliations with a variety of organizations very early on – the David
Duke organization, which was the NAAWP, the National Association
for the Advancement for White People. That was quite early on, maybe
the mid-eighties. I was also very interested in Tom Metzger's group,
WAR, White Aryan Resistance. Again, I didn't formally join these
organizations but I read their newsletters, their literature. I contributed
money and that type of thing, and, of course, I became very interested
in Adolf Hitler. I read *Mein Kampf*, which was really a turning point
in my life. When I read *Mein Kampf*, it completely opened my eyes to
the reality that the white race had been lied to about a number of things,
such as the Holocaust, and for a period of time I referred to myself as
a National Socialist. So I went through, shall we say, some evolutions,
some political evolutions before reaching Creativity. It was a period of
about ten years of personal education and growth before I reached the
point that I am at now.

INTERVIEWER: What impressed you about Hitler's *Mein Kampf*? Many
Americans reading that book today would find it both vulgar and
repulsive, but obviously you reacted to it very differently.

TURNER: Yes. I found it to be a very cogent, truthful, and straightforward
discussion of what Hitler was seeing in his society. I was obviously not
repulsed by what he was saying. It rang a bell with me. I looked around
at my own era, and I felt that the Jews, just as in his time, were running
our media – newspapers, television. I identified with everything he had

to say. I felt that it was not written in an hysterical style. I felt it was a very controlled and highly intelligent – indeed, brilliant – piece of political testimony. So for several years I certainly considered myself a devotee of Adolf Hitler.

INTERVIEWER: Did you come from a white supremacist family?

TURNER: No, I did not. I would say that my family in my growing up years would probably be termed liberal – they voted for the Kennedys and that type of thing. Certainly I was never exposed to any racial views growing up. However, there was a turning point within my family in which we found ourselves living in a neighborhood across the street from a house that was being used as an illegal alien safe house. At any given time, there might be ten or fifteen Mexican males in residence at this house, and this was when we were living in southern California. For the first time, we realized that there was an immigration problem in this country. Prior to that time, we had no idea within our family that there was any kind of out-of-control immigration situation, and while my parents did not become, shall we say, radical prowhite activists, they did become involved in immigration reform. I went on and became, I guess in their view, more of a radical activist. But they, too, understood and recognized that there were problems in this country that needed to be recognized and faced, so I guess what you could say is that when we actually had a real-life experience in our own face, in our own family, our family did acquire a certain racial consciousness. So even though I was not raised that way, we did sort of evolve that way later on.

INTERVIEWER: So you and your family all in one way or another became less liberal on the issue of race?

TURNER: Absolutely. It showed us that we had kind of been living in a dream world. There had been a certain hypocrisy. We had not really had much dealings with nonwhites in our neighborhood, in our own community, and as soon as we did, it was almost like an overnight change with our family. There was quite a radical change, and it occurred very rapidly.

INTERVIEWER: So these first dealings with nonwhites were not positive?

TURNER: No, they absolutely weren't. The house across the street turned our middle-class neighborhood almost overnight into a slum. We also found out that the home was owned by Jewish factory owners who were using it as a safe house, where they would bring Mexican aliens to work in their factories. They urinated on the lawn, they threw trash in the streets, the women threw dirty diapers in the street, so, no, it was obviously not a positive experience.

INTERVIEWER: What are your responsibilities as Women's Information Coordinator for the World Church of the Creator? What sort of things do you do on behalf of your church?

TURNER: One of my primary activities is to make use of the Internet whenever I can as a way of networking among like-minded individuals to
recruit women to the church. I also have a monthly newsletter called
The Women's Frontier, which is a very powerful medium to get the
word out. We have around 700 to 800 subscribers now to the newsletter. The other most powerful device that I have is the Women's Frontier website, which was established, I guess, around a couple of months
after I joined the church. I started one of the most advanced women's
websites on the entire Internet, and I make heavy use of it as a recruiting device. So those are the two primary ways that I recruit and put
the message out of Creativity.

INTERVIEWER: You are something of an anomaly among members of
groups that espouse white supremacy insofar as you are a woman. Most
other white supremacy organizations seem to attract mainly males and
hold traditionalist views regarding the subordinate role of women.
Could you explain your views regarding the role of women both in
society at large and in the white supremacy movement? Does the World
Church of the Creator affirm a male leadership principle or is it acceptable for women to assume leadership positions in the group?

TURNER: Well, first of all, I should explain that we view men and women
as being different. We believe that nature's laws should be adhered to
in that men have their own special role to play, and so do women. We
believe that women's most important role is as wives and mothers to
white children. We certainly, though, encourage women to take on leadership roles. Obviously, I am in a leadership position within the church.
We encourage women to be all that they can be and do all that they
can do, and we do not seek to limit women. However, this is not a feminist stance. We still recognize that women are going to look at things
differently than men do and take a different approach. Women tend to
be more nurturing. We tend to be more diplomatic in some cases, and
we celebrate the difference between men and women.

But, we do encourage women to assume leadership roles in the
church. Women within the church can become reverends, just as the
men can, if they take the ministerial exam. Women can lead their own
church meetings and head up Women's Frontier chapters. So we don't
seek to segregate women from men in the church, and we give a woman
who has leadership qualities every bit as much respect as we would a
man who shows such qualities. This is different, I suppose, from some
of the other prowhite organizations. We believe those other organizations are reactionary in their views in attempting to hold women back
and to restrict their roles. We don't think that's going to bring victory
to our cause. It's really counterproductive for white women to stand
on the sidelines and not fight side by side with their male comrades,

and we feel very strongly that if other groups and organizations are going to continue to take that tack, that they will never see the kind of victory that they want. It's like trying to run a race with one leg. You can't do it. Women must be included as partners – not as equals in the sense that we are the same as men, but partners in this struggle – and more and more people in our cause are beginning to understand that and recognize that. I receive probably hundreds of e-mails, mainly from men, who say that they are thrilled to see that women are finally having a voice, that they are coming forward. I would say that 80 percent of subscribers on my mailing list are men. So we have had overwhelming support from men, and we are very proud of the accomplishments that we've made.

INTERVIEWER: Is it conceivable that a woman would ever become head of the World Church of the Creator?

TURNER: The head position, the pontifex maximus, in the World Church of the Creator is reserved to a man but only for one reason, and that is that we view the top role of leadership as being analogous to the head of the family, which we do see as the male's role. So we see the pontifex as being like the head of our church family, and we do restrict that to a male. However, the next position in line to pontifex, which is hasta primus, and is analogous to a vice president, is open to a woman.

INTERVIEWER: What sort of women join the World Church of the Creator? What demographic groups do you recruit from and what reasons do women have for joining your organization?

TURNER: Well, we have women from all walks of life who join the church. But I would say that they are still predominantly in the eighteen- to twenty-five-year-old age group. We would like to broaden our horizons, but there are women from all ages who join the church, and I don't want to perpetuate a stereotype and say that it's just young women or women from a certain economic background who join, because that's not true. I myself have a college degree, a B.A., and we have many college-educated women coming into the church. We are trying to do a lot more college outreach on the campuses, so we do hope to expand the demographics in that way. But I'm not going to say that it's any one particular age group or economic background that joins. I receive mail from all kinds of women – young women, middle-aged women, working class women, women who have professional degrees – so it's really all over the map.

INTERVIEWER: How successful have you been with the college outreach?

TURNER: Well, we feel that we have been moderately successful. We distribute a great deal of literature on the campuses. I have heard from a girl who is a student at Cornell, I have heard from other students from other Ivy League campuses. One of the problems in that arena, of course, is that there is still a sense of stigma and persecution. Some women are a little bit afraid about coming out and being openly prowhite, so it may be a little difficult for us right now to completely gauge just how many supporters we have on the campuses. We feel that there is a great deal of support; it's just a question of convincing them that what they have to do is stand up for our race and not be intimidated by campus administrators. This is something that we are going to do a lot more targeting of in the next year.

INTERVIEWER: You have said in your literature that your organization seeks to operate within the law and does not advocate violence. Yet a main tenet of the Creativity religion seems to be a call to a racial holy war against dark-skinned people and Jews. This racial holy war under the acronym RAHOWA is proclaimed repeatedly on your website and in your literature. How do you reconcile these two conflicting positions – nonviolence and a call to war?

TURNER: Well, for me personally the word RAHOWA does not mean a literal killing or harming of anyone. It is a symbolic battle cry. For instance, when we speak of a war on drugs, does that mean a literal battle in the streets? Not necessarily. It's a motivating cry. It's also a symbolic understanding that unless we as whites turn this situation around, there will be a racial war – not one that we instigate, but one that is going to come about because we are going to have to defend ourselves against nonwhite violence directed against us. The Women's Frontier and the church are very clear on this subject as far as violence is concerned. We do not advocate going out and killing anyone; we simply say that if there is not a raising of the consciousness of our white people, there will be violence. There will be a racial war. This is something that we want to avoid. We do not want to see this happen, and so I view my position more as being a warning voice, a warning cry, to prevent a racial war in this country.

INTERVIEWER: Who would start this war?

TURNER: We believe that the nonwhite peoples have *already* started the war against the white race. The daily violence against our people, women being raped, murdered – these are things that occur everyday and aren't even being reported in the press. We are under siege on a daily basis, so we consider that a racial war has already been declared against us by the nonwhites. The Mexicans, the mestizos, who declare their intention to take back the Southwest, "We will retake your territory," "We are going to kill you, whitey" – we've had years and years of this kind of rhetoric from the nonwhites. There has clearly been a war against us for many years. So it's already in progress.

INTERVIEWER: To what extent have government policies, in your view, contributed to racial tensions in America? Which government policies would you like to see changed and which retained?

TURNER: Number one would be the total lack of enforcement of the immigration laws. I remember when the Simpson–Mazzoli bill several years ago was first introduced. When I and my family were still trying to approach the immigration problem from that standpoint, we still had confidence in our government that they would through some legal means restrict the overwhelming invasion of illegal aliens, particularly from Mexico. Well, that didn't happen. So certainly the immigration policies have been insane in this country, particularly for the last twenty years. Affirmative action is the other major area that is totally insane; it's ridiculous. It should never have been instituted, so I would say those are the two main areas that I would totally throw out.

As far as my position on the government, of what I would want to see retained in this government – I would want to see *nothing* retained about this government. As far as I am concerned, this government is the Jewish occupational government. I would dismantle it, destroy it, and reform it into a prowhite government based on nature's racial laws. So there's nothing I would retain of this government.

INTERVIEWER: Let's talk more about the Jews. In many of the articles that you have written and in the interviews that you have previously given, you display an intense, visceral, and many would say a truly paranoid and pathological hatred of Jews around the world. Why do you hate the Jews so much?

TURNER: Well, in studying the history of the world, I've seen the way the Jews have in every place they've ever gone, invaded the territory. They have stolen, they have polluted, they have destroyed the civilizations of every place they have ever been. Many people, you know, feel that anti-Jewish feelings started with Hitler. But Hitler was a Johnny-come-lately in this area. The Jews destroyed Rome; they destroyed Egypt. If you read history, if you read the Talmud – the Talmud declares openly that the Gentiles are slaves, that they are inferior, that they are to be destroyed. One cannot look at the Jewish race and see anything but a polluter of civilization, and it certainly is not paranoid to acknowledge this. This view is based on historical fact and the actual reality of what their influence is wherever they go. To every nation they occupy, they bring economic enslavement and civilizational destruction.

INTERVIEWER: If Jews are such polluters, if they are such parasitic people, such uncreative people as you contend, why is it that 25 percent of all Americans who have received the Nobel Prize in science have been Jews, and an even higher percentage – perhaps a third or more – of the Americans who have won the Nobel Prize in economics have been Jews – this despite the fact that Jews comprise less than 3 percent of the American population? Jews it would seem have been enormously creative and have contributed greatly to America culture and civilization.

TURNER: Well, you have to understand that the Jews have a very closed and tight system in which the awards that they award one another, whether it's the Nobel Prize or the Oscars, or whatever it is, is an outgrowth of this ethnic loyalty to one another, their closed ranks. This is no proof of their creativity. It's just more proof that they give each other these phony awards to heighten their own social prestige. As far as the Nobel Prize, that's meaningless to me. These prizes, these awards, these are Jewish inventions that have nothing to do with the white Aryan race, and, you know, they can cite awards forever, and it doesn't change anything. It's just part of their own internal mechanism for keeping their own social prestige and power alive. That's all it is. To me, it's meaningless.

INTERVIEWER: But the Nobel science prizes are conferred by the Swedish Academy of Sciences. There aren't many Jews in Sweden. How do you explain this?

TURNER: Well, there is Jewish power in all countries, regardless of the numbers of Jews. It doesn't matter what country you are talking about. Jews have a hold on power in Sweden, too. As a matter of fact, there is a lot of Jewish power in Sweden, and the Swedes are rising up more and more everyday to protest the kind of Jewish stranglehold that there is in their country. So it's not necessarily a matter of numbers; it's a matter of economic power, of money power, and other types of influence, such as influence over the media. A low percentage of Jews doesn't prove anything.

INTERVIEWER: Unlike most other white nationalist and white supremacist organizations, your organization has taken an extremely hostile stance towards belief in God, and particularly towards the Christian religion. On your Women's Frontier website, you describe the Christian religion as "Christ Insanity." Why are you so hostile to religion in general and to Christianity in particular?

TURNER: Well, first of all we feel that the Bible itself, the chief religious book of Christianity, is a fairy tale, a myth. No one knows who wrote it. Indeed, there is no proof that Jesus even existed, and so right there we can't accept the veracity of anything in this book, which we, of course, consider to be of Jewish origins. The philosophy behind Christianity is utterly poisonous – Turn the other cheek, Love your enemy – these kinds of ideas have put a guilt trip on the white race. The idea of heaven and hell – if you're good, you'll go to heaven, you'll go there if you do what you're supposed to do and play the game the right way and be a good Christian, etc. – our white race has allowed this pernicious philosophy to turn over our entire culture, our territory, our land to nonwhite invaders.

The biggest enemies we have out there are the Christian churches, and on the Women's Frontier website I specifically mention, for instance, the Trinity Broadcasting Network, TBN, which is the largest broadcasting network in the entire world. They are responsible for bringing in refugees and nonwhite aliens hand over fist, and they don't care what it does to our white communities and to our nation. It is Christianity that underlies this notion that we must help the downtrodden regardless of what they are doing to us. They can kill, rape, and maim the whites. But I don't see the Christians out there saying, "Hey, we've got to start protecting the white race." No, it's always someone else's country, someone else's race that they want to protect. It's the Christian philosophy that allows them to justify these types of actions, and so that is why we utterly reject this philosophy as alien to the white culture and the white people.

INTERVIEWER: Is it the egalitarian aspect of Christianity which incenses you the most?

TURNER: Well, certainly that, and this idea that you should love everybody no matter what color they are, no matter what they do to you, that you shouldn't stand up for yourself, that you should give everything away. It's just a completely insane philosophy that taken to its ultimate conclusion would result in the destruction of a people. It makes no sense and so much of it is completely unprovable. We must challenge Christian ministers and preachers about what they mean by heaven and hell – it's a fairy tale.

The World Church of the Creator believes in what we can see around us, what we can prove through our logic, through our commonsense, what we can see in terms of the way nature really works. And for us Christianity is a pie-in-the-sky fairy tale that cannot be proven and cannot be supported by facts and reason. So if you ask me what incenses me most about it is this idea that regardless of who you are, what you are, what color you are, everybody's the same. Christianity says, "Love everybody, no matter what." That type of philosophy is totally poisonous to our people.

INTERVIEWER: The black and brown people of the world are repeatedly referred to in your writings by the epithet "mud people." Why do you use such a venomous term, and why do you want to deny to nonwhites the same presumed dignity and respect that you would routinely accord to white people?

TURNER: Well, we just feel that the word "mud race" sums them up as far as the way they look, the way they behave. We don't accord our inferiors and our enemies the same respect that we do to our own people. That may sound reprehensible to you, but that's the way we view it. We don't ask anything from them. We don't ask them to respect us. We ask of them to live their own lives in their own culture, and in their own nations, and let us do the same. But they refuse to do that. They want to invade our world, our culture. They want to rape our women, kill our people, commit crimes in our neighborhoods. So we don't accord such criminals, such fiends our respect. So, yes, we do use words that they don't happen to like, but we don't make any apology for that. We call it the way we see it. If these lower races would stay out of our nations and out of our culture, that is what would please us, that is what we want. But why won't they do that? They want to benefit from our achievements because they have none of their own, or they are envious and jealous of what we are. So when we stand up for ourselves and we use terms that may sound impolite to people, well, we don't apologize for using terms like mud race, we don't apologize for using the term "nigger." We feel that it's our free speech right to call them niggers. If they act like niggers and behave like animals and apes in our society, then they are not going to be called very nice words, and, that's the way we see it.

INTERVIEWER: Where do East Asian people like Japanese, Chinese, and Koreans fit into your worldview? Are they "mud people"?

TURNER: Yes, they are. Anyone who is not of the white race, who does not have white European ancestry, is considered to be part of the lower races, and we certainly put them in the same category.

INTERVIEWER: Asians in America seem to be outperforming whites in all sorts of academic endeavors. Why do you classify them as a race inferior to the whites?

TURNER: Well, we hear a lot about how East Asians outperform white people. But we have no proof of that. We keep hearing these remarks about how brilliant Asians are, but I can tell you from personal experience that this is not true. I was in college, and I was in a lot of classes with a lot of Asians. I didn't see them performing any better than anyone else in the class. As a matter of fact, most of them were inarticulate and had very little to say in the classroom. This is what I have seen firsthand rather than this hype about how brilliant Asians are. They were the least articulate, the least able to communicate – I could out-communicate any Asian in any class that I was ever in, so how am I supposed to reach the conclusion that they're so brilliant? From some kind of studies that have been released from somewhere? I didn't see that from firsthand experience.

Asians are nothing but imitators, copycats. That's what they're good at. It's monkey-see, monkey-do. And if it weren't for white people, Asians would still be living in huts somewhere. They have copied what white Europeans have done, and that's the only reason that Asians have any kind of a civilization at all. Like I just said, from firsthand experience, I was not impressed by Asians that I saw in my college classrooms.

INTERVIEWER: The Asian superiority is usually seen in the mathematical and technical sciences rather than in verbal skills.

TURNER: Well, is that the only lynchpin of superiority – that they can do math? I am not even saying that what you are telling me is inaccurate. But I don't know where some of these so-called studies come from about Asian mathematical superiority. White people are responsible for most of the inventions of the world. If Asians are so great and so brilliant, why haven't they been responsible for as much of the intellectual achievement and inventions that the white European race has been responsible for? If you match it up achievement-to-achievement, the white race outstrips all other races on all levels, no matter whether you are talking about math, technology, art, music, whatever.

INTERVIEWER: What is your ultimate vision for the racial future of America?

TURNER: What I would like to see is white people living anywhere and everywhere in the world that they would like to live, and to achieve and advance and expand. I do not believe that white people should be assigned some little white area of the U.S., like the Pacific Northwest. I believe we should go and be and live and do anywhere we want to, just like the nonwhites have declared that they intend to do. We should expand and advance any way we want to, anywhere we want to. No one is putting the skids on Mexicans or Asians in terms of their invasion and spreading out all over the globe, and there's no reason that white people should so restrict themselves. If, in the course of that, violence occurs, it won't be because we instigated it. It will be because, again, the nonwhites are going to fight white expansion. They do not want us to expand; they want genocide against us. They want to keep us restricted to some small little area, and we refuse to do that. If violence comes about because of our own rights to expand – whether it's population-wise or with territory or however we wish to live or wherever we want to live – then that will be what will happen.

I suppose your question is, "Do I want to see an all-white world?" Well, that would be a very beautiful world in my opinion, yes. An all-white world would be a paradise on earth because I know that it would be the highest expression of the human creative potential that I could possibly imagine. There would be far less crime – I'm not saying that there would be no crime – but we would have a much cleaner, more crime-free, more beautiful world. Again, I'm not saying that our goal is to go out and commit violence against anyone or to wage war against anyone, but in the course of asserting our rights, our expansionist rights, such as the other races are doing, if violence comes about, then we're ready for it, and we will face it at that time.

INTERVIEWER: Aren't you saying though that whites have a right to unlimited expansion, but nonwhite groups do not?

TURNER: What we are saying is we have a right to expand. They can do what they want to do.

INTERVIEWER: Do they have a right to expand?

TURNER: Well, they are doing it. What I'm saying is we're going to pursue our goals, and if that comes into conflict with whatever they are doing, then there may be a racial war, yes. We are sick and tired of being invaded wholesale by nonwhites who think they have a right to break our immigration laws and do whatever they want to do with impunity. And so, therefore, we think, "Well, if they're going to be permitted to – to break our immigration laws, then we feel like we have the same right to expand into all the world that they're living in." There's nobody stopping the Asians, there's nobody stopping the blacks, nobody is stopping the Mexicans from breaking our immigration laws, our laws of entry. So we feel that, "Well, yes, given this, we have the right to expand anywhere in the world that we want to, and we will do so."

INTERVIEWER: That ends our formal questions. Is there anything else that you would like to tell us that you haven't already talked about, or something that you said but would like to expand upon or reinforce?

TURNER: Yes, I would like to explain again that the most important mission or goal that I have is the recruitment of women, and that is where I spend most of my time, and most of my energies. My overall goal, my mission in life, is to bring more racial awareness to white women because I believe that white women have been used as pawns by the Jewish power structure in this country. They have been co-opted into believing that they somehow have something in common with quote "the minorities." I wrote an essay that was probably considered the most popular piece that I have written – it was reprinted in *Spearhead* magazine for the British Nationalist Party – which was called "The Co-optation of White Women." I made clear in that essay how women have been brainwashed and propagandized into being foot soldiers in the war against the white male. I wrote the essay because I got sick and tired every time I picked up a newspaper and women would be included in this laundry list of individuals . . . illegal aliens, racial minorities, dysfunctional people, blah-blah, and women – as if women were part of this army of nonwhites and dysfunctionals against the white male. I wanted to make clear that women are not part of that. We white women are sick and tired of being included with quote "the minorities." We're not a minority. We're here to fight beside our white male comrades with pride and dignity, and I'm very, very proud of a lot of the breakthroughs that the Women's Frontier has made. It is one of the few women's organizations in the entire prowhite movement. You may have heard of Women for Aryan Unity in Canada, but we're still part of only a handful of women's organizations. I hope to see the prowhite movement grow and expand, and we will continue to spearhead this growth. I'm very excited to be a part of what I consider history in the making, and I want women to finally recognize just how they have been used. More and more white women are waking up and understanding that they have been used by the Jew power structure, and to bring about this continued awareness is my primary goal and mission within the church.

INTERVIEWER: Thank you.

10

William Pierce

William Pierce, the head of the neo-Nazi-oriented National Alliance, differs from the other people who have been profiled in this anthology both in the international reach of his organization and in the successful use that he has made of imaginative novels to propagate his radical racial views. *The Turner Diaries*, Pierce's novel of domestic race war first published in 1978, depicts a triumphal racial pogrom by whites in America that is touched off by the detonation of a powerful fertilizer bomb to blow up a federal building. *The Turner Diaries* quickly attained something of a cult status among militia groups and members of the racist right in America and became the inspiration for a number of acts of domestic terrorism, the most deadly of which was the destruction of an Oklahoma City federal building by Timothy McVeigh in 1995 in which 168 people were killed. *The Turner Diaries* has been translated into German and French, and the high regard in which it is held among the racist right in Europe has resulted in Pierce acquiring an unusually high reputation for an American in European nationalist and neo-fascist circles. Pierce's second novel, *Hunter*, depicts the assassination of interracial couples and Jews, and while not as popular as *The Turner Diaries*, has had considerable impact among white nationalist forces, particularly in Britain. Pierce is certainly an unlikely candidate to head a neo-Nazi organization. A graduate of the California Institute of Technology who holds a Ph.D. degree in physics from the University of Colorado, Pierce worked for a number of years as a college teacher at Oregon State University and was a senior research scientist for a Connecticut aerospace firm. At an early date, however, he became interested in neo-Nazi and white supremacist activities, and for a time in the late 1960s was an active member of George Lincoln Rockwell's American Nazi Party. In 1974 Pierce founded the National Alliance, which has served as the main vehicle for the

The interview of William Pierce on December 27, 1999, by Russell K. Nieli is printed with kind permission of the interviewee.

dissemination of his white supremacist views. Besides its use of race novels, the National Alliance has made effective use of an Internet website, a short wave radio broadcast, and a newsletter, the *National Vanguard*, to spread its message of racial separatism and white supremacy. In the following interview Pierce makes plain his view that nonwhites and Jews constitute an alien racial presence in America, and that America's strength is largely contingent on its ability to maintain a white racial ascendancy. While not advocating violence as a means of obtaining the racial purification and racial separatism that his group hopes to bring about, Pierce is clear that his opposition to violent methods is based on pragmatic and tactical considerations under present circumstances rather than to moral opposition to racial violence as such. Pierce also makes plain his deep, abiding admiration for Adolf Hitler, who he once described as "the greatest man of our era."

Interview with William Pierce

INTERVIEWER: Could you explain the nature of the organization that you represent, the National Alliance. We would like to know particularly how it got started, what is its underlying philosophy, what are its goals, and what activities does it engage in to further these goals?

PIERCE: That's a big question. Back in the 1960s, I was teaching at a university in the Pacific Northwest, and I became concerned about some social trends that I thought might have some profound implications for American society, and I began reading and thinking and talking to people about these trends. In particular, one of these trends was the opposition to the Vietnam War. More than that, it was the pro-Vietcong sentiment openly expressed at a time when the government was drafting young men and sending them to Vietnam, where they were being killed at a substantial rate by the North Vietnamese and the Vietcong. And yet the Vietcong and the North Vietnamese had a fairly large and growing cheering section on the American university campuses. The other social trend that I could see in the sixties that I was concerned about was the civil rights revolution, really the coming out of the closet of the civil rights revolution – the attempt to bring about social integration between the races on a large scale in America.

As I thought about these two things and what their long-range implications would be, I began writing, and eventually I realized that because the questions I was asking were politically incorrect, and many of the answers that I was giving to my questions were politically incorrect, I couldn't reach the public with my thoughts on these matters without building an infrastructure. That is, I couldn't just go to a New York publisher and have him publish and distribute my materials. I couldn't be invited to television programs and express myself at length. I had to build up an infrastructure for publication and distribution of the things that I thought were important to reach the public with. So, I had to build an organization, and that is how the National Alliance first came about, as an organization for the dissemination of ideas, first in the form of printed materials and then in the form of other media. And that's what it remains today, although it has ramified itself substantially and is in fact working in many media. Today, we have weekly radio broadcasts, which are carried around the world by shortwave radio or are broadcast locally in a number of metropolitan areas in the United States. We have a very large and active Internet presence with a great number of our materials available in several languages on websites. We are using music as a medium for reaching people. We recently purchased two record companies, the largest resistance music company in the United States and the largest in Europe, and increasingly we'll be active with these record companies using resistance music to carry our message. And, we will be using other media as they become available to us – video, for example. Did I answer your question completely?

INTERVIEWER: Well, certainly you answered part of it. We would like to know, too, what is the underlying philosophy of your organization? What is the mission of the National Alliance?

PIERCE: I suppose I could answer that question in parts. Our task now is to reach the public – and I'm really talking about the European section of the public, the European-American white section of the public – our task is to reach the public with ideas and facts on a continuing basis in such a way that we will provoke them to put down their funny papers, pay attention to what's happening in the world, think – that is, the ones who are capable of thinking. We're not under any illusions that everybody is capable of thinking independently about these things. But the ones who are capable of independent thought, we ought to provoke them into accepting responsibility for what's going on, to think about where we are headed as a society, as a race, what's happening to our civilization, and to take a position. And, of course, we would like for them to take our position, or some position close to ours. So that's our mission in the short range. It's an educational mission, it's a propaganda mission. It's a wakeup mission. In the long range, of course, we would like to get people moving in unison, get them moving toward certain goals. For example, to eliminate some of the destructive influences in our society, for example, to regain control of the mass media of news and entertainment, to change the type of government that we have in this country, so that it's unthinkable that someone like Bill Clinton could be in the top position of power in the country. So we do have these long-range goals for restructuring our society, restructuring our world, but all of our activities, in fact, are directed toward our short-term mission, which is just to reach, communicate with, and move as many people as possible.

INTERVIEWER: How would you characterize the current state of race relations in America? What are the major problems dealing with race, as you see it?

PIERCE: The major problem that we have in America is that we don't have a racially homogeneous society. Of course, we have had from the beginning different racial groups in North America. We had the American Indians. But we've pretty well solved that problem by moving the Indians onto reservations. We had black slaves, but even after the Civil War, the blacks had their own separate society for the most part, and the Europeans had their separate society. After the Second World War, with the move to break down the social barriers between the races and forcibly integrate them, we began developing the sort of situation that we have today, with large-scale racial intermarriage and with the loss of a sense of racial consciousness and racial identity on the part of our people, on the part of the European people. There is increasing alienation in other words, especially among young people, and all sorts of self-destructive activities. Suicide rates are up, divorce rates are way up, the birthrate for our people is way below the replacement level. We have a very serious long-term situation developing that must be addressed now or we are headed toward extinction.

INTERVIEWER: What form would this extinction take?

PIERCE: I'm using the word in its ordinary sense, that is, that there won't be, if the processes that are visible today continue for another six or seven generations, for all practical purposes there will not be a European population in America. We're headed toward a mestizo population, really. By mestizo, I mean that in the broadest term, a mongrel population as the intermarriage rate continues to increase, as our birthrate stays down, as the immigration from the Third World continues on a massive scale. We will pretty soon become a very small minority in our own country, and then disappear altogether.

INTERVIEWER: Many sociologists and anthropologists believe that intermarriage is a good thing for interethnic and interracial relationships.

PIERCE: Well, yeah, of course, that depends on your values. I realize that there are many people who are pushing for this, who think it will be wonderful when we no longer have a white majority in America, but those are not my values.

INTERVIEWER: What's wrong, in your view, with interracial marriage?

PIERCE: Interracial marriage results in the destruction of both of the races involved, or all of the races involved. It destroys racial homogeneity and results in a cosmopolitan, rootless, alienated society.

INTERVIEWER: And you think that racially homogeneous societies are more deeply rooted and are able to conduct their affairs better than mixed race societies?

PIERCE: Well, I *know* they are. I mean historically that's what we have had in Europe – racially homogenous societies. And we brought that situation to North America with us, and for the first couple of hundred years here in North America we maintained that situation. But we're losing it now. We've been conditioned, we've been brainwashed, we've been propagandized by the mass media primarily, but also by the schools, by the churches, by the government to be – how do you say it? – to be antiracist, to be ashamed of wanting to associate with, wanting to work with, live with, breed with our own kind. And this is a very destructive thing which will destroy the basis of our civilization, which will destroy our culture, and eventually will destroy our race.

INTERVIEWER: Do you think human beings have a natural desire to be with their own kind?

PIERCE: Yes! I certainly do. Certainly, the way it's been historically, not only among human beings, not even just among mammals, but among all of the higher species, they have tended to segregate themselves among their own kind.

INTERVIEWER: In one of your two novels, the novel *Hunter*, you depict the killing of interracial couples in a manner that many people have seen as endorsing those kinds of actions. Was it intended as such an endorsement?

PIERCE: Well, if I thought that that could be done on a significant scale today, why then, sure, I would endorse it. But I don't believe so, and actually that wasn't the purpose of the novel. *Hunter*, just like my earlier novel, *The Turner Diaries*, is not about the action in the book. The action is just something to carry the reader along. It's the ideas expressed by the characters which are important in both novels, and I, of course, chose *types* of action which would be attractive or interesting to the type of people I thought I would be able to most easily reach and influence with my ideas. I wasn't trying to reach liberals and make liberals understand that they were sick and needed to cure themselves. I was trying to reach people who were basically racially conscious, but simply hadn't really put it all together, didn't have a coherent way of thinking yet, hadn't figured out yet the answers to a lot of things. I wanted to clarify the thinking of people who already were more or less amenable to my message.

INTERVIEWER: So it was a novel written for racially conscious white Europeans?

PIERCE: Yes. That's sort of redundant, racially conscious white Europeans.

INTERVIEWER: But you say that you would advocate the killing of interracial couples if it were able to achieve the desired end?

PIERCE: Yes, if it were to accomplish something. But I've never advocated violence or, in fact, any kind of illegal activity because I don't think it would be productive. I think it would be counterproductive at this time.

INTERVIEWER: But you have no moral opposition to such action?

PIERCE: No. I mean when you're faced with the choice between allowing your race to die or causing individual members of your race to die who have transgressed against certain basic and very important principles, the choice is easy.

INTERVIEWER: How would you characterize the membership of the National Alliance? What sort of people join your organization and what are their reasons for joining?

PIERCE: We have a minimum membership age of 18. We have members from that age all the way up into their nineties. I would say the average age of our members is probably early twenties. We're probably about 80 percent male, 20 percent female in our membership. So far as socioeconomic categorization is concerned, that's a little more difficult for me. I have not really made very careful studies or comparisons of our membership with the general population. Being an academic myself, I was interested in the success we had had at recruiting among other academics, university faculty people. And the last survey I did, which was about a year ago, we had seven times the percentage of academics in our membership as exist in the general population.

INTERVIEWER: So you get a lot of well-educated people, not just people at the lower end of the socioeconomic scale?

PIERCE: Well, we get people spread over the whole spectrum. We have university professors, writers, and artists. We have engineers and teachers, and we have unemployed truck drivers.

INTERVIEWER: Is there any regional division? Do you get more people from the South than from the North, or from the Midwest than from the Far West?

PIERCE: Actually, I was a little surprised about this issue myself. I'm not surprised anymore, but I think the initial assumption of people who haven't thought about it much is to believe that the South is sort of a reservoir of racial feeling in this country and therefore that we would exhibit special growth in the South. That has not been so. We do have a pretty good concentration of membership in a few Southern states – North Carolina, for example, Texas (I suppose Texas would be considered a Southern state), Florida – but the South has some negative things from our point of view, too. It's the Bible Belt for one thing, and we're not a religious organization. We've never taken a pro-Christian viewpoint, and, in fact, I've been very critical of many of the activities of the mainline Christian churches. Furthermore, among the educated Southerners, there's sort of a defensiveness, a sort of bending over backwards to show that they have abjured their Southern heritage. So I would say the South is not a better area than the rest of the country. Texas has been good, North Carolina has been good, Florida has been good, Pennsylvania has been good, it is good throughout the Midwest. Ohio is certainly one of our better states, if not our best state; we have a number of members out in California, in the Pacific Northwest – they're pretty well scattered all around. If I got out a map and studied it, I might see some trends, but I haven't focused primarily on looking on that sort of thing. I've focused primarily on formulating and propagating our message.

INTERVIEWER: Do you have any specific strategies for recruiting new members? For instance, do you recruit on college campuses or over the Internet? And what is the major attraction of your organization to new members?

PIERCE: Well, let me start with the second part of that question first. There are millions of Americans who are concerned about the way our society is going. They are not just fat and happy because the economy is good. They're concerned about the decline in moral values, about the breakdown of our society, the atomization of our society. They're concerned about things like they've seen in Washington during the Clinton Administration. They're concerned about the immigration catastrophe in this country. And they're looking for answers. They really are open to answers. And we provide answers. And I think that has a great appeal to people, that we are able to help them fit a lot of things they're concerned about into a picture where it all makes sense to them. And I think that's generally it, that we are able to provide reasonable answers to people that have questions and concerns.

Now to the first half of your question. We have mostly recruited in a nonorganizational context, which is to say, we have depended upon individuals to examine the message that we present to them and make an independent and individual decision to participate with us in our effort. The Internet is probably the single largest source of new recruits for us. People hear about our Internet site or they run into us on the Internet. They read our materials, they listen to some of my weekly broadcasts, which are on the Internet, and then they make the decision to join. But we also distribute a lot of printed materials, and some people receive these printed materials, read them, perhaps order books from us, think about, and then send in an application form. We do some recruiting in an organizational context. I encourage our members, for example, to bring groups of friends to their home or perhaps on a Saturday evening or some convenient weekend time, and then play for them one of my broadcasts, which are accessible at any time through the Internet. Our members are encouraged to have people in their living room, to play a broadcast, to serve cookies and coffee and discuss the ideas that are presented in the broadcast to get people to realize that there is an organization out there which addresses the issues that they're concerned with and has answers.

INTERVIEWER: Is your weekly broadcast over shortwave radio?

PIERCE: The broadcasts go out over shortwave radio to the whole world. They also go out to a number of metropolitan areas through local AM and FM stations, but the main listenership these days, I believe, is by way of the Internet. All of the broadcasts are available in audio form as well as in text form at our website. When I started, I had only printed materials, I had a tabloid newspaper. I was in Washington, D.C., at the time, and I had news racks all over downtown District of Columbia – out in front of the government office buildings and the major hotels and so on. I had seventy news racks. So this tabloid was the main outreach that I had when I started. And then I began a book list, a book service where I had a little catalogue of books, which has grown very substantially now. About six years ago, I began radio broadcasts, and then about that time or maybe a year or two after that we got on the Internet.

INTERVIEWER: Could you describe your vision for the future of America? What would the racial landscape of America look like if your vision for the future were to be realized?

PIERCE: Well, you know, that's a very hypothetical question. You are asking me to describe institutions that might be developed in the future of America, and I think that's something that will require a lot of careful thought and planning as to how we want to change institutions based on the lessons we have learned from the present disaster. So about all I can really say is that we want to have a homogeneous America – a racially homogeneous America consisting of just Europeans. We want to have healthier ways of raising children. I think that the nuclear family, which evolved over many, many generations among our people, way back in precivilized times, I think that we pretty well need that to be healthy again. I think we need to reestablish a family setting for raising children and do away with day-care centers. We need to get mothers back in the home with their principal responsibility to nurture their children and maintain a good wholesome home environment. I think we need to do more than that, though. I think that we have become a soft and indisciplined sort of population. I think we need to have a child development program where we are very much concerned about producing the best possible adults that we can. We need to think about child raising the way the ancient Greeks did; we need a new *paideia* really for America, for a white America, which takes into consideration all of the influences on the development of people from infancy on and tries to make them into the best and the strongest, the most effective adults that we can.

INTERVIEWER: Where do Jews fit in to your picture of a racially homogeneous America?

PIERCE: They don't.

INTERVIEWER: But Jews are white Europeans . . .

PIERCE: No, no. [laughing]

INTERVIEWER: Why don't Jews fit into your view of a European-American society?

PIERCE: Well, Jews have lived in Europe, of course, for a while. They've had Jewish colonies in Europe since Roman times, but Jews really don't think of themselves as primarily European. They identify with the Middle East, at least the ones who are really Jewish, the ones that have a strong Jewish consciousness do. Their whole approach to life, their whole way of relating to the people around them is entirely different from our own. They've played a very destructive role in our society and in virtually every society in which they have been a minority. We can't afford to fall into this trap again. They have to go their own way.

INTERVIEWER: How can you say that when you look at the great number of Jewish contributions to American culture? Take your own field, theoretical physics – from Einstein to the most recent Nobel laureates, Jews have been conspicuously prominent in the development of modern physics. They've been prominent in the economics field, they've made great contributions to all sorts of academic disciplines.

PIERCE: Well, I think we're just going to have to learn to do these things for ourselves. We did it pretty well for ourselves in the past. The nineteenth century really saw an explosion of new thought in science, and in all of the centuries before that, essentially it was *our* effort, our activity which gave us our understanding of the universe. It's really only been in this century that you've seen any substantial Jewish involvement in that. I think that we're going to have to go back to doing it ourselves.

INTERVIEWER: What about Asians? Where do they fit into your racial picture in America?

PIERCE: They don't, they don't fit in at all. They're going to have to do it for *them*selves, too.

INTERVIEWER: Why, though, if you are so concerned about the moral decline of America, would you want to exclude Asians? If one looks at the Asian Americans, they have much lower rates of out-of-wedlock births, of drug addiction, of crime and delinquency, of school failure, and of most other social pathologies that plague white, black, and brown America.

PIERCE: Well, I mean I admire them for that. That's wonderful for *them.* But we have to solve our own problems.

INTERVIEWER: So you believe that Asians belong in Asia. Is that basically your view?

PIERCE: Yes, that's my view.

INTERVIEWER: To what extent have government policies in the United States contributed to racial tensions?

PIERCE: Well, prior to the Civil War, government policy was that blacks and whites were quite different, that they had different roles in society, that it was undesirable that they mix, and even for many years after the Civil War segregation was supported at all levels by statute. It's only really been since the Second World War that there has been a concerted effort to change that, in fact to reverse the role of the government. Whereas the government once supported the keeping apart of the races, now the government has taken the role of forcing the races together whether they like it or not – in neighborhoods, in workplaces, in the schools – and that is destructive of the things that I believe are most important.

INTERVIEWER: So you oppose antidiscrimination law – the Civil Rights Act of 1964, for instance?

PIERCE: All of the civil rights legislation that we've had in this country since the Second World War has been destructive. I'm opposed to all of it.

INTERVIEWER: How about your views on immigration policy?

PIERCE: Well, I'm all in favor of immigration as long as it is restricted to Europeans, and the immigration policy was good for building up this country with kindred stocks back before the war, but the new, the current immigration – I mean, we really don't have an immigration policy now. The government has laws which it deliberately doesn't enforce. The government could cut off illegal immigration virtually overnight if it wanted to, but it doesn't want to because a lot of people in Washington and in New York and elsewhere in this country want a cosmopolitan, racially mixed society, and they see immigration as a way to achieve this. They just don't have the guts to scrap all of our immigration laws, so they simply don't enforce them.

INTERVIEWER: What do you think about current affirmative action policies in regard to race?

PIERCE: Well, I mean affirmative action is one of these issues that wouldn't exist in a healthy society.

INTERVIEWER: A healthy society in your view wouldn't even have a problem of a multiplicity of races and ethnicities?

PIERCE: That's correct. The problem wouldn't exist in the first place. Affirmative action is something that has come about only because we have a racially mixed society and the blacks can't compete on an equal basis. They can't do it by themselves, so they get an extra boost from the government.

INTERVIEWER: Why do you think the blacks can't compete by themselves?
PIERCE: They're biologically different.

INTERVIEWER: And this biological difference, you think, is the major source of their difficulties here?
PIERCE: Yes, that's the major source of their difficulties.

INTERVIEWER: You don't think it's due to discrimination or poverty or a legacy of past injustice?
PIERCE: Well, all of these things are sort of interrelated. If blacks, say, had naturally the same sort of abilities that whites have and they were able to innovate and create and succeed the way whites have historically, I think a lot of the discrimination would have disappeared. That is, a lot of the discrimination is based on a recognition of the biological differences, and of course the economic differences grow out of the fact that blacks simply aren't able to compete. All these things are interrelated, and affect one another, but I think the basic, the fundamental thing here is that blacks and whites are different. They evolved in different parts of the world under different conditions; their equipment for surviving is different.

INTERVIEWER: And because of this difference, you don't think they will ever be able to live together harmoniously with whites?
PIERCE: No, I don't think so. I think that as long as you have these inequalities that are based on race, there will be resentments, there will be hostility, there will be conflict. The government tries to overcome that by giving the blacks an artificial boost. Without government intervention – for example, the government going out and deliberately building up the concentration of blacks in the universities – there would be few blacks in the best institutions. The universities that I went to, for example, there was no law against blacks enrolling as students, but virtually none did until the government began requiring that schools enroll them – and beat the bushes, pull 'em out of the trees, recruit them, build up the numbers . . . you know, meet certain racial quotas. That's the effort on the part of the government to artificially create equality where it does not exist naturally.

INTERVIEWER: Timothy McVeigh, who placed the truck bomb outside the Oklahoma City Federal Building in 1995, which ultimately killed 168 people, had excerpts from your novel *The Turner Diaries* in his possession when he was arrested. He was also said to have called the

National Alliance on a number of occasions before the bombing. What was McVeigh's relationship to your organization and what is your organization's position regarding terrorist acts of this kind?

PIERCE: First, just a clarification of the facts. It's my understanding that he had a Xerox copy of a passage from one page of *The Turner Diaries* along with some Xerox copies – quotes I think – from John Stuart Mill and some other people, in an envelope in his car at the time that he was arrested. I also understand that he distributed copies of my book to people at gun shows or urged his friends to read the book. He did not actually have any other contact with the Alliance other than distributing our book. There have been rumors to the effect that he called the National Alliance, talked with people in the National Alliance. To my knowledge, he never did. We have telephone answering devices around the country – about thirty of them at this time – all over the country, where one can dial a local number, hear a four-minute recorded message introducing the caller to the National Alliance and giving him an address where he can write for further information. We had such an answering service, a message service, in, I think it was Fort Mojave, Arizona. And when McVeigh was in Kingman, Arizona, several calls – four or five calls – over about a three-day period were made from a motel in Kingman, Arizona (using a calling card that had been purchased by Timothy McVeigh) to our telephone message service in Fort Mojave. So far as I'm aware, those are the only telephonic contacts that McVeigh or people using his calling card have had with the National Alliance. The fact that somebody using his card called four or five times to our message service suggests to me that it wasn't just he who was calling, that he perhaps had some other people with him, and called the message, and then had his friends call the message one at a time and listen to it. But I don't really know. I've never spoken with him. No one that I know has ever spoken with him, and so these rumors about telephone calls to the National Alliance are simply erroneous.

INTERVIEWER: In *The Turner Diaries*, though, you depict the bombing of an FBI building, and apparently McVeigh was inspired by *The Turner Diaries*. Mustn't you assume at least some responsibility for his actions?

PIERCE: Well, to say that Timothy McVeigh was inspired by *The Turner Diaries* you really need to clarify your meaning there. I believe he probably was inspired by the ideas in the book. I don't believe that my depiction of the destruction of the J. Edgar Hoover building in New York City had anything to do with the destruction of the Murrah building in Oklahoma City, however. It's clear what Timothy McVeigh's motivation for the bombing in Oklahoma City was, and that was the Clinton Administration's massacre of all those women and children in the church in Waco, Texas, two years earlier. McVeigh had traveled to Waco during that siege. He had expressed his outrage to other spectators down there. He later expressed his outrage to his friends and others back in other parts of the country where he was, and it's clear that he intended to send a message to the government that that sort of behavior, that outrageous behavior of besieging that church and burning all those people to death, simply would not be tolerated, that some people would strike back at the government. And that was his message to the court when he was sentenced to death, when he quoted something from Justice Brandeis to the effect that the government is the teacher of the people and the government teaches its citizens by its example. McVeigh's meaning was that when you have a terrorist government, a government that commits acts of terror against its own citizens, then you mustn't be surprised if some citizens respond with counterterror against the government.

INTERVIEWER: Does your organization condemn terrorist acts of this kind?

PIERCE: No, not really. I do not advocate them because I don't think that they accomplish anything at this time. We're in a war for survival and any and all means are justifiable if they are effective. But if they are not effective, then they are a waste of resources. I hate to see Timothy McVeigh on death row when he might be engaged in much more productive activities outside of prison.

INTERVIEWER: Many of your critics, including groups like the Southern Poverty Law Center and HateWatch pay you a kind of backhanded respect by describing you as an expert organizer and fundraiser and as someone with a reputation for getting things done and for unifying disparate elements of the radical right. How do you respond to this backhanded praise? Are they telling us the truth here?

PIERCE: I guess I'm not as enthusiastic as they are. I cannot compliment myself in the same way that they do. I don't think I've ever been good at fundraising, for example. I'm pretty much a loner. I'm not really an organization person. I don't think of myself as a good organizer. I formed an organization only because I *had* to in order to give me the infrastructure for getting ideas out to the public. If I have had any success, it is simply because I have been totally committed to reaching the public with ideas, to communicating with people, to getting people to accept responsibility for what's happening in the world, and I've worked at it day and night for more than thirty years. And I think perhaps a lot of people – how do you say? – I'm able to communicate to them my seriousness and my sense of commitment in this, and I have certainly had some degree of success recently in building up the structure needed for doing what we have to do, in this country anyway. But it's been a bootstrap process, it's been a long, hard effort. I think if I had the sort of organizational and fundraising skills that people like Morris Dees have attributed to me that I would be a lot further ahead.

INTERVIEWER: Could you explain at greater length your views on Christianity? You said you are critical of Christianity and presumably related religions. What exactly are your criticisms of the Christian religion?

PIERCE: Well, you know, that's a big topic, and I can't really do it justice. I'm not a Christian myself. I have not been since I was a college freshman, although as a teenager I thought of myself as Christian, and in fact I sold Bibles door to door. But I think we need to move beyond that. We need to take responsibility for the world around us. Christianity doesn't do that, at least not the way it's interpreted by most people today. I think that the role which Christian churches have taken in allying themselves with the Jews in supporting the government's efforts to bring about a racially mixed society mean that the church has put itself beyond the pale. It's just the sort of thing that cannot be tolerated in a healthy society. Therefore, I have been very critical not only of the role of the church but of some – how do you say? – some counter-evolutionary, countersurvival aspects of Christian doctrine itself.

INTERVIEWER: Is there any other religion to which you are more attracted?

PIERCE: None of what you would ordinarily think of as religion, certainly not any of the Semitic religions – Islam, Judaism, Christianity, or any of the offshoots of those things. All of these are *revealed* religion. It's hocus-pocus superstition. Moses had God revealed to him in a burning bush – this kind of stuff, this revelation, is to me something that ought to be beneath a civilized, intelligent, and progressive people.

INTERVIEWER: Would you describe yourself as an atheist?

PIERCE: No, I am not really an atheist. I'm certainly not the kind of an atheist who says I can prove there is no God. I'm certainly not a fanatical atheist. In fact, I really don't spend a lot of time beating the Christians over the head. I have friends who are Christians. I am happy to accept the participation of Christians in the National Alliance.

INTERVIEWER: You have Christians in your movement?

PIERCE: Yes, we do. I would say probably 20 to 25 percent of our members think of themselves as Christians. They are just not members of the mainstream churches.

INTERVIEWER: What is your opinion of Martin Luther King, Jr., and the black-led civil rights movement of the fifties and sixties in which he played so prominent a role? Is America a better place or a worse place because of that movement and the nonviolent philosophy of Dr. King?

PIERCE: It's an infinitely worse place as a result of the civil rights movement and the legislation that accompanied that movement. I mean I don't really approve of the sort of segregated situation that we had before the civil rights movement. I think segregation is ultimately bad for society. I think that we ought to cut our own grass, wash our own dishes, carry out our own garbage, take care of our own kids. I do not

approve the separate but unequal societies that we had. I think blacks
have to solve their own problems in their own parts of the world, and
we're going to have to solve our problems in our part of the world. So
I certainly do not approve of the civil rights movement or the effect
that it has had on our society. Of course, King had really not much
choice in the matter. If he had chosen to follow a violent course instead
of a nonviolent course, I don't think he could have succeeded. He
simply was a good strategist and did the best he could with the
circumstances that he was faced with.

INTERVIEWER: Given the situation in America now where blacks constitute
   13 percent of the population, how is ethnic homogeneity possible? Do
   you believe that black people should be encouraged to migrate back to
   Africa?
PIERCE: Well, if I thought that would work, that's what I would be doing.
   I would be encouraging them to do that. You know, we had groups of
   people in this country for quite a while, apparently prominent groups
   who were doing that. We had the American Colonization Society, which
   tried to implement the resettlement of freed slaves in Africa, and that's
   how the country of Liberia got its start as a matter of fact. Altruistic
   white people bought land over in Africa and paid to transport blacks
   from North America to Liberia and get them started over there. But it
   really didn't amount to anything. They're still eating each other over
   there in Liberia. The civil war that's been going on over there has seen
   some of the most barbaric behaviors, as bad as anything in Rwanda,
   for example. There was an entirely black movement in this country just
   a few decades back. Marcus Garvey wanted to lead a migration of his
   people back to Africa, but again nothing came of that, nothing significant anyway. I think any successful return-to-Africa movement is going
   to require a large-scale effort with full government backing.

INTERVIEWER: Speaking of killings and genocides, you once described
   Adolf Hitler as the greatest man of our era. What did you mean by
   that?
PIERCE: Well, I meant by that that he had done more than anyone else to
   show us the way that we need to take in the future. He came up from
   nothing at the end of the First World War; he was blinded, wounded
   in a military hospital; he had no friends, no family; both his mother
   and father were dead. He had no money; he had nothing but a high
   school education; and without any of these advantages at all, he rose
   in a few years' time – from the time he was discharged from the army,
   thirteen years later he was the chancellor of Germany. And he transformed that country. He made it strong and self-confident again. He
   developed many very healthy, positive institutions in that country
   for young people, for education, for a relation between labor and

management, for the development of natural resources, and for the protection of the environment. He was probably the most prominent anti-smoking pioneer in Europe and in many other ways was a leader for the future. If the Second World War hadn't come along, I think he would have had an opportunity to set an example that would have been followed in many other countries.

INTERVIEWER: But wasn't it Hitler who started that war?

PIERCE:* You know, that is a historical question which is probably beyond the scope of this argument. When he was in his military hospital in 1918, he made a resolution that he would try to free Germany from the people that he felt had betrayed Germany and caused her defeat at the end of the war, and then he wanted to destroy communism. Those were his aims. So what would have eventually happened between Germany and Russia, I suspect, would have been a violent conflict in any case. I think Hitler had a very strong desire to free Europe from the threat of Bolshevism, but he did not want to have conflict with England or with France, didn't want to have a conflict with the West, and I believe that the invasion of Poland, which took place almost simultaneously by Germany and the Soviet Union, really, that was just an excuse used by France and the United Kingdom for attacking Germany.

INTERVIEWER: Thank you.

---

*In the summer of 2002, William Pierce learned that he had terminal cancer. Shortly before his death in late July he made provisions to insure that others in his organization would carry out the mission of the National Alliance.

For Further Reading

The white nationalists interviewed in this volume make many controversial assertions and claims regarding a host of topics about which most readers will have little firsthand knowledge. Readers who wish to inform themselves further on some of the many issues, controversies, and claims found in the preceding interviews are encouraged to survey some of the specialty literature on these topics, a selection from which is listed below.

The Affirmative Action Debate

Appiah, Anthony K., and Amy Gutmann. *Color Conscious: The Political Morality of Race*, Princeton University Press, Princeton, N.J., 1996.

Belz, Herman. *Equality Transformed: A Quarter Century of Affirmative Action*, Transaction Publishers, New Brunswick, N.J., 1991.

Bergman, Barbara. *In Defense of Affirmative Action*, Basic Books, New York, 1996.

Bolick, Clint. *The Affirmative Action Fraud*, Cato Institute, Washington, D.C., 1996.

Bowen, William G., and Derek Bok. *The Shape of the River*, Princeton University Press, Princeton, N.J., 1998.

Carter, Stephen. *Reflections of an Affirmative Action Baby*, Basic Books, New York, 1991.

Cohen, Carl. *Naked Racial Preferences*, Madison Books, New York, 1995.

Delgado, Richard. *The Coming Race War and Other Apocalyptic Tales of America After Affirmative Action*, New York University Press, New York, 1996.

D'Souza, Dinesh. *The End of Racism*, The Free Press, New York, 1995.

Eastland, Terry. *Ending Affirmative Action: The Case for Color-Blind Justice*, Basic Books, New York, 1996.

Edley, Christopher. *Not All Black and White: Affirmative Action and American Values*, Hill and Wang, New York, 1996.

Ezorsky, Gertrude. *Racism and Justice: The Case for Affirmative Action*, Cornell University Press, Ithaca, N.Y., 1991.

Glazer, Nathan. *Affirmative Discrimination*, Basic Books, New York, 1975.

Kahlenberg, Richard D. *The Remedy: Class, Race, and Affirmative Action*, Basic Books, New York, 1996.

Klitgaard, Robert. *Choosing Elites*, Basic Books, New York, 1985.
Lynch, Frederick R. *Invisible Victims: White Males and the Crisis of Affirmative Action*, Praeger, New York, 1991.
Nieli, Russell K., editor. *Racial Preference and Racial Justice: The New Affirmative Action Debate*, Ethics and Public Policy Center, Washington, D.C., 1991.
Reskin, Barbara. *The Realities of Affirmative Action in Employment*, American Sociological Association, Washington, D.C., 1998.
Rosenfeld, Michael. *Affirmative Action and Justice*, Yale University Press, New Haven, Conn., 1991.
Rowan, Carl. *The Coming Race War in America*, Little, Brown, Boston, 1996.
Skrentny, John David. *The Ironies of Affirmative Action*, University of Chicago Press, Chicago, 1996.
Sleeper, Jim. *Liberal Racism: How Fixating on Race Subverts the American Dream*, Penguin, New York, 1997.
Sniderman, Paul M., and Thomas Piazza. *The Scar of Race*, Harvard University Press, Cambridge, Mass., 1993.
Sowell, Thomas. *Preferential Policies: An International Perspective*, William Morrow, New York, 1990.
Steinberg, Stephen. *Turning Back: The Retreat from Racial Justice in American Thought and Policy*, Beacon Press, Boston, 1996.
Swain, Carol M., editor. *Race Versus Class: The New Affirmative Action Debate*, University Press of America, Lanham, Md., 1996.
Taylor, Jared. *Paved with Good Intentions*, Carroll and Graf Publishers, New York, 1992.

The Christian Identity Movement

Aho, James A. *The Politics of Righteousness: Idaho Christian Patriotism*, University of Washington Press, Seattle, 1990.
Barkun, Michael. *Religion and the Racist Right: The Origins of the Christian Identity Movement*, University of North Carolina Press, Chapel Hill, N.C., 1994.
Comparet, Bernard. *The Cain/Satanic Seed Line*. Church of Jesus Christ Christian, Hayden Lake, Idaho, n.d.
Kaplan, Jeffry. *Radical Religion in America*, Syracuse University Press, Syracuse, N.Y., 1997.
Zeskind, Leonard. *The Christian Identity Movement*, National Council of the Churches of Christ in the U.S.A., Washington, D.C., 1986.

The Civil Rights Movement

Branch, Taylor. *Parting the Waters: America in the King Years*, Simon and Schuster, New York, 1988.
Carson, Clayborne. *In Struggle: SNCC and the Black Awakening of the 1960s*, Harvard University Press, Cambridge, Mass., 1981.
Franklin, John Hope, and Alfred A. Moss, Jr. *From Slavery to Freedom*, McGraw Hill, New York, 1994.
Garrow, David. *Bearing the Cross – Martin Luther King, Jr. and the Southern Christian Leadership Conference*, Vintage Books, New York, 1988.

King, Martin Luther, Jr. *Stride Toward Freedom – The Montgomery Story*, Harper and Brothers, New York, 1958.

Klinkner, Philip, and Rogers M. Smith. *The Unsteady March*, University of Chicago Press, Chicago, 1999.

Kluger, Richard. *Simple Justice: The History of Brown v. Board of Education and Black America's Struggle for Equality*, Vintage Books, N.Y., 1975.

Lawson, Steven F. *Black Ballots: Voting Rights in the South, 1944–1969*, Columbia University Press, New York, 1976.

McPherson, James M. *The Abolitionist Legacy: From Reconstruction to the NAACP*, Princeton University Press, Princeton, N.J., 1975.

Morris, Aldon D. *The Origins of the Civil Rights Movement*, Free Press, New York, 1984.

Patterson, Orlando. *The Ordeal of Integration*, Civitas, Washington, D.C., 1997.

Sitkoff, Harvard. *The Struggle for Black Equality 1954–1992*, Hill and Wang, New York, 1992.

Holocaust Denial

Anti-Defamation League. *Hitler's Apologists: The Anti-Semitic Propaganda of Holocaust Revisionism*, Anti-Defamation League, New York, 1993.

Duke, David. *My Awakening*, Free Speech Press, Covington, La., 1999.

Lipstadt, Deborah E. *Denying the Holocaust*, The Free Press, New York, 1993.

Smith, Bradley. *The Holocaust Controversy: The Case for Open Debate*, Committee for Open Debate on the Holocaust, Visalie, Calif., n.d.

Weber, Mark. *The Holocaust: Let's Hear Both Sides*, Institute for Historical Review, Costa Mesa, Calif., n.d.

Immigration and Its Effects on the United States

Barone, Michael. *The New Americans: How the Melting Pot Can Work Again*, Regnery Publishing, Washington, D.C., 2001.

Bogen, Elizabeth. *Immigration in New York*, Praeger, New York, 1987.

Borjas, George J. *Heaven's Door: Immigration Policy and the American Economy*, Princeton University Press, Princeton, N.J., 1999.

Brimlow, Peter. *Alien Nation: Common Sense About America's Immigration Disaster*, Random House, New York, 1995.

Higham, John. *Strangers in the Land: Patterns of American Nativism*, Rutgers University Press, New Brunswick, N.J., 1955.

Send These to Me: Immigrants in Urban America, Johns Hopkins University Press, Baltimore, 1984.

Kim, Illsoo. *The New Urban Immigrants*, Princeton University Press, Princeton, N.J., 1981.

Kotkin, Joel. *Tribes: How Race, Religion and Identity Determine Success in the New Global Economy*, Random House, New York, 1993.

Kwong, Peter. *The New Chinatown*, Hill and Wang, New York, 1987.

Light, Ivan. *Ethnic Enterprise in America*, University of California Press, Berkeley, 1972.

Reimers, David. *Still the Golden Door: The Third World Comes to America*, Columbia University Press, New York, 1985.
Schuck, Peter, and Rogers M. Smith. *Citizenship Without Consent: Illegal Aliens in the American Polity*, Yale University Press, New Haven, Conn., 1985.
Waldinger, Roger. *Still the Promised City?: African Americans and New Immigrants in Postindustrial New York*, Harvard University Press, Cambridge, Mass., 1996.

Jews and Anti-Semitism

Arendt, Hannah. *Antisemitism*, Harcourt, Brace, and World, New York, 1968.
Dershowitz, Alan. *The Vanishing American Jew*, Little, Brown, Boston, 1997.
Dinnerstein, Leonard. *Anti-Semitism in America*, Oxford University Press, New York, 1999.
Duke, David. *My Awakening*, Free Speech Press, Covington, La., 1999.
Eisen, Arnold M. *The Chosen People in America: A Study in Jewish Religious Ideology*, Indiana University Press, Bloomington, Ind., 1995.
Gabler, Neal. *An Empire of Their Own: How the Jews Invented Hollywood*, Crown Publishers, New York, 1988.
Hertzberg, Arthur. *The Jews in America: Four Centuries of an Uneasy Encounter*, Simon and Schuster, New York, 1989.
Hitler, Adolf. *Mein Kampf*, Houghton Mifflin, Boston, 1971.
Jaher, Frederic Cople. *A Scapegoat in the New Wilderness: The Origins and Rise of Anti-Semitism in America*, Harvard University Press, Cambridge, Mass., 1994.
Jick, Leon A. *The Americanization of the Synagogue*, Brandeis University Press, Hanover, N.H., 1992.
Katz, Jacob. *Exclusiveness and Tolerance: Jewish-Gentile Relations in Medieval and Modern Times*, Oxford University Press, New York, 1962.
Klassen, Ben. *The White Man's Bible*, The World Church of the Creator, Lighthouse Point, Fla., 1981.
Lerner, Richard M. *Final Solutions: Biology, Prejudice, and Genocide*, Pennsylvania State University Press, University Park, Pa., 1992.
Patai, Raphael. *The Jewish Mind*, Jason Aronson, New York, 1977.
Sachar, Howard M. *A History of the Jews in America*, Alfred Knopf, New York, 1992.
Van den Haag, Ernest. *The Jewish Mystique*, Stein and Day, New York, 1969.

Neo-Nazism, Skinheads, and Militia Groups

Anti-Defamation League. *The Skinhead International: A Worldwide Survey of Neo-Nazi Skinheads*. Anti-Defamation League, New York, 1995.
Betz, Hans-Georg. *Radical Right-Wing Populism in Western Europe*, St. Martin's, New York, 1994.
Bushart, Howard L., John R. Craig, and Myra Barnes. *Soldiers of God: White Supremacists and Their Holy War for America*, Kensington Books, New York, 1998.
Chalmers, David. *Hooded Americanism: The History of the Ku Klux Klan*, Duke University Press, Durham, N.C., 1987.

Coates, James. *Armed and Dangerous*, Hill and Wang, New York, 1987.

Corcoran, James. *Bitter Harvest: Gordon Kahl and the Posse Comitatus*, Penguin, New York, 1990.

Ezekiel, Raphael S. *The Racist Mind: Portraits of American Neo-Nazis and Klansmen*, Penguin, New York, 1995.

Flynn, Kevin, and Gary Gerhardt. *The Silent Brotherhood: Inside America's Silent Brotherhood*, The Free Press, New York, 1995.

George, John, and Laird Wilcox. *American Extremists: Militias, Supremacists, Klansmen, Communists and Others*, Prometheus Books, Buffalo, N.Y., 1996.

Kaplan, Jeffrey, and Tore Bjorgo, editors. *Nation and Race: The Emergence of a Euro-American Racist Subculture*, Northeastern University Press, Boston, 1998.

Kaplan, Jeffrey, and Leonard Weinberg. *The Emergence of a Euro-American Radical Right*, Rutgers University Press, New Brunswick, N.J., 1999.

Kuehl, Stefan. *The Nazi Connection*, Oxford University Press, New York, 1994.

Macdonald, Andrew (pseudonym of William Pierce). *The Turner Diaries*, National Vanguard Books, Arlington, Va., n.d.

Moore, Jack. *Skinheads Shaved for Battle: A Cultural History of American Skinheads*, Bowling Green State University Press, Bowling Green, Ohio, 1993.

Ridgeway, James. *Blood in the Face: The Ku Klux Klan, Aryan Nations, Nazi Skinheads, and the Rise of a New White Culture*, Thunder's Mouth Press, New York, 1990.

Simonelli, Frederick J. *American Fuehrer: George Lincoln Rockwell and the American Nazi Party*, University of Illinois Press, Champaign, Ill., 1999.

The Race/IQ Debate

Fischer, Claude S., et al. *Inequality by Design: Cracking the Bell Curve Myth*, Princeton University Press, Princeton, N.J., 1996.

Flynn, James R. *Race, IQ, and Jensen*, Routledge, London, 1980.

  Asian Americans: Achievement Beyond IQ, Lawrence Erlbaum Associates, Hillsdale, N.J., 1991.

Gardner, Howard. *Frames of Mind: The Theory of Multiple Intelligences*, Basic Books, New York, 1983.

Gould, Stephen, J. *The Mismeasure of Man*, Norton, New York, 1981.

Herrnstein, Richard, and Charles Murray. *The Bell Curve*, The Free Press, New York, 1994.

Jacoby, Russell, and Naomi Glauberman, eds. *The Bell Curve Debate*, Random House, New York, 1995.

Jencks, Christopher, and Meredith Phillips, editors. *The Black-White Test Score Gap*, Brookings Institution Press, Washington, D.C., 1998.

Jensen, Arthur. *Educability and Group Differences*, Harper and Row, New York, 1973.

  The g-Factor, Praeger, Westport, Conn., 1998.

Kincheloe, Joe L., et al. *Measured Lies: The Bell Curve Examined*, St. Martin's Press, New York, 1996.

Levin, Michael. *Why Race Matters*, Praeger, Westport, Conn., 1997.

Lewontin, Richard, et al. *Not in Our Genes: Biology, Ideology, and Human Nature*, Pantheon, New York, 1984.

Loehlin, John, et al. *Race Differences in Intelligence*, W. H. Freeman, San Francisco, 1975.

Rushton, J. Philippe. *Race, Evolution and Behavior*, Transaction, New Brunswick, N.J., 1995.

Seligman, Daniel. *A Question of Intelligence*, Transaction, New Brunswick, N.J., 1992.

Snyderman, Mark, and Stanley Rothman. *The IQ Controversy: The Media and Public Policy*, Transaction, New Brunswick, N.J., 1988.

Racial Discrimination

Alport, Gordon. *The Nature of Prejudice*, Doubleday, Garden City, New York, 1954.

Bell, Derrick. *Race, Racism, and American Law*, Third Edition, Little, Brown, New York, 1992.

Blauner, Bob. *Black Lives, White Lives: Three Decades of Race Relations in America*, University of California Press, Berkeley, 1989.

Feagin, Joe, and Melvin Sikes. *Living With Racism: The Black Middle-Class Experience*. Beacon Press, Boston, 1994.

Frederickson, George. *The Black Image in the White Mind*, Harper and Row, New York, 1971.

Hacker, Andrew. *Two Nations: Black and White, Separate, Hostile, Unequal.* Scribner's, New York, 1992.

Hochschild, Jennifer. *Facing Up to the American Dream*, Princeton University Press, Princeton, N.J., 1995.

Jaynes, Gerald, and Robin Williams. *A Common Destiny: Blacks in American Society*, National Academy Press, Washington, D.C., 1989.

King, Martin Luther, Jr. *Stride Toward Freedom: The Montgomery Story*, Harper and Row, New York, 1958.

Massey, Douglas S., and Nancy A. Denton. *American Apartheid: Segregation and the Making of the Underclass*, Harvard University Press, Cambridge, Mass., 1993.

Patterson, Orlando. *The Ordeal of Integration*, Civitas Counterpoint, Washington, D.C., 1997.

Schuman, Howard, et al. *Racial Attitudes in America: Trends and Interpretations*, Harvard University Press, Cambridge, Mass., 1997.

Smith, Robert C. *Racism in the Post-Civil Rights Era*, State University of New York Press, Albany, N.Y., 1995.

Sniderman, Paul M., and Thomaz Piazza. *The Scar of Race*, Harvard University Press, Cambridge, Mass., 1993.

Thernstrom, Stephen, and Abigail Thernstrom. *America in Black and White*, Simon and Schuster, New York, 1997.

White Racial Advocacy and Segregation

Bridges, Tyler. *The Rise of David Duke*, University Press of Mississippi, Jackson, Miss., 1994.

Carter, Dan T. *The Politics of Rage: George Wallace, the Origins of the New Conservatism, and the Transformation of American Politics,* Simon and Schuster, New York, 1995.

Cell, John W. *The Highest Stage of White Supremacy: The Origins of Segregation in South Africa and the American South,* Cambridge University Press, Cambridge, U.K., 1982.

Chalmers, David M. *Hooded Americanism: The History of the Ku Klux Klan,* Duke University Press, Durham, N.C., 1981.

Clark, Culpepper. *The Schoolhouse Door: Segregation's Last Stand at the University of Alabama,* Oxford University Press, New York, 1995.

Daniels, Jesse. *White Lies: Race, Class, Gender, and Sexuality in White Supremacy Discourse,* Routledge, New York, 1997.

Dobratz, Betty A., and Shanks-Meile, Stephanie L. *"White Power, White Pride!" The White Separatist Movement in the United States,* Twayne Publishers, New York, 1997.

Duke, David. *My Awakening,* Free Speech Press, Covington, La., 1999.

Grant, Madison, *The Passing of the Great Race,* Charles Scribner, New York, 1916.

Klassen, Ben. *Nature's Eternal Religion,* The Church of the Creator, Lighthouse Point, Fla., 1973.

Rose, Douglas, editor. *The Emergence of David Duke,* University of North Carolina Press, Chapel Hill, N.C., 1992.

Stoddard, Lothrop. *The Rising Tide of Color Against White World Supremacy,* Charles Scribner, New York, 1920.

Index